Apprenticeship in England, 1600–1914

Apprenticeship in England, 1600–1914

Joan Lane
University of Warwick

Routledge
Taylor & Francis Group

LONDON AND NEW YORK

First published in 1996

By Routledge

2 Park Square, Milton Park, Abingdon, Oxfordshire OX14 4RN
711 Third Avenue, New York, NY 10017, USA

First issued in paperback 2016

Routledge is an imprint of the Taylor & Francis Group, an informa business

British Library Cataloguing in Publication Data
A catalogue record for this book is available from the British Library.

ISBN 13: 978-1-138-96370-2 (pbk)
ISBN 13: 978-1-85728-249-8 (hbk)

Typeset in Classical Garamond.

In memory of my mother

Contents

Preface

In the course of this research I have become indebted to archivists and librarians in many institutions in different counties for answering queries, both personally and by correspondence, and for photocopying material, but particularly for suggesting sources that might otherwise have been overlooked. I would like to thank the staffs of the following, some for helpfulness beyond the call of duty: Bedfordshire Record Office; Birmingham Central Library; Bodleian Library, Oxford; British Library; Cambridge University Library; Corporation of London Records Office; Coventry City Record Office; Cumbria Record Office; Devon Record Office; Hereford and Worcester Record Office; Ipswich Library; Manchester City Library; Norfolk Record Office and Library; Northamptonshire Record Office; Oxfordshire Archives; Public Record Office; Shakespeare Birthplace Trust Records Office; Sheffield Library; Staffordshire Record Office; Suffolk Record Office, Bury St Edmunds; University of Birmingham, Barnes Library; University of Warwick Library; Warwickshire County Record Office; Wellcome Institute for the History of Medicine Library, London; Worshipful Company of Barber-Surgeons, London; York Record Office.

I am pleased to acknowledge the advice of Professor J. M. Harrington of the Department of Occupational Health, Birmingham University; the constructive advice and friendship of Edward Thompson, for many years, was generously given. The help of Dorothy Thompson, my PhD supervisor, was a constant encouragement. I am grateful to colleagues, students and friends who have provided suggestions and references to sources, as well as to the owners of private papers who have allowed me access to their material. The skilled typing and patience of Deirdre Hewitt have overcome many difficulties.

Finally, I am grateful to my family, especially my son and daughter who, without jealousy, grew up alongside these children from the past.

Leamington Spa,
October 1995

List of tables

List of abbreviations

BCL Birmingham Central Library
BCRO Bristol City Record Office
BL British Library
BLO Bodleian Library, Oxford
CCRO Coventry City Record Office
CLRO Corporation of London Records Office
CRO Cumbria Record Office
HWRO Hereford and Worcester Record Office
MCL Manchester City Library
PP Parliamentary papers
PRO Public Record Office
SBTRO Shakespeare Birthplace Trust Records Office
SRO Somerset Record Office
VCH *Victoria County History*
WCRO Warwickshire County Record Office

Introduction

However ill the practice of a trade may agree with the health, the ability, or the inclination of an apprentice: whether his mind is directed to prefer the study of another, by a riper understanding, which would render him more competent to excel in it; or whether, by the loss of a limb he is disabled from pursuing the first to which he is placed; by *that and that alone* he must abide: he is, in the one case, as irretrievably fixed in that trade, as if he belonged to one of the Castes of India; in the other he has no alternative; he *must starve!*
Anon., *The origin, object and operation of the apprentice laws* (1814)

For at least a hundred years apprenticeship has had a bad press, coloured by such notorious abuses as the sweated and brutal occupations, but also by the disapproving use of the word for unruly youths, equivalent in the present day to "students". However, as an institution it reflects the social history of England to a remarkable degree. Apprenticeship mirrored the change from handicraft, domestic skills to mass-produced, factory goods, it indicated new consumption patterns and above all it failed in responding to England's population growth from the eighteenth century onwards. Its early status of near-fostering, individually arranged, to provide a worthwhile livelihood for a minority was converted into the "cartloads" of very young children transported to distant factories, still, however, called apprentices. The basic faults of apprenticeship changed little. It was inflexible, taking seven years to produce a skilled worker; the child's choice was minimal and parental choice was limited by finance; it was highly traditional, with few opportunities for innovations, and when there were rapid changes in the economy or society, it virtually collapsed, to be replaced by formal education. It had failed by the nineteenth century when it was used as a device of the Poor Law officials to be rid of large numbers of pauper children, who were to be indentured beyond the parish, to reduce the poor rate. The numbers of children bound to housewifery, husbandry and large-scale industry brought apprenticeship into

1

disrepute and what had been effective and respected for a minority was deplored when perverted into a poor relief stratagem. It is also possible that the entry of large numbers of female apprentices, most into the sweated occupations, diminished the status of apprenticeship generally, although there had always been a small group of trades to which non-poor girls could be admitted, with future career prospects.

However, the advantages of apprenticeship when it worked well were considerable. Traditional apprenticeship provided stability for a child, a secure future, with guaranteed employment and limited competition. There were also social benefits for the adult in belonging to a trade or craft organization, including welfare provisions for members and their dependants. Access to charity funds and franchise rights existed in some of the great English trading centres for those who became freemen by right of apprenticeship, both substantial privileges. A good apprenticeship enabled the talented to rise economically and socially, as it was predicted that popular education would do in the present century, and parental sacrifices to secure an indenture are widely recorded. Its importance can be seen in the number of laws made to control both the institution and the participants.

When the Statute of Artificers was formulated in 1563 one of its main clauses was the control of "artificers, labourers, servants of husbandry and apprentices";[1] its strength, tenacity and comprehensive nature are reflected in the fact that it was not repealed until 250 years later. Even in 1814 its critics considered the statute a "poisonous insect" and "venomous reptile" which, though crushed, was not dead but still had "power to sting".[2] Thus a Tudor promulgation, originating as it did from the rules of the medieval craft guilds, created a national system of technical training, with controlled occupational entry, standards of workmanship and trade secrets, as well as influencing adult wage rates and profits for qualified, skilled workers. The population expansion of the later eighteenth century meant that what had been effective for an England of 5.5 million in 1695 functioned with difficulty for nearly double that number by 1801.[3]

Undoubtedly the intentions of the Tudor act were to control apprentices' status, training and personal freedom until the term was complete; they were to be dependent on their masters for the essentials of life (food, shelter, clothes) and to live with the master as part of the family. Clearly this style of apprenticeship meant that the child learned the way of life of the future occupation as well as craft skills, which might be particularly important if a change of social status were involved, as for example, from a tradesman's background to a career in a minor profession.

An apprentice has been defined as "a young person bound by indentures to a tradesman or artificer, who upon certain covenants is to teach him his mystery or trade".[4] The legal theory of apprenticeship was that the master became for the time of the apprenticeship the parent of the apprentice; he exercised the same rights and was liable to the same obligations as a father, and the apprentice became a member of his household. A deed or written contract was essential (an oral agreement was not sufficient), and a premium was characteristic although not vital (see Appendix 1). In response to the master's personal obligation to teach, the apprentice's primary duty was "duly and truly to serve". The master was entitled to exercise "moderate" personal correction to the apprentice, but the most noteworthy feature of an apprenticeship indenture (distinguishing it from a contract of service) was that the master could not summarily dismiss apprentices for misconduct, or be rid of them by paying wages in lieu of notice.[5] Numerous legal cases proved that even deliberate absence, staying out at night, theft or occasional drunkenness were not necessarily grounds for dismissal, although all such offences were punishable by the magistrates.[6] Legislation relating to apprentices was enacted sporadically for three centuries and while a number of new acts were passed, many others were amendments to existing legislation found inadequate in practice. In certain circumstances only pauper children were affected, but other acts governed all apprentices. However, the basic conditions of apprenticeship were those laid down in the Statute of Artificers of 1563 until the Elizabethan statute was repealed in 1814.

The Statute of Artificers ushered in the age of statutory apprenticeship, replacing the medieval system of total control by the guilds. The clauses of 5 Eliz. I which affected apprentices stated that masters should have no more than three apprentices each, a seven-year term was essential before a craft or trade was exercised, a written indenture was obligatory for the non-poor child, local justices could bind the offspring of paupers, vagrants or those "overburdened with children" and anyone under the age of 21 "refusing to be an apprentice and to serve in husbandry or any other kind of art, mystery or science" might be imprisoned until agreeing to do so. Householders with a minimum of half a ploughland in tillage were obliged to take in apprentices aged between 10 and 18 until at least 21 or 24. The act, although devised by central government, was administered almost entirely by local guilds, with emphasis on restricted entry and patrimony in most profitable occupations.

A further act of 1597[7] was particularly concerned with the apprenticing of poor children; it permitted overseers to raise a rate to cover the cost of their premiums and stipulated that 14 years was the maximum age at which a parish child might be bound. The great Elizabethan Poor Law Act of 1601[8] was especially concerned with the indenturing of poor children and empowered the "Churchwardens and Overseers . . . by the assent of any Two Justices of the Peace . . . to bind any such children . . . to be Apprentices, where they shall see convenient". A girl was to serve until the age of 21 "or the time of her marriage", a boy until he was 24. The apprenticeship clauses of the 1601 act seem to have encountered opposition from the beginning, chiefly because pauper children were "put forth very timely" at the age of only seven and apprenticeship disputes involving parish children formed a regular part of the local magistrates' cases throughout the seventeenth century.

3

In spite of these problems, it can nevertheless be said the Tudor system of boarding out plus technical training worked, and that early parish apprenticeship achieved its aims. However, once apprenticeship came to entail the right of settlement after 1662, the whole question became involved with the discredited abuses of parochial "general post" so often seen in the late eighteenth and early nineteenth centuries. A further act of 1691[9] specified that parish apprentices, like non-poor children, required a written indenture, and five years later the maximum age for their indenturing was increased from 14 to 16.[10]

The non-poor apprentice, meanwhile, was affected by no new legislation until the early years of the eighteenth century, when the contract of apprenticeship ceased to be a private arrangement by the terms of the 1709 Stamp Act.[11] This fixed a tax scale (6d in every £1 for premiums of less than £50, 1s in every £1 for larger sums, plus 6d stamp duty) on premiums to the master. To collect the tax, inspectors had to be appointed, indentures listed and financial records kept. Although the act was originally to operate for only five years, it was made perpetual in 1710 and proved to be so regular a source of income that it was not repealed until 1804. There were some quarter of a million apprenticeships entered in the years 1710-62, but there is evidence of considerable under-registration. However, as the numbers of surviving non-poor indentures for the period 1710-60 (when the registers were most completely kept) are so few, it is not possible to estimate the degree of under-registration.

The middle decades of the eighteenth century (1747-68) saw the enactment of four statutes that further controlled apprentices and their masters, which would suggest that certain aspects of apprenticeship were being abused by one side or the other. By the early years of the century economic and social change had weakened the guilds' authority and organization, so that their inspection and control of apprentices' conditions were no longer effective. In 1747 an act was passed[12] to permit any apprentice, pauper or non-poor, whose premium was less than £5, to complain to two local justices "concerning any Misusage, Refusal of necessary Provision, Cruelty or Ill-Treatment". If the accusation were proved, the child was to be discharged, but the master was not punished and was allowed to retain the premium. By setting £5 as the limit below which cases could be brought, the act in practice covered most parish apprentices but not a very wide range of trades; of the 265 occupational premiums listed for London by Campbell in the same year the act was passed, only 27 were in this category. The master himself could complain of a child's behaviour, and the act could easily be misused by the unscrupulous or unsuccessful master to be rid of an unwanted apprentice.

A decade later, in 1757, indentures ceased to be legally necessary, but were replaced by a stamped deed, and increasingly by a printed one, with specified limitations on the apprentice's leisure activities, as well as re-affirming duties and tasks. Apprentices had already been forbidden to hunt in 1692,[13] but from 1757[14] they were also not allowed to play various games of hazard, especially in public houses.

During the Seven Years War opportunities for male apprentices to abscond and enlist were greatly increased, and the frequency of advertisements by masters in the provincial press indicated this trend. So commonplace was the runaway apprentice, that an act of 1766[15] specified that the length of time an apprentice was missing from the master's service should be added on to the original term of the contract, so that the master should not be deprived of the child's labour nor the apprentice lack part of the training. As apprentices apparently became increasingly difficult to control during the eighteenth century an act was passed in 1768[16] that shortened the term of service by three years, so that a male apprentice completed his term of service at the age of 21 instead of 24. This act affected both parish and non-poor boys, and numbers of indentures from 1768 onwards, although still binding boys until the age of 24, have clauses inserted to release the apprentice at 21 or even 18. The act also required premiums to be paid by an instalment method, but this had been, if not commonplace, at least fairly frequently practised since the early years of the century in some parishes.

In the last two decades of the century, four more statutes were passed that affected the apprentice's life in different ways. In 1780 it was enacted[17] firstly that all masters were to provide for them according to the terms of their indentures, which suggests that some masters at least were not fulfilling their contracts, and that no-one should be compelled to take an apprentice not an inhabitant of a particular parish. Eight years later the 1788 act[18] was concerned only with ameliorating the working conditions of boys bound to chimney-sweeps, in practice a minute proportion of apprentices. In 1792 the justices' powers over apprenticeship were very considerably strengthened, as from that year they were empowered to re-assign apprentices whose masters had died and to discharge children for whom masters could not find employment or maintenance if they had less than a £4 premium.[19] Thus apprentices in the less prosperous trades could now be discharged not only because their masters were deliberately cruel, as in the terms of 20 Geo. III c. 19, but also if the trade were not thriving. In the following year a further act[20] increased the range of children to whom its terms applied, by permitting all apprentices to complain of ill-usage if their premium were less than £10, and this limit encompassed a greater range of trades, even allowing for inflation that had occurred since 1747. For the first time a deterrent to the master was stipulated, for he was, if guilty, to be fined £2, which was either to contribute to poor relief in the parish or be given to the apprentice.

The early nineteenth century saw one of the most comprehensive and detailed of all parliamentary measures affecting apprentices and their treatment, the Health and Morals of Apprentices Act of June 1802,[21] which was used to regulate children's conditions in "cotton and other mills, cotton and other factories". Although nationally a considerable number of children were thus employed, they were a minority of the total apprentice population; the owners appear to have complied with the letter of the act but hardly ever with the spirit. The 1802 act applied when three or more apprentices were employed and set out specific conditions for the children; it required that walls should be whitewashed twice a year and that there should be sufficient numbers of windows and a supply of fresh air. In addition, apprentices should have two whole suits of clothes, one new each year. One of the most obvious abuses of factory apprenticeship was the length of a child's working day, which was an important target of reform endeavours. Long hours of work were easier to assess and more apparent than poor food or lack of education, and the 1802 act specified a 12-hour working day between 6am and 9pm excluding mealtimes. All-night work was to be abolished by June 1803, but large factories had longer to effect the change. An important innovation of the act was its requirement that factory apprentices should be taught reading, writing and arithmetic, a more comprehensive curriculum than that taught in many charity schools, by a "discreet and proper" person; from the evidence of newspaper advertisements some masters tried to find teachers. The act also specified that boys and girls should have separate sleeping quarters and that not more than two children should share a bed. On Sundays apprentices were to have an hour's Christian teaching, be confirmed between the ages of 14 and 18 and be examined once a year by the local incumbent to assess what they had learned.

None of the act's provisions was enforceable by central government and two local visitors, a cleric and a magistrate, were to be appointed annually to report on the mills and apprentices at quarter sessions. A fine of between £5 and £10 could be imposed for obstructing the visitors, who were empowered to call in "some Physician or other competent medical Person" in the event of an "infectious disorder" in the factory. The act concluded by requiring two copies of its provisions to be posted in the factory; mills subject to the act were to be listed at quarter sessions.

In the same year, and certainly affecting more children, was the act passed to "require Overseers and Guardians of the Poor to keep a Register of the several Children who shall be bound or assigned by them as Apprentices".[22] This act required two justices to sign each entry, which contained more information about the individual child than the indenture. The register entry included the parents' names, parish and the premium paid; failure to register the apprenticeship by the parish officials could result in a £5 fine. The magistrates signing the register had the final powers of approval and could, like Theodore Price of Birmingham[23] or Dickens's magistrate in *Oliver Twist*, refuse their consent.

In the Statute of Artificers penalties were specific against those who practised a trade without having served their seven-year term, and quarter sessions proceedings illustrate the degree of contemporary concern over this. The repeal in 1814 of the apprenticeship clauses in the Elizabethan statute had one significant result for apprentices; there was to be no prosecution of anyone who practised a trade without having served the seven-year term, and as a result of this clause, cases by aggrieved masters in quarter sessions against workers who had not served their proper terms ceased to be brought. However, the statute in no way abolished apprenticeship but only modified its legal enforcement and the numbers of children apprenticed do not appear to have been affected.

Two years later, however, the press was extremely concerned about the 1816 Factory Act,[24] which set out specific conditions under which a pauper apprentice might be sent to a distant parish. The act was introduced because "many grievances [had] arisen from the binding of poor Children as Apprentices by Parish Officers to improper Persons and to Persons residing at a Distance from the Parishes to which such poor Children belong". Because of the distance, officials and parents could not know how well the children were treated and "the Parents and Children [had] in many instances, become estranged from each other". Greater supervision by the magistracy was intended by this act, for justices had to enquire at a child's binding whether a master resided "within a reasonable Distance" from the child's home, they could ask the parents' views and were to consider the master's "Circumstances and Character". A maximum of 40 miles from home was the greatest distance children might be sent and nine the youngest age at which they might be bound. A child's new settlement rights were cancelled if these clauses were not met and indentures were invalidated if not approved by two justices. Additional control over a master was incorporated in a clause that specified a £10 fine for dismissing a parish apprentice without a magistrate's consent.

Local manufacturing communities could see the dangers of extending the conditions of the 1801 act to all manufactories employing 20 or more persons under the age of 18 and, in May 1816,[25] Birmingham's Chamber of Manufacturers and Commerce sent a petition to the House of Commons to express their "alarm and uneasiness" at the new and unwelcome proposals. They asserted they were unaware of abuses in Birmingham factories, that the existing laws were adequate to deal with any such abuses and that local children aged under ten were employed in various manufactures that did not "require any bodily exertion detrimental to health, but which greatly contributed to form early habits of attention and general industry". Parents would suffer from the loss of their children's earnings and limiting the hours of work would be "most inconveniently felt" in local factories. Furthermore, the town's existing educational facilities were superior to those outlined in the Bill. Visitors were quite superfluous, for they would weaken the masters' authority and cause "vexatious interference", while the prevention of infectious diseases in local factories was thought equally unnecessary by local "medical gentlemen". It is noticeable that only the press in industrial areas expressed concern over the effects of amending the 1802 act, for the *Warwick Advertiser*, for example, noted only that "the Parish Apprentices Bill was committed"[26] with no editorial comment or correspondence. However, the Bill became law and the format of the parish apprenticeship indenture was accordingly altered to cover the amendments it had specified.

The importance and complexity of the apprenticeship laws can be judged by the enormous number of legal disputes in which the institution, its conditions, privileges and customs were discussed and by the frequency with which, outside the courts, men blamed apprenticeship for the depression, low wages or poor trade of their particular occupation. Thus cruelty, inadequate instruction, unqualified practice, enticement and absconding were only some of the more common reasons why apprentices and masters went to law to enforce the original terms of the indenture about which one party or the other felt aggrieved. Less formal breaches of apprenticeship, however, were also resented and the institution itself often blamed for declining prosperity in a trade, frequently unfairly. Thus the Taunton (Som.) weavers attributed their "most unhappy circumstances" in 1700 to overstocking, with masters taking three or even five apprentices for the "luere of a little money".[27] The vastly increased numbers of apprentices in a variety of trades (watchmaking, framework knitting and silk-weaving, for example) were consistently blamed for overstocking and the resulting lower prices.

The control of the numbers of apprentices entering an occupation could be used as a weapon of industrial action on certain occasions, so that the prosperous London Gold and Silver Wire Drawers allowed masters to change the quota of their apprentices from two to three to limit their journeymen's "unjust and illegal practices".[28] Occasionally too as part of a strike, masters would refuse to take apprentices, but in some 412 British labour disputes during the eighteenth century only 20 (4.8 per cent) involved apprenticeship.[29] Even into modern times most trades have been concerned that, in a strike, apprentices should not lose tuition. Permitting a master to take more than the normal quota of apprentices was a considerable privilege, reserved in the craft guilds for the officials, while other members were fined for doing so.[30] In some occupations, such as printing or watchmaking, very large numbers were always indentured with impunity. As different trades experienced economic difficulties, taking in more apprentices who brought premiums, however small, and producing more goods, if of poor quality, seemed an immediate and tempting solution. The long-term effects were usually disastrous for masters, journeymen and the apprentices themselves. However, resistance to the 1814 act was considerable from some honourable and traditional trades, such as the millwrights, but abolition of the necessity of apprenticeship to practise a trade was welcomed by those who, like Adam Smith, regarded it as an archaic institution, epitomized by the unchanged language of the indenture itself. Children continued to be bound and apprenticeship to thrive until modified by the educational reforms of the present century, an institution largely ignored by social historians since Dunlop & Denman's study in 1912.

CHAPTER 1

Characteristics of apprenticeship in England

> The want of affection in the English is strongly manifested towards
> their children . . . at the age of 7 or 9 years at the utmost, they put
> them out, both males and females, to hard service in the houses of
> other people, binding them for another 7 or 9 years . . . in order that
> their children might learn better manners.
>
> Cited in I. Pinchbeck & M. Hewitt, *Children in English society*, I
> (1969)

The practice of sending a child away from home, to live with a host family for
a number of years, usually at a very tender age, had been customary among
the great English families from the medieval period onwards. Such arrangements were not apprenticeships, although in concept and implementation
they were very similar. Slowly this system of free service in return for board
and instruction reached downwards in society, so that the professions, trades
and crafts took advantage of it to train their children in other men's houses
and to receive other adolescents into their own to instruct. Apprenticeship
was roundly condemned by foreign visitors, who saw it as firm proof of
English hard-heartedness towards their offspring. However, by the Tudor
period, apprenticeship was generally accepted as a means of technical training across a very wide range of occupations but still restricted to relatively
small numbers of children. By the seventeenth century it expanded downwards, as a means of social control for the children of the poor, and also
upwards, through economic necessity, as gentlemen's sons became merchants, manufacturers, attorneys and medical practitioners.

By the eighteenth century apprenticeship was common in all but the highest
social levels and by the nineteenth century the system was degenerating into
the scandal of the factory child and the pauper apprentice, bound far from
home to save the poor rate. Thus a method of training for a respectable adolescent minority became a solution for social problems far too complex and
intractable for Victorian parish officials to solve. In spite of its difficulties,
when not abused, apprenticeship was at all periods a successful training

method for new and traditional occupations in which academic skills were secondary to practical ones.

The first problem for the apprentice's parents and the master was matching the two parties and it is apparent that the few ways of child and master finding each other were common to most occupations. Personal recommendation was the most usual way of contact and in some occupations, for example, the London printing trade, complex networks of acquaintanceship can be traced.[1] Since many apprentices and masters are recorded with the same surname, a family connection seems likely; equally, a master might have the same occupation as a child's parent or other relative. Such family links account for a great many distant apprenticeships, so that Christopher Wright, his father a Sussex schoolmaster, was indentured in 1804 to a clockmaker in Tamworth (Staffs.), his mother's home town.[2] Religious connections also, as in William Lucas's case (a Quaker apprenticed to a master of the same faith), secured apprenticeships.[3] Personal contacts may have been by word of mouth or letter; thus one country parson apprenticed a houseboy by speaking to his shoemaker about the lad,[4] while another noted in his diary, "by letter I find a place provided for my son at London".[5] Even a family as prosperous as the Senhouses of Netherhall (Westm.) wrote numerous letters to relations and friends in London to secure an apprenticeship for a younger son.[6]

If personal recommendation were impossible or unsuccessful, the usual alternative was to advertise and notices by masters requiring apprentices and parents seeking places for their children were regularly inserted in local newspapers with a regional readership. Thus Birmingham's *Aris's Gazette* (founded 1741) was read across the Midlands from the Welsh Border to East Anglia in its early years, while Berrow's *Weekly Journal* (1660) printed news from several counties. By the later eighteenth century, when truly local newspapers were established, advertising about apprenticeships was commonplace. The essential facts a master included in his notice were his occupation, the optimum age and social background of the child ("honest parents", "respectable family") and the apprentice's requisite moral and physical qualities, ("of liberal education", "a steady active youth", "unexceptionable character for honesty and sobriety", "a steady, healthy boy"). The more prosperous tradesmen also promised that the apprentice would be well treated and live "in every respect as one of the family". The premium was the most variable element in all the advertisements; very few stated the sum required but some masters mentioned they would need a "substantial" or "adequate" premium, others only that one was expected. Premiums were essentially fixed at what the master thought he could persuade the parent to pay, but as masters were also businessmen, selling products or services to the community, many also used the advertisement for an apprentice to promote themselves. Thus a surgeon-apothecary referred to his "extensive practice", while another master added that the apprentice's "opportunities of improvement will be great". A slightly unusual advertisement for an apprentice was inserted in one local newspaper by a wigmaker:

> Wm Griffin, Perriwig maker, opposite the Red Lion in Birmingham, wants an Apprentice about 11 years. Any Person that has a Mind to set their Son Apprentice to that Business, he will take him on reasonable Terms, may depend on good Usage and . . . being carefully taught.

He added that his reason for advertising was that he was "much confined" to his shop and was a stranger to the area.[7]

As well as individual masters, factory owners also advertised their vacancies for apprentices quite widely, especially once the supply of local children had been indentured and steam power demanded a larger workforce. Benjamin Smart of Warwick advertised in the Oxford, Coventry and Worcester papers, while a notice by Jewsbury's was typical, addressed to overseers and church-wardens for "a Number of Healthy BOYS and GIRLS as Apprentices to the Business of CALICO WEAVING; liberal and humane treatment may be relied upon; and a moderate Premium only expected".[8] Parish officials then wrote to the mill-owner to negotiate terms under which children should be sent. If there were a number of likely apprentices and the journey not too long, the owner or his agent travelled to the parish, signed the indentures and arranged the children's transport.

For the lowest level of apprentices, climbing-boys, advertisements were not used, but legends grew about master sweeps offering large sums to parents or guardians to buy their children. James Dawson Burn claimed to have been kidnapped by a "little hunchbacked gentleman" who offered his mother £100 for him.[9] At the same period the two guineas given to Thomas Cooper's mother seems a more realistic inducement than what Burn quoted.[10] In parishes where even advertising did not find masters for poor children, a rota or lottery was used, as Eden found in Norfolk and Suffolk,[11] and as large communities (Birmingham in 1783, for example)[12] were obliged to operate in years when there were surplus, often unsuitable, apprentices to be bound.

All contemporary writers warned of the importance of securing a good master, morally worthy, humane and able to instruct. Parish officials occasionally made enquiries by letter or visit about a man's suitability to have apprentices, either because they were suspicious about his character or unduly punctilious. Contemporary opinion, however, was divided about the kind of occupation a child should seek, whether to follow the Dick Whittington ideal or, if apprenticed above family origins, whether a child would find only unhappiness in his future life. Undoubtedly apprenticeships arranged through personal contacts were most likely to be satisfactory. A large premium also theoretically ensured the child would be taught occupational skills and be at least tolerably well treated. The apprentice in such circumstances complained only when "unbearably" abused, for the rigours of even a prosperous apprentice's life were considerable, as William Lucas recorded.

Social aspirations in choosing a career varied from one period to another and many occupations changed in general esteem. Thus in the seventeenth century a watchmaker was well regarded as a man of science, but in Victorian England his craft had sunk to near poverty when mass-produced watches, imports and labour dilution all reduced his skills, earnings and status. Across the same period of time the Stuart surgeon, often also a barber, with manual skill but little theory, was held in low public regard, in contrast to his nineteenth-century counterpart, who could command a premium of between £200 and £600. Some trades, on the other hand, seem always to have been well regarded, the silversmith, saddler and cabinetmaker, for example. Such men handled expensive raw materials or created a valuable article with individual talent, impossible to mass produce, and catered for a quality market. These masters were always able to recruit good apprentices and take substantial premiums.

Memoirs and diaries that record details of apprenticeship all emphasize the parental choice in placing a child. Both Ralph Josselin and James Clegg[13] arranged their sons' indentures to urban trades and both were later involved in the arrangements as their sons became unruly and ill. How a child travelled to a distant master varied according to parental prosperity. Josselin and Clegg took their sons to masters in London and Manchester themselves, but William Cookworthy, an orphan bound to a London apothecary in 1719, walked there from Devon.[14] A parish child sent to a Birmingham master in 1768 had his indenture endorsed "The Boy to be left at Mr Wm Stevens's Bricklayer in Carrs Lane", presumably until collected.[15] The importance of apprenticeship within the family may be judged from the regularity with which the fact was entered in contemporary diaries, even if only briefly and with few details.[16]

A child's share in choosing a career varied very considerably, so that an artistic training was arranged for the young George Senhouse by his family,[17] but William Hutton, who wished to be a gardener, was indentured to his uncle, a stockinger, because his father thought gardening "a slavish trade".[18] A boy with artistic talent particularly might change from his original trade and Joseph Farington noted that numbers of eminent nineteenth-century artists had originally been coach or sign painters' apprentices. Many children almost automatically joined their parents' trades, irrespective of personal aptitude. However, some fathers, their own crafts depressed, deliberately sought more secure occupations for their children. Thus George Herbert's father, a plush-weaver in Banbury's failing industry in 1824, "cast about for something . . . and he thought shoemaking was a never failing trade as people must wear shoes".[19] Sometimes, sheer poverty forced a child into a trade with a low premium, while others deliberately rejected their parents' plans. Francis Place refused to be made a conveyancer, even if he were sent to sea for his obstinacy. His father, to his son's surprise, asked what he would like to be. Place replied, "Anything if it were a trade". The same evening, his father, a publican, offered the boy to any master in the inn parlour who would take him;[20] he was apprenticed to a breeches-maker.

The late seventeenth century saw an influx of gentry youths into occupations formerly thought socially unacceptable, particularly trade, manufacture and the professions. They usually had premiums of £100 or more and undoubtedly paved the way for the greater numbers of gentlemen's sons who were to be apprenticed in the following century. Contemporary writers vigorously debated whether a gentleman could remain so if he engaged in trade. After about 1800, however, a different parental attitude can be discerned, eager for a son's advancement above his parents' status, even against the child's own inclinations. Thus Thomas Wood, eldest of ten children, wished at the age of 14 to be an unapprenticed weaver or woolcomber, an almost universal livelihood in Bingley (Yorks.), attracted by working unregulated hours "in the bedrooms or some outbuildings" at home. His father, a hand-loom weaver, "would not hear of it" and Thomas was apprenticed to a mechanic, which caused "as much remark among our neighbours as it would now (1878) if I put a son to be a doctor". He was aware that his parents "must have made a costly effort to get (him) a trade".[21] A more modern parental response can be seen in the career of Paul Evett, a compositor, indentured in 1900, because, following a childhood visit to a printer, he was enthralled by the whole process,[22] an approach advocated by Collyer 140 years earlier.[23] When personal contacts failed, the apprentice's parents or guardians might advertise for a master; such notices usually stated the preferred occupation, the child's age, domestic conditions expected and the kind of premium offered:

> Wanted for a YOUTH, about Fifteen Years of Age, residing in the Country, a Situation, as an APPRENTICE, to a MERCER and DRAPER: a proper Attention to his Morals and Domestic Comforts will be required, as a handsome Premium will be given.[24]

Once child and master had found each other, three basic details about the binding were recorded – the child's age, term and premium. The child's age was the most erratically noted, invariably in pauper apprenticeships, as required by an act of 1708,[25] but seldom in charity and very rarely in normal indentures. In the prosperous occupations the "seven long years" were generally served and the child was usually 14 when indentured. The more exclusive, traditional or profitable the trade, the more likely the apprentice was to be 14 when beginning the term; a child indentured for ten years or more was almost always younger than 14 when bound. In some occupations, in any decade, the older apprentice was an asset. In trades requiring physical strength (tanner, baker, butcher, bricklayer, farrier or blacksmith) the older boy, aged 15 or 16, was far more useful than the younger child. In other occupations greater maturity was an advantage for different reasons, so that milliners, mantua-makers or hairdressers required more sophisticated apprentices for their shops. Occupations apprenticing very young children were, predictably, low skilled, labour intensive and often unable to adapt to new production methods, such as nailing, which, with other Black Country small-metal trades, indentured a substantial number of children aged 7 to 13. Ribbon weaving also bound the younger child, capable of simple quill-winding, but even in this trade the majority of apprentices were aged 13 and 14. In Warwickshire, with considerable ribbon production, the ages of 559 apprentices were recorded; of these 159 were aged 14, 109 were 13, 93 were 12, 63 were 11, 56 were 10 and 30 were 9 years old. There was also one child aged 6 and six who were 17.[26] Children much younger than 14 were apprenticed to framework knitting; William Felkin was only 8 in 1803 when he was bound to a stockinger,[27] but many children in these trades were simply put to the frame or lace-pillow without indentures, especially within the family.

The shoemaker's craft was another universal occupation for very young boys, for even a small village of a few hundred inhabitants supported a craftsman. Although the majority of their apprentices were 14, as Campbell suggested,[28] the trade also indentured boys who were 10 or younger, not necessarily paupers, typified by George Herbert, aged 9 in 1823, since shoemaking required "a moderate Share of Ingenuity" rather than "much strength" or a "mechanic Head".[29] Two other occupations regularly indenturing parish children were husbandry and housewifery, since both provided a range of repetitive, unskilled tasks in the fields or household a small child could manage. Of 337 apprentices to husbandry in Warwickshire, almost three-quarters were aged 11 or younger,[30] while 9-year-olds formed nearly a quarter of the 226 bound to housewifery:[31]

Table 1.1 Ages of apprentices to husbandry and housewifery in Warwickshire, 1700–1834.

Apprentices' ages (years)	Number of apprentices	
	Husbandry	Housewifery
6	3	0
7	8	7
8	45	27
9	85	50
10	68	44
11	29	32
12	44	32
13	38	25
14	10	8
15	4	1
16	2	0
17	1	0
Totals	327	226

Cotton manufacture was another occupation to which it has always been claimed that substantial numbers of younger children were apprenticed and the extreme youth of such apprentices was an important element in reform movements by the nineteenth century. A national survey of factory children is impossible for lack of complete and extant records, both parishes' and employers'. However, during the expansionist years of 1781–1816 some 225 Warwickshire children have been traced as factory apprentices. Most of the county's 215 parishes sent no children at all and some only a handful, leaving certain urban, industrialized parishes to provide the majority of factory apprentices during this period. The ages of 180 of these children were recorded. It may be argued that they are not typical of traditional factory apprentices, but they match almost exactly the age profile of the children entering Quarry Bank, Styal (Ches.) from many counties. Of these 180 Warwickshire children with ages recorded, 124 were girls and 56 were boys; most of the girls were aged 10 (20), 11 (18), 12 (19), 13 (19) and 14 (22). The males were primarily aged 8 (11), 12 (13) and 13 (11), although two little boys were only 7 and one youth was 17.[32] Certain factory masters had a strong preference for older apprentices and, for example, Benjamin Smart of Emscote Mill (War.) particularly favoured 12- to 17-year-old females. One contemporary magistrate, Theodore Price, considered that 8 to 10 was too "tender" an age at which to employ children, since work would be "very destructive of their strength and health", resulting in a "weak and deformed peasantry".[33]

Older boys were a minority in textile factories because they could work in trades requiring physical strength; they were far less suited to the deft work of piecing in a mill than the more nimble-fingered girls of the same age. They were also always a harder group to discipline than females. At Quarry Bank the numbers of male apprentices diminished very markedly; during the years 1800–2, when details of 50 new apprentices were recorded, the ages of 32 were specified, of whom 17 were males. However, 9 of these boys ran away, presumably causing the owners to prefer girls in a later intake, so that in 1815–17, when 89 children were indentured, only 9 were boys, none of whom absconded.[34]

As well as textile work, chimney-sweeping was notorious for apprenticing the very young child. Physical smallness and obedience were essential in such uncongenial work and the older boy, as in other trades, was more likely to abscond. Campbell noted "the black fraternity" all took apprentices and "the younger they are the better fit to climb up the Chimneys".[35] He did not specify an age, but Collyer noted 14 years as a term for these "infant apprentices", generally parish children,[36] which suggests they were between seven and ten when bound. Other children's unfortunate origins caused them to be bound to sweeps; Thomas Steel Vincent was only seven in 1788 when, illegitimate, he was apprenticed for 14 years to a Stow-on-the-Wold (Glos.) sweep with a five-guinea premium, apparently paid by his father, who already had a wife and family.[37] The young illegitimate child might also be sent away to a sweep if his mother subsequently married and he was not accepted by his stepfather.[38] In Coventry, where boys as young as four and five were bound to sweeps,[39] there is also evidence that some of them survived to become masters.[40]

Apart from these occupations, the wide acceptance of the seven-year term is striking, from the professions downwards, suggesting that most children were 14 when apprenticed. Campbell tartly commented that children younger than this were indentured "more for the Advantage of the Master than any thing they can learn of the Trade in such Infant Years".[41] Even if the child's age cannot always be established, the term was never omitted from the indenture, manuscript or printed, from the very earliest record sources until the present century. The term was expressed either as a number of years from the date of the indenture or, primarily for paupers, until the apprentice reached a certain age (18, 21 or 24) or, if female, married. Attempts to change the seven-year term were always strongly resisted, usually with appeals to custom, tradition and usage, rather than that seven years was an ideal training period. The importance of the term may be judged by the number of by-laws enforced by the ancient trading companies to regulate its length.[42]

The value of the term to the master was considerable. It controlled recruitment to an occupation, with numbers of new journeymen qualifying at predictable intervals. Thus wages were kept up and unemployment from overstocking was avoided. The master was also sure of the apprentice's service for a number of years. The term's greatest disadvantage was that, if extra qualified workmen were needed quickly, for a local or national crisis, they could be produced only by shortening the term as an emergency measure or allowing masters to indenture more apprentices than their craft quota allowed. The inflexible term, therefore, was satisfactory in economically and politically stable conditions. When labour or a product was scarce, in wartime or after a fire, for example, the term acted as a brake on expansion. Thus it was possible for a guild to prevent competition by extending the apprentice's term and this was practised by the greatest guilds (the ironmongers, the Newcastle Adventurers and the goldsmiths, for example) at times when their journeymen complained that they could not get work because the numbers in the craft had so increased.[43] Some occupations chose a term that was quite different from those normally served in an area, so that, for example, in 1593 the Coventry mercers reiterated an ordinance that nine years was their term, in a city where seven years was usual.[44]

Variation in the term, from 2 years to 17, appears to have existed widely across trades and regions, although always for a minority of children. Thus the London Stationers' Company bound boys with terms ranging from 7 to 16 years,[45] although 7 years predominated. In Southampton (1610–82) seven years was served by 65.8 per cent of the apprentices, eight years by 21.5 per cent and longer terms by 10.9 per cent, but during the century the seven-year term increased steadily and variations became fewer.[46] In a completely different community, Kendal (Westm.), borough apprentices also predominantly served seven years (1645–1736).[47]

The most comprehensive picture of apprentices' terms in the eighteenth century for non-poor children can be gained from the great London apprenticeship registers. As these were kept after 1710 for tax purposes they illustrate the common problems of tax records as sources, a bureaucratic urge to be complete and the taxpayer's desire to keep payment as low as possible. Unfortunately, they were increasingly defective after 1760, omitting so many essential facts, such as the master's trade, that analysis is possible for only half a century. The returns of five English counties for the years 1710–60 provide a cross section of both local trades (toymakers in Warwickshire, broadweavers in Wiltshire, maritime occupations in Sussex) as well as crafts universally practised.[48] The predominance of the 7-year term is striking and it is difficult to explain Sir Hilary Jenkinson's comment that in the Surrey apprenticeships "nearly all the terms are anything but the usual seven years", citing a range from 2 to 9 years,[49] for in Surrey 87 per cent served 7 years, with a range from 1 to 15 years for the rest.

The counties nearer London or with provincial guilds had more rigid terms, even if different from seven years. Thus tinplate workers, plumbers and apothecaries, with strict control well into the eighteenth century, all served eight years. Apothecaries' terms show a variation between London and the provinces, so that Sussex boys who remained in the county (42 out of 81) served for seven years, while the 29 bound to London masters served a year more.[50] However, by 1818 changes in medical education[51] reduced their term to five years.[52] Occupations with the longer term had distinctive characteristics. Firstly, there were the changing trades, either new and expanding (Birmingham's metalware) or old and declining (Wiltshire's cloth industry); both categories required the longest possible terms masters could negotiate and apprentices' parents accept. Secondly, longer terms were served by children socially unfortunate, not necessarily paupers, such as orphans, bastards or stepchildren, almost as if fostered. They were not bound to the poorest trades, but to butchers, millers, blacksmiths, masons and shipwrights, respectable occupations with adequate premiums. In the third category of longterm apprentices were the poorest children, just above parish level, often bound alongside paupers, indentured for the sake of their labour and a low premium. Such children went to farmers, weavers, carpenters, tailors and shoemakers, all in a small way of business.

In arranging a shorter term than seven years different factors were important, excluding the children who changed masters. Five-year-term apprentices were regularly found with attorneys, milliners and mantua-makers, to which female trades girls might bring premiums as high as £40 from fathers who were merchants and gentlemen. Apart from these minorities, seven years were most generally served at all periods by most children. Apprentices in

Sussex illustrate this pattern, with seven years recorded for 77 per cent of the 243 tailors' apprentices there, 69 per cent of the 112 barbers, 76 per cent of the blacksmiths, 65 per cent of the 57 bricklayers and all 26 barber-surgeons. The tradition is reflected in popular verse and song from "Sally in our Alley" to "The Lincolnshire Poacher".

Parish apprentices' ages and terms differed essentially from those of more prosperous children, but require more detailed consideration when set against the widely accepted historical picture of pauper-apprenticing. The most daunting problem in such an analysis is undoubtedly the quantity of material available, found in overseers' accounts, indentures and, after 1802, apprentice registers. All can be faulty. The registers, ostensibly the most me-thodical record, were not always well kept, so that overseers purchased the new registers, but, resistant to government interference, continued their old ways. Large urban parishes used the new registers more conscientiously than remote rural communities and may have welcomed an orderly means of list-ing their increasing numbers of pauper apprentices. Although often incom-plete, these registers are not at all rare, as has been suggested.[53] The survival rate for factory apprentices' records, however, is variable; for Quarry Bank they are virtually complete, but for the majority of firms, even large-scale, they no longer exist.[54] When it survives, the very quantity of pauper appren-ticeship material is often daunting. Hundreds of loose indentures for a single parish in the eighteenth century are common, grubby, folded or tied in bundles, usually listed in record offices only as "apprentice indentures". Only slightly more disheartening to the researcher is the archive labelled "miscel-laneous Poor Law material".

In spite of such problems, parishes can be found with apparently complete records to illuminate aspects of pauper apprenticeship. All evidence suggests that the industrialized parish, growing in population and poverty after the later eighteenth century, most often used the long-term apprenticeship to be rid of younger children, a major liability. The mining and weaving community of Bedworth, in north Warwickshire, whose population rose from 1,220 in 1730 to 3,161 in 1802, was such a parish. In the early decades of the eight-eenth century the overseers there, like their neighbours, bound 2 or 3 children a year, 6 or 7 by the 1770s and 11 by 1789. These numbers continued to rise, so that in 1810 the parish indentured 22 apprentices. Of the 426 Bedworth pauper children recorded, 378 were bound until the age of 21, 8 until 24, 38 for seven years and 2 for various terms. However, when the ages of the chil-dren were recorded or traced, a harsher picture emerges. Of the 290 whose ages are known, the majority (229 or 78.9 per cent) were 13 or younger, in-cluding 47 aged 11, 54 who were ten, 22 aged nine, 4 aged eight and 1 seven-year-old.[55] Some of the very youngest were apprenticed with a brother or sister or to a master who already had another of the family, and this trend is particularly noticeable in cotton factories. In wholly rural parishes, the very young child was invariably bound to agriculture. Thus at Aymestrey (Herefs.)

24 per cent of the apprentices were aged 10, 20 per cent were 11 and 18 per cent were 12, but 14 per cent were 9 and 10 per cent only 8 years old. Only four per cent were 14 and two per cent a year older.[56] There is a clear county pattern, for other parishes (Felton, Kingsland, Burrington and Leintwardine, for example) apprenticed in the same manner for many decades.

The factory child's term, on the other hand, was governed by different considerations, although also recorded as "until 21". Erratic noting of apprentices' ages makes assessment difficult, but at Emscote Mill, near Warwick, where the terms can be calculated, the girls aged 13 or younger comprised 67 per cent, serving 8 years or more, while at Fazeley (Staffs.) 8-year-old boys were particularly favoured and served for 13 years. Two enterprises binding a large number of children with exceptionally long terms, aged ten or younger, were Harding's Tamworth factory and the Wilkes–Jewsbury partnership at Measham (Leics.). Other owners, such as the Gregs, preferred the older child.[57] Although the length of the term was written into the agreement, it could be amended to suit particular circumstances, in spite of the 1768 act, and numbers of pauper indentures were endorsed freeing the child at various ages after 16. Supporters of binding the very young child, to silk-weaving or chimney-sweeping, for example, maintained that, at the end of the term, then aged 14 or 16, a second apprenticeship could be arranged, giving the adolescent training for an adult livelihood, as William Hutton experienced.

The practice of paying a premium with an apprentice arose, according to Defoe, in the seventeenth century when the optional gift the child brought his new master's wife, "to take motherly care of him", was gradually converted into cash.[58] He noted that in the 1660s and 1670s the highest premium ever paid to eminent Levant merchants in London was £200, although by the 1720s they received as much as £1,000. Before 1640 those same merchants would have taken £100 or less and even "considerable Dealers" (drapers or grocers) had only £50 with a youth.[59] Evidence for premiums in Stuart England, although scattered and irregular, is quite widespread in a variety of trades and regions. As early as 1555 cash premiums existed among the Newcastle Adventurers, for in that year they imposed a fine of £10 on any master who took money or goods with his apprentice.[60] As in other trade legislation, rules were generally enacted against practices which, if not already well established, were becoming accepted. However, premiums were not recorded in the London Weavers' Company until 1730, although "customary long before that date".[61] If premiums were as rare as some comment has suggested, it is inconceivable that the 1709 Stamp Act would have been passed and later amended three times, for the indenture tax produced an income in its first year of £3,792 10s, which doubled by the 1780s and 1790s in spite of evasion and under-registration.[62] Further evidence for the existence of premiums may be seen in the fact that for nearly half a century before the 1709 act, law stationers had sold printed apprenticeship forms with a space left blank for the premium to be inserted.

When disputes occurred between master and apprentice, returning the premium, in part or whole, was normal in legal proceedings. That premiums by the early seventeenth century were not confined to London masters or great merchants may be seen from provincial disputes involving modest sums of less than £5, as at Norwich in 1615 or Nottingham in 1633, and by the masters' trades (a shoemaker, butcher and cutler).[63] Local variations were considerable, so that although only two of the 300 non-poor apprentices at Southampton in the early seventeenth century had premiums paid,[64] in Sheffield the cutlers were receiving premiums regularly by 1644.[65] Premiums were unfailingly recorded in many great London companies, such as the Stationers', from the first decade of the eighteenth century.

In the years after the Restoration younger sons of impoverished gentry, new to trade and the professions, became apprentices in increasing numbers. From such boys, with few personal contacts to secure admission, masters expected premiums; thus the Newcastle Hostmen took £30 or £40 from boys.[66] At the same period Defoe noted that placing an apprentice to any "Shop-keeping Trade will cost in a Countrey Market-Town not less than fifty or sixty pounds, but in London upwards of an hundred",[67] typified in one Lancashire apprentice's £60 to enter cotton manufacture.[68] That such arrangements were not always satisfactory is apparent from apprentices' protests (as at Hertford in 1687) that "great sumes of money" as premiums did not protect them from foreign competition in trade.[69]

The 1709 Stamp Act required the premium to be stated on an indenture and many early-eighteenth-century observers commented disapprovingly on the rising costs of binding a child. Defoe thought apprentices with large premiums were uncontrollable. Their masters were obliged to treat them as gentlemen, not servants, and such adolescents would no longer "stoop" to clean their masters' shoes, fetch water from conduits, wait at table or attend the family to church. Only rarely would they "condescend to open or shut the Shop windows, much less sweep the Shop or warehouse". The "humble apprentice" was transformed into the "lucrative pupil" who had to be "persuaded rather than commanded to do his work", so that by the early eighteenth century such prosperous, unruly adolescents were "too high for reproof or correction".[70]

In exceptional circumstances an unusually high premium would be necessary, as in the case of the Russian apprentices who came to English masters in the early eighteenth century, not entirely welcome because they were to learn the secrets of English skills. Thus in January 1719 the Birmingham ironmongers and smiths petitioned parliament against the newcomers, basing their complaint on the "large and unusual sums" paid by "Muscovites [who have] lately put apprentices to this place to learn the arts of making our iron manufacture". The Birmingham metal workers naturally feared the Russians' return to "his Czarist Majesty's dominions to instruct others to the prejudice of the artificers of Birmingham".[71] Their complaint about premiums was exemplified by the £70 Theodore Klepanicen paid in 1718 to Samuel Freeth, an edge-tool maker, for five years; other English apprentices to the trade paid £5 or £10 and served seven years.[72] This Russian child is interesting as an example of under-registration, because the Birmingham men's petition referred to numbers of apprentices, but only Klepanicen was registered. At least 15 other apprentices to various ship-building trades also came from Russia to Surrey and London masters during the years 1716–18 as part of Peter the Great's Westernization schemes. For all such boys premiums were many times those paid by English apprentices to the same trades and a shorter term was served by most:[73]

Table 1.2 Russian apprentices to English masters, 1716–18.

Trades	Number of Russians	Premiums for Russians	Other premiums	Terms for Russians	Other terms
Anchorsmith	3	£40, £60	£10	5, 7 years	7 years
Augur maker	2	£70	–	5 years	–
Boat builder	5	£30–£80	–	3, 5 years	–
Painter	2	£60	£4–£10	7 years	7 years
Ship's joiner	1	£60	–	7 years	–
Upholsterer	1	£120	£10–£40	3 years	7 years
Joiner	1	£40	£5–£10	5 years	7 years

Undoubtedly these masters had to overcome language and culture difficulties in teaching Russian apprentices and premiums were high as a result; none of these men is recorded as having other apprentices at the same time as the Russian boys. Perhaps ostracized by their fellow craftsmen for passing on skills to foreigners in trades that were important in England's economy and defence, a high premium may have been compensation for the loss of other apprentices' premiums and even for difficulties in trading afterwards.

The importance of the premium in securing an apprenticeship can be seen in bequests made by fathers of young families, who left specific sums of money in their wills for this purpose. Such provisions might be expected in the eighteenth century, but to find them in the early seventeenth suggests that premiums were far more general than has been supposed, especially as examples of this practice exist in remote, rural villages. Thus in 1633 William Evitts, a Warwickshire husbandman, bequeathed £10 to his second son, Richard, to be paid by his executors when "his Apprentisship comes forth and one quarter of corne the one half wheate the other barley to be payd hym . . . when he setts up his trade of hymself half a quarter of the first yere and the other half quarter the second yere". The third son, Thomas, was also to have £10, of which half would be paid "at the tyme when he will purpose to goe Apprentice and the other ffive Pounds at the age of Eighteene years"; if he chose not to be apprenticed he was to have the whole £10 at the age of 18. Two younger children, a boy aged five and a girl of nine, each had money bequests but with no mention of apprenticeship, while the eldest son inherited the land and all five shared the family chattels. Although described as a husbandman, Evitts was quite a substantial farmer; his goods were valued at £81 4s and included luxury items.[74] The two sons intended for apprentices did not die as children and presumably were indentured, for their names disappear from the parish records. Such testamentary provisions, in a remote midland village of less than 300 inhabitants, as early as 1633, indicate an unexpected awareness and acceptance of the apprenticeship premium. Earlier, a premium was presumably intended though not specified in the will of Robert Wood of Little Staughton (Beds.) who had requested his executors to use income from some of his land either to send his son to school or put him to some "profytable craffte".[75] Less surprising were the eighteenth-century businessmen who made similar bequests for their sons; John Gulson, a leather-dresser, in 1741 left £1,000 for apprenticing his 13-year-old son,[76] and responsibility for binding a child was often put upon a particular person in a will. Very occasionally children were left money for a premium by a friend or prosperous patron; for example, in 1661 a Cambridgeshire yeoman, John Welbore, left £3 6s 8d each to two village boys "towards their being put out apprentice",[77] and, although not common, such bequests indicate that premiums were widespread.

The range of premiums for the non-poor child by the late eighteenth century was huge and, in spite of attempts to tabulate these for the guidance of intending apprentices and their parents by such writers as Campbell and Collyer, factors that could not be measured often seem to have controlled the situation rather than simple market forces. Ambitious parents, newly prosperous, sought superior apprenticeships with merchants and in the professions, masters of standing who charged what the parent would pay. Certainly a famous master could attract exceptional sums, so that William Cheselden, the well-known lithotomist, with Newton and Pope among his patients, received £150, £210 and £350 as premiums in the years 1712–30. By 1800 Astley Cooper, once a pupil of John Hunter, with an annual income of £15,000, took £630 with one apprentice.[78] Artists of note also had higher than normal premiums; Arthur Devis would take an apprentice for seven years with 150 guineas, "supposing him to be a Boy of Genius, otherwise not at all", while William Hoare of Bath required £105, excluding board and lodging, and Charles Grignion, the London engraver, expected a similar sum.[79]

Some masters took children from good families with a lower premium for the cachet of having a well-bred apprentice in a business or practice and one such recruit encouraged other parents to place their offspring with the same man. Others received very high premiums whatever a child's social origins, so that Richard Manby, a London bookseller in Ludgate Street in the 1730s and 1740s, had three apprentices, each with £150. One was the son of a deceased London grocer, another a Worcester cleric's son and the third had a Norfolk gentleman as his father. Bookselling clearly attracted more sophisticated customers for whom educated apprentices were essential. Sir James Hodges, a bookseller on London Bridge, took 12 apprentices in the years 1737–77; of these, 5 had premiums from £100 to £157 10s, the sons of a broker, physician, schoolmaster, bookseller and mercer. Four other boys had premiums in the £50 range (their fathers a papermaker, salesman, bricklayer and merchant), while two had charity premiums and one was his own son, for whom no money was paid.[80] Certainly a father's early death could mean a low premium and poor trade for a child of quite prosperous parents if provision were not made in a man's will. Thus the son of a deceased Devizes apothecary, Walter Seager, was indentured in 1716 to a local currier with a £15 premium, although Seager himself had received £49 to take a boy into his own occupation;[81] a bequest to pay a premium usually secured the kind of career that would have been chosen if the father had lived. In the London Stationers' Company in the eighteenth century 28 apprentices were apothecaries' sons; of these, 9 were orphans, 3 with high premiums (£80 and £100), while 2 widowed mothers paid £40 and £50. In the same company, a variety of uncles, aunts and grandparents paid for fatherless boys to be bound.

Other masters who regularly took high premiums were those dealing in valuable raw materials, the professions, fashion trades with a wealthy clientele and industries with a large amount of capital tied up in stock and premises. In all these categories a large premium recompensed the master for an apprentice's errors he made as a novice and the clients he would offend; it provided a child with instruction and entry to a profitable livelihood for 30 years or more, establishing him in a prosperous niche with appropriate marriage and social prospects. There is little evidence that a high premium was in proportion to the length or brevity of the term or that it ensured luxurious living conditions for a child. Examples of very high premiums were listed by Campbell for the London trades in 1747, some with a very wide range:[82]

Table 1.3 High premiums in London trades, 1747.

Range of premiums	Trades
£20–£200	Apothecary, attorney, hosier, jeweller, draper
£30–£100	Ironmonger
£50–£100	Artist, coachmaker, conveyancer, coal factor, insurer, laceman, notary public, sugar baker, timber merchant, wool stapler
£50–£200	Brewer, mercer, scrivener, woollen draper
£50–£300	Banker, all kinds of merchants
£100–£200	Soap boiler

Nearly twenty years later Collyer altered these estimates only slightly and even by 1818 in some trades there was little change, with an apothecary receiving £210 and a draper £105, although such sums were then arguably worth less.[83] However, some extraordinarily high premiums were recorded,

23

particularly in the early eighteenth century, and writers such as Defoe continued to condemn both masters and parents for participating. It is possible, however, that his protests were sharpened by the modest premium, £10 15s, his own father paid on his behalf in 1687.[84]

Even if not famous, a master of good repute in a flourishing trade, especially in London, could expect to attract substantial premiums and apprentices from far afield. Thus in 1787 a London coachmaker, John Browne, took £200 with the son of a Worcester wine-merchant; four years later he received two more premiums, £500 from a Limehouse brewer and £525 from a Herefordshire gentleman, with their sons.[85] In 1783 a Suffolk gentleman's orphan son could be apprenticed to a silk broker in Aldermanbury with £1,000, the entrée to a future prosperous career.[86] Not only provincial parents paid large sums for children to enter city trades. Thus in 1713 £1,075 was paid by a London fishmonger binding his son to a Levant merchant in the City,[87] while another master took an Esher boy with £800 in the same year;[88] in 1721 an Exchange Office attorney received £450 with an apprentice from Putney, one of the many law entrants with high premiums.[89] Provincial masters in the high-premium trades were paid considerably less than city men; Sussex boys bound to London attorneys had premiums of between £200 and £345 while local masters took only £100.[90]

Further away from London premiums fluctuated less, so that in Wiltshire the largest sum paid, out of nearly 3,000 apprenticeships, was £262 10s to a Devizes attorney in 1720.[91] Some masters of course took more than one child at a high premium, for example, a Salisbury surgeon in 1753 and 1759 received £210 with each of his two apprentices.[92] Generally, however, country premiums were lower and for only 66 Wiltshire children (2.2 per cent) were sums of £100 or more paid, although Bath and Bristol masters regularly attracted larger amounts.[93] In Warwickshire at the same period the traditionally prosperous occupations consistently cost parents more: attorney and chemist (average £100, highest £150), surgeon (£62, £105), draper (£48, £105), mercer (£47, £120), ironmonger (£46, £150), apothecary (£44, £90) and grocer (£30, £105).[94] It has been suggested that in one London company, the Weavers', clerics paid much smaller premiums for their sons,[95] but there is no evidence of such preferential treatment elsewhere. Thus of the 81 apothecaries' apprentices listed for Sussex, 10 were the sons of clerics but their premiums fell exactly in a middle range (£30 to £80).[96]

Next to these profitable occupations came a group of trades requiring either a high level of individual ability (the saddler or cabinetmaker), considerable outlay on workshops and space (the tanner, dyer or chandler) or new manufacturing processes that took advantage of contemporary changes in fashion and technology (the toymaker or japanner). Their average premiums ranged from £10 to £20, but could reach £50 if to masters of distinction, such as Matthew Boulton of Soho.[97] In this category of trades maximum premiums included £105 (plumber, toymaker), £70 (saddler), £50 (brass founder) and

£30 (tanner, currier, dyer, cooper).[98] It is noticeable that the clothing and food trades were not in the two most prosperous categories, although well represented in the third group, with average premiums of between £6 and £9, but with considerable numbers of poor and charity apprentices. Certain of these trades illustrated the fashion changes of the eighteenth century in their depressed premiums (breeches-, button and bucklemaking), while others, such as gun smithing, experienced both boom and slump. Also in this category were trades almost unaffected by external forces, with a regular supply of apprentices, a steady but modest profit and little variation in premiums (carpenter, wheelwright, miller), although they undoubtedly suffered from rising prices and unchanged premiums. Figures for Warwickshire are representative of many such humble trades. Very occasionally a child's premium consisted of goods as well as cash, so that, when a gentleman's son went to a Wiltshire apothecary in 1719 his premium was £60 and four hundredweight of cheese, valued at £5, on which tax was paid,[99] while, at the other end of the scale, a pauper girl took a feather bed as part of her premium when bound at the same period.[100]

There were two permanent problems in the whole issue of pauper apprenticeship premiums. Firstly, because such sums were raised by the overseers of the poor, understandably preoccupied with saving the poor rate; secondly, because premiums had to be high enough to attract masters to take children whose labour, when young, was generally unprofitable and not balanced by the cost of their maintenance. A further consideration was voiced by the opponents of parish apprenticeship, such as Bernard Mandeville, who protested that the numerous offspring of the "incorrigeable" poor received training by means of a premium that the respectable parishioner, paying poor rates, could not afford. So that paupers were not preferred to other children, cash limits were sometimes set for parish apprentices, as at Nottingham in 1702, when an upper figure of £4 was fixed for poor boys' premiums.[101] Occasionally the parish would find the premium by selling the possessions of the child's parents and at Dickleburgh (Norf.) in 1682 the parish sold Michael Carsey's goods for £5 and used it to bind his nine-year-old daughter to housewifery for eight years.[102] At Kenilworth (War.) in 1703 the overseers raised 15s from Jane Newey's possessions towards apprenticing her son.[103] Occasionally the father of a pauper bastard would be ordered to pay the premium. Two such children were provided for in Warwickshire in 1675 and 1677[104] and also at Diss (Norf.), where Edward Oadham, liable for Rebecca Wharton's child, was forced in 1713 to pay £5 for her premium as well as maintenance until she was eight;[105] in 1720 an Ilminster (Som.) merchant tailor received a £5 premium the parish had extracted from a putative father.[106] Such cases illustrate the contemporary view that paternal responsibility for illegitimate children included arrangements for their livelihood.

It has been suggested that pauper premiums were paid "long before they became general with the population at large . . . the poor law apprentices were a class apart",[107] a crucially important view if it could be substantiated. The main problem in comparing parish with non-poor apprentices is the varying amount of surviving source material on which to base any conclusions. Early overseers' accounts are fairly rare; for example, of the 215 parishes in one midland county, Warwickshire, only 13 now have overseers' accounts earlier than 1700 and a further 31 for the next half century. Many counties, such as Staffordshire, have virtually none before 1750. Exceptions, however, were the great Stuart trading centres that kept their own apprenticeship records, pauper and prosperous, long before any kind of national registration began. Thus of the 1,072 poor children bound at Southampton (1609–1708), the majority had premiums, in a range from 3s 4d to £8, but with £1 or £1 10s most often paid, irrespective of trade or decade. Clearly the borough authorities acted on the 1563 and 1574 statutes and indentured destitute children, such as one ten-year-old orphan "having noe friends or meanes to relieve or maynteyne her" with her four-year-old sister, "lefte uppon the towne to be kept of almes".[108] A number of the paupers' premiums at Southampton were paid in instalments, in some cases to be reimbursed if the master or child should die. In spite of widespread economic disruption in the Civil War and the erratic keeping of records, in Southampton the indenturing of children continued at a steady rate.

Record material for assessing poor apprenticeships is unfortunately scattered and incomplete for many communities; at Old Swinford (Worcs.) only 18 of the 638 pauper indentures (1670–1794) have premiums entered, all in the decades 1672–1702. The premiums ranged from 15s to £6, but the majority were £3; for the rest of the eighteenth century they were either omitted or not paid. However, at a public meeting in 1735 £2 was allowed with a nailer's apprentice, which suggests that this was an unusual procedure.[109] Even within a county great variety existed from one parish to another in the range of pauper premiums and some were generous, £9 17s 6d in 1719 at Tredington, £8 at both Stoneleigh in 1715 and at Polesworth in 1684, all Warwickshire villages.[110] No pattern in premiums is discernible, for some parishes always paid premiums from an early date, some ceased doing so during the late eighteenth century while others never gave money. Of 6,709 Warwickshire pauper apprentices (1700–1834), premiums were paid by the parish for only 29.3 per cent. Within this group, after 1801, theoretically all premiums should have been recorded, but in practice only industrial or large parishes (Atherstone, Bedworth, Warwick) did so.[111] In some rural communities, such as Stoneleigh,[112] premiums were fairly regularly paid, but complex factors influencing the overseers' decisions included parish solvency, numbers of children to be bound, willing masters and the general state of the local or national economy.

The premium's flexibility may be seen when it was offered at a generous level to induce a master to take a child in some way incapacitated; when Hannah Wright, an orphan, was bound to a yeoman some five miles from her home, the premium was to be returned if she became blind.[113] In 1750 the fairly high sum of £5 was offered by Almeley (Herefs.) overseers "In case any p[shoner] will take Ann Murrell an apprentice on acc[t] of her weak understanding"; this was a remote parish where children were normally bound to local farmers on a rota basis with no premium.[114] It was, of course, better for ratepayers if a handicapped child went beyond the parish boundaries to secure settlement rights elsewhere; to facilitate this the occasional very high sum was offered. Thus £18 was given to put Henry Bannister, a lame boy, apprentice to an Epsom cordwainer in the 1730s by a parish where premiums were usually £3.[115] In spite of fluctuations in prices, wages and occupational prosperity at any period, the premium remained a reliable yardstick of craft, trade or professional status, a means of controlling competition and the size of the adult workforce. Payment of premiums survived all the anti-apprenticeship sentiments of the nineteenth century, when premiums were seen as contrary to the worker's interests, a protection for traditional crafts that prevented the entry of men of talent. The existence of premiums in the twentieth century, although in a narrow range of skills (hairdressing, couture houses, some engineering trades), illustrates the strength of the practice for over three centuries.

The responsibility for clothing an apprentice during the term was clearly the master's, as it was the parents' or overseers' if the child had remained at home or in parish care. Clothes were a requirement common to all categories of apprenticeship, along with bed, board and washing. Children were clothed before leaving home by parents, charity or parish, although only for paupers is there abundant detailed evidence. How prosperous apprentices were clothed is rarely described, although their unsuitable dress frequently caused offence. Attempts, through the sumptuary laws, to control their fashionable appearance are regularly recorded in medieval guild activities. Failure to clothe the apprentice adequately was a common breach of the indenture, especially in the poorer trades, but a noticeably ill-clad child could cause a master adverse public comment and even official enquiry. One of the clauses to improve the lot of factory apprentices was that they were to be paraded in church every Sunday, ensuring that they had at least some adequate clothes. Poor dress was less severe an abuse than insufficient food or violence to the child, although more likely to occasion critical comment by acquaintances.

Evidence is scarce about the clothes a prosperous apprentice was given on leaving home, although Ralph Josselin spent £5 on his son's when indenturing him to a London grocer in the 1660s.[116] Being well dressed was essential for apprentices who served the public in expensive or fashionable trades. However, advice manuals suggested that "Apish Affectation and Vanity of Dress" were as deplorable as "negligent Slovenliness" in the apprentice.[117] Collyer stressed the need for "cleanliness in his person and neatness in his dress, which seem to demand a suitable decorum of behaviour . . . and the advantages of dress are what he owes to others and not to himself".[118] When

John Coggs, a boy of means, was indentured to a London stationer in 1702 for seven years his mother and relations gave him money and clothes, a hat (7s 6d), wig (£1 2s), gloves (2s 4d), shoes (3s 6d) and 4½ yards of cloth (£2 5s). To prepare for winter his mother bought him "a new great coate with double rooes of buttons", a pair of breeches and two shirts. John Coggs bought himself accessories, however, silver buckles, a ferrule and new head for his cane, a clasp-knife with tortoiseshell handle, silk handkerchiefs and cap; he spent 1s on "dressing a hat". Coggs also paid for six pairs of shoes in one year.[119] His fashionable dress was matched by his unruly behaviour, almost the epitome of the youths Defoe criticized.

Other non-poor apprentices who wrote memoirs gave little account of their clothing; Francis Place described the dress of youths aged 16 to 20. In the 1780s all wore breeches, stocking and shoes, before the advent of trousers or pantaloons,[120] a style of dress, with a wide-sleeved shirt and collarless coat, common in the work of Hogarth, Morland and Rowlandson. Apart from their ordinary dress, many apprentices also wore distinctive hats or aprons, marking them as members of a particular occupation. Josselin's son "put on the blue apron" when bound,[121] while other apprentices were recognizable by aprons of leather (blacksmiths, farriers, shoemakers) or distinctive fabrics when away from their masters' shops (butchers, bakers, carpenters, watchmakers). The most accurate and immediate picture of apprentices' dress, however, was when they absconded and their masters advertised for their return. Clothes were important for the runaways' survival and most took their spare garments as they fled (Appendix 3). When William Hutton recalled the severe winter of 1740 he had only a thin, unlined waistcoat and no coat to wear; he absconded a year later, aged 17, taking with him the "genteel" suit he had earned by overwork, a shirt, stockings and his best wig.[122]

Charity children at school wore their distinctive uniforms and, like Blake's "flowers" in red, blue and green, were instantly recognized in their own community.[123] Charities varied whether cash or clothes were provided with the apprentice; at Bablake Boys' Hospital, Coventry, each apprentice had a £2 premium and clothes worth £3 13s 6d,[124] while at Warwick only 3 per cent of apprentices were bought clothes by the different borough charities, as well as their premiums of £5 to £12.[125] Sometimes the child's parents and master would share the cost of clothes or the master provide those items he himself produced, so that a cordwainer made his apprentice shoes and leather aprons, while the boy's parents bought other clothing.[126]

More is known about the dress of pauper apprentices, as are other details, because the overseers of the poor were accountable to the parish ratepayers and the justices for their expenditure. Clothes for apprentices appear in overseers' accounts from all English counties, in some cases only as a total figure, but in the majority of instances individual items of dress, with prices, were recorded. It was always cheaper to spend £1 or £2 fitting out a pauper apprentice than maintain a growing adolescent in the home parish for some years. Certain basic clothes were provided, irrespective of rising prices. A boy received a shirt, waistcoat, breeches, stockings and shoes, with a coat and hat for outdoors. A girl was given a petticoat, one or two shifts and, when worn, a pair of stays as underwear, with a gown, apron, stockings and shoes as indoor clothes; she might also have a cap. Handkerchiefs were shawl-like squares of fabric worn over the shoulders; by the later eighteenth century they were substitutes for short cloaks, for indoor and outdoor wear.[127] Coats and cloaks were hardly ever bought for female pauper apprentices; as girls did not travel to work and were generally employed indoors (except in husbandry and brickmaking) outerwear was not thought necessary. In the late seventeenth century a typical pauper girl's clothes cost 18s 1d and comprised:

to Goody James for a paire of stockens for Anne Heath	1s 3d
for Anne Heath's clothes & for an Apron for her	2s 2d
Goody Ambler to buy linens for Anne Heath	1s 0d
for cloth . . . to make her a suite being 4 yards	6s 6d
for linen & Clasps & Keepers for her Clothes	6d
a Shift for Anne Heath & an Apron for her	3s 9d
pr of bodies for Anne Heath	2s 8d
Goody Ambler for making Anne Heath a Shift	3d

The same parish ten years later provided a similar set of clothes for "Vernons daughter", whose apprenticeship premium was £2 5s, including three aprons, three coifs and a shift (7s 3d), a mantua and petticoat (2s 6d) made from six yards of tammy (10s 6d), two whisks and a pair of shoes (3s 10d).[128] The fashionable whisk was a broad, cape-like collar. (See also Appendix 4.) At this period many parishes bought quantities of fabric for local women and tailors to make the apprentices' clothes, woollen material for gowns or waistcoats, finer tammy for underskirts (petticoats). Paupers were better clad if their masters could bargain with the parish. Thus in 1734 one orphan, bound for only three years, had quite a large wardrobe, although some of the items were secondhand; the shorter term and the purchase of a stomacher suggests she was about 18: "five shifts two of which are new: Two Paires of Shooes one of which is new: Two paire of Shostrings one of which is new: Six Capps: Two Handkerchiefs: a New Paire of Boddice & Stomacher: & one New Straw Hat".[129] As a relevant comparison at the same period the girls at Leeds Charity School each had a new coat, petticoat, two shifts, apron, cap, band, two handkerchiefs, a pair of stockings and a pair of shoes.[130]

Many parishes, especially rural ones, clothed their apprentices even in the later eighteenth century above the most basic level; some indentures were endorsed with a list of the child's clothes. In 1786, for example, 11-year-old Ann Martin's indenture noted that her outfit comprised hats, caps, shifts, neckerchiefs, aprons, outer and under petticoats, stockings and shoes (two of each item) and a new pair of stays.[131] As the eighteenth century progressed some parishes increasingly gave cash instead of clothes to the master, an arrangement obviously open to abuse, with the risk that the child became "like a beggar having nothing but rags and wearing no shirt".[132] Sometimes money was given to a parishioner, not otherwise poor, to meet the cost of a child's clothes when indentured. Clothing and binding a poor child could be a substantial proportion of a small parish's expenditure, especially if the master lived far away. In one hamlet in June 1776 the total spent was £5 18s 4d, out of which indenturing a pauper girl cost £3 1s 6d (52 per cent) as well as 13s 4d for her clothes.[133]

Male apprentices' clothes were always less varied than girls', with only six basic items regularly provided. Typical of a pauper boy's dress was John Glover's outfit, costing £1 10s 1d in 1679, as well as his £4 premium: cloth for apparel (11s 9d), 4 ells of cloth for shirts (4s 6d), a hat (1s 6d), a pair of shoes (2s 8d), two pairs of stockings (2s 2d), trimming for his clothes (2s 0d), tailor's charge for making (5s 6d).[134] Most entries do not record the purchase of underwear for boys, although fabric bought by the parish may have been used for this; a rare example of such an entry was 5s spent in 1688 on two shirts and a pair of drawers "for young Ansill", out of which the shirts cost 4s 6d.[135] By the nineteenth century, however, boys' outfits cost nearly three times as much, £3 4s for one youth in 1805, for example.[136] The most striking aspect of fitting out a poor child was the variable level of cash spent on any one apprentice and, in a difficult year, only a pair of shoes for 3s or 4s was provided. However, as all clothing prices rose in the eighteenth century, the value of the apprentice's outfit to the master also increased.

The dress of factory apprentices was frequently uniform, provided by the child's overseers. Benjamin Smart's apprentices at Warwick had two new dresses each as well as "three articles of each kind which require weekly washing, it being more convenient to wash once a fortnight only". His girls had a satisfactory level of dress and even a critical magistrate visiting the mill considered their clothes "very good and comfortable".[137] Smart would not accept girls without adequate clothes and when one Oxford pauper arrived at the mill with poor clothing provided by her parish, he returned the garments as "they are not quite suitable or like the other Girls' dresses".[138] The importance of two dresses as the most expensive part of the female wardrobe is emphasized when Smart advertised for workers in 1806 and 1812. In the first instance he required two new dresses but no premium;[139] six years later, "because the times are much worse", he expected dresses and a £5 premium.[140] The provision of clothes for factory apprentices was widespread; Blincoe reported that St Pancras workhouse provided two outfits for each child[141] and Cuckney Mill (Derbys.) also dressed the children alike.[142] At Collycroft worsted mill (War.), a contemporary illustration shows both boys and girls of different ages dressed alike at their work in the mid-1790s.[143]

The value placed on a child's clothes may be seen if the apprenticeship were cancelled, for the return of clothing, or its value in cash, was usually arranged. When silk-weaver Thomas Ryland "much misused and abused" his apprentice, the boy was discharged and the master ordered to return all his clothes.[144] Sending away an apprentice but keeping the clothes was a serious offence and, when one master did so, his guild immediately ordered him to release the boy's clothes, a jerkin, two shirts, two bands and a pair of frieze breeches, to the beadle.[145]

An unusual provision in an indenture for more prosperous children was that either masters or parents would be responsible for medical attention if the child were ill, perhaps inserted only for children who were a known health risk. Apprentices were a category often excluded from eighteenth-century voluntary hospitals, for they were seen as their masters' responsibility. However, even healthy children were an expense to masters if they contracted smallpox, and a handful of indentures made provision for this eventuality, so that parents should bear all or half the cost.[146] Before inoculation was widespread, the risk to children, entering a new community as apprentices, was considerable, as Josselin's sons found.[147] However, there was awareness of the dangers, and one country gentleman's son, joining his uncle, a London merchant, was advised to catch the disease and recover before leaving home.[148]

Thus an apprenticeship was arranged, a master found, the premium paid and the child clothed, ready to begin the long term of the indenture, to live for many years in a strange environment, often far from home, with negligible family contacts, until adult journeyman status was attained and an individual, independent life possible. Such essential conditions were common to all categories of English apprenticeship for some three centuries, a method of technical training that included the wealthiest to the poorest child, the grandest to the humblest occupation, which survived in spite of abuses, criticism and economic changes, to be finally overturned only by education reforms of the twentieth century.

CHAPTER 2

The choice of a career

Pride, avarice or whim are too often the chief counsellors of the father, the mother, or the guardian, when they deliberate on the most serious concern in life, the proper settlement of their children in the world . . . parents think it a dishonour to put their children to any branch of business which they do not consider as a genteel trade, or that has not something in it suitable to their notions of grandeur.

J. Collyer, *The parent's and guardian's directory* (1761)

When guardians and parents chose a life-long career for their wards or children, certain factors were common in their selection, almost regardless of historical period or social status. Although such eighteenth-century writers as Collyer, Campbell and Defoe tried to explain to parents the importance of choosing apprenticeships so that children would be happy and spend their adult life in work suited to an individual's "genius" and temperament, this particular consideration did nomt seem to have been paramount for the majority of parents. Of prime practical importance in selecting an occupation was its prospect of long-term security, both of work available and its earning potential, as well as the regard accorded to an occupation by contemporary society. The factor of employment security was particularly significant when the traditional apprenticeship restrictions applied, for adults might not practise a trade to which they had not been bound and to do so was a criminal offence.

Indenturing children was committing them in an inescapable way to an adult working life perhaps of 30 years or more, in one particular occupation, in prosperous or hard times, when ill or well, even against their own inclinations. The parent's choice was, however, less difficult than might now appear, at least until the later eighteenth century, for trades and crafts until the Industrial Revolution were surprisingly stable in England, even static, both in products and in profits or wages, so that a parent would expect an occupation that was prosperous at the time of indenturing to remain so. After about 1800 this essential stability could no longer be relied on, and a trade that was at least adequately profitable in a child's apprenticeship (such as handloom weaving, nailing, watchmaking or ribbon-weaving) could, with the introduction of factory methods, mechanization and unskilled labour, become impoverished almost overnight and certainly not provide a comfortable or respectable existence for the future journeyman or master. However, certain goods and skills were always in demand and this must have influenced the choice of the more thoughtful parents who, like George Herbert's father, in selecting his son's apprenticeship "cast about for something for [him] and he thought shoe-making was a never-failing trade as people must wear shoes".[1]

The actual money wages an adult would earn may not have been the most significant factor in choosing a career in the pre-industrial period for, as Campbell makes clear, there were four basic categories of those who earned income: the impoverished labourer, the lower but not pauperized tradesman, the highly skilled craftsman and the professional or quasi-professional.[2] In all four groups earnings were in direct ratio to both the apprenticeship premium and the cost of setting up as a master. In spite of an apparent rigidity, both contemporary comment and record evidence indicate that, by various means, apprentices could move from their family status up or down, into a recognizably different social category. Collyer condemned parental social aspirations and avarice that often guided the choice of a child's future career:

> From this motive, a father who will have 500 l. to bestow on his son, will give 200 l. with him to a linnen draper, a wholesale hosier, or a sugar baker, and by this preposterous step oblige the young man to be a journeyman as long as he lives; when he might in some other trade easily become a master, make a good figure in life, and by the blessing of heaven, bring up a family and perhaps acquire a fortune for his children.[3]

The social estimation accorded to trades varied considerably depending on whether the occupation were assessed by its practitioners or those who comprised its clientele and at what historical period their judgements were made. Certain trades were highly esteemed from within; the shoemakers always referred to themselves as a "gentle" occupation, rather than as common tradesmen, and indeed the craft seemed to produce a high proportion of thinking, literate men, frequently active in religious and political dissent. There was, however, a practical reason for their above-average literacy. Shoemaking was a suitable skill for a physically small or even disabled boy. Campbell had noted it as a trade that "does not require much Strength"[4] and such apprentices were more likely to become literate since they might spend their leisure time in sedentary pursuits.

Other occupations expressed high esteem of their own status often as their skills declined in value and the members nostalgically recalled an earlier golden age when times were prosperous and wages high. The Leicestershire framework knitters, for example, greatly impoverished by the nineteenth century, remembered the years before the Napoleonic Wars when "each had a garden, a barrel of home-brewed ale, a working suit of clothes and one for Sundays, and plenty of leisure, seldom working more than three days a week. Moreover, music was much cultivated by some of them."[5] Even one of the nineteenth-century's most depressed trades, ribbon-weaving, had formerly been so prosperous in the "Big Purl Time" that the Coventry weavers could employ the less well-paid watchmakers to shell their peas.[6] The watch trade, too, suffered a similar decline, for its members had once considered themselves a "fraternity" who thought "parish relief dishonourable, since the profession of a watchmaker had always been deem'd that of a gentleman, and the higher order of Mechanics".[7]

As the eighteenth century progressed, a number of trades suffered a considerable decline with the introduction of mass-production methods and a cheaper, if less well-made, commodity. Most leatherworkers and metal craftsmen, such as the gunsmith or nailer, were harmed by mass production, and lowering premiums, with the introduction of pauper and charity apprentices, reflected the trades' own loss of security and popular esteem. However, as certain trades were descending others were rising. An interesting example of improved status may be seen in the transition from farrier to veterinary surgeon, brought about by outside pressures (agricultural changes, breed amelioration and foreign wars) and by the ambition of the practitioners themselves to improve their own status. The surgeon also experienced a rise in status at the same period with the recognition by medical schools that surgery, though manual, was an important branch of medicine to be taught. External factors also improved medical status with enhanced employment, the introduction of new drugs and more sophisticated, scientific techniques as well as patients' raised expectations. Thus both veterinarians and surgeons rose to become closer to the university-educated men (physician, lawyer and cleric) and so increased the proportion of professional careers open to the prosperous child or ambitious parent. A similar process was experienced by engineers, architects and artists, who all indentured apprentices with greatly enhanced premiums by the late eighteenth century. At the same period the tertiary occupations, particularly in finance, expanded and grew, providing a new range of careers for boys from a prosperous background.

Some measure of the social regard for various occupations can be gained by examining the public offices held by particular craftsmen. Thus, as Birmingham's leather crafts declined, to be replaced by the metal trades, so public office was held by a japanner or bucklemaker, while in Coventry the importance of watchmaking was reflected in the numbers of the trade who became mayors of the city during the industry's prosperous years. At a lower level of public service, trustees of small local charities were usually from the lesser professions (the apothecary) or the superior crafts (the upholsterer or saddler). Parish officials were largely chosen from local tradesmen, the carpenter, tailor or wheelwright.

Whatever an occupation may have thought of itself and its own practitioners, the opinion of society as a whole did not necessarily concur. Particular trades were widely acknowledged to be dishonest, with popular ballads, literature and the visual arts reflecting these views. There were two main categories of occupations in which cheating was widespread; those that converted raw materials into goods (the tailor or shoemaker) and traders who sold commodities that could be adulterated (flour or milk), short-measured (groceries or fabrics) or that were of poor quality (meat or bread). Contemporary comment on different crafts is unevenly represented, with some occupations frequently discussed, but there was generally a consensus of opinion that men in some trades were dishonest, cheerful, hard-drinking, cowardly or lecherous. Of all the English trades, tailors were the second most numerous, and perhaps for this reason they were often mentioned or figured in different activities. Prosperous enough to have their own section in the great Corpus Christi play at Coventry, they were widely considered to be cowardly and often thought to be physically disabled.[8] They were participants in St Monday's festival and, like several occupations that worked another craftsman's product, were suspected of being less than honest.[9] Perhaps Francis Place accurately assessed his own social status and that of the whole trade for "neither he nor his enemies ever forgot that he was that most ungentlemanly of things, a tailor".[10] Even more numerous than tailors, shoemakers belonged to a respectable occupation, equally subject to St Monday, and always noticeable by their numbers in any popular disturbances.

Apart from craftsmen who worked other men's materials, those who dealt in food or textiles that could be either adulterated or short-measured for greater profit were thought to be particularly dishonest. In spite of their comparative rarity, for not every village had a mill, millers were frequently the subject of rhymes and songs, most of them uncomplimentary.[11] Aside from their reputation for being gross and lecherous, millers were often thought guilty of adulterating their flour and thus were the object of mob hatred in times of bread shortage and high prices. Community disapproval could be forcibly expressed, as in 1756, a famine year, when local colliers marched on Coventry,[12] destroying mills and raiding bakeries as they passed. The miller's proverbial dishonesty linked him in street literature with the grocer:

> The grocer sands his sugar and he sells sloe leaves for tea,
> And there's the dusty miller, where's a bigger rogue than he?

Other occupations were also thought guilty of short measure and of selling inferior goods. The butcher, "underneath whose scale is stuck a dirty lump of fat", or the baker, with his "alum bread and starch", were obviously equally distrusted by their poorer customers.[13] However, at the prosperous end of the retail trade, men such as mercers, drapers and grocers saw themselves providing good career prospects for boys from affluent backgrounds, with apprentices living "as family" during their term. In all these occupations big premiums reflected the high status that merchants enjoyed in society.

The general esteem in which the professions were held is perhaps the most difficult to assess, if only because popular concepts changed considerably between Tudor and Victorian times. Traditional apprenticeship remained the only means of entry into the occupation of attorney and all branches of medicine, except the physician's, until the early years of the nineteenth century. Their clientele came from a very wide range of society and their fees were frequently greatly resented. Law and medicine increasingly attracted boys from good family backgrounds, but contemporary opinion was distrustful of their professional skills. The popular estimation of such occupations was

> Now first it is a lawyer, to bother and to jaw,
> He knows well how to cheat you with a little bit of law;
> And next it is a doctor, to handle you he's rough,
> He will charge you half-a-crown for sixpennyworth of stuff.[14]

In time of need all classes were obliged to use the services of the medical practitioner,[15] but Garth's "Dispensary" or Hogarth's "Mon^r de la Pillule" suggests the low esteem in which fringe practitioners were held. Campbell considered it was "a Degree of Madness to trust them upon any Consideration".[16] Generally considered to be of lower status than the surgeon, the apothecary was summoned to treat the servants in wealthy households while a physician attended the family, as in *Pride and prejudice, Jane Eyre* and *Vanity fair*; there were also, however, apothecaries in large towns with a considerable wholesale trade who lived a prosperous existence among their fellow merchants. Both surgeons and apothecaries attracted apprentices from comfortable homes, who were prepared to travel far to secure a training for a profitable career, since illness would always require treatment. Of lower status, and proportionately lower income, but requiring "as much Judgment and Sagacity, though not so much Learning",[17] was the veterinary surgeon. His status was considerably enhanced in the nineteenth century from his earlier farriery origins, but he was responsible for a valuable source of transport, entertainment and power, the horse, in both town and country. The prosperity of his trade can be seen in the substantial veterinary premises that still survive in many town centres.

In the highly respected trades, even more than the premium as a yardstick of status was the craftsman's product, so that the silversmith, saddler and cabinetmaker, although working with their own hands, created individual, quality goods, impossible to mass-manufacture. At a lower level on the scale, the shoemaker, tailor, milliner and hatter could serve either a high-fashion or utilitarian market, with proportionate profits, and yet all such trades could suffer from the competition of inferior and cheaper factory goods, with only the luxury part of the trade secure.

The majority of apprentices, however, were not bound to the professions or the superior crafts but to a wide range of town and country occupations that changed little from the Tudor period until the later nineteenth century, and in 1747 Campbell could list over 350 trades for apprentices in London. Most of these occupations required only moderate premiums and did not involve high setting-up costs. Equally, the profits were never very great, but trades such as those of the plumber, tinman, fellmonger, staymaker, mason or turner would always be sure of at least an adequate livelihood. These and many others were "respectable" trades, regarded by society as honourable, and comprised the majority of occupations to which non-pauper children were bound.

At the lowest level of public esteem there was a further category of employment recognized by all as humble, even demeaning, impoverished and unappealing, with poor or non-existent career prospects for the apprentice. Such dead-end occupations were recognized as suitable for only the poorest, the orphan, the parish apprentice or the child from a very large family, for whom the chief consideration was securing a place where they would no longer be an expense for the parish officials or parents, providing an essential, cheap labour force for factories and small masters. The trades to which they were sent fall into four main categories. First, the labour-intensive, mostly traditional occupations, where even the youngest child could perform useful tasks, untrained, such as agriculture or silk-winding. Secondly, there were those crafts greatly overstocked with hands, especially the clothing trades, in which females were the majority of apprentices. Thirdly, there were also those occupations where small physique was essential, such as chimney-sweeping or cotton manufacture, and fourthly, the trades where machinery was depressing the adult's earning capacity, such as handloom weaving or nail- and chain-making, in which the domestic working unit, the family, required even the youngest pair of hands to help maintain its earning capacity, if necessary with apprentices. In most of these trades the apprentice was unwanted at the end of the term and could not find adult employment. These were the lowest grade of occupations for apprentices, deplored by many writers and philanthropists, but defended as essential in a rapidly industrializing economy. The fact that most of these occupations were also extremely hazardous to health meant that only the least prosperous child was indentured to them. All trades show that increasing numbers of pauper apprentices tended to attract yet more, while children from good homes in an occupation meant that other parents or guardians were drawn towards that master or trade for their own children.

Apart from the obvious economic factors that made a trade socially esteemed, an occupation was not well regarded if female apprentices predominated. Girls were apprenticed to housewifery, agriculture and the female fashion trades (millinery and mantua-making or dressmaking); they formed a considerable proportion of the textile workforce, both in the factory and home. A minority of girls were apprenticed to some occupations requiring considerable physical strength (mining, the small metal trades, brickmaking). They were rigorously excluded from apprenticeships in the building or leather trades and the heavy metal skills (wheelwright or blacksmith), the profitable crafts, the professions and the high-capital manufacturing industries or prosperous trades. Although not apprenticed, a number of women ran their late husbands' or fathers' firms, shops and practices, often well into the nineteenth century, although usually not taking apprentices in their own right.

At all periods, the largest number of female apprentices were indentured to housewifery, girls chiefly from a poor background, bound by their overseers, often remaining in their own community as a source of cheap labour to the ratepayers. The unsuitability of such girls as servants can be seen in the frequency with which the more prosperous parishioners agreed to be fined rather than have pauper apprentices join their households. An act had been passed in the late seventeenth century to cover this contingency,[18] and, according to the 1834 Poor Law Commissioners, fines raised in this way were an acknowledged and regular form of parish income.[19] Domestic service for girls was not generally well regarded and there was a reluctance on the part of some families to indenture their daughters to housework when alternative employment, such as silk-weaving, was available. The girls themselves were said to "look down with scorn upon it, and prefer the liberty of Monday and Saturday, and the exemption from confinement, and the little finery, with the liberty to wear it, which the loom procures them".[20] Parents were warned in the eighteenth century that they had "better turn out [their] daughter into the street at once, than place her out to service. For ten to one her master shall seduce her, or she shall be made the confidante of her mistress's intrigues."[21] Even though housewifery apprenticeship might have been little more than a source of cheap labour, it did at least ensure the prospect of adult employment after the term was finished and provided training and experience that would be useful in her own home after marriage, for all agreed that factory work made young girls domestically incompetent. The problem of making pauper girls acceptable domestic servants was recognized by those in charge of them; the governors of one Gloucestershire workhouse, at Stroud, announced that their girls available as apprentices were all "virtuously and Christianly brought up, and made fit for good service".[22] Girls bound to agriculture were equally liable to do harsh, rough work in bad weather but they too could be employed as adults.

The trades that supplied the female fashion industry, mantua-making and millinery, were exclusively for girls. Both occupations were urban and condemned by contemporaries as little more than instruction courses for prostitution, unsuitable for girls of respectable family. Girls were also apprenticed in considerable numbers to textiles, held in low public esteem because of the small premiums, bad working conditions and poor career prospects. The few predominantly male occupations to which girls were apprenticed, the small metal trades, for example, were so impoverished that only the parish girl would be bound. The coarsened state of female apprentices in such trades caused amazed, adverse comment from all who saw them, particularly foreign visitors.

The narrowness of girls' career choices and prospects, even for the more prosperous, can be seen from the non-poor apprenticeships recorded during the years 1710–60 from three different counties, where their occupations were primarily those connected with needlework (mantua-maker, milliner, gloveress, sempstress), but also weaving, housewifery and agricultural work:

Table 2.1   Proportion of non-poor female apprentices, 1710–60.

County	Total number of apprentices	% of females
Sussex	2,989	2.9
Warwickshire	2,454	3.1
Wiltshire	2,759	6.9

In these areas, Wiltshire's higher rate of female apprentices is due to the proximity of Bath, with many more openings in the fashion trades in the eighteenth century than the other rural counties. A similar pattern, although for a narrower timespan, has also been recorded for Bedfordshire and Surrey, each with below five per cent female apprentices from non-poor families.

Clearly, one of the problems of indenturing apprentices, especially young girls, living away from home, was the risk of their being sexually abused. Campbell noted that millinery and mantua-making were equally unsuitable in this respect, and that the title of milliner was only a "more polite Name for a Bawd".[23] Collyer was as emphatic about the dangers to girls, who

> put to this employ should have their minds strongly tinctured with a high degree of the dignity of chastity; for in all this, as in all shop-keeping business, they will be exposed to the attempts of designing men; many of whom glory in one of the most shameful acts of baseness, that of betraying to ruin heedless and unwary innocence. Women's best defence is private life; but where circumstances oblige them to come into the world young, the utmost care ought to be taken of their morals; and they should be taught to revere themselves, or, in other words, not to render themselves cheap, by little coquettish compliances. The girl that will patiently listen to, or join in the laugh with the young spark who makes loose allusions or impudent jests, is not far from falling a prey to the first artful seducer who shall take it in his head to seem enamoured with her beauty or wit.[24]

Millinery and mantua-making undoubtedly appealed to girls of good family who had fallen on hard times and who hoped to earn a living with their needle, especially if they could eventually run their own business. Such apprentices, of good appearance and used to polite society, were an asset to a fashionable establishment, perhaps attracting their own acquaintances as customers.

Contemporary opinion was aware of the risks of sexual abuse to the poorest female apprentices; William Bailey pointed out the dangers for girls whose masters indentured them only for "pecuniary considerations", who were subsequently turned adrift "in a more destitute condition at a riper age for mischief than they were when first they became the care of the parish officers".[25] Fielding sought to amend this state of affairs in 1758 by founding a female orphan asylum, to which came "Poor Girls put out by the Parish Officers from the Workhouses, as they are generally placed in the worst of families and seldom escape Destruction".[26] In Bristol, however, absconding female apprentices, "Idleing about the Streets", were caught and brought before the mayor and aldermen.[27]

Lack of adult supervision was blamed by many eighteenth-century critics for youthful misbehaviour, and this was one reason, apart from economic considerations, why out-apprenticeship was deplored. Clearly a master could control an apprentice in every respect when the child lived in, impossible when the apprentices were free in the evenings and at night. Francis Place has described the young girl prostitutes, some of whom were formerly apprentices, and his own unsupervised leisure hours, in London in the 1780s, although this was not apparently a provincial problem until well into the next century. In Coventry the half-pay system was thought to have a "most pernicious effect upon the morals of youth of both sexes" since, when turned off for lack of work (impossible in a traditional apprenticeship) the female apprentices either went on the parish or became prostitutes, with resulting pregnancies a burden on the city's poor rate.[28]

The morals of Birmingham's female apprentices were also condemned, and the town's prison-keeper noted that "badness of trade always tends to prostitution" as did the fact that all apprentices left work at the same hour. A local police constable, observing the popularity of the theatre among the town's apprentices, commented that "in general the girls employed in the manufactories of this town [were] not virtuous".[29] In the Worcestershire carpet and glove industries by the early nineteenth century it was possible to observe "a great increase of drunkenness and prostitution" with an unfavourable state of morals among the young female apprentices there.[30] Other official reports, more sympathetic to the apprentice girls, illustrate how many of them were abused, almost as a matter of course, at their place of work by the adult factory workers. Undoubtedly for the deserted or runaway female apprentice it was easier to turn to prostitution in the city than in rural areas; many poorly paid female occupations were town trades and cities also provided a potential clientele for the "abandoned creatures".

41

As well as the sexual risks for female apprentices in domestic work or the fashion trades, there was also public concern at the reputed lack of chastity among factory apprentices and in 1802 the Health and Morals of Apprentices Act was passed.[31] Girls in factories were at risk from their fellow male apprentices, the adult overlookers and, occasionally, the factory master himself. Their living and working accommodation caused concern at its lack of privacy so that middle-class factory visitors, both unofficial and the government inspectors, condemned the general immodesty of factory life for girl apprentices.[32] Such abuses may have been no worse than the poorest apprentice would encounter in a domestic workshop or even in her own home, where severe overcrowding broke down many sexual restraints; the age of consent in the eighteenth century was 12 for girls and this was not changed in English law until the 1870s.[33]

Although the risk of sexual abuse of female apprentices was widely recognized and openly discussed, a matter of concern to the child's parents and social commentators alike, the chance of a male apprentice's being at risk was apparently never considered. All apprentice handbooks advised boys to behave chastely towards the master's wife, family and female servants, but the risk of homosexual practices was not mentioned in print; only one case of the 74 brought before the Coventry Quarter Sessions in the years 1757–80 involved a master's "sodomitical practices" towards his male apprentice. In this case the apprentice, George Farmer, was discharged as a result of William Burgess, a ribbon-weaver and merchant, "misusing and evil intreating" him by such behaviour; the master did not appear in court but the boy gave "full proof of the said complaint" and was duly freed from Burgess to seek another master.[34] Public disapproval when a male apprentice was sexually exploited could be very clearly expressed by a community on the rare occasions when legal action was taken. Thus a woman currier, Alison Boston, was pilloried for three days for an hour a day, to the accompaniment of rough music, as well as serving a prison sentence, for having "let to hire for immoral purposes" her innocent young apprentice lad.[35] The scarcity of such cases, especially in contrast with heterosexual ones, may indicate the rarity of homosexual practices involving apprentices or the great difficulty of bringing a prosecution.

Apart from homosexual abuse, a male apprentice might also be seduced by older women in the host household, either of the family or employees, a hazard acknowledged by several contemporary writers. Evidence for such seductions is understandably scarce but perhaps typical was a youthful hatter's apprentice, aged 18, five weeks in a new household who, in his master's absence, described how he had been "as much teaz'd as ever Joseph was" by the man's young wife. After this incident he felt the situation to be "painfully uncomfortable" and decided to leave to avoid further difficulties.[36]

A master's responsibility for his apprentice's moral code, in the widest sense, was emphasized by writers on the subject at all periods; Campbell reminded parents that being a good workman is not the only Qualification a Master ought to be possessed of; He must be honest, good-natured, and communicative. If he is not an honest Man, the Boy's morals are certainly debauched: He may learn his Trade, but forget his Religion: and his Master may instil with the Mysteries of his Profession all the Seeds of Vice and Profaneness.[37]

A further protection should be provided by the justices, as "Guardians of the morals of the People [who] ought to take care that the apprentices are not placed with masters who may corrupt their morals".[38] Certainly some masters took this responsibility seriously; in the Coventry watchmaking trade it was possible for a master with "one or two apprentices, not more" in his care to watch over the boys' morals, thus "preserving them from many bad habits, to which they are exposed in large factories". One watchmaker, William Mayo, considered that the morals of indoor apprentices were better than those of outdoor boys, both as "the best workmen and as their moral characters have turned out better". The factory system meant that their morals "became corrupted, and they manifest[ed] less subjection to their parents". Another master in the city considered large establishments of apprentices as the "asylum of vice and profligacy: for where youth are horded together in such numbers, they contaminate the morals of each other". A third master, John Powell, with chiefly indoor apprentices, said that he always felt it his duty to watch over their morals and interests as if he had been their father, and condemned the outdoor system for the immoral state of Coventry's youth.[39] Such views were repeated in evidence to the 1834 Poor Law Commissioners, who heard how "the practice among them is to idle during the first part of the week, and to recover the time by working day and night during the remainder, a system which is said to be injurious both to their health and morals".[40]

As a measure of the regard in which certain trades were generally held, it is striking in how many occupations workmen had a widespread reputation for heavy drinking, deplored perhaps by society at large but valued as a sign of manliness within their own circle. Tradesmen particularly noted for their intemperance were the brazier, hatter, glass-blower, plumber and tallow chandler, all of whom worked in very hot conditions, as well as the plasterer, whose raw material, lime, caused great thirst.[41] All these workmen thought "that there [were] very few soft drinks which alleviate this so effectively as spirits and beer".[42] Alcohol increased the risk of industrial accidents, either with tools or machinery, and of falls, while masters who drank excessively were more likely to ill-treat their apprentices. However, apart from alcohol, most occupations contained health risks to masters and apprentices, caused by four factors, the raw materials used, the environmental conditions, muscular effort and posture, as well as accidents as a result of the work process itself. Two thousand years before industrialization Hippocrates recognized that there were "very many Arts and Callings which are useful and pleasant to those who stand in need of their Assistance, but occasion a great deal of Trouble and Labour to those who practise them",[43] a view that found remarkably little support among medical practitioners of the eighteenth and nineteenth centuries. The work of Bernard Ramazzini, *A treatise on the diseases of tradesmen*, written in Latin in 1700, was translated into English by Dr Robert James. It was said to have been eagerly "bought up at any price and justly became a standard-book". Even before the inventions of the Industrial Revolution added considerably to the range of dangerous occupations, such non-medical writers as Campbell and Collyer indicated trades with associated health risks. The hazards of the midland industries were described from personal experience by Dr William Richardson, of Newton Street, Birmingham,[44] whose *Chemical principles of the metallic arts* was published in 1790. Although Charles Turner Thackrah of Leeds produced his major work, *The effects of arts, trades and professions on health and longevity* in 1832, another Birmingham practitioner, John Darwall, had prepared his MD thesis, *De morbis artificium*, a decade earlier, based on the patients he had treated in the midland trades.[45]

Workmen themselves do seem to have been aware of some of the risks they took, so that Nicholas Paris worried at the effects of using too much aqua fortis (nitric acid) in regilding the great tomb of Richard Beauchamp at Warwick in 1683:

> I could have hartily wished that I had gave a hondred pound so that I had not never medled with it for it hath done me more harme than ever I shall get by it, for it hath cost me allmost my life twise a bout the doing of it as the Docters will aferme.

In spite of his concern, Paris did not die until 1716, aged about seventy.[46] Campbell noted the risks to the gold-refiner's lungs and the engraver's sight, while stressing the need for physical strength in certain trades, the plasterer, locksmith, brazier, plumber, baker and butcher, and also indicating the occupations for the weaker child. Collyer added other crafts to this survey, observing that a carpenter needed to be robust, while a bluemaker's nerves were harmed by his work. It seems likely that such advice manuals, directed at the apprentice and his parents, had a wider readership than specifically medical texts, and some enlightened non-medical comment was forthcoming. Thus a correspondent to the *Gentleman's Magazine*[47] and the occasional foreign traveller in England commented adversely on "professions and manufactures, which are very laborious or pernicious to health, shorten also the lives of thousands".[48] However, the general contemporary response to occupational disease was that it was inevitable; less prosperous apprentices and masters had little choice in selecting a livelihood that was free of risks, either immediate or long term, to their health. The life-long commitment was a further important factor, since workers could not leave a craft to work at other occupations to which they had not been bound. The number of occupations that might be safely followed in the eighteenth century, to judge from Ramazzini's *Treatise*, were few indeed.

With the coming of industrialization in Britain, the range of raw materials, especially chemicals, increased greatly and many of these were far more dangerous than the traditional wood, leather or metal had been. Although the eighteenth century brought a considerable increase among workers in metal poisoning, especially with lead and mercury, there was almost no awareness of protective clothing for those who used toxic substances. The plumber and glazier needed a "strong and healthy Constitution to withstand the Effects of the Lead" which was "apt to unbend his Nerves and render him paralytic". Campbell had observed that glaziers were

> subject to the Palsy more than any other Trade, except the Gilders and Plumbers, from that much handling of Lead. Whether it is the Fumes of the Soder or handling their Putty that occasions this Disorder, I cannot determine; but . . . it is more owing to the White-Lead they use than to anything else.[49]

In fact both the beating of the lead and the application of solder were harmful, causing "nausea and tightness at the chest . . . colic and palsy . . . it is nevertheless apparent that the occupation undermines the constitution for plumbers are short lived. A small proportion reach the age of 50."[50] The plumber's low expectation of life is reflected in the pattern of apprenticeship to the trade, for a surprising number of indentures are to plumbers' widows, running their late husbands' firms and continuing to bind boys to the trade. Glaziers were equally subject to palsy as a result of a damaged nervous system; one glazier's apprentice in 1787 complained of not having a proper bed but that he slept where the lead was melted.[51] Painters also suffered from the effects of lead. There was a degree of medical awareness of the hazards of lead and Sir George Baker's paper to the Royal College of Physicians on the subject, noted that

> almost every day's experience furnisheth physicians with examples of painters and plumbers and the other numerous artificers employed either in manufacturing the several preparations of lead, or in applying them to their respective uses; who after having suffered the most extreme torment from the collic of Poitou, are restored to health and remain free from that disease, so long at least as they quit their usual business or pursue it with greater caution.[52]

Other metal craftsmen also suffered and, travelling in the Midlands, Robert Southey described the brass workers as having "red eyes and green hair, the eyes affected by the fires to which they are exposed, and the hair turned green by the brass-works".[53] Even the traditional blacksmith was adversely affected by his trade, for the iron he worked gave off sulphurous fumes, that caused him to become "blear eyed" and, "like other Artificers that work by fire", he suffered from constipation, for which "beets in the diet" were prescribed.[54] The remedy of protective clothing was almost unknown to the eighteenth century, but Richardson advocated workmen to "put on something like a wag-goner's frock while at work, laying [it] aside when they have done". He also emphasized the importance of washing at the end of work and before eating, but most commentators added that craftsmen would not do so. Richardson actually suggested remedies for lead poisoning, camomile, laudanum and brimstone electuary, but these were only palliative.[55]

Another group of workers at risk from their raw materials were hatters, who used mercury and sulphur to prepare the liquid in which felts were steeped; they too were the victims of brain and nerve damage. Campbell noted hatmaking as a "very dirty business", suitable for children of "mean education".[56] Two parts of their process were particularly harmful to health. Felting was "very slavish work, being continually obliged to be stooping over the steam of a great kettle"; after the dyeing, at a later stage, "a vast quantity of dust, very prejudicial to the workmen" was a further hazard.[57] In addition, part of the process involved dipping the felt a number of times in a mixture of water and sulphuric acid, "heated rather higher than unpractised hands could bear".[58] General recognition of the dangers of hatmaking can be seen in the common phrase, "mad as a hatter", since brain damage was the result of in-haling mercurial fumes. Thackrah also noticed that hatters' nails and cuticles were often "corroded and sore" from the solution of sulphuric acid they used.[59]

Although many new and expanding trades in the eighteenth century became more hazardous with the introduction of innovatory processes, machinery, materials and an expanded market demanding higher output, the traditional building industry also had its share of risks for the workman and his appren-tice. Bricklayers and plasterers were affected by the slaked lime they used, that caused roughness of the mouth and throat as well as congestion of the lungs but also wrinkled and ulcerated the workmen's hands. Thackrah noted that he had seen bricklayers suffering from ophthalmia and cutaneous eruptions, although he quoted a popular workmen's adage that bricklayers' and plaster-ers' labourers, like asses, never die.[60] Another of the oldest craft groups were the leatherworkers, of whom those engaged in the early stages of processing and treating animal skins were at greatest risk from anthrax, usually fatal, as well as such minor diseases as ringworm. Ramazzini made no comment on these hazards, but for some tradesmen (the tallow chandler, oilman and tanner) he noted the "killing smell" of their work, indicating that eighteenth-century medicine was more aware of miasma than infection. Workers in animal skins and fats experienced respiratory complaints, headaches and inappetence, while their complexion was "death-like" and their appearance splenetic and puffed-up.[61]

Another ancient trade, flax-dressing, was equally harmful to health as a "foul mischievous powder" flew out of the flax and hemp when heated, causing continual coughs and asthma, as well as pale complexions and bleary eyes.[62] With the introduction of machinery the problem was reduced, but the amount of dust was still so great that a visitor

> cannot remain many minutes without being sensible of its effects on respiration . . . dressers of flax . . . are generally unhealthy . . . They are subject to indigestion, morning vomiting, chronic inflammation of the bronchial membrane, inflammation of the lungs, and pulmonary consumption.[63]

A polluted environment caused little contemporary concern, so that the cotton factory filled with "flew" (cotton down) and the windows, required by the 1802 act, remained closed. Needle grinding and the cutlery trades filled the air with extremely fine particles of stone and metal, causing extensive lung damage.[64] Climbing-boys were "very liable to cough and inflammation of the chest", while the narrow chimneys caused a child's elbows and knees to become "cartilaginous". The carcinogenic properties of the soot caused chimney-sweep's cancer; one London surgeon had operated on several cases of scrotal and lip cancer, but "in general they are apt to let them get too far before they apply for relief" and "the dread of the operation which it is necessary to perform, deters many from submitting to it".[65] Darwall remained unsure about the cause of sweeps' cancer, noting that "the cause of this disease is still obscure".[66]

However, not only industry was responsible for a polluted environment that caused or exacerbated workers' diseases, for two of the most traditional occupations were those of the baker and the miller, whose raw material, flour, combined with the physical labour of their trades to produce unhealthy working conditions. Flour particles caused congestion of the lungs and throat, pleurisy resulted from extremes of temperature and kneading caused the baker's hands to become "swell'd and pain'd";[67] both bakers and millers suffered from lice. By the 1830s Thackrah was able to cite a variety of adverse working conditions, many more than earlier writers had noted. He listed those who worked in industries with polluted air, such as miners, textile workers and straw bonnet makers (at risk from sulphur fumes), as well as masons, who all suffered from respiratory difficulties, nausea, impaired digestion and general debility.

Even the professions were hazardous, for veterinarians (farriers and blacksmiths before 1790) in their work with horses were at risk from glanders, from which the founder of the London Veterinary College, Vial de St Bel, died.[68] All zoonotic infections were unpleasant, but glanders and rabies especially so, involving as they did ineffectual but painful treatment, prolonged suffering and finally death. Surgeons and apothecaries could also be victims of epidemics and, with the chemist, "receive injury in preparing Remedies for the Health of others".[69] In addition, the "meaner sort of surgeons" who treated venereal infections were at risk from the mercury preparations they used, while apothecaries suffered from preparing laudanum, opium and cantharides-based medicines.[70]

However, since muscle power was essential in most trades, much occupational illness was the direct result of the physical activity involved in the daily repetition of particular procedures and movements. Physical deformity easily developed in the growing child or adolescent who regularly used certain muscles for 14 hours a day, six days a week and such deformities were widely recognized. Thus nail-making in the Black Country caused the workman's one shoulder to be higher than the other and the region was known in local slang as "Humpshire", while weaver's deafness has existed until the present century in Lancashire. A number of trades for both male and female apprentices involved sitting, with heads bent over their task, for the whole working day. Among the sedentary trades such as tailors, shoemakers, milliners, watchmakers and weavers, a crooked back, lameness and sciatica were proverbial. When two apprentices absconded in the 1740s, one, a shoemaker's boy, was described as "lame on the right side", while the other, bound to a tailor, was "lame of the left leg, steps on the toes of the same side, and does not set his heel to the ground".[71] In addition, a "scabby and ill-complexion'd" appearance was the fate of tailors and "needlewomen that work at home Night and Day".[72] Thackrah commented that shoemakers

> work in a bad posture, by which digestion and circulation are so much impaired, that the countenance marks a shoemaker almost as well as a tailor. From the reduction of perspiration and other excretions . . . the blood becomes impure and the complexion darkened . . . In the few shoemakers who live to old age there is often a remarkable hollow at the base of the breast bone, occasioned by the pressure of the last.[73]

The risks to female apprentices in the sedentary trades were greater than to males, since the wearing of tightly laced stays was customary for girls of all social classes from the age of nine or ten.[74] Medical writers, including Thackrah, vigorously condemned the practice. However, the posture of lacemakers caused a late-eighteenth-century visitor to the English lace-making areas to describe the "frequent sight of deformed and diseased women" in Buckinghamshire and Northamptonshire. "Many of the workers of lace are deformed", he wrote, "occasioned by their uneasy posture, and many more are diseased, seemingly owing in great measure, to their inclined posture while working, which prevents their lungs having a free play."[75] As an occupation, weaving was widespread but Ramazzini noted that weavers complained of "pain in the loins" and he advised exercise on holy days as a remedy, adding that, among the sedentary trades, weavers were relatively healthy, since they exercised their hands, feet and whole bodies.[76] However, one weaver described how he suffered "excessive pain" in his chest, could not sleep, and still had chest and back pain although he had left weaving two years ago, his physique "wasted by over Labour and low Diet".[77] Epitomized by Silas Marner, the weaver's "bent, treadmill attitude" caused fear and suspicion. Ribbon weaving was also "very laborious indeed as well as injurious to the health, producing great pressure on the chest".[78] One midland medical practitioner observed that two out of five weavers suffered particularly from diseases of the lungs, as well as indigestion and consumption, while dyers in the same community were "a fair specimen of the hardier class of artisan". Opinion about the occupational hazards of ribbon-weaving were far from unanimous, as another contemporary observer considered there was nothing in ribbon manufacture injurious to health.[79]

Although watchmaking was clean, indoor work, requiring neither great physical strength nor repeated muscular actions, it too threatened the craftsman's health; an early-nineteenth-century master reported how the trade

> produces disease and premature decay . . . where boys of the most robust appearance, have come to the trade and been speedily attacked with fits, and become sickly and emaciated, and have carried that appearance throughout their lives.[80]

Thackrah expounded the contemporary medical opinion of all sedentary work, that

> the posture which curves the spine, affects the abdomen, rather than the chest; for this is protected by the ribs, while that has no firm support except at the back. The regions of the navel and stomach sustain the pressure which a bent posture produces.[81]

If tasks that involved a bent, seated posture were harmful, those that were performed standing, with great physical effort, were no less so. Tradesmen such as the cooper, quarryman and paver all suffered in this respect,[82] while the carpenter, sawyer, bricklayer, blacksmith and engraver could have a weak stomach, swellings in the veins of their legs and kidney ulcers as a result of standing for a long time.[83] Some trades, such as framework knitting, involved the repeated push and pull of the machine, while plasterers, with much overhead work, suffered severely from the repetitive physical actions the worker performed innumerable times a day.

Apart from the specific trade risks, a wide range of artisans were obliged to lift, carry and move very heavy weights as a normal part of their work, and a high incidence of hernia was the result. As late as 1842 it was estimated that ten per cent of the labouring population were sufferers,[84] and in earlier centuries the proportion must have been even higher. Adam Smith observed that a London carpenter could not last in his utmost vigour at work for more than eight years (until he was about 30).[85] When steam power came to Sheffield in the late eighteenth century a contemporary commented that the town no longer abounded in "cripples and weak deformed people" as when iron and steel were forged by hand.[86] The National Truss Society was formed in 1786, the Rupture Society ten years later and the City Truss Society in London in 1807. However, apprentices still complained that they were "bursten" as a result of heavy work[87] and Thackrah noted hernia among porters, millers and warehousemen. All the building trades, the heavy metal crafts, mining and most agricultural work involved great muscular effort with chronic hernia as a result. The importance of a workman's strength was ruefully recalled by George Sturt, who remembered that in his early years in the family wheelwright's shop he was not strong enough even to grind up the Prussian blue he used for painting wagons. His father had a "hard place on his waist" from shaving wheel spokes for a lifetime and not wearing the tradesman's protective pad.[88]

Other non-fatal injuries were caused by certain trades to workers' eyes and ears. Sight could be damaged both by "mechanical annoyance" or by close application to minute objects. The first kind of injury might either be from raw materials such as stone, brick or wood, with particles flying into the eyes, or by an atmosphere polluted with lime, soot, fumes, brickdust, coaldust, cotton down or flour that caused conjunctivitis.[89] Ramazzini had observed that bakers and millers suffered from "the particles of the Flower or Meal that stick to the Eyes, . . . and sometimes occasion a Blear'dness",[90] while a worker such as the bottom sawyer was constantly covered with falling sawdust. Ophthalmic work was perhaps the first medical specialism to develop in the eighteenth century and the coming of eye-hospitals, as at Birmingham early in the nineteenth, was a direct response to eye injuries in a heavy industrial area. It is doubtful whether close work actually damaged the workers' sight, in spite of contemporary beliefs, but undoubtedly workers were unable to continue making very tiny products or continue at fine work into middle age. Among the male trades, only watchmaking was populous, for printing, engraving and instrument-making employed relatively few men, and all were fairly prosperous occupations. Ramazzini described the problems of close work:

> By keeping the Eye constantly in this one Position, they contract such a habit, that the Retina, being inur'd and harden'd to one Form and Figure, persists in it, and can't be mov'd at Pleasure for the Perception of remoter Objects: . . . while the Eyes are kept immoveable, and perpetually fix'd upon one Point, the Humours grow thick, and lose their Transparency along with their Fluidity, which gradually makes

way for a Weakness of the Eye-Sight; so that tho such Tradesmen may naturally have nimble and clear sighted Eyes, they become short sighted in process of time. So great is the Calamity intail'd upon this sort of Work, and the finest Pieces of Workmanship, such as Clocks and Watches, are so apt to produce this Weakness of the Eyes, that many of the Workmen are almost Blind before they arrive at old Age.[91]

Even the non-medical Campbell commented that although a watchmaker required no great strength, "there was scarce any Trade which requires a quicker Eye or steadier Hand".[92] After the factory system had been established for nearly 50 years in Coventry, a master there commented that by middle age many watchmakers had lost "that acuteness of sight which is necessary to enable them to follow the trade with advantage". The parish was a source of assistance when a craftsman's sight had failed but, as relief meant loss of franchise rights, as well as of personal pride, watchmakers founded their own friendly societies as a form of security.[93]

The needlework trades to which females were apprenticed were widely regarded as harmful to the workers' sight after a period of years; a normal day in these sweated trades was often 14 hours long and inadequate artificial light was used throughout the winter months. An assistant surgeon at the Royal London Ophthalmic Hospital, Moorfields, John Dalrymple, described the working conditions of one fashionable milliner's apprentice whom he treated:

> a delicate and beautiful young woman, an orphan, applied at the hospital for very defective vision . . . she had been apprenticed to a milliner, and was in the last year of indentureship. Her work-hours were 18 in the day, occasionally even more; her meals snatched with scarcely an interval of a few minutes from work, and her general health evidently assuming a tendency to consumption. An application was made, by my direction, to the mistress for relaxation: but the reply was, that in this last year of her apprenticeship her labours had become valuable, and that her mistress was entitled to them, as recompense for teaching. Subsequently, a threat of appeal to the Lord Mayor, and a belief that a continuance of the occupation would soon render the apprentice incapable of labour, induced the mistress to cancel the indentures, and the victim was saved. It was not until many months afterwards that her health was re-established.[94]

Lace-making was particularly notorious for its harmful effects on the workers' sight, both because it took in a large number of young girls as apprentices but also, to some critics, because the product was non-essential. One medical practitioner, Dr Williams, stated that he had personally treated at least

10,000 cases of diseased sight in Nottingham during the years 1829–43 (an average of 13 patients a week). Lace runners and menders particularly suffered from amaurosis and many women were forced to give up the trade before the age of 30 or lose their sight completely.[95] Half a century earlier, Eden had seen young pillow-lace workers become "necessitous" in old age because they were not accustomed to any other work.[96] Many lace-makers who gave up fine work as their sight failed could later do only coarse and badly paid sewing for framework knitters, seaming stockings and stitching "cut-ups".[97] The different branches of needlework were second only to housewifery as an apprenticeship field for girls, for, until the later nineteenth century, all garments and furnishing, even the cheapest, were hand-sewn. The wide range of needlewomen can be seen in Mayhew's interviews (1849–50), when he talked to women and girls who made all kinds of clothes, from gaol uniforms and shrouds to peers' robes and *haute couture*, perhaps epitomized in Hood's "Song of the Shirt", published in *Punch* in 1843. The girl apprentices in the luxury part of the needlework trades, fine embroidering waistcoats or bugle bead decorations, were particularly prone, Thackrah noted, to ophthalmia, myopia and palsy of the nerves of the eye.[98] Marriage, prostitution or unskilled work were widely acknowledged as these women's future.

Damaged hearing as a result of particular occupations was less frequently recorded and did not prevent workers continuing at their employment, but Ramazzini noted that millers became "deafish" from the noise of their waterfalls, wheels and grinding machinery.[99] As well as millers, Thackrah observed impaired hearing in frizers, who worked the nap on worsted cloth, and whose hearing had become "obtuse".[100] All industrialization must have increased the incidence of deafness, for hand processes made far less persistent noise than the continuous sound of power-driven machinery.

Since so many occupational hazards were accepted as normal, it is difficult to find a trade in which physical injury or long-term deformity was avoidable. Even robust apprentices would be harmed by wet outdoor employment, a polluted environment, dangerous substances or harmful posture, while less sturdy children were also at risk from confined working conditions without sunlight or fresh air. All apprentices, prosperous or poor, worked at least a 12-hour day for six days a week, with few local or national holidays. Since virtually all occupations carried a health risk this factor was little regarded by intending apprentices or their parents. The readership of works such as those by Ramazzini or Thackrah was extremely limited, but both Campbell and Collyer warned of some risks inherent in certain trades to the intending apprentice. Undoubtedly the superior trades and professions were less harmful to an apprentice's health than either the middle-range artisan occupations or the impoverished, overstocked crafts that, by the early nineteenth century, in a polluted urban environment, were particularly so. Perhaps medical unawareness of the problem by the middle years of the nineteenth century is its most surprising aspect:

There is, we will venture to say, no country in the world where the effects of trades on the health, and longevity of the workmen who follow them, are so extensively pernicious as in Great Britain. For there is none where the proportion of the people employed in hurtful trades is so great, none where the workmen are congregated so much in towns, and large manufactures, . . . where the working hours occupy so large a part of the day. It is then melancholy to reflect how little has been done in this country by medical men or philanthropists out of the profession, towards ascertaining the nature and extent of these effects, as well as the means of correcting them, and how little encouragement has been held out by our government for such investigations. English medical literature has been till now destitute of a single general treatise on the disease of trades and professions . . . on one occasion only has this government interested itself in the fate of the sickly and short-lived artizan. No one will feel surprised at the apathy of a government, which has long been notorious for indifference to scientific inquiries.[101]

In almost all factories and trades accidents were commonplace, the inexperienced apprentice particularly likely to be injured by tools, unused to lifting heavy weights skilfully, even unable to foresee a dangerous situation. Unguarded machinery, especially for girls with long hair or loose clothes, was a considerable risk. At Fazeley when an apprentice was "caught by the drum-wheel", her arm was "so severely lacerated as to render amputation necessary".[102] A year earlier, another girl at Tamworth aged 17 was "so badly mangled by the machinery . . . as to cause her immediate death".[103] Boys were less often recorded as factory accident victims, because they were a minority of apprentices there, but occasionally, as at Fazeley in 1805, an incumbent noted a boy's death, "hurt in the cotton mill", in the parish burial register.[104] Aware of public concern the Gregs listed, c.1833, the 17 apprentices who had died at Styal in the last 22 years: these comprised 8 boys and 9 girls out of a regular work force of 80–90. Only one of these died as the result of an accident, "at play, not in the Mill"[105] and at Emscote no accidental death in the factory was recorded, although one girl apprentice was drowned in the River Avon.[106]

Although the building trades were virtually untouched by industrialization, they remained dangerous occupations, with injuries from falls, moving heavy weights or using sharp tools, and mishaps to apprentices and men were often chronicled in local newspapers. The wide variety of accidental deaths considered by coroners and the injuries in hospital admissions registers indicate the many hazards the workman or apprentice could face:

as Thomas Edmonds, a young man about 18 years of age, apprentice to Mr Gray, turner of Coventry, was assisting another person in carrying a heavy piece of timber, his foot slipped in passing along Much Park Street, and the timber fell with such violence upon his temple, that he expired in a few minutes. The accident was occasioned by his crossing the road for a waggon to pass. Coroner's verdict – Accidental Death.[107]

Many crafts had their own "tricks" for alleviating minor injuries that an apprentice discovered, so a wheelwright's apprentice learned to cover his chapped hands with a protective film of cobbler's wax and thus continue at work.[108]

Medical and lay response to occupational disease was perfunctory. Safety measures, protective clothing and washing facilities were costly and often reduced a worker's output. Resistance to such measures by the tradesman himself was noted by Ramazzini, who commented sharply that a sick craftsman preferred medical treatment (purging, bleeding, vomiting, or drugs) to changing his way of life.[109] However, concern about two minority but well-publicized groups of apprentices, climbing-boys and factory children, brought a wider awareness of health risks, with shorter hours, better working conditions and higher wages as the non-medical remedies, while greater sobriety in the workplace slowly contributed to a reduced accident rate.

According to many contemporary and modern commentators one of the most deplorable aspects of pauper apprenticeships was the sending of children many miles from home, so that contact with family and friends was minimal if not impossible. Evidence to parliamentary enquiries recorded the transport of young apprentices to distant masters, in some cases by the cartload. Most memoirs of the period emphasized the harsh conditions the children endured, especially the homesickness of the very young. However, this complaint against pauper apprenticeship is not completely substantiated when examined for those factories for which record material has survived and when compared with non-pauper indenturing. At Emscote, near Warwick, all the apprentices came from less than 20 miles away while the Coventry firm of Nickson and Browett took all but two of their 39 apprentices from the city. Of the 269 children apprentices at Styal for the period 1784–1841 the majority had homes less than 30 miles away (Table 2.2).[110]

When several factories were grouped in a fairly small area it was inevitable that masters searched further afield for apprentices once the local children had been indentured; thus in the years 1786–1805 only 8 per cent of the Cuckney apprentices came from the area but 63.8 per cent from London.[111] The labour requirements of such large-scale masters as Peel, Jewsbury or Chambers would have been impossible to fulfil from neighbouring parishes, as their advertisements in regional newspapers show. Certain parishes regularly supplied a particular mill with apprentices, so that newly arrived paupers joined other children from their home area already at the factory. Greg had several groups of apprentices from Newcastle under Lyme and

Table 2.2 Pauper apprenticeships at Styal, 1784–1841.

	1784–94 %	1794–1802 %	1815–41 %
Home in:			
Cheshire	51	17	23
Staffordshire	39	80	4
Lancashire	1	2	7
Liverpool	nil	nil	58
Beyond 30 miles	3	nil	.1
Not stated	4	nil	7
Total apprenticeships	143	95	31

Liverpool, Chambers took children from Nuneaton, Toplis from London and Wilkes from Stratford-upon-Avon, while Harding of Tamworth had numbers of paupers from Bedworth. Styal records show that not only overseers of the poor consigned children to distant mills, for parents sent their children there as apprentices from as far away as Herefordshire and Hertfordshire. Except for the very largest firm, it seems that factory children were sent no further from their homes than other apprentices, but this was the aspect of pauper apprenticeship of which nineteenth-century philanthropists most often complained. For all apprentices, poor or prosperous, contact with their homes was minimal, even if indentured in an adjacent parish or town, since irregular transport, low literacy and a very long working week all precluded family visiting.

An interesting picture of indenturing during a quarter of a century can be seen in Coventry in the period from 1781 to 1806, when the city apprenticeship registers listed all boys bound, whether prosperous, charity or poor, but not girls, since apprenticeship brought freeman status and franchise rights. During this period the homes of 3,888 boys were recorded out of a total of 4,811; of these a majority, 3,036 (78 per cent) came from Coventry homes, while 674 (17.3 per cent) were Warwickshire boys from no further than 30 miles away and only 176 (4.5 per cent) lived beyond the county boundaries. Of the non-Warwickshire apprentices the majority came from the neighbouring counties:[112]

Table 2.3 Homes of midland apprentices in Coventry, 1781–1806.

County	Number of boys
Northamptonshire	44
Leicestershire	33
Worcestershire	14
Staffordshire	13
Derbyshire	10
Oxfordshire/Gloucestershire	6 each

There were also 21 boys from London, chiefly bound to the silk industry, but also to relatives or to the professions. In addition there were boys indentured in Coventry from 16 other English counties:

Table 2.4   Homes of non-midland apprentices in Coventry, 1781–1806.

County	Number of boys
Middlesex	5
Buckinghamshire/Yorkshire	4 each
Cheshire	3
Lancashire	2
Bedfordshire, County Durham, Cumberland Devonshire, Ely, Hampshire, Kent, Lincolnshire, Norfolk, Nottinghamshire, Shropshire	1 each

Another example of apprentices' homes and the distances they travelled to find masters can be seen in the indentures to Norwich masters during the period 1500 to 1752. During these years 5,580 boys were indentured in Norwich, and, like the Coventry children, a number came from the counties bordering Norfolk:[113]

Table 2.5   Homes of East Anglian apprentices in Norwich, 1500–1752.

County	Number of boys
Suffolk	170
Lincolnshire	33
Cambridgeshire	15

However, because Norfolk is a coastal county, with fewer neighbours than inland Warwickshire, there were also considerable numbers of boys from further afield (Table 2.6), especially the northern counties, as well as one from Rotterdam (see Table 2.6).

Thus there were 485 (8.7 per cent) from non-Norfolk homes, nearly twice the Coventry proportion at a later period, but both sets of figures emphasize the fact that, pauper or prosperous, nine out of ten boys remained in their home community when apprenticed. Not only in ancient trading centres is such a pattern apparent, for in Sheffield too it has been shown that whereas a minority of apprentices (6.4 per cent in 1624–49 and 8 per cent in 1775–99) came from beyond a ten mile radius, nearly half (47.5 and 48.7 per cent in the same decades) had homes ten miles away or less.[114]

Interesting patterns may be seen in the indentures listed in the London apprenticeship registers for Wiltshire, Warwickshire, Sussex, Surrey and Bedfordshire in the eighteenth century. The apprenticeships covered boys and

Table 2.6 Homes of non-East Anglian apprentices in Norwich, 1500–1752.

County	Number of boys
Yorkshire	119
Westmorland	22
Lancashire	18
Leicestershire	17
London	16
Essex	10
Cumberland	6
Berwickshire, Northamptonshire	5 each
Cheshire, County Durham, Hertfordshire, Huntingdonshire, Northumberland, Staffordshire	4 each
Bedfordshire, Derbyshire, Kent, Nottinghamshire	3 each
Cornwall, Middlesex, Warwickshire, Worcestershire	2 each
Berkshire, Buckinghamshire, Gloucestershire, Oxfordshire	1 each

girls, but excluded parish children, for whom no tax was paid; they show a wide variety of occupations, premiums and social status in five dissimilar areas. During the period 1710–60 there were 2,735 apprentices listed for Wiltshire, leaving, entering or remaining in the county.[115] Of these, a large majority, 2,256 (82.5 per cent) were Wiltshire children indentured to Wiltshire masters. Apprentices entering or leaving the county were primarily from the adjacent areas, while a significant minority were sent from Wiltshire to the ancient trading centre of Bristol, as well as the newly expanded spa of Bath, where medical and fashion occupations attracted a variety of boys and girls (Table 2.7). It is apparent that the majority of these children, like the Coventry apprentices, remained within their own area when bound, at a maximum distance of 25 or 30 miles from their homes, difficult but not impossible to travel and not a totally strange locality for the child (see Table 2.7).

Figures for Warwickshire for the same period show a nearly identical pattern. During this pre-industrial half century there were 2,314 non-poor children listed as indentured to Warwickshire masters. Of these, 1,586 (65.1 per cent) did not have their home parish recorded, but this information was given for 728 apprentices. Of these 574 (78.9 per cent) came from the county of Warwick and were sent to masters within its boundaries. Two boys came as apprentices to Warwickshire from overseas; in 1714 John Beale from Antigua, in the West Indies, was bound to a Coventry apothecary, Thomas Herbert, for nine years with a typical substantial premium, £53 15s.[116] Three years later he indentured another local boy with the same premium and term.[117]

In Warwickshire the 574 apprentices bound to masters within the county boundaries can be considered in three groups: those who stayed in their home

Table 2.7   Homes of apprentices entering and leaving Wiltshire, 1710–60.

Apprentices' homes	To Wiltshire from	From Wiltshire to
Bath, Somerset	5	23
Berkshire	4	7
Bristol	–	79
Carmarthen	–	1
Cornwall	1	1
Dorset	35	54
Flintshire	1	–
Gloucestershire	8	41
Hampshire	44	82
Kent	1	1
Lancashire	–	1
London	5	5
Northamptonshire	–	1
Oxfordshire	1	3
Somerset	25	46
Sussex	–	1
Warwickshire	–	2
Waterford, Ireland	1	–
Worcestershire	1	–
Totals	132	348

community, those sent to the larger industrial and trading centres (Birmingham, Coventry, Stratford-upon-Avon and Warwick) and those who moved from one small village to another, often only a few miles away. There were 66 children (11.5 per cent) in the latter category and 198 more who remained in their own large town when apprenticed, a total of 46.0 per cent. In Sussex, a quite different county, at the same period a similar picture emerges. Of 2,989 children bound during these years, the apprentices' and masters' homes were recorded for a majority, 1,771 (59.3 per cent) of whom two-thirds (1,158) had their homes in Sussex and went to masters living in the county. A further 197 boys and girls went to masters living in the adjacent counties (88 to Kent, 69 to Surrey, 40 to Hampshire) out of 494 who went to non-Sussex homes. In addition, 252 children were bound to London masters and 42 to Middlesex men, with a single master in Essex, Lancashire and Suffolk. Apart from these apprentices, 119 also came to Sussex masters, the majority from the neighbouring areas (Surrey, 39; Kent, 35; Hampshire, 34) and a handful of children from more distant homes (Wiltshire, 4; London and Suffolk, 2 each; Devon, Middlesex and Somerset, 1 each).[118]

In Bedfordshire for the decade 1711–20 there were 370 apprentices out of a total 436 (84.9 per cent) who remained within the county. There were also

66 going beyond the county boundaries (15.1 per cent) to find masters, although half of these went to Bedfordshire's five neighbours (London 32; Buckinghamshire, Hertfordshire, 10 each; Northamptonshire, 9; Cambridgeshire, 2; Huntingdonshire, Middlesex, Surrey, 1 each). The children who went to London were indentured to the fashion trades (mantua-maker, milliner, sempstress, peruke-maker), to the professions (attorney, barber-surgeon), and the City's specialist occupations (goldsmith, armourer), as well as the usual artisans.[119]

Many more varied apprenticeships existed for the provincial child in the City of London than at home and the capital was always a magnet for the ambitious parent or child, with the well-known example of Dick Whittington as an incentive to these betterment migrants.[120] Of the 3,780 apprentices to the Stationers' Company, 1563–1700, only 694 (18.4 per cent) came from the City itself. Of the rest, the four adjacent counties provided 393 apprentices (10.4 per cent) and the next ring of counties outwards from London (Hertfordshire, Buckinghamshire, Berkshire, Hampshire and Sussex) a total of 300 apprentices (7.9 per cent), while most children came from the rest of Britain (2,393 or 63.3 per cent), with even the remotest rural counties, such as Herefordshire, Cumberland and Cornwall, represented.[121]

In other London companies a changing pattern of apprenticing across different decades can be seen; thus the Carpenters and Fishmongers, in the years up to 1649, recruited about 40 per cent of their entrants from the north and west of Britain, but by the last years of the century the contribution of these areas had halved. At the same time there was a striking rise in the numbers of boys from London and the Home Counties who, before 1649, had comprised less than 20 per cent, but whose numbers rose to 50 per cent by 1700 and to 70 per cent by 1750.[122] In exceptional circumstances a craft could alter recruitment patterns quite dramatically, as the London Carpenters' Company was obliged to do after the Great Fire, when extra boys were speedily indentured and older apprentices freed before their time to solve a desperate shortage of workmen in London.[123] In Oxford too there was a noticeable change in the distances boys travelled to find masters, with short-distance recruitment (five miles or less) increasing very strikingly after the 1690s. In the eighteenth century some 16 per cent of Oxford's apprentices came from further afield, with only about 5 per cent from homes 25 miles or more away.[124]

A quite different pattern of apprenticing emerges from the records of a provincial company, the Newcastle upon Tyne Shipwrights.[125] From the mid-seventeenth to the mid-nineteenth century the shipwrights recorded the homes of 773 of their total 871 apprentices (88.7 per cent). Of these, 273 (35.3 per cent) were from beyond Northumberland, while 500 were local boys. Except for two brothers, whose father was serving with the East India Company in Bengal, the majority of non-local apprentices came from neighbouring areas:

Table 2.8 Homes of non-local Newcastle upon Tyne shipwrights' apprentices
c. 1650–c. 1850.

Home of apprentice	Number of apprentices
County Durham	237
Yorkshire	11
Scotland	8
London	5
Cumberland	4
Berkshire, Essex, Lancashire, Middlesex, Norfolk, Surrey	1 each

This pattern of provincial apprenticeship is echoed in such different communities as Worcester, which drew apprentices in the sixteenth century from a 10-to-25 mile radius of the city, or Bristol, whose apprentices came chiefly from the adjacent counties or the Severn valley.[126] At Sheffield too the recruitment areas changed from the early to the late seventeenth century; in the period 1625–50 there were 22 per cent of boys bound to the Cutlers' Company with homes further than 31 miles away, but by 1675–1700 only 5 per cent of their apprentices were in this category, with a noticeably increased recruitment from the local community.[127]

There is considerable evidence from different areas that apprentices were prepared to travel quite long distances to be indentured to one of the high-premium, prosperous occupations or to be bound to relatives (masters with the same surnames). In the first category were such children as the Hereford pipemaker's son bound to his father's trade in Bristol,[128] the 11 boys who travelled to Coventry to be indentured to chemists there during the years 1781–1806[129] and the many provincial children whom London always attracted. Exceptional circumstances could send English children overseas as apprentices in the lucrative occupations. Thus a Dorset gentleman's son joined a Cadiz merchant in 1714, with a £400 premium, for five years, while in 1803 two New York druggists, Puffer and Back, took the young Thomas Fairchild as their apprentice.[130] In all such distant apprenticeships parental participation was, of course, essential.

Apart from prosperous children, paupers might also have distant apprenticeships and the evidence for them is fairly substantial, for among parish papers the apprentices' records were usually carefully retained in order to prove the child's right of settlement elsewhere in adulthood. Of 918 pauper apprentices in Cambridgeshire (surprisingly few, if for the whole county for two centuries, 1631–1830), 35 per cent remained in their home villages, 64 per cent went to a neighbouring parish, while the rest, 1 per cent, were sent further from home.[131] Figures from other individual parishes, however, show a far larger proportion of children indentured where they were born, as in Gnosall (Staffs.)[132] and Doveridge (Derbys.),[133] where 83.5 and 69.5 per cent respectively have been cited, as well as in Loes and Wilford Hundreds

(Suffolk),[134] where 65 per cent of pauper apprentices remained at home in 1770–83 and 56.1 per cent in the period 1821–6. All these parishes, however, like those in Warwickshire or Herefordshire, were almost entirely rural, where ratepayers, either farmers or craftsmen, themselves usually took numbers of pauper apprentices.

If these remote rural parishes were typical by the late eighteenth century, the philanthropists' protests against distant apprenticeships for young paupers seem greatly exaggerated and the 40-mile legislation less necessary if only a small minority were thus sent far from family and friends. The apprenticeship patterns of ten Warwickshire parishes under the Old Poor Law can be used to illustrate the extent to which children were near to home after binding (Table 2.9). All were large parishes, some highly industrialized(Bedworth and Nuneaton), others less so (Atherstone and Kenilworth), while also represented were ancient market towns (Stratford-upon-Avon and Warwick), entirely rural parishes (Tanworth-in-Arden and Temple Balsall) and those close to a very large community (Allesley and Walsgrave-on-Sowe, both near Coventry). All ten parishes have good collections of apprenticeship records, with few gaps and with other corroborative source material (see Table 2.9). It is apparent from these parishes that less than a third of pauper apprentices remained in their home parishes, that only a small minority went to adjacent parishes and that just over half travelled to masters living more than one parish away.[135]

Apart from economic factors, demography too played a part in apprenticeship, for in periods of high adult mortality more orphans needed masters and

Table 2.9 Destinations of Warwickshire pauper apprentices.

Parish	Area (acres)	Population (1802)	Total	Apprenticeships					
				Own parish		Next parish		Distant	
				no.	%	no.	%	no.	%
Industrial									
Bedworth	2,165	3,161	463	82	17.7	74	15.9	307	66.3
Nuneaton	6,112	4,769	812	293	36.1	182	22.4	337	41.5
Semi-industrial									
Atherstone	944	2,650	198	61	30.8	5	2.5	132	66.6
Kenilworth	5,914	1,968	266	77	28.9	12	4.5	177	66.5
Near city									
Allesley	4,257	752	104	16	15.3	51	49.0	37	35.5
Walsgrave	2,713	823	77	7	9.1	19	24.6	51	66.2
Market									
Stratford	109	2,418	235	41	17.4	4	1.7	190	80.8
Warwick	5,613	5,592	367	90	24.5	20	5.4	257	70.0
Rural									
Tanworth	9,808	1,695	490	301	61.4	22	4.5	167	34.1
Temple Balsall	5,095	853	112	26	23.2	20	17.8	66	58.9

in decades of rising birth-rates and lower infant mortality more adolescents were surviving, available to be apprentices, while increased consumerism encouraged indenturing in many trades. For the orphan of all classes, apprenticeship could provide a replacement home and bequests of money for premiums indicate parental concern for a child's future in the event of a father's untimely death. Most non-poor apprenticeships indicate whether a child were an orphan, either by the entry "father deceased" or "mother, widow" and adult male mortality rates can be discerned from apprenticeship sources. In Southampton (1610–1710) the numbers of orphan apprentices steadily declined, with 36 per cent in 1620–31 the highest level, falling to 20 per cent by 1710.[136] A similar picture emerges for other towns in the seventeenth century, with 34 per cent orphan apprentices at Bristol, 20 per cent in the London Stationers' Company and 25 per cent in the City's Fishmongers' and Bakers' Companies.[137] Adult mortality figures varied within trades, however, so that an exceptionally high number of fatherless apprentices are recorded in the London Weavers' Company during the years 1655–1795, with 57 per cent orphans in 1655–64, 34 per cent in 1736–45 and 17 per cent in 1786–95.[138] As weavers' apprentices came increasingly from poorer families (textile workers, labourers and mariners) with few from professional and merchant homes, such mortality figures are not surprising.

As the eighteenth century passed, fewer apprentices were orphans; as male life expectancy was increasing, so the Newcastle shipwrights indentured 8.9 per cent fatherless boys before 1750 but only 4.2 per cent in the next hundred years.[139] County apprenticeship records show a similar pattern of fatherless children. It is difficult to know why only a mother's name was given for some children; they were, bound to the upper crafts and professions, unlikely to be illegitimate, but it is possible their mothers had remarried[140] and were responsible for indenturing their sons rather than the stepfathers:

Table 2.10   Orphan apprentices, 1710–60.

County	Total apprentices	Father dead	Mother widow	Mother only	% of total
Warwickshire	2,452	1.8%	2.6%	3.6%	8%
Wiltshire	2,759	5.9%	2.3%	3.5%	12%

Many apprentices substantially modified their social status as well as their residence by being indentured, moving from gentry to trade or from craft to profession as a result of altered family circumstances, employment opportunities or changing public estimation of various occupations. As an example of such social mobility the numbers of gentry sons entering professional or merchant careers can be measured, even allowing for a generous use of the category "gentleman". Especially after the Civil War surviving younger sons, often with reduced opportunities of marrying well, increasingly found a career essential, at the same time that mercantile connections became more socially acceptable. Gentry participation in trade and the professions, it has been suggested,[141] gave foreigners the impression that English society was less static than their own. In the period before the Civil War only 3.9 per cent of Bristol's apprentices had fathers who were gentlemen.[142] During the seventeenth century the numbers of gentlemen's sons bound in Southampton rose steadily from 6 to 20 per cent,[143] while in the 1660s in the Shrewsbury Drapers' Company nearly half the freemen were from gentry homes[144] and almost a fifth of the London Stationers' apprentices were so described.[145] The eighteenth century shows a distinct reduction in these figures, either because fewer gentlemen's sons recorded their parentage thus or, with wider economic opportunities as a result of the Industrial Revolution, boys from such families entered careers for which apprenticeship was not essential. In Surrey, early in the eighteenth century (1711–31), 5.2 per cent of apprentices were the sons of gentlemen and clerics.[146] By the middle decades in Sussex and Wiltshire only 2.6 and 1.5 per cent respectively[147] of apprentices had fathers recorded as gentlemen, while in Warwickshire the proportion was less than 1 per cent at the same period.[148]

Although the apprenticing of boys of good family undoubtedly raised the status of the occupations they entered, encouraging others to follow, not all social mobility was of this kind and apprenticeships can indicate seriously reduced family prosperity. Thus deceased merchants', clerics' and gentlemen's sons could find themselves bound to quasi-professions or upper tradesmen, just as orphaned artisans' sons might be bound to weavers, husbandmen or other impoverished occupations unless an apprenticing charity were to intervene. The tenuous hold on prosperity for many families needed reinforcement by parental survival, for disease and death could as easily destroy a family firm or workshop as economic factors. Apprenticeship records amply illustrate the transition "from shirtsleeves to shirtsleeves in three generations" with distressing frequency, but equally show the rising fortunes of many through trade, manufacture and the professions into the landowning gentry by the nineteenth century, a step made possible by an ancestor's apprenticeship.

CHAPTER 3

Education and training

For as a twigge will best bend when it is greene, so children are fittest
to be bound when they are young, otherwise by reason of their idle
and base educations, they will hardly hold service: but as they have
wavering and straying mindes, so they will have wandering and
unstaid bodies, which will sooner be disposed to vagrance than
activitie, to idlenesse than to worke.

Anon., *An ease for overseers of the poore* (1601)

Since the period of apprenticeship did not begin for most occupations until
the age of 14 the problem of the child's education before this was not the
master's but the parent's concern. Clearly educational levels and requirements varied enormously from the poorest crafts, through the prosperous
trades to the professions, but no occupation normally specified in the indentures that the apprentice would be taught anything more than the master's
"art and mystery"; formal education was either presumed in some occupations or unnecessary in others. Education, therefore, for apprentices could
comprise any or all of the skills of reading, writing, counting and craft
instruction, as well as religious and social training. Not all of these were necessary or taught in every occupation and of them only literacy can in any way
be estimated. Assessment of literacy is, however, difficult, since signing a
name cannot be taken as proof of the apprentice's ability to do much more
than this. Although an estimate of 30 per cent literacy for English males has
been made for 1642,[1] it is difficult to tell how far apprentices were able to
read and write at this period. It has been noted in the late sixteenth and seventeenth centuries that apprentices to a particularly literate trade, the Stationers' Company, tended to come from towns where grammar schools were
established, although special provision was made in 1602 for one boy whom
a printer was only allowed to apprentice provided the child was first sent to
school to learn to read and write.[2]

A certain level of literacy must have existed among apprentices by at least the later seventeenth century, if only to judge from the numbers of chap-books and broadsheets produced for them and sold by both provincial and London printers. These publications, cheaply and crudely printed, usually in large type, told traditional stories with uncomplicated plots, often with the "rags to riches" or apprentice-hero theme. Others were simplified versions, only 24 pages long, of newly published works, such as *Robinson Crusoe, Moll Flanders* or *Jack of Newbery*, as digests intended for a readership whose literacy level was low, whose vocabulary was fairly narrow and whose wages did not permit the purchase of a bound volume. There were also special alma-nacs printed, for example, for weavers, in this crude form and certainly the propaganda value of chap-books in social control must have been consider-able. One correspondent to the *London Magazine* recognizing their potential, wondered why

> no administration in this country for their own good, or no worthy magistrates for the public good, have been at pains to have ballads of a proper tendency circulated among the people. I am sure money could not be better employed, and I am certain that no placement, or pensioners, can be of so much service as a set of well chosen ballad singers might be.[3]

A useful yardstick for literacy in the London trades of the mid-eighteenth cen-tury can be seen in both Collyer's and Campbell's insistence on it. The variety of crafts they mentioned suggests quite widespread ability, for Collyer insisted that "the business of Education [was] the most important duty of the parent and guardian".[4] Certain trades, such as shoemaking, baking, tailoring or carpentering, relied heavily on the rule of thumb and judgement of the work-man's eye, rather than written instructions and measurements. However, an educated apprentice was clearly essential in the professions, for writing accounts, reading of all kinds, and in the retail and wholesale trades where numeracy was vital. In advertising for an apprentice a bookbinder predictably required a boy who "understands English" and "writes a tolerable hand" but, perhaps surprisingly, a spurrier also requested that his apprentice "writes a very good hand",[5] while a milliner, "in genteel business" wanted a "Person who has had a liberal Education, of a good Family, and can be well recom-mended".[6]

Campbell carefully delineated the different skills that various tradesmen required in guiding children and their parents in the choice of a career. Among the trades, he named only 12 for which literacy was needed, and noted scorn-fully that a cutler might have an education "as mean as you please", while a brazier needed strength, ingenuity and drawing, but little other education. A cabinetmaker needed to know only drawing, a mason geometry and drawing; other craftsmen, the carpenter, locksmith and engraver, should be able to read

English and write, but a saddler and a cooper needed only "the common Education of a Tradesman".[7] Campbell, in fact, was more aware of personal qualities in the apprentice than literacy, so that strength, eyesight, ingenuity and alertness were all specified for different occupations, as well as skill in "plain English", polite conversation or common arithmetic. Only slightly different requirements were set out by Collyer 16 years later for the trades he described.

Among the prosperous occupations, the goldsmith, grocer and woollen draper needed only English, according to Campbell, but the engineer required also mathematics and designing. The apothecary should have had an "early and liberal education" and be "Master of the Languages",[8] although these were not specified, but Collyer mentioned a knowledge of Latin among the apothecary's abilities. Both Latin and Greek were thought essential for surgeons by Campbell and Collyer,[9] and the Barber Surgeons' Company required in 1727 that future apprentices "shall be called in and examined by themselves touching their skill in yᵉ Latin tongue". As knowledge of Latin for their apprentices had been one of the company's orders 170 years earlier, the need to repeat it perhaps suggests that Latinity had been declining among entrants.[10] Campbell, however, noted that a compositor needed grammar, Latin and Greek.[11] Apart from the physician, cleric and attorney, the highest educational standards were needed for the merchant, who had to

> understand his Mother Tongue perfectly, write it grammatically, and with Judgment; he must learn all the Trading Languages, French, Dutch and Portuguese, and be able to write them accurately ... [also] Geography, Navigation, a fair hand, Figures and Accompts.[12]

In order to provide a vocational training, schools were established for mercantile apprentices, as at Bristol, where "J. Jones, writing master and accomptant" advertised his curriculum in 1740 as spelling, reading, writing, arithmetic and bookkeeping, with geography a special subject.[13] At Leeds too "Young Gentlemen will be carefully and expeditiously instructed in every Branch of Genteel Literature, necessary for Trade, the Merchants' Compting House, the Public Offices and the Sea."[14]

Skill in a foreign language for trade purposes, however, was always the master's responsibility, so that a handful of boys in Southampton were to learn French and Spanish, spending one or two years abroad to do so.[15] An East Anglian merchant at the same period needed to converse with the cloth traders of the Low Countries and so sent his apprentice for a year to Flanders to learn to speak Dutch.[16] Ability to "cipher" was also to be taught to one Southampton apprentice.[17]

Until the nineteenth century there were three main sources of education outside the home for less prosperous boys: the grammar school, for skilled artisans' and emergent middle-class children, the charity school, frequently founded by a Tudor or Stuart philanthropist, and the Sunday school. Only the Sunday school was open to any child, however, for entry to the grammar school was restricted by the fees that had to be paid and entry to the charity school was by means of a recommendation from one of the school's trustees or patrons. In the eyes of contemporaries the charity school not only educated children but also disciplined them to accept their station in life, an attitude reinforced in a practical way by the children's distinctive uniform:

> The very garments that in some places are given them to wear, and their maintenance in all of them by charity, are the constant badges and proofs of their dependence and poverty; and should therefore teach *them humility* and *their parents* thankfulness; the frequent contributions made for their support shows them their obligations to their benefactors and friends, and naturally leads them into gratitude and submission; and must, if anything, inspire them with a desire to please, by their faithfulness, diligence, and industry, that they may not forfeit protection and assistance they need in any future station in life.[18]

The view of charity schools as supporters of social order, however, was not universal, for Mandeville wrote passionately against them, not only that they encouraged self-esteem in the governors of such establishments but, more seriously, because education made the poor child unfit for labour. Schools merely kept children from working and

> are more Accessory to the growth of Villainy, than the want of Reading & Writing, or even the grossest Ignorance & Stupidity ... where People's Livelihood has no dependence on those Arts, they are very pernicious to the Poor, who are forc'd to get their Daily Bread by their Daily Labour ... Going to School in Comparison to Working is Idleness, & the longer Boys continue in this easy sort of Life, the more unfit they'll be when grown up for downright Labour ... Men who are to remain & end their Days in a Laborious, Tiresome & Painful Station of Life, the sooner they are put upon it at first, the more patiently they'll submit to it ever after.[19]

At the period of Mandeville's criticism a group of charity schools, named Bluecoat after the pupils' dress, was being established in the provinces, of which some had specific apprenticeship provisions. Those for girls only were not concerned with apprenticing, merely "placing" their pupils in domestic service (for example, Hereford, founded in 1710,[20] and Coventry in 1714).[21] Others, however, were mixed schools (Nottingham, 1707)[22] and many were for boys only (Chester, 1706,[23] and Birmingham, 1724).[24] The numbers of pupils were not large (30 at Birmingham, 35 at Chester, 40 at Nottingham) when the schools were founded but by the mid-nineteenth century had greatly expanded (200 at Birmingham, for example). In all these schools strict standards of behaviour and religious instruction were emphasized and the children taught there were fitted to enter any of the respectable trades. The fairly high premiums the Bluecoat schools provided facilitated entry to these trades and local voluntary support enabled the trustees to increase premiums as prices rose during the eighteenth century, so that at Nottingham, for example, the premium of £3 in 1717 had risen to five guineas by 1784.[25]

The effect of all charity schools on general literacy, however, was quite widespread, and 30,000 children were estimated to be attending them by 1760.[26] Mandeville's doubts on the merits of educating the poor child in 1714 were to be echoed a century later by William Cobbett, the self-educated son of a labourer, who emphasized the necessity of enabling children to earn their living by labour:

> The taste of the times is, unhappily, to give children something of book-learning, with a view of placing them to live, in some way or other, upon the labour of other people . . . what disappointment, mortification and misery to both parent and child! The latter is spoiled as a labourer; his book-learning has only made him conceited: into some course of desperation he falls; and the end is but too often not only wretched but ignominious . . . I am wholly against children wasting their time in the idleness of what is called education; and particularly in schools over which the parents have no control, and where nothing is taught but the rudiments of servility, pauperism, and slavery.[27]

The schools against which Cobbett inveighed so passionately, however, were almost invariably for the children of non-pauper, respectable parentage and most foundations set an upper limit of pupils to be taught, often as low as a dozen. Such numbers were not unreasonably few when the original benefactions were made but must have been effective for only a very small proportion of children in the population increases of the later eighteenth century and, as the Charity Commissioners noted, most schools had fewer than 50 children each. However, a number of such schools were intended specifically to apprentice children at the end of their education, with funds from the school's endowment to provide their premiums. All six charity schools in Coventry, inspected by the Charity Commission in 1833, were apprenticing boys aged 10 to 12 to city trades. One school, in Cow Lane, required them to be able to read and write their own names before admission. The largest foundation was Bablake Boys' Hospital, with 70 pupils, "the sons of respectable poor persons of Coventry, but not necessarily of freemen". These boys were taught reading, writing and arithmetic, using books supplied by the Society *for Promoting Christian Knowledge (SPCK). These children were "clothed* annually, in an ancient and peculiar dress".[28] There were also numerous dissenting academies founded during the later seventeenth century, but these too catered for the non-pauper child, with pupils such as Defoe and John Howard. Although dame schools flourished for the poorer classes, it is difficult to accept them, if *The water-babies* is at all accurate, as anything more than "minding schools" or crèches for working mothers able to afford a few pence a week.

There is, however, evidence of educational requirements and the master's obligation to provide instruction, at least in reading, in the occasional apprenticeship indenture. Scattered indentures for the seventeenth and early eighteenth century mention teaching the child to read as a condition of apprenticeship. For example, the young illegitimate John Thomas, indentured to a Stoneleigh husbandman in 1704, was to be "Educated & taught to Read English" as well as "Instructed in yᵉ Art & science of Husbandry". In the same county a Hartshill husbandman was to teach his parish apprentice to read the Bible and a Warwick girl, bound to three women in the town in 1711, was to learn to read a chapter in the Bible well, apart from domestic work.[29] At the same period, a Derbyshire miller's charity apprentice was to be taught by his master "to read English well if hell learne".[30] Of the 1,072 apprentices in Southampton (1609–1740) instruction in reading was specified for only five (including three girls who also learned knitting, spinning and needlework) and reading and writing for only three.[31]

It is, of course, possible that these illiterate children were exceptions to the majority who had learned to read and write before being indentured. Personal responsibility for instruction varied greatly, so that in one Yorkshire family in the late seventeenth century an elderly aunt was responsible for instructing "several servants . . . and apprentices that could not read a word, nor perhaps know a letter, when they came to her, and she taught them to read very distinctly. She was industrious in that, and successful in it."[32] If the master were himself only partly literate, the indenture could specify that the apprentice was to be taught by someone else, so that one Norwich grocer was to send his apprentice to the grammar school for two years and a worsted weaver's apprentice was to go to a writing school in the city, one month in his seventh and one month in his eighth year.[33] Such writing schools specifically catered for boys entering crafts and shopkeeping trades, especially in acquiring the correct copperplate handwriting needed for commerce.[34]

Even in the humble trades a boy might become literate if there were some local person who took an interest in his welfare. Thus, the Reverend William Cole intended to apprentice his young houseboy, James Wood, to his own shoemaker, but before doing so, after discussing the matter with the master in July 1761, in December he "put Jem to Schole to Wm Chenils for Writing & Accounts, as I design to put him out Apprentice & hoped to have done so last summer before he was so much spoiled as he is now".[35]

At least some country parsons appreciated the importance of education and personally gave instruction in their parish; William Best, vicar of Kenilworth in 1718, wrote that as there was not a charity school in the town he had himself "for about ten years taught them gratis in the church vestry to read English well and to write and copy accounts fit for apprentices".[36] Mathematical skill seems hardly ever to be specified, although Collyer noted certain humble crafts for which it was essential (bricklayer, carpenter).[37] However, informal ways of counting and measuring in crafts and trades have existed for centuries. Thus the "faggett-marke" for five (卌) was commonplace,[38] as was recording a measurement taken not in inches but by a series of marks on a long flat wand of wood, still used by carpenters in the present century.

The variety of poor people interviewed by Mayhew illustrates the uneven levels of literacy by the mid-nineteenth century and the different ways that labouring apprentices learned to read and write is very striking. Most who could write well enough to leave memoirs described how they were educated. All were taught when very young (Hutton, Place, Shaw and Lovekin before the age of five) and cottage or dame schools were most commonly mentioned. However, some boys (Charles Newnham at the Rochester Mathematical School,[39] Joseph Gutteridge at a Coventry charity school[40]) were able to progress beyond basic tuition, while Thomas Wood at Bingley Grammar School learned Latin but no mathematics for two years before being apprenticed to an engineer.[41] Except in these literate artisans, however, estimates of educational attainments among apprentices are extremely difficult to make, especially in assessing what levels of numeracy or literacy they achieved beyond the most basic, apart from those occupations where such skills were obviously intrinsic. It may be, however, that many more diaries and memorandum books were kept by apprentices and artisans than have actually survived, and ones newly discovered, such as those of Joseph Hill of Stratford-upon-Avon or John Whittingham of Stoke (War.), a barber and gardener respectively, may have been typical of their fairly basic literacy, but of lively, interested and observant men.[42] Not all masters in poor trades were illiterate but passed on their skills to their apprentices. William Felkin, indentured to a stockinger at the age of 14 in 1809, recalled that

> as several of us were fond of literature . . . it was his frequent custom (while the work was done) to ask what works we were reading, what we thought of them, and to throw out ideas, often of value in drawing attention to important or difficult points, or aiding to form a correct estimate, or helping to make the best of what we read . . . By this a stimulus was given to the first employment of my pen in writing some short papers to be read and discussed at the weekly meetings of seven apprenticed youths held in the schoolroom and supplied with dim tallow candles, barely sufficient to make the manuscript legible.[43]

In spite of the prevalence of the anti-school arguments put forward by such persuasive writers as Mandeville or Secker, who thought apprenticeships for the poor lessened the number of suitable trainee domestic servants,[44] a surprising number and variety of charity schools existed in England by the eighteenth century. Stone has identified 410 schools in ten counties by 1660,[45] and a century later in one typical county at this period, Warwickshire, out of the 215 parishes, 99 (46 per cent) had some kind of charitable school foundation. These schools varied greatly; in Alcester, for example, a small market town with needle- and rope-making industries, there were two charity schools; the one founded in 1581 was for poor men's sons from Alcester and Harbury, who were to be taught for three years from the age of nine, but the Charity Commissioners noted that there were only five pupils, and that the school was "greatly neglected" by the master. The other school there, founded in 1700, was for teaching reading, writing and arithmetic to the children of the parish poor not in receipt of relief, which precluded pauper apprentices; pupils entered aged 8 to 10, and remained until they were 14.[46] In this case the children's apprenticeship indentures support the commissioners' estimate of the school's effectiveness; during the years 1800–29 a total of 154 boys and girls were bound by the town's two charities, and of these only 70 (45.5 per cent) were able to sign their own names on the indentures.[47] Of those signing only 16 were girls and 54 were boys. An interesting comparable level of apprentices' literacy can be seen in a series of some 650 settlement examinations during the years 1815 to 1826 at Cheltenham (Glos.), where the applicants for assistance were of varied social status, although all in difficulty of one kind or another. Of these cases, 70 involved persons who had once been apprenticed and of these 31 (44.3 per cent) could sign their statements.[48] It has been shown that, as reading was taught before writing at this period, those capable of signing could also read.[49] There were, however, family literacy patterns from at least the mid-eighteenth century and a number of working men who subsequently wrote their memoirs were taught to read and write at home, for example James Dawson Burn.[50] Apart from family instruction and charity schools, there were other means in the eighteenth and nineteenth centuries by which the poor child might become literate and numerate. The parish workhouse could employ a schoolmistress or master to teach the children before they were apprenticed at the age of 12 or 14,[51] and since 1780 there were Sunday schools, growing in number and popularity, where children were taught "reading, and the great principles of religion".[52] It is almost impossible to measure the effectiveness of such Sunday tuition; the evidence to Sadler's committee, for example, was contradictory, but gave the general impression that factory children in the north of England were not literate, in spite of the 1,000 Eccles children said to attend Sunday school.[53] However, separate depositions for other areas gave a more favourable impression. When Leonard Horner reported on conditions in Coventry he observed that, in general, "children were well attended to in their education, as there are many excellent schools for the lower orders, and that the children employed by their parents usually attend Sunday schools". The situation in the city seemed sufficiently satisfactory that "it was unnecessary to spend any more of our time in Coventry".[54] At the time of Horner's visit the city had a total of nine schools, seven charity and two grammar schools, and yet Joseph Gutteridge, who was certainly not a pauper but of the respectable working class, recalled his own difficulties in learning to read. He had been taught by a Quakeress and a Wesleyan preacher before attending a charity school, and, at the age of 14 when beginning his apprenticeship, still found it necessary to practise his reading skills on the names of the shops he passed on his way to work. His own assessment of popular literacy in the city about 1821 is an interesting one; he thought that "at that time perhaps not ten persons in a hundred could read or write".[55] His estimate was supported by a parliamentary survey of 1816 that reported that only seven per cent of the total population of England and Wales were attending day schools.[56] At the same period in Birmingham a number of witnesses agreed that "in a general way [the children] could read, through the medium of Sunday schools and evening schools, and a vast number can write. They usually go to the Lancasterian, National and other schools before they are set to work, and they keep up their education by attending Sunday-schools."[57] One witness then added that there "were more schools for the lower orders than in any other town . . . and the children are well instructed".[58]

Education for factory apprentices was a separate problem (Ch. 8) but one young boy described the instruction provided and his own difficulties in attending:

> I was obliged to make overtime every night but I did not like this as I wanted to learn my book we had a school every night but we used to attend about once a week (besides Sundays when we all attended) 8 at a time I wanted to go oftener to school than twice a week including Sundays but Richard Bamford (the Overlooker) would not let me go tho' the mill had stopt, but this was the time that the straps and frames wanted mending.[59]

In spite of such provisions, the level of factory education cannot have been very high, since any competent schoolteacher would presumably prefer to work elsewhere. The low standard of attainment was recorded by Maria Edgeworth of a Derby factory child who could not understand what she was reading, and thought a bee was "something like a cow".[60] On the other hand two young sisters, apprenticed with Blincoe, were able to write a letter to their mother describing their harsh treatment.[61] In spite of scattered surviving evidence of literacy, it seems that the average poor apprentices, bound to the lower, less skilled trades by their parish officials, would not have been able to read and write at the beginning of their term and the responsibility for any such instruction fell upon their masters in the years before the mid-eighteenth century. Indentures specifying that the master should teach the apprentice to read and write presume a degree of literacy in the master himself, not always borne out by his mark at the end of the indenture. After this period, however, pauper children increasingly became apprenticed, both as a total number and as a proportion of the whole apprentice population. There is no evidence that greater numbers of them became literate as the eighteenth century progressed, rather, in fact, the reverse. Paupers could not attend charity schools because they came below the social category for whom such schools were intended and they were potentially helpful to their families, to tend younger children or assist their parents in the family occupation. Indeed, the desirability of education for the poor was not generally accepted. Many men in the eighteenth century, otherwise of a philanthropic disposition, would have agreed with the MP who considered that education would make the poor

> despise their lot in life, instead of making them good servants in agriculture, and other laborious employments to which their rank in society had destined them; instead of teaching them insubordination, [sic] it would render them factious and refractory, as was evident in the manufacturing counties; and it would enable them to read seditious pamphlets, vicious books and publications against Christianity.[62]

One craftsman who suffered because he was literate was a young saddler, just out of his time, "of studious habits and an enquiring turn of mind" who read *The black dwarf* aloud to "a few of the more intelligent working people" at the village cross in Bellingham (Northd). The local farmers thought he had "imbibed a spirit of radicalism" and would not employ him, a serious loss of trade in a country area.[63]

In addition to literacy, as the master was legally *in loco parentis* to the child, religious instruction was also necessary. Thus the sixteenth-century adolescent candidate for Anglican confirmation was required to have learned the catechism, for which "Fathers, Mothers, Masters and Dames" were to prepare their "children, Servants and Apprentices".[64] As the Reformation reduced priestly authority in society but elevated lay heads of households, some form of guidance for masters was needed, and books such as Edmund Coote's *The English schoolmaster* (1595) were intended for craftsmen and tradesmen responsible for teaching their servants and apprentices.[65] As early as 1543 merchant householders had been encouraged to read the Bible aloud to their families, whilst withdrawing this privilege for artificers, apprentices and journeymen.[66] In the last decade of the sixteenth century masters were to ensure their apprentices attended church, with £10 a month fine for failure to do so.[67] The virtues of an apprentice "well instructed in piety" were described by William Gouge as "most profitable, not only to the family, but also to the

74

Church and commonwealth" and a contemporary pamphleteer advised apprentices "let your study be, first to please your heavenly Master, and then your masters on earth". At the same period Westminster Abbey published its shorter catechism to help masters teach their apprentices to read,[68] although clearly it was possible for a child to learn the catechism by rote and still be unable to read. However, the master's own practice of Christianity must, in all ways, greatly have influenced the apprentice living with the family, so that boys or girls in an ungodly household, even though their parental home was different, would have found public and even private worship difficult. For this reason the SPCK in 1714 insisted that

> The Trustees shall see that the Masters to whom the children are apprenticed are persons of a sober and religious life and conversation, who will cultivate and improve their christian disposition. Hear them read the bible and some other good books; make them repeat what they have learn'd at school, see they are constant in their morning and evening devotions and not only carry them to Church to be catechised there . . . but sometimes send or go with them to their Minister to be catechised and instructed by him in private.[69]

Only 20 years later, however, Richardson devoted over a third of *The apprentice's vade mecum* to the "Scepticism and Infidelity of the present Age" setting out the "Essential Principles" of Christianity for young apprentices to follow. That not only prosperous children attended communion may be seen in the records of one borough apprenticing charity whose boys, at the end of their terms "did receive the holy sacrament of the Lord's Supper" and each apprentice had a signed certificate to that effect. These apprentices were bound to such craftsmen as a weaver, shoemaker and joiner in the first decade of the eighteenth century; similar records, significantly, have either not survived or never existed at a later date.[70]

Apart from the problem of assessing apprentices' education and religious instruction, the occupational teaching they received is even more difficult to estimate. In spite of the numbers of publications from the seventeenth century onwards advising the apprentice how to behave in the new host family, similar volumes directed at the master, suggesting how he should instruct the newcomer, do not seem to have been produced. Although the craft guilds provided supervision of apprentices during their term, this was intended only to ensure that the adolescent was being instructed (not used as a domestic servant) and treated properly, that the apprentice was behaving suitably and that only the permitted number of apprentices were being taught. The guilds, of course, finally judged the success or failure of the apprentice's training by inspecting his "proof piece" before he was made free of the company. Until the coming of technical institutes in Britain in the later nineteenth century, training for any occupation was based on the traditional method of "watching

Nellie", with apprentices beginning the term carrying out the most menial, progressing to unimportant and then major skills during the course of the seven years. Some apprentices, masters and observers (like Campbell) acknowledged that after five years many apprentices could perform most of the tasks at least as well as a qualified adult worker. It was, however, generally recognized that apprentices could not be trusted with the responsibility of expensive materials unsupervised or deal with valued clients who expected the master's personal attention. The untheoretical method of learning by observing a skilled practitioner was, except for the university man, in general use for centuries.

Exactly how an apprentice was taught varied considerably even within one occupation, for curricula did not exist; however, there was in all skills a corpus of knowledge to which each master would add his own "tricks" and personal innovations. The different stages through which apprentices passed during the term were rarely recorded, but memoirs generally described the first part of the term and the resented non-craft tasks the apprentice was expected to perform. Thus unskilled, demeaning work was a common experience to all apprentices at any period across a wide range of trades in the first year of their term. Advice to the young apothecary's apprentice early in the nineteenth century listed the routine tasks he should expect to perform:

> When there is not a man or boy kept, your first care after opening the shop, will be to sprinkle and sweep it, if your bed is in the shop, turn it up; and put everything that is not immediately wanted to be made use of, into its own proper place. If lamps are used, take this time for trimming your lamps, for packing up such unsightly things as are to be carried into the store-room, or be put entirely out of the way.[71]

Similar tasks fell to the young William Lucas, at a Haymarket, London, pharmacy where he began his term in 1819, only to complain how he, as the youngest, "had to do the most menial work and be at the beck and call of the elder". He added that what went most "against the grain" was having to "go out with a basket and deliver medicines" when there was an "interservitium of errand boys".[72] A watchmaking apprentice, William Masters, also ran errands, collected orders and delivered goods in Coventry before beginning to learn the skills of the trade to which he was indentured.[73] Other menial tasks included sweeping the floor for a gold-beater and washing up for a compositor.[74] Robert Blincoe's first task at Lowdham cotton mill was to pick up the loose cotton that fell on the floor, than which, he thought, "nothing could be easier, and [he] set to with diligence". Terrified by the machinery, suffocated by the cotton dust and flue, he felt nauseated and his back ached from constant stooping. He continued picking up cotton for seven or ten days.[75] Providing the adult workers with beverages of all kinds was also the lot of the new apprentice; most boys seem also to have resented the personal nature of this service. Henry Broadhurst, a mason's apprentice, recalled how in 1853

> as the youngest employee many duties besides the acquisition of a trade fell to my lot. At eight o'clock in the morning I had to see that hot tea and coffee were ready for thirty or forty men. Then at ten I must start on my tour of the shop to see how many pints of beer would be wanted at eleven, and this task had to be repeated at three o'clock . . . I must fetch the beer from one [public house] nearly a mile away.[76]

As well as brewing tea for the men, a young cabinetmaker's apprentice also was obliged to deliver customers' orders, sometimes with disastrous results.[77] However, William Masters remarked in his memoirs that in this way he had come to know many watchmakers, journeymen and customers in the community, and these acquaintances had helped him as an adult workman.[78] The next stage of work for the apprentice generally involved tasks connected directly with the craft and using its raw materials, involving only a low level of skill but giving apprentices practical experience of the materials they would be handling for the next seven years. Thus manufacturing glue brushes out of cane,[79] making wrought nails[80] or thousands of brass watch pins[81] and "closing" boots (a task also suitable for the shoemaker's wife)[82] were all beginnings in different crafts. Even a surgeon's apprentice in 1806 began work by rolling up pills and painting bottles in the dispensary before progressing to tooth extraction.[83] In ribbon-weaving the new apprentice began work "by helping others to change their patterns, and doing odd jobs about the shop . . . the journeymen in return would, practically show [him] how to manage things that [he] might have asked the foreman in vain to instruct [him] in". This particular apprentice, Joseph Gutteridge, was highly critical of the instruction he received, since the foreman was "more given to drinking than to teaching . . . a talented and capable workman, but . . . extremely unfit, either by precept or example, to have the care of young people".[84] Preparatory work for the adult was also part of the apprentice's early training period, so the mould runner prepared the potter's stove that work could begin at 6am.[85]

After this initial period an apprentice could be trusted with more responsible tasks, but still not involving expensive raw materials or valued customers. Thus clock-cleaning was a suitable task for the novice,[86] and George Sturt commented that "Apprentices, after a year or two, might be equal to making and painting a wheelbarrow. But it was a painful process with them learning the whole trade. Seven years was thought not too long."[87] Sometimes instruction was reluctantly given, the apprentice fearful to ask and the skilled men unwilling to be bothered with the adolescent, as Henry Broadhurst discovered; however, he secured a journeyman's advice with "the persuasive power contained in a pint of beer".[88] Some masters, although severe, were competent workmen and instructors. George Herbert's was such a master, with his own "pleasant way of getting a good deal of work" out of his three shoemaking apprentices:

> He used to hang up his watch where we could all see it and he would then handicap us according to the length of time which we had served, and he was the judge to see which was done the quickest and the best. He used to say, "Your arms ought to fly like bees' wings", and I have been very thankful many times that he did so as it made us very quick at our trade.[89]

The young apprentice entering a merchant's business was given specific advice on how he should receive some parts of his training. In the first years the boy learned to weigh, measure and pack his master's commodities and then was taken from attending the counter and sweeping the warehouse into the counting-house. There he would learn what goods cost, and exercise his own judgement about their quality, which Defoe thought the most useful skill of all, to be acquired as early as possible. The apprentice should, near the end of his term, become acquainted with his master's suppliers, the chapmen, his customers and methods of bookkeeping, "and if he finds his master either backward or unwilling to teach him, he should complain in time to his own friends, that they may somehow or other supply the defect".[90] John Coggs's experiences in London exemplified Defoe's advice.[91] In other prosperous occupations, especially medicine, watching and then imitating a skilled man was a widespread method of instruction. Thus a surgeon's two apprentices watched a post-mortem examination carried out before attempting one themselves.[92] Another parish surgeon took his 19-year-old apprentice with him "on his rounds to the poor and Poor House to visit the sick". This particular apprentice, Henry Jephson, wrote home in delight,

> I can with just pleasure add that he behaved like a Gent and has promised to let me visit them alone. I assure you it has happened exactly right in my last year, as I can visit them more than I did before, indeed he advised me to pay attention to the various diseases I see, and you may depend upon my taking it.[93]

Because of a master's absence or illness an apprentice, however, was often required to carry on the business himself although only partly trained. Such an occasion must have given the ambitious apprentice an opportunity to show his skill, and it is said that James Brindley, bound to a Macclesfield millwright in 1733, left to work alone in his master's frequent absences, was preferred by the millers "in execution of their orders to the master or any other workmen".[94] Even a physician as eminent as John Coakley Lettsom began as an apprentice who, in the 1760s, took charge of the practice and visited patients "often . . . when [his] master was out of town or engaged on midwifery", but was very conscious of his incompetence, "never having heard a lecture or seen any anatomical figure, except a skeleton".[95]

In many masters' minds, however, a skilful apprentice, about to become a journeyman, was a risk, for the younger man might either actively seek to attract his master's customers when setting up for himself or actually be preferred by a clientele dissatisfied with the older man's attention or products. The risk was unimportant if the new journeyman returned to his family home to practise his skills, became a partner with his former master or married into the master's family, a favourite solution in reality and myth for the ambitious apprentice at the end of his term.

CHAPTER 4

Pauper and charity apprenticeships

The practice in some towns, pursued systematically is to bind the parish apprentices into out-townships . . . When I enquired of the assistant overseers . . . how the apprentices turned out after they were bound, his answer was, "We have nothing to do with them afterwards."

PP, XVIII (1834), Appendix 1

In spite of the wide variety of occupations to which children might be bound, the basic intentions of apprenticeship at any period were twofold, economic and social, affecting three separate categories of apprentices: pauper, charity and normal. First, apprenticeship provided children with an adult livelihood, enabling them to support themselves and their dependants for 30 years or more, without recourse to parish relief. Secondly, apprenticeship controlled the supply of entrants to any occupation, which limited the numbers of adult journeymen and masters who would ultimately practise a craft, and so avoided overstocking and resultant low wages. As a training method, apprenticeship regulated the skills of an occupation and prevented dilution by unqualified workers, who would bring the craft into disrepute and depress wages. Politically, pauper apprenticeship was intended as a form of social control, a means of removing the dreaded swarms of beggars that Tudor legislators feared would grow uncontrollably. By the eighteenth century both inhabitants and parish officials acknowledged apprenticeship as a reliable method of keeping down the poor rate. At any period, however, apprenticeship relied for success on stable economic conditions.

Both pauper and charity apprentices were created in the sixteenth century and, although the word "apprenticeship" covered all three categories of children, they differed from each other very considerably (see Table 4.1). Unfortunately, great differences also exist in the survival rate of records relating to the three groups of apprentices, with pauper and charity sources far exceeding those for non-poor children. In every apprenticeship two copies of the indenture were made, one to be held by the master and one by the binding authority

Table 4.1 Comparison of the main clauses in typical apprenticeship indentures.

Pauper	(Charity)	Normal
Parish officials bound child with justices' consent	Apprentice bound himself	Apprentice bound himself
Parentage not recorded	Parentage recorded	Parentage recorded
Term: until child reached stated age	Term: years specified	Term: years specified
Apprentice to serve master faithfully in all lawful business	Apprentice to serve master faithfully	Apprentice to serve master faithfully
	Apprentice to keep master's secrets	Apprentice to keep master's secrets
	Apprentice to obey master's lawful commands	Apprentice to obey master's lawful commands
	Not to harm the master or see him harmed	Not to harm the master or see him harmed
	Not to waste or lend the master's goods	Not to waste or lend the master's goods
	Not to sell or buy without the master's consent	Not to sell or buy without the master's consent
	Not to enter tavern, inn or alehouse	Not to enter tavern or playhouse
	Not to gamble	Not to gamble
	Not to marry	Not to marry
		Not to commit fornication
Apprentice to behave in honest, orderly and obedient way to master and his family	Apprentice not to leave the master night or day	Apprentice not to leave the master night or day
Premium from parish officers	Premium from trustees	Premium from parent or guardian
	Master to teach art and skill of the trade as best he can	Master to teach art and skill of the trade as best he can
Master to provide the apprentice with adequate meat, drink, clothes, lodging, washing and all other things fit	Master to provide sufficient meat, drink, clothes, lodging, washing and necessaries	Master to provide sufficient meat, drink, clothes, lodging, washing and necessaries
Master to ensure that apprentice did not become a charge on the home parish during the term		
At the end of the term the master was to provide double apparel for the apprentice		

or parent. As institutional records, therefore, overseers' and trustees' copies have survived in far greater numbers than privately owned papers. The most substantial sources for non-poor children are the great London apprenticeship registers, kept to record the stamp duty paid on indentures, but these are reliable for only 50 years (1710–60), although they were maintained irregularly until 1818.

Of the three groups, the pauper apprentice has received most attention from both contemporaries and modern historians, and yet much comment is based on the small minority of parish apprentices noticed because they broke the law or were the victims of violence. Contemporaries regarded the pauper apprentice in various ways: as a parish burden to be given settlement rights elsewhere; as an object of compassion; as a source of biddable, cheap and unskilled labour. With increasing industrialization, a characteristic of pauper apprenticeship came to be the narrow range of trades to which parish children were bound, unacceptable occupations with low premiums. Thus certain trades became increasingly pauperized and this stigma deterred children of respectable families from entering. It is apparent that certain unhealthy trades, such as hatmaking or brickmaking, were highly pauperized, as were those providing poor adult career prospects, particularly textiles (cotton, lace, framework knitting), an abuse contemporaries frequently noted.

Table 4.2 Proportion of paupers apprenticed to occupations in Warwickshire, 1700–1834.

50% and over	30 to 49%	10 to 29%	Below 10%
99 housewifery	47 tailor	28 brass founder	8 toymaker
97 husbandry	46 mason	25 woolcomber	7 cooper
96 ribbon-weaver	44 ribbon-weaving	23 hairdresser,	6 dyer, whittawer,
95 horn comb	branches	carpenter	wheelwright
maker	40 cordwainer,	22 milliner, miller	5 plumber
93 brickmaker	bucklemaker	18 turner, engine-	4 chandler
81 silk-weaver	38 breeches-maker	weaver	3 printer, clothier,
63 hatter	37 bricklayer,	16 staymaker	grocer
58 weaver	buttonmaker	15 mantua-maker,	2 saddler,
	33 glover	butcher	cabinetmaker
	31 gardener,	13 heel maker	1 ribbon
	chimney-sweep	12 joiner	manufacturer
		11 baker	
		10 currier, dresser,	
		collar maker	

The children most obviously marked for removal by parish authorities were those likely to become burdens on the ratepayers: the unsupported child who might live many years, the handicapped, the bastard or member of a large poor family were all obvious choices for removal by apprenticeship. Illegitimate children were almost invariably indentured by their parish; even if bastard status were not recorded in the apprenticeship sources, it can often be deduced by indemnity payments from the putative father or by overseers' marginalia, for example, "this be Ted Heritages child". However, an apprenticeship premium of £2 or £3, even of £5 in the eighteenth century, was a considerable economy for the parish when a weekly maintenance payment for a child was 1s 6d, a yearly cost to the ratepayers of £3 18s. Boys and girls with only one parent, a widowed or deserted mother, or a widower unable to care for his children, were usually apprenticed by the parish. The greatest burden for the overseers, however, remained the hard core of intractable paupers, whole families who needed support at all points in their lives, and their names recur in parish records across several decades. Such families were the Smiths or Bucks of Stratford-upon-Avon, five of whom were pauper apprentices in the 1760s, with others indentured by the parish 30 years later,[1] while in Felton (Herefs.) families named Bush, Bowcott and Oliver had children who were parish-bound during three decades.[2]

Parish officials were also eager to indenture a child likely to be a health risk and a number of indentures carried the additional clause "if he so long liveth". If apprentices could no longer work because ill or disabled, masters sought to return them to their home parishes, often engaging in expensive legal disputes to achieve this. Overseers could negotiate special conditions for incapacitated apprentices, as in 1768 for Charles Edwards, whose indenture was endorsed

> whereas . . . [he] has but one Eye, be it remember'd that before the Signing, Sealing and delivering this Indenture it is agreed by and with the Churchwardens and Overseers of the Poor aforesaid and the said John Harrison that if his other Eye should fail so as to render him incapable of doing his Business the Parish . . . is to take him again and Provide for him and the said John Harrison is to be entirely free of him.[3]

Overseers also acknowledged that an inducement had to be offered to make masters take particularly unsuitable apprentices at all, and one overseer noted in his accounts in 1750 that "in case any p^shoner will take Ann Murrell an apprentice on ye acct of her weak understanding he shall be allowed 5 pound wh her".[4]

Physical strength and good health were aspects of pauper apprentices available for indenturing that Overseers regularly stressed in their newspaper advertisements from the mid-eighteenth century, while Melton (Suffolk) offered only children who had had smallpox.[5] However, physical disability could successfully be cited by a master who wished to be rid of a child and a pauper apprentice's blindness in Coventry in 1790 was noted when he was bound, as the master might have sought to cancel the indenture in the future.[6]

Pauper premiums were clearly a factor that separated parish apprentices from charity or non-poor children, not only in actual sums paid but as an indication of trades to which they might be bound. Contemporary opinion was aware of masters who were "drunken, dissolute and incapable of teaching any trade . . . induced to receive the apprentice solely for the sake of the premium",[7] but in very few parishes, such as Birmingham,[8] was the master's character investigated, while a master to a non-poor child was likely to be assessed by the child's parent or guardian, as Campbell advised.[9] Some masters would not take children without money, but many children were indentured solely for the sake of their labour, and a contemporary noted that parish children were "put to laborious trades, and no other; with many of them, no money at all is given; with most of them but forty shillings; with some few, five pounds; but more with none".[10] Dunlop & Denman suggest that parish apprentices were given premiums before the practice was usual for other children, but record evidence does not confirm this. Premiums were certainly paid in the early seventeenth century with non-poor indentures and scattered instances exist of premiums for paupers at this period, as, for example, £1 10s paid with a young girl bound to a labourer in 1666.[11] Such payments were certainly common by the early years of the next century in a wide variety of trades and places. The parish apprentice also differed from the non-pauper child in that the term was usually longer. A pauper was generally bound much younger than 14, the age at which other apprentices were indentured, and could be required, before the 1768 act, to serve until the age of 24. However, many indentures were endorsed with a penalty clause setting the apprentice free at the age of 21.

Pauper apprentices, especially if from an urban parish, were more likely than other children to travel long distances to be indentured and to enter a narrow range of occupations, often with unhealthy conditions and poor adult employment prospects, all reinforcing their general unacceptability. Ratepayers wished to place a child beyond parish boundaries for obvious financial reasons, but also because, in the remote, rural enclave many parishioners preferred a pauper apprentice who was a stranger to one with existing parish connections. Two remedies were devised to overcome ratepayers' reluctance to take parish apprentices – ballots and fines. Pauper children were to be allocated by ballot among the ratepayers, a practice the Poor Law Commissioners noted in the rural counties of Herefordshire, Monmouthshire, Shropshire and Suffolk. The method employed at Knaresborough (Yorks.) was widely used:

> The practice is to have a meeting of the ratepayers once a year, who select 30 persons who are considered suitable to receive apprentices; then the meeting select 12 out of the 30 as the most suitable, and then the parties have notice to attend before the magistrate and show cause why they should not take an apprentice, and then they either take one each or pay £10. In Harrogate they give notice in the church that they have a certain number of children to put out, and they put them upon the ratepayers nearly in rotation, according to the length

of their residence, giving preference, however, to those who are liable to some offices, and saving those who are thought not able.[12]

Although the indenture and later the apprentice register were intended to record a pauper apprenticeship, parishes often noted the details of a binding in other account books, even if the reasons for doing so are not always clear; some of the arrangements thus recorded appear to be quite straightforward, for example,

> It was Agreed yt Tho: Kemble uper Churchwarden should dispose of Jno Michaell a nurse Pish boy to a Master yt should giue bond to discharge ye pish from him & to bind him apprentice to Learne his Art & Trade of a painter and that he should Agree with the said Master as cheape as hee could for his soe doing not exceeding seuaen pounds.[13]

Apart from allocating apprentices to unwilling ratepayers, the overseers also fined inhabitants who refused to take a parish child. The practice still survived in 1834 and many parishes saw it as a regular form of income; Defoe had identified it as an example of "birding" and the fine for refusal was £10 under the 1696 act (8 & 9 Wm c.30). Understandably the 1834 commissioners disapproved of fines raised in this way:

> The power of binding parish apprentices, upon an unwilling ratepayer, is very capriciously exercised, and is in many places the ground of just complaint. In several towns it is made a means of raising considerable sums annually, in the shape of fines for refusing to take apprentices. In Leeds one thousand pounds has been raised in this way within the year, and in several places one apprentice has been the means of raising thirty pounds, forty pounds and in one instance fifty pounds.[14]

The extent of such fines is difficult to estimate, but Halifax raised £100 or £150 a year by this means and one child in Ovenden, presumably completely unacceptable, regularly added £50 a year to parish funds by his unsuitability as an apprentice.[15] The commissioners noted that, after the 1819 Factory Act, when wholesale apprenticeship to manufacturers practically disappeared, overseers increasingly relied on their powers of compulsion to force ratepayers to take pauper apprentices.[16] Enforced apprenticing undoubtedly caused resentment, especially if the ratepayer felt that other issues were at stake in the arrangement:

> I became known as a Radical, and I have no doubt whatever that my trade with the aristocracy of the town suffered most severely in consequence. I daresay I was a marked man in the books of the

authorities for a long time; indeed, feelings engendered then are not eradicated now, after thirty-five years have passed by. I was summoned on juries, saddled with a parish apprentice, and had to pay £10 to be quit.[17]

A rota system seems to have worked better in rural parishes, where the largest ratepayers were substantial farmers who could easily absorb extra unskilled labour. In one big midland parish there were 15 such farmers who each took between two and five children during several decades; for example, one man indentured four male parish apprentices in the years 1787, 1801, 1810 and 1822, all to husbandry, a pattern seen in many similar parishes.[18] Many overseers feared that incoming pauper apprentices would make claims through the settlement laws; one solution was for their master to sign a bond making him liable, as Thomas Shaw at Elloughton (Yorks.) did for the sum of £100.[19] As well as fines and rotas, parish apprentices might also be placed as a result of inducements, as at Thirsk (Yorks.) where in 1700 a parishioner was paid £1 as a "further gratuity for taking a poor boy apprentice". Two years later the same overseers offered £3 as an incentive with "a vagerent boy . . . as an apprentice to some trade".[20] Civic privileges could also be used as an inducement to accept pauper apprentices; in 1575 an Ipswich tailor, Peter Ray, was made a burgess in exchange for taking an apprentice from the hospital and in the same town a "fforainer" was allowed in 1599 to trade on market days provided he took and kept a local child as an apprentice.[21]

Advertising apprentices as available was common in the eighteenth-century press; in one newspaper local carpenters, wheelwrights, shoemakers, tailors and manufacturers were required as masters for

> several healthy, well disposed BOYS, from the age of Ten to Fourteen Years, who for the last Three years have been educated at a Free School, and can make themselves useful. They must be apprenticed until they attain the Age of Twenty One Years. A fair Premium will be given.[22]

Finding a second master for a parish apprentice was often extremely difficult, since good apprentices were rarely discharged:

> The Master of a Girl about 15 years of age, a parish apprentice, is desirous of parting with her to any person of good credit in the country, to whom a handsome premium will be given, on giving security for her apprenticeship. She is a strong healthy girl, and capable of doing a great deal of hard work.[23]

Contemporary opinion about pauper apprenticeships was often vigorously expressed, both favourable and critical; a master's powers of abusing his apprentices was widely acknowledged and in 1794 Gisborne condemned the binding of a "friendless child" to an "unfeeling and profligate master [and] . . . a trade [that] will manifestly be ruinous to his health".[24] In 1800 the Middlesex bench, concerned at the treatment of apprentices in the London fashion trades, required closer supervision from the local magistracy, especially over the master's fitness to maintain his apprentices.[25] It is difficult to assess whether such pronouncements were the result of well-publicized cruelty cases or an attempt to preclude abuses. As early as 1697 the Bristol guardians appointed a committee to enquire into the binding of corporation apprentices; the first stipulation was that the master should be a "man of ability and honesty also of some sort of employment or faculty lest otherwise the Child be ill-treated . . . or else consume his time idly without learning anything whereby he may live thereafter". They proposed asking the mayor and aldermen by their own example to encourage suitable masters to take poor children as apprentices. In Bristol the corporation did not indenture children to chimney-sweeps and manufacturers' applications for batches of pauper apprentices were carefully considered before acceptance,[26] in contrast to Robert Blincoe's experiences.

Unlike the non-poor child, little or no supervision of pauper apprentices during the term might be expected nor any assessment of the master's suitability to take parish children. In a minority of cases, record evidence has survived to show that enquiries about potential masters were undertaken by the parish, either because of genuine concern about the pauper apprentices or because the master might be rumoured to have an unacceptable character. A handful of certificates have survived, for example, among the parish material for two north Warwickshire parishes, Bedworth and Bulkington, indicating that their officials made enquiries about Leicestershire masters to whom their paupers were to be bound. In January 1799 a magistrate and an incumbent from Hinckley certified that Thomas Green was a fit person to take an apprentice while other masters' certificates declared they were men of "good fame and of sober life and conversation".[27] Although the 1816 act to improve the conditions of parish apprentices required a certificate of a master's humanity and trustworthiness, the scarcity of these documents in record collections suggests that either they were rarely given or that they were destroyed as of little value. Concern for the welfare of parish apprentices could occasionally become a community matter, as in the case of a Stratford-upon-Avon boy at Measham in 1796 (Ch. 8). In this case, rumour and gossip in the borough resulted in the parish officials travelling to Leicestershire and interviewing their 29 pauper apprentices; a pamphlet describing their visit was printed and advertised in the local press, but such enquiries and publicity were very rare.

More than the other categories of apprentices, parish children consistently attracted criticism for their unsatisfactory behaviour, as unsuitable for certain tasks and whose pauper origins made them unfit to live at close quarters with a host family. A child from a very poor home could not expect to attain the status of a higher servant in a good household, but would perform the rougher domestic tasks; on a farm the more agreeable work in dairy or kitchen was unlikely to be for parish apprentices, although by the later eighteenth century the new agricultural societies tried to remedy this by awarding prizes for successful male and female husbandry apprentices. In 1795 the Devon Agricultural Society offered a prize of £3 3s to a "female parish apprentice (who has been for the greatest part of her apprenticeship employed in the different branches of agriculture) who shall produce the best character from her master of her behaviour in the last three years of her apprenticeship".[28] The unmanageable older male parish apprentice was a persistent problem for masters, who only rarely maintained contact with the child's overseers; one man, an Essex oyster dredger, however, wrote to his apprentice's former parish officials to tell them that they had got rid of a "loose, idle youth".[29] When a child was apprenticed by the overseers but the procedure was supervised by a parishioner personally, it seems likely that the arrangement was more satisfactory. Thus the incumbent of Bletchley, William Cole, noted in his diary in 1766 that he was meeting parish officers about "putting out the Bastard Son of Alice Worsley to one Rogers a Taylor of Soulbury", suggesting a degree of individual concern.[30]

From its inception a pauper apprenticeship had very different characteristics from the other two categories. The child's future master might be unwilling, chosen by parish officers for financial reasons rather than by the child's parents or by charity trustees with greater motives of goodwill. Sheer numbers became a problem for overseers as the eighteenth century progressed, and the pauper child could often be placed only in the particularly overstocked trades, such as ribbon-, nail- or lace-making, with poor adult employment prospects, with even a low premium a temptation to the "needy tradesmen" deplored by Crabbe.[31] Paupers also were apprenticed to excessively unpleasant occupations, such as chimney-sweeping, horn comb-making or cat-gut dressing, and to trades that were, before steam power, highly labour-intensive, especially textiles. Parish apprentices were more likely than others to be abandoned by absconding, insolvent masters, and certainly to suffer physical abuse than the more prosperous child, but parochial authorities failed to protect the most notoriously abused child, as in the cases of Elizabeth Bott Robbins and Ann Hands (Ch. 10). As early as 1764 Burn commented that it was the object of the overseers to "bind out poor children apprentices, no matter to whom or to what trade, but to take especial care that the master lived in another parish". It is not surprising that paupers were unsatisfactory apprentices; it is remarkable, perhaps, that any such arrangements were ever successful.

Much more successful for both master and child was the apprenticeship arranged by a charity endowed for this purpose. Charity apprentices took with them a reasonable premium and had often been prepared for apprenticeship by a charity school education, so that they were both literate and used to discipline. The child was likely to be well motivated; many charity apprentices were orphans, whose fathers had been respectable traders or craftsmen in the community and for such children a decent apprenticeship was the means of restoring the prosperity they had lost by their fathers' death. The master also must have welcomed such an apprentice, with an adequate premium, often with clothes provided by the trustees, a child from the community whose background he knew. Charity apprenticeships were selective, not available to all applicants. Most charities stated they were for children but some specified only boys were eligible: in Warwickshire there were 55 apprenticing charities noted by the Charity Commissioners in 1837 of which 14 were for boys and only one exclusively for girls.[32] These 55 charities represented 5.3 per cent of the county's 1,037 total, half of which were established for the general purpose of aiding the poor. However, bread charities comprised 15.7 per cent and those for clothing 5.9 per cent of the bequests. Charities for apprentices therefore ranked fourth, ahead of those for teaching (4.9 per cent), widows and spinsters (4.5 per cent), poor not receiving parish relief and schools (3.7 per cent each), almshouses (2.4 per cent), books (1.5 per cent), fuel and church repairs (1.1 per cent), with miscellaneous objectives comprising 2.8 per cent. Apprenticing charities were concentrated in certain communities, presumably since philanthropists followed the example of earlier benefactors, and most were founded in the larger towns. Warwickshire's charities were in only 29 of the county's 215 parishes, the majority in Coventry, Warwick, Alcester and Atherstone. Some were for surprisingly few children. Six of Warwickshire's charities were for only one boy a year and two for one child every other year; even the well-endowed Coventry charities could bind only some 30 children a year from their bequests. Most benefactors did not, in fact, specify for how many children their gift was intended, since premiums were always what the market would bear and, as time passed, the original value of the bequest in rents especially might bring in much more or considerably less in income than the benefactor envisaged. Some charities set out detailed conditions for the child, so that, for example, Webb's charity of Warwick, founded in 1722, did not allow an apprentice to be bound to his father, brother or mother. Many charities specified the town or parish from which an apprentice should come and a number were for children of alternative places: thus Monk's charity of Austrey could benefit children both from that parish and from Measham (Leics.) and several charities were open to both London and Warwickshire applicants. In Exeter, sons of the poor, aged from 7 to 14, were educated, fed and clothed in the Blue School, then given a premium of £6 when indentured, from the late seventeenth century.[33]

The intentions of the charity's founder were usually clear from the criteria set out in the bequest; apart from a desire to aid children from the home parish, some charities specifically required a master to be outside or within the parish, others allowed or forbade the master to be the child's own parents,

Figure 4.1 Wall tablet, All Saints, Northampton, showing a child from the charity founded by Mrs Dorothy Beckett (d. 1747) and Mrs Anne Sargeant (d. 1738) for 30 poor girls.

while a substantial number refused apprenticeship to children whose parents had received parish relief. A small minority of charities insisted that the apprentice should be an active member of the Church of England and a handful of founders left money for apprentices who were already literate, boys who could recite the catechism by heart and read from the Bible. Very rarely ability to write and cast accounts was also expected. Many charities mentioned an apprentice's parents in their conditions, and in some, parental involvement was expected; in Herbert's charity of Stretton-on-Dunsmore parents paid the same sum as the charity towards the boy's premium (between £5 and £10), thereby ensuring their son a "good trade". In one charity, with high premiums at £12 or £14, a certificate of the master's character was required by the trustees, who, at the indenturing, arranged a dinner for all concerned, the master, parents, trustees and apprentice, but such occasions, noted by the Charity Commissioners in 1837, were extremely rare. Some charities provided assistance to former apprentices at the end of their term, sometimes cash for setting up or for tools (£2 at Coleshill, for example). Occasionally conditions were attached to the gift, such as having been a communicant while apprenticed. The intentions of founders can only be guessed after two or three centuries, but a sense of parochial or civic loyalty was very strong, especially in those who had prospered in trade, often far from their birthplace, and wished, at their death, to aid other young people in their careers. Aristocratic or gentry founders of charities were more inclined to leave bequests for the poor as a whole or for disadvantaged members of the community, such as widows, or for a grander concept, a parish school or almshouse. Those who founded apprenticing charities would have shared the view of Thomas Puckering of Warwick, who died in 1637:

> the increase of trading and education, and bringing up of young men in trades and sciences, did not only tend to the general good of the commonwealth, but also to the profit and benefit of such as were trained and brought up therein, and was a principal means to avoid idleness, and consequently beggary.[34]

However, even these sentiments were marred in practice, for Puckering also left money for houses where the masters might live, but, when work was scarce, the apprentices were sent out to collect wood for fuel, from which they learned to "pilfer and steal". The craftsmen's houses were eventually rented out to tenants who did not take apprentices.

Although the rate at which apprenticing charities were established was uneven in different periods, with the years 1680 to 1730 especially rich in foundations, awareness of apprenticeship as a worthwhile charity was surprisingly consistent in English philanthropy, combining as it did moral, Christian, economic and educational ethics with a desirable degree of social control. In addition to those charities specifically for apprenticing, a number of other foundations spent residual funds on indenturing children, but even when these are included, the numbers of children who were charity apprentices remain very few out of the total bound. Only a minority of charity apprentices could be distinguished in public by any form of special dress, like Blake's children in their London procession, but some charities made public announcements in the parish church naming those chosen by the trustees. Charity apprentices who did well in later years were often cited as models for others to copy; thus when one Coventry boy, apprenticed by Duckett's charity in the city in 1688, became an alderman there in 1733, a contemporary commented, "from [which] we may observe how advantageous a small charity may prove".[35]

Although benefactors wished to help poor children to be apprenticed, they were almost universally opposed to apprenticing paupers from their funds; indeed, the binding of charity children was not without critics, anxious that charity children thus had advantages the struggling labourer or craftsman might not afford for his offspring. When a local physician visited Wells charity school in 1724 he was opposed to apprenticing any of the boys there unless they were "lame" since it "injur'd the Persons of Small Estates, by rendering it insignificant to their Children to place them in Handycrafts".[36] However, as with all eighteenth-century charities, a strongly practical, pragmatic emphasis finally decided how, and to whom, benefactors were generous; in a sermon preached at Oxford in 1755 William Sharp advised his congregation

If Compassion cannot move you, let Consideration of interest prevail with you. For neglect this poor Man's numerous Family, leave them to follow their own imagination, and to make the wretched Shift they can, and experience the sad Consequence. They will grow up soon into publick Nuisances, infect your families with their idle dishonest disorderly Behaviour; fill your streets with Vice and Violence; break in upon your Comfort and your Security; take the same Persons under your Patronage, teach them what is right – and hear how you will be repaid. They will be serviceable to you in many Ways, by themselves, and by their Examples; Industry, Sobriety, Good Order and Good Manners will get Ground amongst you; your City will be stock'd with honest, laborious, ingenious Artisans, some of the most useful Members of a Community. Wealth will increase.[37]

CHAPTER 5

Work and leisure

Take sloth from my fingers and drowsiness from the lids of mine eyes; whether I rise early or lie down later, so gladly let me doe it, as if my prenticeship were to be consumed in thy service.

The Dove in Thomas Dekker's *Fowre birds of Noah's arke* (1609)

Of two important aspects of an apprentice's existence, the hours of work and general living conditions, only the latter were even broadly defined in the indenture that bound the child. The master was to provide "meet, competent and sufficient meat, drink . . . [and] lodging" while no hours of work or rest were agreed. By the nineteenth century hours of work, especially for adolescents, had become a prominent reform topic. Before 1800, however, there was in all occupations a general acceptance of the need to work daylight hours in summer, nearly as long in winter with the aid of artificial light indoors, and to do additional work, even all night, if an emergency demanded a craftsman's product. For example, fashion changes, war or a royal death all brought the unplanned chance of extra sales to particular trades, and the adult, working 14 hours or more for six days a week, saw nothing wrong in an apprentice's doing so as well. Indeed, long hours and over-work taught the apprentice what a future career involved. A fairly complete picture of hours worked in different trades in the mid-eighteenth century is given by Campbell and Collyer; there is never any suggestion that apprentices worked shorter hours than adults, rather the reverse. Apprentices' duties included opening up and closing the shop, preparing raw materials for the craftsman to use, cleaning tools and general tidying, all of which were done very early or late in a working day.

In the medieval period late night work was forbidden by the guilds, the goldsmiths and leathersellers, for example, because in bad light poor work escaped detection by the craft's "searchers" (inspectors). In the late fifteenth century the leathersellers' rules decreed a 12-hour working day from 6am but on Saturdays and festivals work could cease at 3pm.[1] Normal hours of working in many honourable trades were from 6am to 8pm, at least since the sixteenth century, and in certain occupations longer ones were common. Thus in the sixteenth century the Sheffield scissorsmiths negotiated a two-year experiment of a shorter day, reduced to 6am to 8pm, as an improvement on their former conditions. They noted that the excessive hours and hard labour caused many to "become lame and in a little tyme whollie disenabled to follow their callings".[2] The hours worked in the mid-eighteenth century, listed by Campbell for 262 occupations, show a distinct pattern:[3]

Table 5.1   Hours worked in London trades, 1747.

Hours worked	Number of trades	%
6am–8pm	137	52.3
Not specified	37	14.1
6am–9pm	25	9.5
7am–8pm	18	6.8
6am–6pm	10	3.8
Daylight	8	3.0
Various	7*	2.6
7am-10pm	4	1.5
8am–8pm	4	1.5
By Tydes	4	1.5
6am to dark	3	1.1
8am to dark	3	1.1
7am to dark	2	0.7

* 1 each of trades

Among trades working the 14-hour day were all kinds of occupations, but after the mid-eighteenth century prices were very low for some crafts and masters sought to increase profits and production by extending the apprentice's day. Thus the stockinger's hours were in the 6am to 8pm category, but by the last quarter of the eighteenth century times were so hard that shops remained open from 5am to 10pm and pauper apprentices worked until 11 or 12 at night.[4] Shoemakers also theoretically worked a 14-hour day, but George Herbert's memoirs recorded that he often worked "for three weeks together from three or four in the morning till ten at night". Herbert's father, who accepted that "a shoemaker's hours are from six to eight", finally took legal advice on his son's behalf. The master's response was an interesting one: Herbert reported that he said, "I will see you d . . . before I will teach you any more of your trade" and withholding instruction was a serious threat to the apprentice. In a few days their disagreement "all passed over".[5]

Trades that generally worked a longer day, 6am to 9pm, were already, at this early stage, showing sweated tendencies, a number predominantly for girls. In this group were the silk trades, bucklemaking, calico printing, gloving and such poorly paid work as child's-coatmaking. In the Coventry silk trade Gutteridge's hours as an apprentice in the early 1830s were 6am to 8pm in winter but an hour longer in summer,[6] although 6am till dark were the hours worked by the 15-year-old Elizabeth Robbins in 1810, shortly before her death, as a ribbon-weaver's apprentice in the city.[7]

Trades that began earlier did not necessarily mean a shorter day for the apprentice; thus farriers began work at 5am because the forge had to be prepared. Other men began at 6am but had to stop as light failed, so that 6am to 6pm were the hours for the carpenter, mason, paviour, bricklayer, cabinetmaker and coachmaker. Fashion trades worked a 12- and 13-hour day, beginning at 7am; milliners, bodicemakers and mantua-makers were all in this group, but seasonal work could extend these hours very considerably.[8] Apprentices bound to tradesmen who kept retail or wholesale businesses could expect not to open until 7am but remain at work until 10pm, including grocers, drapers and oilmen. Campbell did not give a chemist's hours, but Lucas noted,

> The hours of work were long in those days. All had to be in the shop from nine to nine and each in turn for a week at a time from 7 a.m. to 11 p.m. At one time there were only two who were considered qualified to make up prescriptions and then the confinement was very close indeed.[9]

These conditions, however excessive they seemed to Lucas, were exactly as set out in an advice manual for those entering the apothecary's trade.[10] Traders selling less essential goods closed earlier at 8pm, for example the stationer, ironmonger, china shop, haberdasher and perfumer. A substantial group of Campbell's trades had hours of work that were "uncertain", and these included such prosperous occupations as the banker, apothecary and attorney as well as the butcher, tanner and miller.

Occupations involving factory conditions did not, of course, concern Campbell, but the hours of the factory apprentice interested philanthropists and parliamentary enquiries for half a century, producing emotional witnesses and damning evidence on a large scale. However, recent re-evaluation of Blincoe's memoir against other material may present a less dramatic picture.[11] That even contemporaries could err in their judgement of factory children's conditions may be seen in Theodore Price's retraction of his criticisms of Peel's factory in 1816.[12]

Apprentices in textile factories worked hours that became a clearly defined cause of public concern. Robert Blincoe reported a 14-hour day for the Lowdham Mill children, with a "bribe" of ½d to work through the dinner hour; at Litton his hours were longer, including 5am till midnight on Saturdays.[13] Evidence given to Peel's 1815 committee showed that a 13- and 14-hour day was common for factory apprentices, and records of individual mills support this estimate. At Bott's Tutbury (Staffs.) mill the female apprentices worked a 13-hour day or 11-hour night in 1802,[14] while in 1815 at Rock

Mill, Warwick, they began at 6am and worked for 12 or 13 hours, eating breakfast at their machines and with an hour for dinner.[15] Aged eight, Thomas Wood in a Bingley (Yorks.) mill worked from 6am to 7.30pm with 40 minutes for dinner, in 1830, when there were "no inspectors, no public opinion to put down flagrant cases of oppression, or of cruel usage".[16] Undoubtedly the nature of the factory apprentice's work, rhythmic and controlled for the whole day, made it particularly harsh for a child. Even long hours in less regulated conditions, in the craftsman's shop or outdoor employment, were more congenial for children.

The apprentice's hours of work in agriculture and domestic service never caused the same concern as the conditions of factory children. Indeed, many farmers' own children worked hours as long as the apprentices did, but the parish apprentice's tasks were inevitably the least pleasant on the farm. Thus a nine-year-old Devon girl apprenticed in the early nineteenth century worked with three other female and four male apprentices. Both boys and girls began work at 5am or 6am, but rose at 3am on two market days a week; their bedtime was 9.30pm. Girls capable of better employment than field work could be taken into the dairy, although cheesemaking was exceptionally hard work with very long hours, and milking was essential twice every day. Female apprentices were finally excluded from much farm work by the 1840s with the increase of mechanization.[17]

However, if legislation and public opinion could reduce the hours of work for many apprentices by the mid-nineteenth century, the conditions of their daily lives depended entirely upon their masters. For their comfort and diet the master's wife was all-important but, as the case of Elizabeth Robbins emphasized, it was the master who was legally responsible for apprentice welfare. Many of the complaints of dissatisfied apprentices who wrote memoirs concerned the food they received as perpetually hungry adolescents. They complained of poor quality and small quantity and seem not to have received the essential daily calories and proteins to promote growth and perform laborious work in most cases. Living-in apprentices, without earnings, were entirely dependent on the master's wife for food and even in a prosperous household this could be as "coarse as workhouse diet".[18] One apprentice of very good family bound to a wealthy merchant recalled how, although a "tender youth", when he came home from a long journey and "had driven packs, [he] might have had nothing but a mess of broth, or cold milk and bread".[19]

Presumably diet was thought suitable for apprentices if the master shared it, as were long hours. Thus, in the early eighteenth century one "eminent manufacturer" used to be in his warehouse before 6am, accompanied by his children and apprentices; at 7am they all

> came in to breakfast, which consisted of one large dish of water-pottage, made of oatmeal, water, and a little salt, boiled thick, and

poured into a dish. At the side was a pan or bason of milk, and the master and apprentices, each with a wooden spoon in his hand, without loss of time, dipped into the same dish, and thence into the milk pan; and as soon as it was finished they all returned to their work . . . but though the little country gentry did not then live in the luxurious manner they have done since, the young men found it so different from home, that they could not brook this treatment.[20]

An interesting legend, surprisingly widespread, relates how apprentices living near salmon rivers objected to the frequency with which they were fed on salmon, but examination of indentures has revealed no examples of the so-called "salmon clause".[21] The apprentice particularly dissatisfied with his diet might, as John Coggs did, raid the larder; on one occasion he ate steak after his master and mistress had gone to bed and stole a bottle of Rhenish from the wine cellar. He also objected to eating up the cheapest joint of mutton, boiled neck, at his mistress's insistence.[22]

Among poor urban apprentices, however, bad or insufficient food was a constant problem; William Hutton recalled that his aunt "grudged every meal [he] ate" and "kept a constant eye upon the food and feeder".[23] At least he was not starved to death, the fate of a Coventry ribbon-weaver's apprentice, Elizabeth Robbins, whose diet was described by a fellow apprentice, 13-year-old Elizabeth Tucker. Breakfast was bread and dripping or lard, with a cup of tea, sometimes with milk in it. Each child had a round of bread from a six-penny loaf. Dinner was potatoes or bread and meat, generally beef but also bacon. The child illustrated the size of the meat by measuring across her hand; the approximate amount was two to three ounces. Elizabeth Robbins had been punished by having this diet reduced; she used to "pick potato parings off the muckhill and eat them" and had stolen a loaf of bread. Three local medical practitioners said that Elizabeth's food was

> not sufficient to support the health and strength of a girl of her age who worked as she did . . . [and that] the small quantity of food . . . with the work she performed would have produced much debility and impaired her constitution.

In his summing up the judge reminded the jury that to provide "wholesome and proper nourishment" was the "duty of masters and it should be distinctly known so".[24] The combination of long hours and low protein diet must have been the lot of many poor apprentices,[25] especially severe for town children in non-food trades, since bakers' or grocers' apprentices had access to scraps and country children had some free addition to their diet from the hedgerow. The modest cost of feeding even a prosperous apprentice can be judged in the few indentures that specify a sum of money for this purpose; thus in 1724 one apothecary's apprentice was to have diet worth £8 a year, or 5d a day,[26] while the cost of feeding a clockmaker's apprentice in Sussex in 1717 was slightly less at £6 a year.[27]

Of all apprentices, the diet of those in textile factories has been fairly well documented. However, Blincoe's diet was clearly very different from that at Mellor Mill, with its "abundant food, including meat and fruit" or the menu at Quarry Bank. At Measham the food was said to be "very good" and at Emscote "good", and certainly there the owner employed a man to tend the kitchen garden and milk the cows. There is, of course, no proof that the cotton apprentices ate the garden produce or drank the milk, but the death rate there, as at other mills of the period,[28] was not so high as to arouse suspicion of the apprentices' dying from starvation.

The lack of clean living and sleeping accommodation was a further complaint of apprentices and clearly children from better homes especially suffered in new, uncongenial surroundings. The lack of physical comfort and the "little attention paid to rendering the evenings of apprentices agreeable at home, where they were considered rather as servants than pupils" caused boys to abscond, enlist or patronize local taverns.[29] However, Lucas commented that, as the shop was open until 11pm there was not "much time for recreation".[30] Across a wide range of occupations and periods living-in male apprentices slept in the shop. Even a prosperous apprentice, William Stout, indentured in 1700 to a Quaker ironmonger in Lancaster, was "frequently caled up at al times of the night to serve customers [which] obliged [apprentices] to have a bed in the shop".[31] In London Francis Place and his fellow apprentice also slept in the shop in the style of Oliver Twist.[32] The more prosperous Lucas and the four other apprentices, however, slept in an attic, where, he maintained, the beds were infested. When not asleep they lived in "a most squalid manner, always sitting in a little dirty dark room at the back of the shop".[33] The importance of proper bedding could concern a craft company in certain circumstances, so that, for example, when two London weaver's apprentices complained that they had "lain in one pair of sheets three months or more" their master was ordered to provide clean sheets every month or else the apprentices would be taken from him, a standard of hygiene that applied to Bridewell apprentices at the same period.[34] Apprentices sleeping in the shop was largely unavoidable before the architectural changes of the nineteenth century, since craftsmen's houses before this period usually had only one bedroom, for the master and mistress, sometimes partitioned with a separate area for young children or older daughters of the family.[35] Apprenticing has been seen by some modern observers as an important means of preventing incest, with adolescents living away from home during the crucial years of puberty.[36]

Long hours of work, of course, meant little time in which to enjoy adequate living accommodation, and William Stout recalled that his duties at 15 involved "attending the shop in winter with the windows open, without sash or screen until nine in the evening and with the windows shut and the dore open till ten o'clock without coming into the house except to our victuals or to the fire".[37] Apprentices began to live at home in some trades as the eighteenth century progressed, a change noted by masters such as Joseph Brasbridge, who regretted his loss of control over his apprentices after the day's work ended,[38] but Francis Place certainly led an extremely unsupervised life in the 1780s although living with his master.

Factory children were of necessity provided with purpose-built living and sleeping rooms in apprentice houses, usually with a woman, and sometimes also her husband, in charge, but accommodation varied greatly. In the apprentice house at Quarry Bank, with 42 boys and a larger number of girls, separately lodged, the rooms, said to be "very clean", were aired every day, washed frequently and whitewashed once a year, an early, but largely ineffective form, of disinfecting.[39] At Rock Mill, Warwick, a local JP considered the house "very clean", while his daughter described the apprentices' "living-place" as a "comfortable room", their dormitories "clean and comfortable" and the beds "very good". All assessments about accommodation, of course, were highly subjective, whether made by the inhabitants or visitors. Thus a child from a workhouse or very poor family might find even a shared bed in a factory dormitory preferable to a former existence. However, most evidence of factory apprentices' living conditions was critical rather than complimentary and even at Rock Mill the visiting magistrate said he would rather send his four daughters to Bridewell than to the mill for seven years, although the proprietor was a "very respectable man".[40] Undoubtedly such children could not easily protest at their living conditions, as Mayhew later noted about London millinery apprentices, poorly fed and housed, because the girls were all "from a long way off in the country" and could not communicate with their friends.[41]

In the original concept of apprenticeship the master provided technical training in exchange for labour; money, as a premium or wages, had no part in the transaction. Theoretically, the apprentice had no need of money for the master provided all the necessities of life and in practice long hours left little time in which to spend it. However, evidence of apprentices with money exists from a fairly early period and a number of crafts consistently opposed wages for apprentices. These payments usually took four forms. The longest-established were small sums, such as a penny a month, intended as pocket money. In the reign of Henry VIII an act decreed that, if a master paid an apprentice, both could be disenfranchised, but this regulation was widely ignored. Many craft companies were opposed to any kinds of payments so that, in 1692, for example, a weaver, was fined for paying his apprentice 2s 6d a week[42] and in 1745 the pewterers decreed that "a master by oath could not give his apprentice wages and the apprentice thereby forfeits his freedom".[43] The various lists of craft wages, many of which specified apprentices on the scale of earnings, indicate that such restrictions were flouted. Thus in 1655 the Carpenters' Company quoted 2s 6d a day for a skilled man,

2s for an apprentice who had served for over two years and 1s a day for an apprentice who had served less.[44] In 1710 the Warwickshire Quarter Sessions instituted a scale of wages for building and other workers that gave an apprentice aged 18 or more bound to a mason, ploughwright, cartwright, bricklayer, tiler, plasterer or shingler a daily rate of 4d with meat and drink, or 8d without, while boys between 12 and 18 in those trades were paid 3d with meat and drink, 6d without.[45] Such scales indicated a widespread acceptance of money wages to apprentices and an attempt to control them.

The second way of paying an apprentice, for work done over the normal amount expected, applied only to the older, more skilful child, and piece rates were negotiated for apprentices in Norwich as early at 1556.[46] William Hutton demonstrated that it was just possible, even with a very demanding master, to earn money in this way; he saved enough from overwork to buy a suit.[47] Not all apprentices could meet their masters' work demands, however, as in the case of Elizabeth Robbins, whose earnings fell below subsistence level. The third type of payment was money in lieu of one of the master's normal responsibilities, especially clothes, that the apprentice undertook to provide. Thus in 1627 a shipwright's apprentice for the last four of his seven years was to have £2 a year to buy apparel, while a brewer's apprentice a year later had £1 a year more; earlier in the century a sergeweaver's apprentice had only £1 8s 6d a year for clothes.[48] An unusual arrangement in a 1647 indenture allowed a shoemaker's charity apprentice to have 10d a week instead of clothes (£2 3s 4d a year) but be able to earn a further 30s a year by "delivering shoes within the said term".[49] The fourth kind of payment was a regular wage, a proportion of a journeyman's, paid every week or month to the apprentice or his parents. This has generally been considered a nineteenth-century device for living-out apprentices, sometimes called the half-pay system or "colting", but clearly practised at least in the seventeenth century in some occupations. Thus in 1714 a Gloucester weaver's apprentice was to find himself in food, drink, lodging and apparel, but might go home every Saturday to Monday. His wages were to be, out of every shilling made by his master, 2½d in the first year, 3d in the second and third years, but 4d in his fourth and final years.[50] As an incentive to an apprentice in a very long term wages were occasionally agreed for the final years; for example, a labourer's son bound to a Knowle (War.) weaver in 1718 for nine years was to be paid 15s in his eighth and 16s in his final year's servitude.[51]

The apprentices most likely to receive pay were those who lived at home, although others, like Francis Place in the 1780s in London, lived at his master's house and had 6s a week.[52] Such a rate was considerably more than that paid at the same period by a Wolford (Glos.) carpenter to his apprentice, who received 3s a week for the first year, increasing by 6d a year throughout the term.[53] Some trades, such as needlemaking, regularly gave wages to their charity and poor apprentices, but most of these children lived in their home parish. Sometimes the apprentice's father was paid during the child's term;

thus in 1825 Joseph Dolby, a tailor, took an apprentice to whose father he was to pay 2s weekly in the first year, increasing by 1s a year until the sixth and seventh years were reached, when the apprentice kept half the earnings, the rest going to his father.[54] Another version of the scheme was for the apprentice to pay half his earnings to the owner of the factory where he worked and whose machinery he used, as Joseph Gutteridge recorded.[55] At the same period James Burn, a hatter's apprentice, after being boarded and lodged, had a small wage of 1s a week, increasing by 6d a year; he welcomed the chance of two weeks' work at harvest to be able to buy clothes.[56] The prosperous apprentice normally had money from his parents or guardians, but occasionally a wage was agreed; thus in 1809 Thomas Rootes, bound to a surgeon, apothecary and man-midwife, was to have £6 in his first year (2s 3d a week), £7 in his second and £11 in the third year of his term.[57]

An exceptional way of an apprentice's earning money was possible only to those bound to the wealthiest merchants, for such apprentices might be allowed to trade on their own behalf. Thus a mercer's apprentice in 1649 was permitted to "traffique for himselfe with a stock of 50 li when he goes to sea, which is to be in ye two last yeares". Occasionally too merchants' apprentices were able to invest their own money, even £40 or £50, in their masters' overseas ventures.[58]

At the furthest end of the scale from the merchant's apprentice, factory children occasionally too had money to spend. At Measham they received "pecuniary rewards" and at Quarry Bank children bound by their parents were paid 9d a week for the first year and 1s for subsequent years. Parish apprentices were not paid by agreement but were able to earn overtime, so that Joseph Sefton, a runaway, had earned 2d a week for an extra nine hours' work. Apprentices did not always receive the money earned at Quarry Bank, but it was "set down in a little book; They have only a little of it: the rest is sav'd till they come out of their times".[59] By 1830 at Bingley (Yorks.) the apprentice's wage was 1s 6d a week, which rose to 4s 9d when he left the mill, "this point being reached by additions of 3d from time to time as an advance".[60] In the same decade a small silk factory in Warwick paid from 2s to 3s 6d a week for apprentices there whose wages were paid quarterly to their parish overseers to defray the cost of supporting them out of the poor rate.[61]

It was, of course, possible for apprentices to be given money by parents or relatives. Francis Place regularly received 1s a week from his mother and frequently the same amount from his sister.[62] John Coggs's wealthy "Antt ffryer" held £1 11s 6d on his behalf while both she and his uncle gave him various sums of money, even £5 or £10 at times.[63] Thus although in theory an apprentice could live without money during the term and so not be tempted to break many of the clauses of the indenture (gambling, attending theatres or taverns, even marrying), there is considerable if scattered evidence that adolescents acquired money to spend by various means. The intrusion of money into the master–apprentice relationship as an incentive first enabled the master to get more work from the apprentice. It finally destroyed the customary concept, allowing apprentices to break free of restraints and sell their labour for the best rate possible, as Adam Smith had advocated when apprenticeship was still traditionally enforced.

In almost all personal recollections of apprenticeship, the lack of leisure time seems to have been very greatly resented. It is possible that the literate young were particularly aggrieved at their long hours and impaired personal freedom, although the apprentice's indenture specified no hours of work or holidays. Flexibility was equally crucial to the small poor master, the skilled craftsman or the professional man, all of whom worked entirely to the demands of trade, customer or client to provide goods and services when necessary. A boy or girl was expected to work at the master's behest for six full days a week but in slack periods the apprentice might have extra but unpredictable free time. The apprentice could expect only the established national or local festivals as leisure occasions. Apart from Christmas and Easter, apprentices also celebrated Shrove Tuesday, Mothering Sunday and May Day, widely accepted as specifically adolescents' festivals. In addition, there were such local celebrations as the church or craft patronal festival, harvest home, Hallowe'en, Guy Fawkes night, Plough Monday and fairs throughout the year; in any or all of these the apprentice might take part.[64] There was also, in certain occupations, the celebration of St Monday, but this form of holiday was to diminish rapidly with the coming of steam power, factory-style employment, regular hours of work and the reduction of piece-rates.[65] Irregular public entertainments varied greatly, in number and frequency, from hangings and donkeyings to street football, elections and general mass rowdyism, all possible for apprentices to enjoy when messengers or when working outside the shop. Certainly rural and urban entertainments varied for the apprentice, but such differences do not seem to have become institutionalized until the mid-nineteenth century, since before that period country amusements were taken into the towns and practised there by the new inhabitants, so that many ancient city festivals (for example, Hocktide) had rustic origins.

Of all these occasions, Shrove Tuesday, which could fall between 8 February and 9 March in the church's year, was the most important to apprentices. Contemporaries themselves acknowledged the occasion as an adolescents' festival by ancient custom when authority ignored their otherwise unacceptable behaviour. Thus in Staffordshire in 1636 it was reported at quarter sessions that "the apprentices, and servants, and young boyes of the town . . . were sporting them selves according to the accustomed manner and liberty of that day"[66] while in Gloucestershire the "prescriptive right of ancient custom" was the apprentices' excuse for their behaviour on Shrove Tuesday.[67] In the eighteenth century John Brand noted that Shrovetide was the apprentices' "particular holiday" and advised them that, as they were on several accounts so much interested in the observations thereof [they] ought, with that watchful jealousy of their ancient rights and liberties . . . as becomes young Englishmen, to guard against every infringement of its ceremonies so as to transmit them entire and unadulterated to posterity.

He added that Shrove Tuesday was typified "so happily . . . by pudding and play" that from time immemorial this day was a holiday for "apprentices and working people".[68]

One of the important rituals of Shrovetide was eating the special foods of the feast; these ranged from bannocks to doughnuts in different regions, but pancakes were almost universally prepared. The Pancake Bell was rung (originally the Shriving Bell) to summon parishioners to confession, but even after the Reformation it was still the signal for the holiday to begin, usually at 11am or noon, and in some parts of England its tolling was particularly associated with apprentices. Dr Lake of York successfully stopped the apprentices assembling in the Minster at 11am and taking turns to toll the bell there. At Newcastle upon Tyne the bell of St Nicholas rang at noon; shops were "immediately shut up, Offices closed and all Kind of Business ceases; a sort of little Carnival ensuing for the remaining Part of the Day".[69] A similar practice continued at Hedon (Yorks.) until the late nineteenth century and there are scattered examples of the Shrovetide bell in the present century, for example, at Scarborough (Yorks.)[70] and at Claverdon (War.).[71]

Apart from enjoying the special foods on Shrove Tuesday, apprentices also took part in the ancient amusements of cock-throwing and cock-fighting with which the day was particularly associated. The popularity of cock-throwing in many regions of England may be judged by the widespread references to the practice and its general association with apprentices. Throwing at a cock differed from cock-fighting in two important respects: first, it involved only one bird at a time, rather than the pair of birds that fought each other in a main of cocks. Secondly, it required some skill on the part of the human participants. The boy who was the thrower had "three shys, or throws, for two-pence . . . [and] wins the cock if he can knock him down and run up and catch him before the bird recovers his legs".[72] Opposition to cock-throwing as a sport seems not to have been expressed before the mid-eighteenth century, for in 1673 at York, the apprentices of the city "being at liberty for recreation, plaid in the Minster yard, throwing at a cock".[73]

In his advice to apprentices' parents Collyer condemned those who allowed the "juvenile butcher" to throw at cocks,[74] a view supported by Hogarth (*The first stage of cruelty*, 1751) and many letters to the provincial press and the *Gentleman's Magazine* in the 1750s and 1760s. The popularity of this apprentices' pastime and its tenacious survival, in spite of enlightened opinion, may be seen from measures repeatedly taken to suppress it throughout the later eighteenth and nineteenth century. At Northampton the local press hoped that "Persons in Power, as well as Parents and Masters of Families, would exert their authority in suppressing a practice too common at this season – throwing at cocks", although it was, "to the Credit of a civilized People . . . annually declining",[75] while in a letter to a Leeds newspaper a reader was able to claim that "the absurdity of throwing at cocks at Shrove-Tide has been so repeatedly exposed that a great deal of that barbarous custom is abolished".[76] Magistrates in various counties acted to stop the practice, but it survived actively in Warwickshire until quite late. In 1799 a Stratford-upon-Avon diarist noted, without any adverse comment, that the snow was "so deep on the grownd that the boys could not find no other place to throw at cocks but on the ice on the river",[77] while at Coventry in the early nineteenth century it was still practised on Shrove Tuesday "in the Windmill Fields at Spon Wake".[78] As late as 1814 and again in 1824 magistrates in the county tried to discourage "so disgraceful a practice".[79] In London they had been more successful much earlier, for one newspaper reported that "yesterday being Shrove Tuesday, the orders of the justices in the City and the Liberty of Westminster were so well observed that few cocks were seen to be thrown at, so that it is hoped that this barbarous custom will be left off".[80]

It is apparent that the essential characteristics of cock-throwing ensured its decline, while cock-fighting continued to thrive. The former was an adolescent, plebeian pastime, supported by small groups on special festive days only, with no large wagers placed; it also seemed basically unfair. Cock-fighting was a contest between equals; it attracted all classes and, with high stakes, was difficult to suppress. It too appealed to apprentices, for example, at Messingham (Lincs.) and Skipton (Yorks.) on Shrove Tuesday, when cock-fighting and football were "sports inseparable from the day".[81] Cock-fights were unsuitable for apprentices because they encouraged gambling (specifically forbidden by the indenture), while participating in a potentially unruly group distracted attention from learning an occupation. A Coventry mayor, John Hewitt, deplored cock-fighting as an apprentices' amusement in the 1750s, urging his fellow magistrates to suppress it along with "cards, dice, tables, tennis, coits, skittles, nine-pins, billiards, shuffleboards, horse races, footraces . . . dog matches and other unlawful games",[82] an interesting range of activities in which apprentices might offend their masters.

Street football was another Shrove Tuesday sport apprentices enjoyed, but the craft guilds recognized how dangerous participation might be, so that in 1595 the Carlisle shoemakers agreed that "no journeyman or apprentice shall make any foot balle to sell or play withal without consent and knowledge of his or their maisters and that they shall not play at football within the liberties of this cittie".[83] In Manchester the Court leet heard a complaint in 1609 that apprentices played "giddye yaddye or catts pallett and ffoote ball"; nine years later they appointed three "officers for ye foote ball" whose duty was to prevent apprentices from playing the game.[84] Various descriptions of the game confirm its violence and the chance it provided for settling grudges, but also its popularity and longevity; William Hutton noted how it made temporary heroes of humble participants:

> I have seen this coarse sport carried to the barbarous height of an election contest; nay, I have known a foot-ball hero chaired through the streets like a successful member, although his utmost elevation of character was no more than that of a butcher's apprentice.[85]

As well as celebrating Shrove Tuesday with pancakes and football, another apprentices' diversion on this day was attacking bawdy houses and the women who lived there. It was, however, a London practice, since brothels were not usually found in the English countryside and widespread organized prostitution was rare in provincial cities. It also had political overtones, for although the practice was revived in the years after the Restoration, when brothels reappeared in London, it had certainly existed in the early years of the seventeenth century, for example, in 1619, when apprentices were responsible for causing "spoyle in Shorditch" on Shrove Tuesday.[86] The most detailed description of apprentices attacking brothels was in 1668 when, with the excuse that they were removing temptation before Lent, the London apprentices rioted and pulled down the city's bawdy houses. Government response was vigorous and Pepys described the two nights of disorder in the London streets. None of the bystanders found fault with the apprentices, "but rather of the soldiers for hindering them". Pepys thought bawdy houses were "one of the great grievances of the nation" and that the apprentices should not have stopped pulling down the little brothels but have destroyed the great one at Whitehall.[87] Apart from any religious views, these London adolescents presumably felt frustration and resentment towards the prostitutes they could not afford and from whose company they were in any case forbidden by their indentures. Early in the eighteenth century, however, a popular rhyme referred to this practice as no longer fashionable,[88] and similar riots in the eighteenth century, when the press would certainly have noted them, do not appear to have taken place. As well as attacking brothels, apprentices also vented their frustration on London theatres, from which they were barred by their indentures and in 1617 they had attacked the queen's players on Shrove Tuesday at a new playhouse in Drury Lane, tearing costumes and burning scripts.[89]

In Lent there was, however, another day of relaxation for all adolescents, including apprentices, when their activities were less reprehensible. This was Mothering Sunday, when apprentices were allowed to return to their family home; it was not normally a full working day in any case. It is difficult to estimate how many apprentices were physically able to visit their family on Mothering Sunday, since long journeys were impossible in a single day's absence from the master's house and only apprentices indentured close to home could have taken advantage of this day as a holiday.

Apart from Shrove Tuesday, May Day was the most important holiday in the apprentice's calendar, celebrated in all parts of England. Although there were local variations, the most common elements in May Day were dancing, especially round a maypole, and gathering branches and flowers to make garlands or for decorating houses. The great number of customs associated with May Day indicates the importance of this particular festival in the community year, and only Christmas has more rites and practices associated with its celebration.[90] May Day was condemned by Puritan writers for the sexual licence it encouraged; the phallic symbolism of the maypole was noted by many.[91] John Aubrey thought "the Civille Warres comeing on have putt out all these Rites or customs quite out of fashion"[92] but the vigour and tenacity of May Day can be seen in the number of prosecutions during the Commonwealth against those who still followed the old customs. In the more remote counties May Day was celebrated regardless of Puritan legislation so that, for example, in 1655 Warwickshire Quarter Sessions had to suppress

> several unlawful meetings of idle and vain persons . . . for erecting of maypoles and may-bushes and for using of morris dances and other heathenish and unlawful customs whereof tendeth to draw together a great concourse of loose people and consequently to the hazard of the public peace besides other evil consequences.[93]

That apprentices participated, with or without their masters' consent, may be judged from the case of a Bedfordshire apprentice accused of stealing. At the vital time when the theft occurred he had, with other youths from his parish

> upon May day in the morning last past stucke several May bushes at the doores of divers people in our said Towne, and at the very instant . . . when the money was lost, were drinkinge and makinge merry at those houses where the May bushes were formerly stucke.[94]

Such celebrations were essentially rural, but in the cities they had their counterpart in the May Day processions in which chimney-sweeps' apprentices were the most important figures. Urban May Day celebrations, with Jack-in-the-Green as the central figure, have been recorded in communities as different as Cambridge, Coventry, Hereford and London in the eighteenth century. These processions contained a strong element of role reversal, for in some the sweeps dressed as females (Coventry), in others they whitened their faces (London), but music and collecting contributions from bystanders were common to all.

In addition to such occasions, there were also regional fairs that apprentices might attend, either with their masters' consent or when working away from the shop. There were a large number of fairs spread across the calendar, either for special commodities (cheese or wool, for example) or as general markets, usually in the spring or autumn, based on a region's ancient trading centres. Thus Somerset had 94 fairs established by charter before 1500 and more than a hundred annual fairs by the early eighteenth century.[95] In the Midlands, Warwickshire had a total of 60 fairs in 15 centres by 1828,[96] while Herefordshire had 56 markets in 16 communities at the same period.[97] As well as goods for sale, there were also entertainments and sideshows, and for this reason fairs were condemned as a temptation and distraction to the young apprentice. Fairs were particularly criticized for the quantity of alcohol available and "debauching of Servants, Apprentices and other unwary people".[98] To what extent apprentices attended fairs is hard to judge, but that they resented not doing so may be seen from George Herbert's experiences in Banbury. Near the end of his term, Herbert recalled that his holidays were "few", comprising only Christmas Day and Good Friday. One year, on Michaelmas Fair day, his master had given the younger apprentices a half-holiday but insisted that George should remain at work until he had completed a pair of top-boots and then go to the fair. The task would take four hours, and George resentfully thought "as he has given the others a holiday I will take one". As a result of his unauthorized absence from work the master took George Herbert before the local magistrate, who ruled that a shoemaker's apprentice's hours were from "six in the morning to six at night". In spite of this pronouncement George found himself subsequently working until 8pm, but he noted that "in a few days it all passed over as though nothing had happened".[99] It may be that George Herbert was bolder and more resourceful in defying his master than the average apprentice near the end of the term, and certainly his later career shows these characteristics. Attendance at the local fair was also allowed to some factory apprentices, so that those from Lowdham Mill went to Nottingham Goose Fair, held in October, "the whole of them conveyed in carts . . . and regaled with frumenty, and sixpence in money was allowed to the very youngest".[100]

It is clear from available evidence that the apprentice's official holidays were strictly controlled by his master; Place had only "three holidays at Easter, Whitsuntide and Christmas" during his London apprenticeship in the 1780s.[101] He recorded how much he had also enjoyed Twelfth Night, "a great fete day with boys", when they used to "divert themselves and others with a most mischievous practice, now [1824] discontinued, of nailing people's clothes to Pastry Cooks Shops", and admitted he had formerly been the leader of such a gang.[102] Guy Fawkes Day was also a "great festival among boys . . . very many masters permitted their apprentices to play the black-guard on this day";[103] the other amusements he described, available to apprentices, clearly contravened the terms of any indenture.

An important consideration about apprentices' amusements was that they were seldom "with their masters' profit"[104] and the theme was a popular one in didactic literature. Defoe's dialogue between a master and his wife on the state of their apprentice's behaviour and his leisure activities could have been spoken by John Coggs's long-suffering master and mistress. The mistress advised her husband that, in dealing with their often absent apprentice, he should

> oblige him to do as becomes a servant, viz., give you an exact account of his behaviour; his time is yours, and you ought to know how he spends it; if any of his time is employed out of your business, you ought to exact an account of it from him how it has been disposed of, as much as you would with money that you had trusted him with and how he had paid it.[105]

Music and dancing were particularly deplored as amusements for apprentices, partly because these activities brought apprentices into undesirable company, especially the opposite sex, although the enlightened Locke saw the advantages of dancing, than which "nothing appears . . . to give children so much becoming confidence and behaviour".[106] At the same period, however, one large trading company forbade its apprentices to "get to fencing or dancing schools, nor to music houses, lotteries, or playhouses, neither to keep any sort of horses, dogs for hunting or fighting cocks", which suggests that apprentices may already have been infringing these rules.[107] The association of music and dancing with sensuality was a long-standing one, by no means only a Puritan preoccupation. It seems that music and dancing were condemned as much for their powers of diverting the serious apprentice from work as for being the cause of promiscuity. Richardson summed up this attitude in *The apprentice's vade mecum* when he advised the apprentice that such entertainments

> too much detach his Mind from his Business, and fill it with light and airy Amusements. His thoughts and Conversation will generally turn upon what had so strongly impress'd him in its favour; and he may be taught in time to sit loose to those narrow Ties to which his Business necessarily binds him. If he has any Taste for those Diversions, the Musick will always play upon his Ears, the Dancers will constantly swim before his Eyes.[108]

There is little evidence of the extent to which apprentices joined or watched the variety of popular disturbances that occurred on the streets of England at any period. They were presumably discouraged by their masters from taking part, unless in support of the master's cause, but they certainly participated when their own occupation or class interest was involved. For example, at Banbury in 1793 the shag weavers stopped work and marched an unlawful apprentice, his blackleg work carried on a donkey, through the streets, accompanied by a fife band and garlanded supporters. This corporate disapproval, a warning to all, was watched by a crowd of 1,500, nearly half the population, and was not dispersed until a troop of Blues arrived from Coventry, 27 miles away, the next day.[109] It has been shown that one of the most important functions of youth groups was their public ridicule of deviant behaviour,[110] and their participation may be presumed in the donkeying or pillorying of those who committed craft offences, abused apprentices or paid very low wages, more than in other instances of "rough music". Much amusement for apprentices in their strictly limited leisure hours must have been of an informal, *ad hoc* kind, such as the 40 apprentices and other boys who met frequently to play together "in a spacious place" in Elizabethan Salisbury.[111]

It is clear from the terms of the apprenticeship indenture that it was thought desirable to keep apprentices away from public places of amusement, and perhaps even more important, although unacknowledged, to prevent their associating with each other. Corporate activity involved the risk of shared trade secrets and of apprentices comparing their working conditions. That the prohibition was ignored can be seen from the popularity of the theatre with adolescents at all periods from the seventeenth century. Apprentices attending the London theatres from 1731 onwards were able to watch the cautionary tale of George Barnwell, a merchant's apprentice, his downfall and death, the result of disloyalty to his master. Lillo's *The London merchant*, the third most popular play in the capital, referred in its epilogue to the occupancy of the cheapest seats by apprentices. By the mid-eighteenth century it was the traditional offering for Easter and Christmas holidays, since it was judged "a proper entertainment for the apprentices, etc, as being a more instructive, moral, and cautionary drama, than many pieces that had usually been exhibited in those days with little but farce and ribaldry to recommend them".[112]

Not only London apprentices were theatregoers, however, for in the eighteenth century the English counties were regularly visited by travelling companies, so that *Barnwell* appeared at Walsall in 1755 in the repertoire of the Warwickshire Company of Comedians and *The apprentice*, by Arthur Murphy, was billed as a new farce at Birmingham three years earlier.[113] By the nineteenth century the Birmingham police complained that, on Mondays, the majority of a theatre's gallery audience were boys and girls aged from 12 to 18, for "it was a very frequent case for an apprentice, a very numerous class of mechanics in this town, to obtain leave to quit his work at half-past five . . . to go to the theatre, and keep a place for a female companion, when she leaves work at 7"; gallery seats cost 6d each.[114] It is noticeable that while St Monday was less widely observed, apprentices were still obliged to ask permission to leave work early.

Francis Place's memoirs indicate the riotous clubs and entertainments enjoyed by young labouring apprentices in London even though they were living in; he emphasized how little their masters cared about their leisure activities so long as they performed the required amount of work in a day,[115] while the anonymous author of *Low life* described apprentices' leisure pursuits that contravened their indentures. As attending concerts was not permitted for apprentices, on one occasion some who bought tickets were obliged to take their money back and return home.[116] Even a prosperous apprentice such as John Coggs amused himself in ways unacceptable to his master, staying out late at night, getting drunk, gambling and deliberately breaking tradesmen's windows.[117]

Some apprentices do seem to have had irregular holidays, individually arranged by their masters, so that Ralph Josselin's son, Thomas, spent at least two periods at home during his apprenticeship, including six months when plague raged,[118] while the Sheffield cutlers gave apprentices four weeks annual holiday.[119] Very rarely apprentices were allowed a period of time to spend at their family home to help with seasonal farm work. Such a child was Thomas Gray, bound in 1556 to a Norwich worsted weaver, Edmund Peekover, who was to allow Thomas "in harvest tyme yerely to go home to his freendes in Bedforthshire and to remayne there one month".[120] For no apparent reason special holiday terms might also be given to factory apprentices; Ann Mayson, for example, in 1795 was allowed one week a year to visit her father in Cheshire from Quarry Bank Mill, while another apprentice there, Bessie Night, was permitted to go home for six days at Christmas.[121] Such arrangements, so specifically detailed, were clearly exceptions, however. Even by the mid-nineteenth century apprentices' holidays were irregular, so that although William Andrews might celebrate the end of his term with a morning visit to watch a local hunt, in the last year of his apprenticeship he noted in his diary (6 June 1855) that "Mr Bray says that I can have 2 or 3 days holiday next week – thinks it will do my health good. I have had scarcely any holiday during my apprenticeship. Decide to go to Nottingham"; there he stayed with his uncle, visited the castle, walked and went fishing for chub.[122]

Apart from public holidays, fairs and festivals, there was one other form of entertainment, closely associated with work, that the apprentice would encounter. In most occupations there were traditional festivities in the workplace when the apprenticeship began and ended. There were two elements in initiation common to most occupations, the consumption of alcohol by all the workforce and various "tricks" to make the newcomer feel foolish or even cause physical suffering. None of the advice manuals for the young apprentice refers to these rites, presumably because the secrets were kept from authors such as Defoe, Richardson and Collyer, or they thought the nature of such rituals offensive to the reader. Craftsmen's memoirs are relatively scarce before the mid-nineteenth century and, since the ceremonies were intended to humiliate the novice, most writers would have preferred to omit such embarrassing or painful experiences from their recollections. George Herbert, Charles Shaw, Robert Blincoe and George Sturt all give no mention of any initiation ceremonies.

From the early eighteenth century buying alcohol or "footing" was commonplace when a new apprentice was indentured; Joseph Gutteridge noted that, in 1829, every newcomer was expected to pay for a gallon of ale, each of the other men adding a pint . . . sometimes the men would adjourn to a public house to drink the beer, but oftener it would be brought into the shop. The older apprentices were allowed to share in these orgies, and the younger ones, lounging about, would get an odd drink now and then.

The amount paid for footing varied, but the necessity of paying it was emphasized by Gutteridge, who commented that "the men would either strike or at any rate prevent the new hand from getting on with his work until he had complied with this custom, so that it was morally impossible to resist".[123] Certain tradesmen, such as hatters, had impressive and complex drinking rituals, with very large quantities consumed, and 10s paid with each new apprentice.[124] Even in trades with modest footing sums, the shipwrights with 2s 6d, for example, there were penalties for not contributing, in their trade, flogging with a handsaw.[125]

The other part of initiation, personal humiliation of the apprentice in the presence of fellow-workers, was far more varied than the "maiden garnish" payments; some activities were clearly related to the occupation the apprentice was joining, so that the printers' songs and the stonemasons' rituals all referred to trade practices. However, some initiations were intended only to make newcomers feel foolish and reduce self-esteem so that they accepted a lowly place in the work hierarchy. In 1713 a young printer's initiation involved "striking [him] kneeling, with a broadsword; and pouring ale upon [his] head"; he was then given the title "Earl of Fingall".[126] However, scatalogical and sexual initiation rites survived in some trades into the modern period. In one Birmingham printing firm, about 1885, it was common practice to tell new boys "they must be weighed on a stone slab which was on top of the weighing machine. As the unsuspecting boy was seated on the slab a large sponge, well soaked with water, was slipped beneath him, and he was well pressed down on it". The new apprentice then spent the rest of his working day being teased for having wet trousers.[127] The sexual humiliation of a young cabinetmaker's apprentice early in the twentieth century involved the liberal use of the craft's essential materials, glue and sawdust; he could not tell his mother what had happened and his father did nothing since "all boys had tricks played on them; if fathers went complaining then boys would be called 'cissies' . . . but there are tricks and tricks", he added.[128] A recent survey of the survival of these initiation practices into the present century has revealed their surprising tenacity; all retain their eighteenth-century elements, with humiliation (usually sexual) and alcohol of equal importance. Victims' reminiscences indicate how degraded they felt and how physically dangerous some practices were, occasionally necessitating medical attention (Appendix 2). Even in a prosperous trade, with a Quaker master and a premium of £250, teasing as initiation existed. William Lucas, bound to an apothecary, experienced the whole household's commiseration at how ill he looked, "from the fat old woman in the kitchen to the first assistant in the shop, in various modes, condoling with [him]". The sensitive Lucas was so affected by this that he wrote home saying that it was evident London did not agree with him, that his health was failing and that he must leave. This "led [his] friends to inquire and the hoax was discovered".[129]

There were, however, more agreeable diversions for the apprentice that centred on the craft, especially those marking its patron saint. These were particularly urban celebrations, promoted by the masters as displaying the craft's role in the community and the apprentice's place within the craft. Although most crafts had their own patron saints, only the wealthier occupations could stage their own processions; smaller crafts often collaborated for this purpose. The London processions were the most splendid, but many smaller provincial towns celebrated a local craft's patron in this way, with pre-Reformation saints changing their names but not their roles. The craft processions reflected very clearly the apprentice's place in the hierarchy; thus in one illustration of a Bishop Blaise procession, the woolcombers' patron, the smaller walking figures are apprentices carrying symbols of the wool trade, crooks and a lamb. There may have been a revival of such parades in the mid-eighteenth century, as noted in Worcestershire in 1751,[130] but Blaise processions took place as far apart as Leeds in 1769 and in Coventry 60 years later. The coming of factory discipline and its link with the keeping of St Monday affected only a proportion of apprentices, since many were bound to trades totally untouched by mass production, in which domestic conditions of employment still applied. By the 1830s in Birmingham, St Monday was so little valued that two apprentices were given a month's hard labour because they had been celebrating St Monday at their masters' expense.[131]

Another institutionalized leisure event for the apprentice was the coming-out ceremony at the end of the term, but completely different in emphasis from the footing; celebration rather than humiliation was the intention of the coming out, marking a newly acquired status within the craft. However, the printers' "banging out", the coopers' "trusso" and the silversmiths' practice of standing the apprentice on his head, continued communal horseplay of a fairly unpleasant kind.[132] The feast at the end of his term was described in 1843 by one young engineer as beyond his means:

> In consideration of my poverty they agreed to have the supper in the shop instead of a public house. The master, or rather now the foreman, cooked it in his house hard by. It was a quiet, economical affair, but I had to borrow the money to defray the expense.[133]

A more elaborate celebration took place in the Birmingham gun trade, where the former apprentice's fellow-workers contributed their share towards the expenses, work ceased a few minutes before noon and "on the first sound of the clock striking twelve, a salvo of improvised artillery would rend the air, and three rounds of hearty cheers would be given to welcome him who had arrived at man's estate". The gunfire continued for an hour and ale was served to all; on many occasions the employer himself would attend. Work was resumed between 2pm and 5pm. The "outcome supper" was held at one of the tavern tea gardens in the Birmingham suburbs, men brought women guests and, after supper and speeches, the employer left the celebrations, "the remainder of the evening to be enjoyed in dance and song". The oldest workman presided and, at midnight, the new journeyman was led to a chair, raised on a table, circled by the company, and crowned. All drank from a loving-cup and sang "a welcome to their new associate in manhood. At the close of the singing, what was left in the loving-cup would be poured over the head of him who was then honoured with the title of manhood" and the special song for the occasion was sung:

> Here's to him that's now set free,
> Who was once prentice bound;
> And for his sake this holiday we make,
> So let his health go round,
> Go round, brave boys, until it comes to me,
> For the longer we sit here and drink
> The merrier we shall be.[134]

Even in the higher status, non-manual occupations coming-out celebrations existed; in 1785, for example, a wholesale bookseller's apprentice in London was obliged to entertain his fellows on his return from being enrolled at Stationers' Hall. He provided a grand supper at which "two immense bowls ... of negus and punch graced the head and foot of the table".[135]

Since most amusements were forbidden to apprentices by masters, indentures or guilds, there were few pastimes a boy or girl might legitimately enjoy when not working. Reading was not always easy even for the literate minority; Samuel Richardson recalled that he "stole from the Hours of Rest & Relaxation [his] Reading Times for the Improvement of [his] Mind".[136] William Lucas relied on reading for pleasure during his few leisure moments, miserable in his attic.[137] However, reading cannot have been a pastime for the majority of apprentices and Joseph Gutteridge described how, with difficulty, he practised reading by spelling out shopkeepers' names and trades on his daily walk to the silk factory.[138] John Coggs's journal is a rare example of diary-keeping as an apprentice activity.

Apart from the leisure activities forbidden to apprentices, there were also the traditional boys' amusements that did not contravene the indenture; not all were without personal risk, however. Flying a kite must have seemed a harmless amusement, but in 1774 a clockmaker's apprentice "climbed on a tree to disentangle a lantern which had been tied to the tail of a kite, and fell to the ground, whereby his neck was dislocated".[139] Swimming was permitted, but apprentices occasionally drowned, their mishaps reported in the local press.[140] The more serious apprentice, interested in natural science, might collect minerals, fossils or plant specimens. The young Henry Jephson, apprenticed to a Mansfield apothecary in 1812, had his own geological collection,[141] while Gutteridge roamed the countryside near Coventry collecting and pressing wild flowers, engrossed in "the pleasures of science".[142] Some sympathetic masters allowed their apprentices to participate in their own hobbies, so that Gideon Mantell, a Sussex surgeon-apothecary, took his apprentice fossil-hunting, while Farington's diary for the early nineteenth century indicates that young men apprenticed to leading London artists led an active social life, often accompanying their masters on visits.

By the later nineteenth century it is obvious that, with the coming of a shorter working week and national bank holidays, the traditional apprentice holidays of Shrove Tuesday and May Day became less necessary either as safety-valve occasions or, with growing urbanization, to perpetuate accepted and established community values and craft practices. Yet both occasions are still, in however debased a manner, celebrated in present-day England. Significantly, the essential spirit of May Day, as a non-religious, workers' festival, was recognized by its establishment in 1889 as International Labour Day and its recent revival in England as a public holiday.

CHAPTER 6

The service industries
and the professions

Mac-Donald, Staymaker, Opposite the Black Horse in St Clements, OXFORD

Will make small or middle-sized Womens STAYS, of Ticken or
Callimanco, for those that will come to his house to be measured,
and to try their Stays on, at one Guinea a Pair; from this Time till the
first of Dec^r, of the best Goods and neatest Work, for Ready Money
only. Large Womens and Childrens Stays cheap in Proportion.

Oxford Journal (5 October 1765)

Until the later nineteenth century many occupations that took apprentices
were both makers and retailers of their products, especially in food and clothing, while others provided a personal service, such as hairdressers or apothecaries, selling goods only as a part of their income. Attorneys and surgeons
sold advice and skill rather than goods; physicians, of course, did not have
apprentices. At the lowest end of service occupations, children bound to
domestic duties and chimney-sweeps also provided a service, although usually not of a personal kind. Of all the food trades, the baker's was the most
widespread and evenly distributed, and as his commodity was "so necessary
for Life, he seldom wants Customers". More prosperous and less common
than tailors or shoemakers, since much bread was made at home, bakers' apprentices were 14 or 15 before they were bound, since the "great Burthens
they are obliged to carry out in serving their Customers requires more
Strength than is ordinarily to be met with in younger Years".[1] Francis Place's
father was a baker, "strong for his height", who could carry two sacks of flour
weighing five hundredweight at the same time.[2] As a trade, most bakers'
apprentices served a seven-year term; Campbell suggested a £5 to £20 premium,[3] exemplified in Birmingham in the years 1719–66 where 35 bakers
apprenticed boys; all but 11 took premiums of £10 or more, similar to
sums received by staymakers in the town. The relative prosperity of bakers'
apprentices can be seen in their parents' occupations; in Coventry, a high proportion were farmers and yeomen. Some city bakers were in a large way of

117

business to judge from the numbers of apprentices they took, thus John Lane of Bull Street, Birmingham, bound four boys during the years 1746–61 with whom he received premiums of £9 to £15; Lane, a Birmingham man, had himself been apprenticed to a master in the town in 1720 with a £15 premium.[4] Thus in 1767 there were 49 bakers in Birmingham, 29 of whom were masters with 13 apprentices indentured to them[5] and in Coventry in 1828 5 of the 29 masters had apprentices, of whom one, George Eld, had nine boys bound between the years 1784 and 1805.[6]

Although the baker's trade was untouched by fashion changes, fluctuations in corn prices greatly affected his profits and, in the years of poor harvests, high prices and food riots, far fewer apprentices were bound. Thus in October 1766, civil disorder in Coventry was reflected in only one baker's apprentice being indentured and in another riot year, 1800, no boys at all were bound to the city's bakers.[7] It seems that bakers in small communities were less inclined to take apprentices; for example, in Melbourne (Derbys.) in 1696 the single baker had neither an apprentice indentured to him nor a servant or journeyman, only a wife and daughter as the rest of his household.[8] At the same period in a London ward four of the bakers each had an apprentice and two had not.[9] As well as the cost of setting up, Campbell noted that bakers were almost unique in the food trades in preferring credit to cash customers, but that they made amends for this by "making Dead Men" or "cutting double Strokes on their Tally".[10] Bakers seem to have made their greatest profit from the poor, who were the main purchasers of rolls and small loaves, over which there was no government control. Bakers were generally held in low public esteem because of their "tricks", especially adulterating flour, giving short weight and profiting from poor people's hunger in harvest failure.

The butcher's trade was, in many ways, very similar to the baker's. Both provided a basic food, existed chiefly in large communities and indentured few poor or charity children. Premiums too were similar; both trades were for male apprentices, often from agricultural families. Bakers and butchers even shared the same patron, St Peter. A butcher's skill was far more than serving his customers in the shop; he was responsible for slaughtering, cutting up and dressing a carcase, and for selecting animals at a market or on the farm, and experience was vital in choosing a profitable beast to buy. Butchering was recognized as a necessary nuisance in towns; unlike tanning, it was not forced beyond a city's boundaries and many ancient trading centres still have their Shambles or Butchers' Row. Butchers' apprentices in cities were similar to bakers' in their distribution; Campbell suggested 14 or 15 as the youngest age at which a boy might be bound,[11] and Collyer noted it as a trade not to be chosen for a boy of "delicate sensations".[12] The trade was noticeably a family one, prosperous men indentured a series of apprentices and it was an occupation in which journeyman status was easily attained, with regular employment, but for which capital was needed to become a master. A strong link can be seen between butchers' apprentices and agriculture, presumably as the producers of cattle, sheep and pigs recognized the trade's profitability, and farmers' sons were a distinct group among these apprentices. Like bakers, butchers were affected by general farming conditions, but less adversely than bakers, since weather had less influence on the production of livestock than on the growing of cereals. However, in the eighteenth century several epidemics of cattle plague (rinderpest) seriously diminished the supply of beef available to butchers and a government policy of total slaughter, with compensation, was ruthlessly followed. Thus in 1714, a year of national "distemper among the horned cattle", and again in the 1740s apprenticeships to butchers were either not arranged or greatly reduced in numbers, for quarantine restrictions made the trade far from prosperous. Theoretically an entirely male trade, as symbolized by Hogarth's butcher in *Beer Street*, there were a number of women trading as butchers and taking male apprentices, running their late husbands' or fathers' firms, in spite of considerable and widespread superstitions against women's handling of meat.

After the baker and the butcher, the third most important purveyor of food-stuffs was the grocer, who traded in "Tea, Sugar, Coffee, Chocolate, Raisins, Currants, Prunes, Figs, Almonds, Soap, Starch, Blues of all Sorts, etc. Some of them deal in Rums and Brandy, Oils, Pickles and several other Articles fit for a Kitchen and the Tea Table",[13] in fact, in most raw materials for the household. Because they sold goods in bulk, they traded in only the larger communities and in the Middle Ages, as "spicers", they had also been apothecaries. In the provinces the dual description "mercer-grocer" survived into the eighteenth century; there were 12 in Kendal in the years 1645–1736, for example.[14]

One of the grocer's most distinct characteristics, setting him apart from other food traders, was the size of premiums paid by apprentices, such uniform sums in certain areas that some kind of masters' agreement seems indicated. For example at Kendal (1711–28) premiums were recorded for nine apprentices; for five boys £40 was paid, three masters took £31, £35 and £37 each, while one child, indentured to a relative, had only £5 paid on his behalf. Of these nine boys, two became masters themselves in this period, taking the same premiums their own fathers had paid.[15] Their substantial premiums were maintained throughout the eighteenth century; in Birmingham masters took £30 most frequently, although £105 was also recorded,[16] but of 19 Surrey boys indentured to grocers, 5 had premiums of £100 or more and 7 had £30 to £50,[17] just as Ralph Josselin had paid for his son in the 1660s.[18] In Wiltshire too high premiums predominated, with 5 of the 44 apprentices having £100 or more paid, 7 between £60 and £86, 22 in the £30–£50 category and 10 with £20 or less. The lower premiums were presumably paid for the future shopmen rather than traders on their own account.[19] Grocery was also a trade, because concentrated in towns, to which apprentices often travelled some distance to find a master; of the 9 boys bound to Kendal grocers, 4 came from beyond the borough,[20] while 8 of the 31 Sussex boys left their county to join London masters.[21] Grocers frequently indentured several boys each, usually with overlapping terms and, as the term was often shorter than the normal seven years, the value of the premium was enhanced. Campbell considered that a boy might learn the trade "in a Month or two as well as in seven Years" and that it was "scarce worth while to serve a Seven Years Apprenticeship, to learn the Art of buying and selling the materials they furnish their Shops with: They have nothing to learn but the Market Price of Goods". The grocer's apprentice was expected to be able to write a good hand, count and be "alert at weighing out, to give his Master the Advantage of the Scales".[22] For the grocer either a partnership or setting up was an expensive business, and capital was needed to buy stock, acquire premises and support bad debts, for there is considerable evidence from family papers and bankruptcy proceedings that although the gentry were good customers of a grocer, they tended to complain and defer payment, often for years.[23]

In the clothing trades much of the craftsman's work involved a personal relationship with the client, especially in the fashionable sector of tailoring, mantua-making and related crafts. All clothing trades extended across a very wide range of social groups as customers, but there was little in common between exclusive tailors, milliners or staymakers in London or Bath and their counterparts in provincial market or industrial towns. Tailoring was largely unaffected even in the later eighteenth century by increased industrialization; a highly traditional occupation, with apprentices aged 13 or 14, serving a seven-year term, the tailor's premiums were generally within Campbell's range of £5 to £10.[24] By the mid-eighteenth century a substantial proportion of tailors' apprentices were parish boys, although before that period numbers of respectable, non-pauper boys had been bound, with modest but adequate premiums. Thus at Kendal (1707–36) of the 42 tailors' apprentices, premiums were paid for 31 ranging from £2 to £7. Of these only five were charity boys; other apprentices' parents were such borough craftsmen as a tailor, glazier and carpenter.[25]

The population increases of the eighteenth century linked to a rising standard of living meant that work for tailors and mantua-makers grew in proportion. Disposable income could be spent on clothing that was more than the basic essentials; the new rich, the expanding middle class and even the aspiring artisan were all customers for clothing in a thriving economy. By the later eighteenth century the numbers of tailors and dressmakers noted in the *Universal British directory* show a remarkable and growing occupation. The tailor's trade was carried on in both large and small communities in all areas; in 1696 of the 5 tailors in Melbourne two had apprentices[26] while in one London ward at the same period there were 16 craftsmen of whom six had boys indentured.[27] Tailors are noticeable in apprenticeship records for the number of masters who had several boys each; of the two Melbourne masters one had three apprentices,[28] while three Kendal tailors each had seven, five and three boys respectively indentured.[29] Some tailors' shops were therefore quite large establishments; in 1695 Joseph Lee of London had a household consisting of his wife, three sons, two daughters, maidservant and three apprentices.[30] Tailors were usually a numerically substantial group in a community and always well represented among apprenticeship records, even though they ranged from the fashionable to the poorest craftsman. The number of boys indentured grew as the eighteenth century passed, so that whereas in the early decades only 2.3 per cent of non-poor Surrey apprentices went to tailors, by the later decades in Sussex and Wiltshire the proportion had grown to 7.8 and 8.4 per cent respectively.[31] Their numbers were very considerably increased by charity and pauper boys, but for these apprentices complete figures are impossible. Where parish and charity apprenticeships to tailors have been examined they appear to have been most numerous in the last two decades of the eighteenth century and the early nineteenth century, with tailors taking apprentices in even very small communities (for example, in half the 208 towns and villages of Warwickshire at this period).[32] Many of these masters had a varied clientele, doing work for the overseers of the poor, for local farmers and occasionally for the clergy and gentry. The tailor's employment prospects were not particularly good, for the trade was overstocked, and seasonal work encouraged erratic hours, always hard on apprentices. In their community tailors were often radicals, but rarely held important office, although they might serve as overseers or churchwardens. If only because they were numerous, tailors and their apprentices were fairly frequently involved in litigation, often cruelty cases, and their general reputation for both cowardice and physical deformity was an unenviable one.

The female equivalent of the tailor was the mantua-maker or dressmaker, the term in use by the nineteenth century. Her business was to

> make Night-Gowns, Mantuas and Petticoats, Rob de Chambres, etc. for the Ladies. She is sister to the Taylor and, like him, must be a perfect Connoisieur [sic] in Dress and Fashions; and, like the Stay-Maker, she must keep the Secrets she is entrusted with, as much as a Woman can: . . . she must swear herself to an inviolable Secrecy: she must learn to flatter all Complexions, praise all Shapes, and, in a word, ought to be compleat Mistress of the Art of Dissimulation.[33]

Like the tailor she too worked for a wide variety of social classes, from the poor to the aristocratic. Although Campbell wrote of the mantua-makers as exclusively female, there were a number of men practising the craft in the eighteenth century, some in partnership with their wives, but their apprentices were all females. Generally a short term was served, five years or less, and by non-poor girls; thus in Wiltshire (1710–60) a premium of £10–£12 was commonly paid.[34] The social origins of mantua-makers' apprentices varied little; of the 37 Surrey apprentices to the trade three had fathers with a regional occupation (mariners), seven were respectable tradesmen (butcher, farrier, leatherseller, for example), while two had yeomen and one a gentleman for a father. A further group, seven, were orphans and eight had fathers living, but with no occupation recorded.[35] A similar pattern exists for other counties at the same period.

In only larger communities was there enough work for a mantua-maker to have several apprentices simultaneously. However, mistresses like Catherine Pulsford of Chippenham, with three apprentices, each with a £10 premium,[36] or Ann Lambert, whose four apprentices brought sums from £15 to £20,[37] or Jane Leafe of Lambeth, all presumably had prosperous clienteles.[38] Frequent newspaper advertisements for mantua-making apprentices indicate the labour needs of this particular trade, with a quicker than normal turnover of apprentices. The term was generally a short one, partly because the 15- or 16-year-old girls bound had already acquired some sewing skill at home or charity school, unlike boys bound to many traditional trades. Thus apprenticeship to a mantua-maker provided instruction in making garments, fashionable taste and pleasing the customer, rather than simply in sewing and, for girls of respectable family, the prospect of a genteel later career after marriage or in widowhood.

Although the mantua-maker provided women's clothes for all social classes, the milliner catered for the prosperous customer only. Many of them sold haberdashery (ribbons, trimmings, materials for needlework) as well as hats, caps and luxury accessories. In the seventeenth century they were importers of Milan goods and generally male; of the nine listed in London in 1696 only one was a woman and, as a widow, may have been running her husband's business.[39] It was also a trade in which several apprentices were bound to one master, so that of the four milliners in one London ward at the same period only one man had a single apprentice, two had two each and one master had three.[40] By the early eighteenth century milliners were established in provincial centres; for example, Wiltshire masters were trading at Devizes, Salisbury, Trowbridge and Marlborough. The cathedral city clearly had the most prosperous milliners and high-premium apprentices, for in 1750 and 1751 sums of £40 and 52 guineas were paid with girls bound to two Salisbury women.[41] Of the ten milliners in Birmingham in 1767[42] seven had apprentices, also with quite substantial premiums, and such girls often served only two to four years. Apart from prosperous apprentices, there were also poor and charity girls bound to the trade with £5 premiums, which was, however, more than poor female apprentices had in many other trades, to become the essential adult workers of the future.[43]

In 1747 Campbell estimated that it cost between £100 and £1,000 for a woman to set herself up in business as a milliner,[44] more than five times the mantua-maker's expense, presumably because of the luxury stock she carried. This capital outlay was comparable with that for the male trades of tanner, gunsmith or upholsterer, and the most expensive for a woman mentioned by

Campbell. Such investment required high profits for the milliner and long hours of work, especially at such busy periods as the "Season" or royal mourning. Millinery, however, remained a trade in which a girl from a respectable family, in unexpectedly reduced circumstances, symbolized by Kate Nickleby, might earn a living, avoid domestic service, and for which she already had essential needlework skills.

A further personal service was provided for women of all ranks by the staymaker, who taught apprentices to construct the boned stays that created the fashionable contemporary silhouette. The widespread wearing of stays by all females was noted by foreign and English travellers. In the eighteenth century there was regular work for the staymaker, since even paupers had stays provided by their parish overseers. Originally staymaking, like habit-making, was a branch of tailoring, a garment impossible to make at home. Campbell noted the qualities essential for a staymaker; he should be a

> very polite Tradesman . . . possessed of a tolerable Share of Assurance and Command of Temper to approach [ladies'] delicate Persons in fitting on their Stays, without being moved or put out of Countenance.[45]

Clearly discretion was essential when he was "obliged by Art to mend a crooked Shape, to bolster up a fallen Hip, or distorted Shoulder", an estimate of the trade echoed by Collyer.[46] Staymakers visited clients at home and attended those who came to their workshops. Essentially a trade for men in the early eighteenth century, it was increasingly for women after about 1760. By 1818 it was not sufficiently important an occupation to be listed in a contemporary *Book of trades*. The change occurred because, in the first half of the eighteenth century, stays were made from canvas, strengthened and shaped with whalebone or steel strips, and the work was "too hard for women"; it required "more Strength than they are capable of, to raise Walls of Defence about a Lady's Shape, which is liable to be spoiled by so many Accidents". At this period, women's work was limited to stay-stitching, "but poor Bread",[47] and it was to this branch of the trade that its few female apprentices were indentured, with less than £10 premiums. After the mid-eighteenth century, stays were lighter, using less whalebone, and the craft came within a woman's capabilities. By the nineteenth century also it was no longer thought suitable for a man to measure and fit a woman for so personal a garment as stays. The flowing fashions of the period needed less extensive corsetry and by the early nineteenth century royal ladies had female staymakers.[48] Thus, whereas in 1767 Birmingham had 16 staymakers, including one woman,[49] by 1828 for a much increased population, 18 of the craft traded there, of whom only five were men.[50] Staymakers worked in the same large towns that supported milliners and mantua-makers and the importance of stays to the contemporary wardrobe can be estimated from the number of references to the purchase and fitting of stays in diaries and letters of the period, as well as from the staymakers' own advertisements for their services. By the early nineteenth century mercers and haberdashers increasingly sold ready-made stays, reducing the craft's status, premiums and profitability.

Two important sectors of commerce to which wealthy apprentices were bound were the wholesale trades of the draper and the mercer. They were "as like one another as two Eggs" but the draper dealt chiefly with male customers, and was in consequence "the graver Animal of the two", while the mercer "traficks most with the Ladies".[51] The draper dealt in wool or linen cloth, supplying tailors and private customers alike, and needed considerable capital for both stock and credit. Premiums were high; Campbell quoted £50–£200 in 1747,[52] Collyer £100–£400 by 1761 for apprentices to woollen drapers, but linen drapers, dealing in a less valuable product, took slightly lower sums.[53] Certainly great city drapers were men of substance, and of the 12 woollen drapers listed in London in 1696 nine were men worth £600.[54] Drapers frequently bound several apprentices, and of the 13 masters listed for one London ward in 1698, only five had a single apprentice; all the others had between two and four boys indentured and employed a couple of maidservants.[55] Such boys also often came from distant homes but always prosperous ones. Even in the early seventeenth century, without recorded premiums as a measure of status, the number of country gentlemen's sons bound to drapers is noticeable, with no apparent stigma at entering trade and before lost fortunes in the Civil War made such careers necessary. Thus in Southampton of the 19 boys bound (1610–64), four had gentlemen as fathers, four had yeomen, while two had clerics and merchants. At this early period, a substantial master such as Henry Bracebridge could regularly attract apprentices from beyond the town itself, indenturing the sons of three yeomen, a baker and gentleman in 1619, 1627, 1629, 1639 and 1649, all for eight or nine years. Presumably in 1639 his own health was in doubt, for the indenture was endorsed with a note that if the master were to die, the apprentice was to serve the rest of his term with the widow Bracebridge.[56] In the early eighteenth century drapers' apprentices in Sussex were able to offer masters premiums between £40 and £105; as a measure of a country draper's prosperity a Lewes trader could indenture one son to a London apothecary with a £50 premium in 1715 and another to a City mercer with £126 in 1733.[57] The minority of boys, bound with premiums in the £10 range to drapers, were the book-keepers and shopmen of the future, not masters. Campbell insisted it was

> scarce any man's while to serve seven Years to learn to measure or weigh out Goods in a Retail Shop; but that it is absolute Madness in any Parent to bind his Child to such Shop-keeper, except they have a rational Prospect of being able to set them up for themselves.[58]

The mercer's trade was another occupation to earn Campbell's disapproval, as indeed he deplored all who profited from fashion and human vanity. The mercer dealt in

> Silks, Velvets, Brocades, and an innumerable Train of expensive Trifles, for the Ornament of the Fair Sex . . . He must be a very polite Man . . . he ought, by no Means, to be an aukward clumsey Fellow, such a Creature would turn the Lady's Stomach in a Morning, when they go their Rounds, to tumble silks they have no mind to buy.[59]

Campbell suggested a larger sum than that required by a draper was necessary to set up as a mercer, £1,000–£10,000.[60] Because mercers dealt with the general public and as wholesalers, they were more numerous and traded in more communities than drapers. Thus in the mid-sixteenth century 55 of the 1,800 Bristol apprentices were indentured to mercers in contrast to only 24 bound to drapers.[61] In seventeenth-century Southampton 33 boys were indentured to mercers compared with 19 to woollen drapers[62] and in a major clothing area, Kendal, of 427 apprenticeships in the years 1645–88 a tenth (44) were to mercers.[63]

Although prosperous, mercers ranked slightly below drapers in the premiums they took, the social origins of their apprentices and the trades to which they themselves indentured their own sons. Although the occasional premium was £100 or more, £50 was most commonly paid, and a noticeable minority of boys had only £25 to £40. Of all prosperous trades theirs had a very wide range of premiums, reflecting the clientele, quality of goods and size of community where the master traded. Thus the 17 early-eighteenth-century apprentices in Kendal had premiums of between £10 and £50; of these boys, four had fathers who were gentlemen and seven who were yeomen, including John Stout of Bolton, whose uncle, an ironmonger, paid his £40 premium.[64] In London mercers were very substantial citizens, although less wealthy than the drapers, judging from the 1696 marriage tax assessment.[65] Most of these London mercers with apprentices had at least one servant and lived among other prosperous merchants; inventories of their goods indicate the extensive overseas trade many of them had, with valuable stock and a large clientele. Mercers bound their own sons to occupations that indicate their prosperity; sons of men in a small way of business might go to a tailor, glover, butcher, baker, plumber or clocksmith with only £8 or £12 premium, while the larger traders bound sons to a draper (with £45), London armourer (£30) or barber-surgeon (£90).[66] In Coventry in the eighteenth and nineteenth century mercers were second only to silkmen as mayors and many traders were founders of local charities. However, they suffered from bad debts and overlong credit and their names frequently appeared in bankruptcy lists. By the nineteenth century a number of provincial mercers entered manufacturing (textiles and watchmaking, for example) and apprenticed their sons to law or medicine.

A far more personal but less prosperous individual service that took considerable numbers of apprentices was given by the hairdresser-barber-wigmaker (peruke-maker). It was primarily an urban occupation, but not confined to large cities, since quite small market towns had their own hairdressers, often itinerants, visiting clients at home to cut and dress hair or measure and fit wigs. Most hairdressers practised all three branches of the craft, specified on the apprenticeship indenture. Much contemporary opinion from the seventeenth century onwards disapproved of wigs and their makers; for "forty or three score pounds a year for periwigs and ten to a poor Chaplain to say Grace to him that Adores Hair is sufficient demonstration of the Brains [wigs] keep warm".[67] Perukes were an object of amusement especially in the outrageous styles of the early eighteenth century. More significantly, as foreign visitors noted, they were an important sign of status, so that "farm servants, clod hoppers, day labourers . . . all labouring folk wore wigs".[68] Since the cheapest wigs cost a guinea, these must have been third or fourth hand, made of tow or wool, rather than human hair. Wigmaking was exclusively a male occupation, although from the 1750s women were their main customers; by the 1760s men were beginning to wear their own hair, but exaggerated female fashions brought a period of prosperity for wigmakers generally. Some country craftsmen served their communities as barber-surgeons as well and Richard Arkwright's father, for example, was thought "clever in his peruke-making business and very capital in Bleeding & toothdrawing".[69] Campbell suggested a premium of £20 or below, with £10 to £200 to set up as master and equip a shop.[70]

The trade was not highly pauperized, with premiums of £10–£14, until the profitable wigmaking side of the business declined, with fashion changes, leaving only the barber-hairdressing work. The apprentices to the trade paid premiums that varied according to the level of fashionable clientele the master had. In one market town, Kendal (1716–34), premiums ranged from £5 to £15, but £9 and £10 were most often recorded.[71] Masters who were only wigmakers commanded higher premiums than those who were also barbers. Thus in Wiltshire (1710–60) the barbers' commonest premium was £10, with a large minority of boys paying less than this, while masters who were solely wigmakers received up to £20, with 15 of the 19 boys paying £10 or more and £15 the commonest sum recorded.[72] The proportion of men who took apprentices is difficult to assess, but in Birmingham in 1767 of the 54 wigmakers trading, 11 had apprentices indentured.[73] Wigmakers tended to bind several boys each so that, for example, the 14 Kendal apprentices in the early eighteenth century were indentured to eight masters.[74]

An interesting example of a wigmaker's life and clientele in a small market town in the eighteenth century is given in the diary of Joseph Hill of Stratford-upon-Avon.[75] He arrived there from Lutterworth (Leics.) in 1769 with a settlement certificate and established a business. In 1790 he indentured a Warwick pauper, William Boddington, with a three-guinea premium,[76] an example of how the craft was declining by the later eighteenth century. Hill visited clients in the surrounding villages, and allowed extended credit for hairdressing, shaving and making wigs. Literate enough to keep a diary, he noted many national and local events, but was chiefly concerned with clients' measurements, his mileages, bad debts and income. He supplemented his wigmaking by farming a smallholding and owning fighting-cocks; at the time of his death in 1821 he was prosperous enough to live in Sheep Street, one of the town's main thoroughfares. His career may be typical of other craftsmen of the period who have left no written record of their livelihood.

Other forms of service for the apprentice were of an entirely different and domestic nature, to which chiefly poor children were bound, housewifery and chimney-sweeping. Housewifery was exclusively for girls and almost solely for parish children, either orphans or from a very large family supported by the parish. The girls bound to housewifery were strikingly younger than those entering other occupations, with nine-year-olds most often recorded. Girls were indentured to housewifery until the age of 21 or marriage and the level of premiums was predictably low, usually £2 or £3, but until the mid-eighteenth century many parish girls also had outfits of clothes or single items provided by their overseers (Appendix 4). Poor girls were bound to farmers and a wide variety of occupations, from small craftsmen such as tailors to wealthy merchants. They were often unwelcome in private households, their poor home conditions an impediment to service in a prosperous family and so could expect to do the roughest work. At least these apprentices could find employment at the end of the term, in contrast with girls bound to factory work. It has been suggested that only seldom were parish apprentices placed in respectable families, since girls from homes of "habitual poverty" made unacceptable servants.[77] However, in Warwickshire (1700–1834) 22 per cent of housewifery apprentices went to masters whose occupations were all reasonably prosperous, and included inhabitants such as drapers, surgeons and chandlers. Local clerics and schoolmasters also indentured housewifery apprentices and very few of these Warwickshire girls went to impoverished labourers. Some ratepayers still chose to pay a £10 fine rather than accept an allocated parish housewifery apprentice.[78]

In spite of the numbers of poor girls bound to housewifery, not all girls apprenticed were paupers. For some girls from good families training in domestic skills provided for their future, either as the kind of superior companion Mrs Pepys employed or running their own homes. Thus in Bristol in the mid-sixteenth century, 17 non-poor girls were indentured to housewifery with the wives of city tradesmen, the majority for seven years. These girls came from London, Gloucestershire, Wiltshire and Worcestershire, with fathers in respectable trades.[79] Even a girl such as Ralph Josselin's second daughter, Anne, at the age of 14 in 1668 was "bound . . . her time out June 24 1674" and Josselin paid her mistress £50.[80]

Such arrangements were a minority, however, and by the seventeenth century most girls bound to housewifery were paupers, indentured to the wives of less prosperous men with premiums of 10s to £3 to save the poor rate. It was not until the population growth and changes in Poor Law administration of the second half of the eighteenth century combined that many more young girls were available as housewifery apprentices either within their own parish or further afield. Clearly apprenticeship prospects varied according to local industries but wholly agricultural parishes had to devise different solutions for placing their poor girls and be as flexible as possible when population and industries changed. One such parish, Tanworth-in-Arden, with a large collection of Poor Law apprenticeships, was increasingly obliged to indenture girls to inhabitants as the eighteenth century passed, but by 1809 these girls were entering Worcestershire needlemaking rather than housewifery. The overseers' experiment in apprenticing girls in the Coventry ribbon trade, as in 1758, was not continued, perhaps because the masters' premiums were too high or because apprentices from nearer the city were preferred:[81]

Table 6.1 Female parish apprentices from Tanworth-in-Arden, Warwickshire, 1686–1835.

	1686–1700	1701–50	1751–1800	1801–35
Total apprentices	15	91	245	150
Number of females:	8	21	95	29
to housewifery	4	8	67	18
to husbandry	3	8	10	–
to needlemaking	–	1	3	10
miscellaneous	1	4	15	1
in Tanworth-in-Arden	7	16	82	18
to other villages	1	3	8	–
to Birmingham	–	–	3	1
to Coventry	–	–	8	–
to Worcestershire	–	2	9	10

In an even more remote area, Herefordshire, parish girls were bound to housewifery and husbandry in their home or adjacent parishes, for villages such as Burrington, Felton, Leintwardine and Kingsland were all far from Hereford's few industries and those of the neighbouring counties.[82] In the Devonshire parish of Yealmpton, with some 555 children apprenticed (1638–1840) the pattern of binding girls to housewifery was equally distinct; of these children only 26 were girls but all were bound to housewifery, in contrast to the wide variety of trades for boys.[83] A similar distribution of girls as apprentices to domestic service can be seen in most rural areas, but at least housewifery provided both the opportunity for adult employment and some instruction in running a home if the girl married.

The service provided by the chimney-sweep was of a domestic, not personal nature; it was one to which apprentices were bound and was certainly not a production occupation. Its obvious abuse of the concept of apprentice-ship was important because the children, unlike those in factories, were seen by the general public, plying their trade in city streets, reinforcing philan-thropists' attempts to abolish the activity. Numbers of sweeps and their apprentices grew in the later eighteenth century as architectural styles nar-rowed flues to burn coal not wood, with apertures only 8 or 12 inches square. Campbell noted that "the Black Fraternity" all took apprentices, "the younger they are the better fit to climb up the Chimneys", but added that he would not recommend a friend to "breed a Son to this Trade", although he knew some masters who lived comfortably.[84] Apprentices were of necessity small, and either extreme youth or undernourishment ensured this. The sweep traded entirely in urban communities, for many country chimneys were of the old-fashioned wider style that could have soot burned away or scraped from below. By the mid-eighteenth century the climbing-boy was a familiar sight in city streets, as in Hogarth's *The march to Finchley* (1745); the child's appearance had changed little, in spite of legislation in 1788, when 60 years later, Rowlandson depicted a climbing-boy listening to a street ballad-singer. This boy in 1805 also carried a scraping-brush, wore a cap, and was black from head to foot, with a bag of soot at his feet.

In 1788 a London master sweep, David Porter, had successfully petitioned parliament to introduce measures to improve the conditions of climbing-boys, but in the Lords powers to license masters, register apprentices and pro-hibit "calling" in the streets were removed, rendering the act virtually powerless. In spite of these alterations, the act ordered that no apprentice was to be younger than eight and no master should have more than six appren-tices, each of whom must have the master's name and address on a brass plate stuck in front of the leather cap (a large metal semicircle, as in Seymour's car-toon (see Fig. 6.1)). Apprentices were not to be let out for hire, call the streets after midday or work before 7am in winter or 5am in summer. The tradi-tional wording of the indenture was modified, so that the master agreed that apprentices should be "thoroughly washed and cleaned from soot and Dirt at least once a Week", to send them to church on Sundays, not force a child to climb a chimney actually on fire and to treat the apprentice "with as much Humanity and Care as the Nature of the Employment of a Chimney-Sweep will admit of".[85]

Although evidence to parliamentary enquiries particularly indicted London sweeps for cruelty, that they indentured parish children very young, and took large numbers each, different conditions appear to have operated in the prov-inces. Thus, of the 22 apprentices to nine masters in Coventry (1765– 1823) only six were parish children, although others' parents were predictably poor (labourers and silk workers). The ages of eight boys were specified, from 7 to 13, with terms from 5 years to 14, and four boys bound until the age of 21. Three premiums only were recorded, £3 2s, £4 and £5 5s,[86] although chim-ney-sweeping was one of the few occupations for which neither Campbell nor

Figure 6.1 Robert Seymour's cartoon of chimney-sweep's apprentices, early nineteenth century.

Collyer indicated a premium. One of these Coventry masters unhappily exemplified the cruel sweep of Kingsley's novel *The water-babies*; in 1765 Thomas Morgan indentured two Warwick paupers, of whom one, aged ten, had parents living.[87] A decade later Morgan had two other apprentices removed from his care and their indentures cancelled because of cruelty, the only sweep to appear among 73 court cases.[88] The abuse of masters taking large numbers of apprentices was practised by only one Coventry family, the Campbells, with eight apprentices bound (1786–1803), so that in 1800 they had five boys indentured.[89] The 1788 act did cause at least some parishes to follow its requirements, with additional clauses in the indenture for the child's dress and cleanliness, but the rarity of these indentures is significant.[90] The concern of individuals such as Blake and Hanway for climbing-boys gained wider support from the disclosures of the 1816 parliamentary select committee, especially the medical evidence. However, the euphemistically

130

named "chimney-sweep's cancer" was less debated than the lack of adult employment prospects for climbing-boys, the physical dangers of the trade and their irregular hours of work, permitting "idleness and depravity".[91] There were attempts to replace boys with sweeping machines, but not all customers accepted the innovation, and parish disputes could prevent the re-apprenticing of former climbing-boys to other healthier occupations.[92] In spite of the risks to young male apprentices, some survived to be masters themselves. Thus a Claydon (Oxon.) child, bound to his stepbrother in 1820, was still working as a sweep in Coventry 30 years later,[93] symbolizing young Tom's dream that he would one day be a master himself, making the apprentices "carry home the soot sacks, while he rode before them on his donkey, with a pipe in his mouth and a flower in his button-hole, like a king at the head of his army".[94]

At the other extreme of society were apprentices entering the professions, medicine and law. They were distinguished by certain characteristics from those in humble occupations, yet identical in the essential terms, paying of premiums and service in the master's household. There the similarities end, however, for although the term might be seven years, the premiums were the highest of the non-merchant occupations and future career prospects were good. The professions also differed from other livelihoods in that, during the eighteenth and nineteenth centuries, their status within society changed quite strikingly, especially the surgeon's.

The main division in medicine was between the physician, always a university man, his medieval origins in the church, and the surgeon, trained by apprenticeship to perform basic surgery, treat injuries, set limbs and attend childbirth. There were also apothecaries, always more numerous than other medical personnel, who dispensed the physicians' prescriptions, sold drugs and attended patients, although theoretically allowed to charge only for medicines and not advice. The early eighteenth century saw the final phase of the barber-surgeon, his professional status impeded by his hairdressing activities, and the middle decades were a period when men-midwives (*accoucheurs*) established themselves in fashionable practice both in London and the provinces. Thus important changes in status were made possible by a growing professionalism and a desire to remove the less-qualified from practice, but also by scientific improvements in medicine itself, making the practitioner a more skilled man. The increased life expectancy of the eighteenth-century population and the coming of new therapies available to wealthy patients all enhanced the surgeon's status, his rise in society reflected in larger premiums and the recruitment of apprentices from gentry, mercantile and clerical homes by the 1720s.

Surgeons' status in the mid-sixteenth century is well illustrated by the boys apprenticed to Bristol men (sons of a yeoman and husbandmen, both deceased) while surgeons' own children were bound to fellow craftsmen, a spurrier, saddler and tailor, for example, at this period comparing unfavourably with apothecaries' apprentices from merchant homes. By the mid-seventeenth century the surgeon's status was slightly improving, for at Southampton the orphan sons of a cleric and gentleman were bound to surgeons, while a surgeon indentured his own son to a dyer.[95] London medical practice was traditionally more lucrative, and of the seven surgeons listed there in 1696 two were worth £600 each and one was described as a gentleman.[96] The establishment of Thomas Gardiner, surgeon to the royal household, comprised his wife, daughter, two apprentices, a coachman, two maidservants and Toby, a Black boy,[97] while Gratian Bale, worth £600, had a chambermaid and cook as domestic staff, as well as his two apprentices and children.[98] In contrast with such men, in the remote provinces much medical care was still in the hands of barber-surgeons so that, for example, at Kendal (1649–1734) the apprentices bound to practitioners were all the sons of craftsmen (cordwainer, blacksmith, weaver and the like) with premiums below £12.[99]

The prosperous state of surgeons in the southeast can be seen in the 12 apprentices bound to Surrey masters in the years 1712–26; these boys were the sons of clerics (three), an apothecary, currier, vintner and deceased gentleman, with homes as far away as Cambridgeshire, Lancashire, Denbighshire and Norfolk and a range of premiums from £20 to £107.[100] A group of boys bound to Wiltshire masters in the first half of the eighteenth century emphasize the differences between substantial and less prosperous men. Thus a country surgeon at Pewsey took only £35 with a boy while the newly evolving consultant, with hospital appointments, could attract several times this sum. The leading practice at Salisbury, Thomas Tatum and Co., already a partnership in 1753, received £140 with one apprentice, while Edward Goldwyre in the city took 200 guineas with each of his two apprentices at the same period;[101] both masters became consultants at the new Salisbury Infirmary.[102] Although these were exceptionally high premiums, all but four Wiltshire surgeons received £50 or more with each apprentice. In the later eighteenth century a similar pattern can be seen in Warwickshire, where the Birmingham hospital staff apprenticed boys in the higher premium range; a number of these men (John Freer and Kimberley Moore, for example) had themselves earlier been apprentices to Birmingham surgeons.[103] Campbell had suggested premiums of £10 to £100,[104] Collyer from 20 to 100 guineas, but added the important comment that though setting up required "no great sum", the youth should have a "fortune sufficient to support him like a gentleman, till he becomes known, and renders his merit conspicuous".[105] In a county with no hospital, lower premiums were recorded, so that in Sussex sums of £20–£60 were common at the same period.[106]

Partly as a result of growing professional consciousness, a register of qualified medical practitioners was published in 1779; a fuller edition of 1783 makes it possible to trace some of the apprentices after they had completed their term. Thus John Clare, bound to Joseph Needham of Devizes in 1740, was still practising in the same town in 1783, while John Merewether, apprenticed in 1751 to George King of Calne (Wilts.) was in practice in Chippenham three decades later, although John Pearce, one of Mr Goldwyre's wealthy apprentices in Salisbury, by 1783 had moved to another cathedral city, Canterbury.

Throughout the eighteenth century and the early decades of the nineteenth many surgeons derived part of their income from working for the overseers of the poor, either on an individual fee or contract basis, and a number of well-qualified men, apprenticed to reputable masters, are known to have done so. Of all occupations, medicine showed a particularly strong tendency to remain in families, often in the same town or area, for two centuries or more. The Brees of Warwickshire exemplified this trend; in 1676 a gentleman's son from Kenilworth, Thomas Bree, was bound to a London barber-surgeon, Edward Cockayne, for seven years;[107] members of the family continued to enter medicine and practised in the centre of the county until well into the nineteenth century, as did the Welchman family in south Warwickshire. The later eighteenth century saw the development of certain modern characteristics of medical practice, particularly the growth of partnerships, the concentration of urban practices in small areas of a community and a considerable expansion in numbers and distribution of practitioners. Apart from the traditional apprentices to surgeons, the sons of prosperous tradesmen, farmers and clerics, a noticeable group of boys were recorded as widows' sons, perhaps because, once out of his time, a young man might find immediate employment with an established practitioner, requiring little parental support, before putting up his own plate.

As an example of the provincial surgeon, training apprentices and in general practice at the turn of the century, Bradford Wilmer of Coventry (1747–1813) illustrates the many aspects of the master's work of which his apprentices would gain experience. During the years 1772–1810 Wilmer served a total of nine parishes as surgeon, regularly for three villages near Coventry, and saw a variety of pauper patients as a consultant. He attended difficult parturition cases, usually for two guineas, carried out amputations and a limited range of surgical procedures, including couching.[108] His interest in surgery was considerable, and he wrote a small textbook of observations on over 30 of the most striking cases he had attended, indicating the wide range of all social groups he treated.[109] He saw many patients referred to him by other local surgeons and participated in at least two murder trials, the poisoning of Sir Theodosius Boughton with laurel water in 1783[110] and the murder by starvation of a young silk-weaver's apprentice in 1810,[111] on both occasions as a prosecution witness. He took four apprentices in the years 1773–95[112] and their premiums illustrate the increasing sums a reputable master might command; with his first apprentice he received £130 for a seven-year term, with the next (1792) the premium was £120 for only three years, presumably a boy assigned from another master. However, with his last apprentice in 1795 he took 200 guineas for only a five-year term, and clearly these apprentices, although with a provincial master, had a wide and extensive training.

The distinction between dispensing drugs and advice on their application was a fine one, and certainly some practitioners were qualified both as surgeons and apothecaries. The selling of small quantities of drugs had been a separate occupation since the Middle Ages, and originally the apothecaries had close links with the spicers and pepperers. Apothecaries frequently indentured several apprentices and were more numerous than surgeons in all kinds of communities; for example, there were only two surgeons as masters in seventeenth-century Southampton but five apothecaries,[113] while the 21 apothecaries trading in London in 1696 were three times the number of surgeons practising there.[114] Of these London men, Thomas Hudson may be typical; apart from his wife and maidservant, his household consisted of a bachelor apothecary, presumably a journeyman, and three male apprentices.[115]

The parentage of apothecaries' apprentices was prosperous, and a tendency for surgeons to bind their own sons to apothecaries has been noted;[116] in the first half of the eighteenth century, however, gentlemen and clerics were predominant:

Table 6.2   Parents of apothecaries' apprentices, 1710-60.

	Beds.	Surrey	Sussex	War.	Wilts.
Total apprentices	12	37	82	42	50
Parents recorded	8	24	41	10	23
gentleman/esq.	2	7	13	–	5
cleric	1	5	11	–	5
surgeon	1	–	2	2	–
orphan	1	3	3	–	6
miscellaneous	3	9	12	8	7

At the same period apothecaries were binding their own children to an assortment of trades, so that Sussex boys with very prosperous apothecaries as fathers were indentured to an attorney with an £80 premium or a London skinner with £100, but at the poorer end of the trade one apothecary's son was to serve a carpenter with only a £15 premium, although this was three times the normal sum to enter a humble craft.[117]

As in other occupations, the apothecary's premium indicated his status, the scope of his business and the apprentice's parents' prosperity. Thus a London master could command premiums of £80 or more by the early eighteenth century, and even £157 10s in one instance, while in the same year, 1730, a Reigate (Surrey) trader received only £50 with a boy.[118] Although Campbell suggested a very wide range of premiums, £20–£200, for apothecaries' apprentices,[119] the sum most frequently paid was £50 but with £30 fairly often recorded. Once a boy had finished his term as an apprentice apothecary, he could quite quickly set himself up as master, and many men who did so announced the fact in local newspapers, usually naming the master to whom they had been indentured. Apothecaries also worked for the overseers of the poor, supplying medicines and treating parishioners, but many practitioners were men of substance, living in large houses, holding civic office and endowing charities.

The boys apprenticed to attorneys differed from surgeons' apprentices in that the profession charged for advice only, selling neither product nor manual skill to justify high fees, and perhaps for this reason the most genteel of all apprenticed occupations. By virtue of their large premiums for only a five-year term attorneys had the highest-status apprentices by the eighteenth century, but Campbell warned that the practitioner's reputation was all-important when choosing a master, for the parent who was "resolved to breed his Son to this Business ought to be very solicitous to find out a master, of known Integrity and with sufficient Practice, without which the Youth is certainly lost".[120] He thought that attorneys were too numerous and easily became dishonest, a view clearly shared by Hogarth in *Marriage à la mode* (1745) and *The rake's progress* (1735), and their numbers certainly increased in the litigious eighteenth century.

Essentially an urban profession, most attorneys practised in a handful of communities in each county, particularly the assize towns, and in London. Thus in the first half of the eighteenth century in Wiltshire 8 of the 24 recorded apprentices went to four masters in Salisbury[121] and at the same period in Warwickshire 6 of the 15 boys bound went to three masters in Birmingham, while a further five men in Coventry took one boy each.[122] As far as apprentices' origins were recorded, boys from mercantile families were noticeably absent and their parents were without exception gentlemen, clerics and widows, some of whom sent their sons far from home to find a master. London, of course, was the attorney's magnet, where the highest fees might be earned and the largest premiums paid. The shorter five-year term was almost universal and made any premium proportionately more valuable; the sum of £100 or £105 was paid in about a third of recorded cases (36 per cent in Sussex, 35 per cent in Warwickshire, 33 per cent in Wiltshire, 25 per cent in Surrey and Bedfordshire). However, even more striking were the larger premiums than this, so that for three Sussex boys sums of £315 each were paid, including in 1748 Bysshe Shelley's premium, with whom an additional £30 was paid for his "dyet",[123] presumably to secure better food than the apprentice usually received, since such extra payments were rare. A number of masters took several apprentices each and their increasing premiums, often across a decade or more, reflected the individual attorney's personal status and clientele. Apart from the gentry's willingness to go to law against their neighbours, the eighteenth century also saw considerable expansion of legal practice as a result of Poor Law disputes, with parish officials often paying large fees to attorneys to enforce settlement or bastardy laws, and increasing litigation must have encouraged attorneys to take apprentices.

The cost of setting up in practice was said by Campbell to be from £100 to £1,000;[124] premises were usually the master's own house, but books, office materials and a clerk's wages were essential expenses, as well as the cost of extended credit to clients. A strong family thread ran through many provincial law firms; some attorneys grew wealthy by property or transport speculation, while many married into landowning families. Their growth in numbers was quite remarkable in only a century so that, in Sussex for example, in the years 1710–19 9 boys were indentured, in each of the next two decades 19 were apprenticed and in the 1740s their numbers had again increased to 22.[125] Perhaps because of their progress, attorneys seem never to have been held in general regard, profiting, by the nature of their work, from the misfortunes of others. As in other aspects of eighteenth-century life, Samuel Johnson's comment on the profession succinctly embodied all the prejudices of the age when he remarked of an acquaintance that he "did not care to speak ill of any man behind his back, but he believed the gentleman was an attorney".[126]

CHAPTER 7

The production industries

Not Europe can match us for traffic,
America, Asia, and Afric':
Of what we invent each partakes of a share,
For the best of wrought metal is Birmingham ware,
Birmingham ware,
None so rare,
For the best of wrought metals is Birmingham ware.
  John Freeth, *The Warwickshire medley* or *Convivial songster* (1780)

The line that could be drawn between service and production industries varied from one trade to another and in different decades, for many workers were craftsmen who bought raw material, made a product and then personally sold it to the customer, for example, the saddler, blacksmith or cabinetmaker. Further down the craft scale were such men as shoemakers, with products that ranged from the high fashion, individually made, to the cheapest footwear, and this latter group were, like watchmakers and textile workers, to find their livelihood threatened as machine techniques replaced hand skills. Essentially, however, production industries included those who worked in leather, metal and textiles, as well as the building trades and agriculture, some of these localized, others virtually universal.

The leather trade comprised craftsmen found everywhere in small numbers, those who were among the most numerous of all workers and a third group with strong regional connections in areas such as Northampton that specialized in leather products. The elite of the leatherworkers were undoubtedly the saddlers, their essential quality product maintaining their status and income. They worked chiefly in trading centres, indentured more than one apprentice each and never took paupers. Saddlers were primarily a provincial rather than a London trade, so that while there was one craftsman in Melbourne in 1695 for less than 700 inhabitants,[1] there were only four men listed for London at the same period. The pattern continued into the eighteenth century so that, although Sussex children were sent to London masters in considerable numbers in other trades, boys bound to saddlers went not to the capital but to masters in Lewes, Chichester and Rye.[2] Wiltshire saddlers were also concentrated in a few communities (Devizes, Warminster, Salisbury, Chippenham and Malmesbury) with 23 masters taking 30 apprentices,[3] while in Warwickshire saddlers traded in Coventry, Birmingham and Warwick.[4] In this area particularly saddlers benefited from the local metal trades to carry out essential riveting work on their product.

The cost of setting up as a saddler Campbell assessed as between £50 and £500;[5] fairly rapid progress to master in the craft is illustrated by the details recorded of two apprentices, Henry Kemm and Benedict Ithell. In 1741 Kemm was bound to William Brinsden of Chippenham for seven years with a £20 premium; 16 years later he himself was a master in Chippenham, to John Stevens, with whom he received 20 guineas.[6] Earlier in the century a Coventry widow's son, Benedict Ithell, was bound for the same term and premium to a city master in 1717; out of his time in 1724, he indentured a Coventry innholder's son five years later with £20 from the boy's father.[7] The majority of boys bound to saddlers were from a prosperous trading background, with parents who were ironmongers, maltsters, farmers and yeomen, able to afford premiums that Campbell suggested should be £20–£30.[8] A master able to attract premiums in this range from several apprentices received useful additional capital; thus Abraham Vaughan of Birmingham indentured three boys in 1719, 1723 and 1729 with premiums of £21, £35 and £20, each for seven years.[9] For both Warwickshire and Wiltshire, however, £20 was the most commonly paid premium, with £35 the highest and £5 the lowest sums recorded. Campbell recognized the need for saddlers to have a "large Stock of ready Money to deal considerably" since the gentry among their customers were "no more solicitous about paying their Saddler than any other Tradesman"; the trade was never overstocked.[10]

Although a large variety of trades used leather, its preparation by the currier, whittawer and tanner was highly specialized, involving relatively few men and apprentices. Considerable capital was required to buy and store the raw leather and chemicals, large premises were needed (as for tanning) and slow return on capital was inevitable. The currier's job was vital, for while a tanner could prepare leather for hard, stiff shoe soles, it could not be used for harnesses, shoes or other products. The currier took tanned leather and produced leathers of different colour, thickness and suppleness before the dresser and whittawer could begin work. The currier's premiums were very similar to the saddler's, although Collyer thought it a "black, greasy business, and requires no other abilities in the youth designed to be put apprentice to it but strength".[11]

From the pattern of apprenticeships, the currier's trade was distinctly regional and, with strong guild control, indentured boys whose parents worked in other branches of the leather trade. A few leathersellers were trading in London in 1696 and by the early eighteenth century a number of curriers there were indenturing boys from Surrey and Sussex. Their premiums were in the £10–£20 range, although Collyer had noted £10–£15 as sums paid.[12] There were a few very exceptional apprenticeships for which higher premiums were paid, for example, a Clayton (Sussex) gentleman's son bound to a London citizen-currier in 1716 with £30,[13] a Guildford boy, also of gentle birth, to another city master in 1725 with £40[14] or John Freame of Devizes (Wilts.) who took £40 with Robert Godwin in 1755.[15] However, John Smart of Birmingham was far more typical, with three apprentices in 1752–9 and premiums of £20 and £30.[16] A member of a prosperous Quaker family, the son of a Warwick tugerer, he was one of the town's curriers trading in 1767[17] and as late as 1791 at the age of 77.[18]

By far the largest but poorest group of leatherworkers in all English counties were the cordwainers and shoemakers. Although the term "cordwainer" originally meant a worker in fine Spanish goatskin, making shoes and other leather goods, the two terms by the sixteenth century at least were interchangeable, but with "cordwainer" more generally used than the English "shoemaker", and no distinctions of premium or apprentice status discernible. By the time of the 1841 Census members of the "gentle craft" comprised the largest single artisan trade (excluding textiles) with 133,000 adult male workers.[19] In London by the late seventeenth century the term shoemaker was universally used and a typical craftsman's home into which an apprentice went was recorded in St Mary-le-Bow, a prosperous parish, in 1696. There the master was Thomas Acreman, with a wife, daughter, an apprentice and spinster as other members of the household.[20] In this parish 9.7 per cent of the total population were apprentices, who lived in nearly half (44 out of 106) the households (41.5 per cent). Even in the remote Derbyshire village of Melbourne there were seven cordwainers trading, of whom one, Nathaniel Hazard, had two apprentices as well as a wife, journeyman and two sons in his household.[21] The choice of shoemaking as a trade for pauper children can be seen in Southampton in the seventeenth century where 46 quite prosperous boys were bound to shoemakers but also 35 poor children, including 4 girls, at the same period.[22] The trade's increasing impoverishment in the eighteenth century is reflected in the increasing numbers of parish apprentices bound to shoemakers so that, for example, in Warwickshire, of the 603 children bound, over half (372) were paupers, 159 were charity apprentices and only a minority were indentured by their parents to shoemaking.[23] However, in four other counties non-poor boys were bound to shoemaking in substantial numbers in the first half of the eighteenth century, so that of 1,012 apprenticeships recorded for Bedfordshire, Surrey, Sussex and Wiltshire, 11.7 per cent were to shoemakers and cordwainers. A trade with longer than normal terms suggests an apprentice aged less than 14, and younger children could be usefully employed in shoemaking. Of all the trades, the shoemaker's was perhaps most widely distributed, with men in even small villages by the eighteenth century. Always in work, even if poorly paid (only 9s or 10s a week in the mid-eighteenth century)[24] because shoes and boots could not be made at home, although some repairs could be carried out by the poor themselves.

Shoemakers were noted for their irregular habits and their celebration of St Monday; one of their number was depicted as symbolic of this weekly holiday in a contemporary print,[25] and later advice to the trade stipulated a workman should be "sober and industrious",[26] as if this were not the usual state of the craft. However, shoemakers had a reputation for being among the most intellectual of working men, frequently literate, articulate and even musical.[27] Such a man was Benjamin Satchwell of Leamington Priors, son of a miller, born in 1732, and bound to a shoemaker in neighbouring Offchurch about 1746 after his father had died. His master taught him to read and write and, in 1753 when out of his time, he returned to his widowed mother's home where he worked as an "honest mender of boots and shoes". Between 1753 and 1764, when he married, he had saved £200; he loaned money to his neighbours and bought his own cottage. Satchwell was a figure of some importance in the parish: he established a Friendly Society in 1777, reported for the London and Coventry newspapers as well as being local postmaster.[28] In 1767, at the age of 35, he took in a charity apprentice for seven years with a £5 premium.[29] Although Satchwell was perhaps a more significant local figure than many of his craft, he typified the counselling, philosophical and literary aspect of the shoemaker.

However, not all cordwainers were of the respectable, orderly kind; it is noticeable that they often appeared in disturbances, as did their apprentices, since they were relatively numerous in any gathering. Certainly when the case of Joseph Day came before Warwick Quarter Sessions, it exemplified the very reverse of Satchwell's image of the "gentle craft". The local press reported in June 1806 that, "on Tuesday last, some words arose between two boys, apprentices to Mr. Dudley, a respectable shoemaker of Coventry, when the youngest plunged the knife he was making use of into the belly of his companion and cut him in a shocking manner; but there are hopes that the wound will not prove mortal. The offender, in the confusion, escaped." A month later Joseph Day was sentenced to two months' imprisonment in the House of Correction.[30] Day was the son of a Coventry weaver, indentured to Stephen Dudley in 1804; he was presumably aged about 16 when the stabbing occurred, and his victim was William Lucas, a Coventry boy, bound to Dudley in 1801. After he was released from prison, Day did not return to his master, but was re-assigned to another Coventry cordwainer, William Hulm, who already had one other apprentice. However, he remained with Hulm only six months and in March 1807 was assigned to a third master in the city, Richard Whatnell, with whom he remained, although he was presumably not a very satisfactory apprentice after the events of 1806.

Apprentices who were bound to the various building trades from the earliest period were joining a group of crafts that were intensely traditional, unmechanized, in constant demand, with masters of all levels of skill and prosperity. The building tradesmen comprised the bricklayer, mason, carpenter-joiner, plumber-glazier and plasterer. The interior of the house was completed by the upholder or upholsterer, who was an interior designer as well as a craftsman, and the cabinetmaker, whose work was frequently custom-made for an individual client. Of all these skills, the bricklayer and carpenter were the lowest in status, chiefly because few became large-scale masters. Their premiums were small, they neither worked valuable raw materials nor had, like the stone carver or decorative plasterer, a superior personal skill to sell. Bricklayers worked almost everywhere, but tended to concentrate in certain areas where building styles favoured the use of brick. Their numbers grew in periods of urban or rural expansion, for example, after a fire had devastated the centre of a town, or when a great country house was built. However, bricklayers had erratic work periods because of unsuitable wet weather. Campbell described the work as "only in carrying his Bricks even upon the Top of one another, and giving them their proper Bed of Cements",[31] although Collyer advised that a boy should have "a good genius, and before he is put apprentice, should learn not only arithmetic, but be taught trigonometry, geometry and drawing", so that he might draw plans, survey and estimate buildings.[32] Many examples of highly ornate and elaborate eighteenth-century brickwork survive as proof of the contemporary bricklayers' skill, especially in towns such as Lewes or Warwick where brick was a usual building material. In London in 1696 there were 21 craftsmen listed, typical of whom was William Gardner, whose household consisted of his wife, son, three daughters and one apprentice.[33] In Southampton at the same period bricklaying was chiefly a trade for only a handful of poor or charity children, with whom a premium of £1 10s or £2 10s was paid. The exceptional expansion of building in northern Surrey in the early eighteenth century is reflected in the numbers of apprentices (48 of 2,945) and masters (38), particularly in Richmond, Epsom, Croydon, Guildford and Leatherhead, but also in 17 other communities. Of these men Edward Exell of Richmond was the largest master, with six apprentices bound in the years 1716–23, always with two or three boys indentured, their premiums £6 to £10, except one orphan, with whom the sum of £30 was paid in 1723. The highly traditional nature of bricklaying is reflected in Surrey as elsewhere by the frequency of the seven-year term; in Surrey only three of the boys served longer or shorter terms, while in Sussex of the 47 apprenticeships in the early eighteenth century, 16 varied from the seven years, but all six boys in Wiltshire were bound for this term.

The distribution of bricklayers varied considerably from one area to another, so that in Surrey they were concentrated in a few towns, in Sussex only Northiam, Brighton, Buxted, Battle and Chichester had several apprentices and masters each, while a single child was bound in 31 communities in the county. In an area such as Warwickshire, where brick was an important local building material, 26 communities had masters with apprentices, whereas in Wiltshire they were outnumbered by masons. Although the numbers of poor apprentices were noticeable towards the later eighteenth century, it was the older, and therefore physically stronger, boy who tended to be bound everywhere. Campbell observed that it was a "very profitable business, especially if they confine themselves to work for others, and do not launch out into Building Projects of their own, which frequently ruin them".[34] The building trades in all periods and regions provided employment and apprenticeships for many, especially the work of the carpenter and joiner. Houses of all building materials needed a frame, doors, windows, floors and staircases. Sometimes the terms "carpenter" and "joiner" were interchangeable, but usually they were separate men. Their work differed in skill and cost, for joinery was finer than carpentry; both Campbell and Collyer made the distinction that "a Joiner's work requires a nicer hand, and a greater Taste in Ornament, his Business requires that he should be acquainted with Geometry and Mensuration; and, in these Respects, an accurate Accomptant".[35] These abilities were clearly desirable for any craftsman, but essential for a man to be clerk of the works and pay workmen. Although carpenters and joiners often had responsibility for the site and were generally well respected by other craftsmen and in their own communities, their style of life was usually modest. Of the 23 carpenters in London in 1695, Job Edwards of St Mary-le-Bow had a small household consisting only of his wife, daughter, maidservant and apprentice, Thomas Sharpe.[36] In the same year at Melbourne the village carpenter had three sons, a servant and one apprentice.[37] An equally small household was that of Francis Ragg, a joiner, of St Michael Bassishaw, London, who had a wife, daughter and two apprentices, but no servant, in 1696.[38]

The distinctions between joiners and carpenters were less pronounced in their premiums, however. For non-poor boys the premium most often paid in the first half of the eighteenth century was £10 (27.2 per cent in Surrey, 24.6 per cent in Sussex and 23.3 per cent in Wiltshire) but substantial numbers paid £5 (26.3 per cent in Surrey, 11.6 per cent in Wiltshire and 7.6 per cent in Sussex). In the upper range of premiums (£20 and over) there was considerable variety, with £50 the highest sum recorded. A Russian boy, bound to a Rotherhithe joiner in 1716 for only five years, however, paid £40 to his master,[39] as in other trades at least double the normal amounts paid for British apprentices. A similar emphasis on £10 and £5 premiums can be found among carpenters, but in this trade very few men received more than £20 with a boy (only three out of 322 apprenticeships in Surrey, for example) while sums below £5 were increasingly paid. Carpentry was by no means a pauperized trade, but one to which poor or charity boys might be bound if the overseers or trustees could afford the premium and a master were willing to take a less prosperous boy. Thus in Warwickshire (1700-1834) of the 158 carpenters' apprentices, 37 were paupers and 17 were charity boys with some masters indenturing children from different backgrounds with similar premiums. Thomas Stokes of Ashow bound a Leamington Priors carpenter's son in 1763 with a four-guinea premium, in 1767 a labourer's son from Hampton-in-Arden with £5 and a Warwick charity boy the same year also with £5.[40] As strength was important, slightly older boys (aged 13–15) were frequently indentured and this traditional trade remained in families for a century or more.

The range of work the village and town carpenter covered was very wide: large country houses provided steady employment for local men (Thomas Stokes of Ashow was adjacent to Stoneleigh Abbey), many of whom also made furniture and coffins for the overseers of the poor. Campbell insisted the carpenter should be literate, "know how to design his work" and "understand as much Geometry as related to Mensuration of Solids and Superficies",[41] while Collyer noted that an apprentice should learn the skill of lifting heavy weights.[42] Although a carpenter's pay was little more than that of a common labourer, the trade suffered less than other branches of building from uncertain weather, since many tasks were indoors. The skill of some carpenters can be identified through the building accounts of the larger houses on which they worked. In Warwickshire, John Maunton, the carpenter of Compton Verney chapel, working under Capability Brown in the 1770s,[43] had been an apprentice to Henry Southam at nearby Kineton in 1744 for seven years with a premium of £8.[44] In the same county, a Warwick carpenter, David Saunders, worked under the gentleman-architect, Sanderson Miller, in building the new Shire Hall in 1754, his status reflected in the premium of £15 he received in 1763 when he indentured Henry Elliott for seven years.[45]

The carpenter's was a trade in which it was fairly easy for a boy to become a master even in a small way of business, thus in Wiltshire John Wheeler was bound in 1741 to a joiner in Dorchester with an £18 premium for seven years. When he had been out of his time for five years he himself was a master and took a premium of £10.[46] Carpenters and joiners were widely and evenly distributed across towns and villages in all decades; 18 men in Southampton in the seventeenth century, for example.[47] By the early eighteenth century there were single apprentices to joiners in 13 Sussex communities as well as 38 boys bound to masters in such centres as Chichester, Arundel, Lewes and Petworth;[48] a similar pattern can be seen in other English counties. It is difficult to assess how carpenters sought apprentices for, unlike painters or plumbers, they rarely advertised in the local press. Presumably a trade that was both widespread and honourable could rely on word of mouth. Carpenters' apprentices, although numerous, were rarely runaways, in spite of opportunities to abscond, and very few complained of their masters' cruelty. The trade was traditional in most respects, presumably also in satisfactory master–boy relationships, with abuses such as overstocking not generally practised.

A far more substantial workman, often before the nineteenth century also a builder and architect, was the mason or stone carver. His building material was more costly and he needed a spacious workshop to prepare the stone.

Building accounts from innumerable country houses illustrate his role as adviser to the owner and often as clerk of works or site foreman, overseeing others, buying materials and paying the labourers; many such men began life as apprentice masons. The distribution of masons across the country was uneven, since they worked primarily one type of highly local building material, and quarrying villages like Painswick or Ketton were nurseries for craftsmen. However, in 1696 London had at least 12 masons, of whom John Thorne may be typical, with his wife, two daughters, servant girl and two apprentices in his household,[49] which was similar to that of William Taylor of Melbourne in the same year. Another craftsman in the village, however, had no apprentice, only a servant.[50] The distribution of masons in certain counties reflected to a large extent the supplies of stone, either in the area or easily transported there, so that while only 4 Surrey masters and 6 in Sussex were taking apprentices in the early eighteenth century, 20 men in Wiltshire and 23 in Warwickshire were indenturing boys to the craft. Masons also flourished when extensive new town schemes developed (as at Bath), after fires (Warwick and Northampton) or when churches and country houses were built or remodelled.

Campbell described the mason's as "an ingenious genteel Craft, and not unprofitable"[51] and a wide but quite substantial range of premiums give him status clearly above the bricklayer's. In Wiltshire, for example, sums of £2 to £8 were recorded, but with £5 and £10 most often paid. Boys bound to London masons paid more, so that Sussex and Surrey boys regularly had premiums of £10 and £20 when indentured to City masters. According to Collyer's and Campbell's exacting standards, the stonemason

> ought to be of a robust Constitution: His work requires Strength as well as Ingenuity. He must have so much Judgment as to take in a large Compass of Figures; Geometry is absolutely necessary; he must learn Designing, and to draw all the five Orders of Architecture, according to their several Proportions; his Skill in Drawing is likewise employed in taking down with his Chalk upon the Block of Stone, from the Architect's Plan, the out-lines of any Figure, Moulding or Scroll, that is to be cut. In a word, without Drawing and Figures he cannot make a Stone-Mason, unless he is to be employed only in cutting and squaring Flag-Stones.[52]

The level of skill such men attained may be seen in the local "schools" of craftsmen that developed, as at Warwick in the early eighteenth century, under the aegis of one exceptionally talented mason, Francis Smith (1672–1738) and his family. Supported by a variety of other skilled men in the building trades, they and their apprentices worked at many large houses. Thus Job Collins, son of a Warwick man, was bound in 1726 for seven years, with a £10 premium, to John Dunkley, a mason in the borough;[53] in 1743 Collins indentured a charity boy, Thomas Morris, for seven years with a three-guinea premium.[54] From the 1740s Collins carried out some important work in Warwick. Later in the century another local man, John Morris (perhaps related to Collins's apprentice) built the new Judge's Lodgings under the direction of the nationally known Henry Hakewill.[55] Morris in 1803 took a pauper child from the town, Matthew Pare, with only £2.[56] The mason who was also a contractor-surveyor could become very wealthy and hold responsible posts within the community; Francis Smith owned an estate worth £10,000, was mayor of Warwick twice and a local charity trustee.[57] A five per cent fee, with three or four major houses in progress simultaneously in some years, gave such men as Smith a substantial income. Their pupils too often developed prosperous architectural practices: thus Smith's apprentice, Nathaniel Ireson, built Stourhead House. Even if masons were not of Smith's calibre, many played a considerable part, collaborating with the owner, in building a country house. At Arbury Hall, in Sir Roger Newdigate's Gothic transformation, a Coventry mason and his son, Joseph and John Alcott, were paid sums such as £21, £15 and £44 18s in the years 1791–1801 for a wide range of work, including chimney-pieces, the east front, the tower and setting up "scagliola columns" specially brought from London.[58] John Alcott indentured eight apprentices between 1799 and 1820, of whom three were his own sons, two were charity boys and one a pauper, as well as a carpenter's and a yeoman's son.[59] Their premiums were not recorded, but one of these apprentices was still working in Coventry in 1850.[60]

Other men who might also become builders, although practising a simple craft themselves, were plumbers-glaziers and plasterers. Both were of lower status than the mason, however, although some of their highly decorative lead or plasterwork still exists to indicate their artistic skill. Although the tasks performed by a plumber and glazier might seem different, and were to become increasingly so by the later nineteenth century, they were usually performed by a single craftsman, linked by the raw material, lead, common to both trades. The plumber was responsible in a house for such lead objects as water cisterns and sinks, milk coolers and troughs in the dairy or buttery, as well as flashing on the roof, gutters and such interior piping as existed at this period. Glazier's work was of two kinds, dictated by building taste in the early years of the eighteenth century, when fashionable sash windows replaced the medieval mullion style. For sash windows, at first with only the lower half moveable, the glazier "cuts the Glass, with a small Diamond, fixed in the End of a Pencil, and fixes them with Putty, made of Whiting and Linseed Oil", and Campbell noted a decline in trade since the introduction of sashes.[61]

By the early eighteenth century London masters and their apprentices increased in numbers with the changes in architecture involving greater use of lead and glass, and in only two decades (1711–31), of 13 Surrey boys bound to plumbers, 10 went to City masters and 21 of the 34 glaziers' apprentices also were indentured in London. In the provinces, however, both trades were practised chiefly in larger towns, but also in smaller communities where an adjacent country house gave employment. Thus in Surrey there were glaziers with apprentices in Kingston, Leatherhead, Richmond, Carshalton and Reigate in the early eighteenth century,[62] while in Wiltshire (1710–60) masters were recorded in Salisbury, Devizes, Bradford, Trowbridge and Warminster, but also in Wilton, the seat of the earls of Pembroke.[63] In Sussex too plumbers' and glaziers' apprentices went to masters in Lewes, East Grinstead, Northiam and Midhurst, but also at Arlington, near such houses as Glynde and Firle.[64] Quite a prosperous trade, to judge from the premiums paid, so that of 73 apprentices bound in three counties (Wiltshire, Sussex, Surrey) in the first half of the eighteenth century, the sums most often paid were £10 (19 boys) and £5 (15), but with 35 premiums of £11 or more, up to £49 and 4 boys with only £3 each. Of the various building trades, the plumber's or glazier's seems particularly to have had women as masters, presumably because of the high health risks of the trade. In Coventry of 31 masters in the eighteenth and early nineteenth century three were women in partnerships with men and three were widows in business on their own account;[65] in Sussex too the occasional woman was recorded as a master in these trades.[66]

The trade of the plasterer could be practised as a highly skilled craft, with ornamental work at great houses, or at the lowest level of simply applying a smooth coat of plaster to ceilings or walls before decoration. Plasterers were a small trade numerically, and some English craftsmen, with their apprentices, travelled far from home to undertake work, but others had patrons close at hand. Robert Moore of Warwick, who took a single apprentice,[67] John Lane, in 1761, worked on over a dozen midland houses and was a prominent citizen in his own community. Plasterers' premiums varied considerably according to the calibre of work and clientele they had, but by the early nineteenth century highly decorative work was no longer fashionable. In spite of the health risks, Campbell considered the trade to be "very profitable" to the master and the work could generally be carried on indoors in all but frosty weather.[68] Although 11 plasterers were listed in London in 1696, none apparently with an apprentice,[69] by the early eighteenth century four of the five Surrey boys bound to plasterers went to City masters with premiums of £2 to £10.[70] However, plastering as a trade took relatively few apprentices, which precluded overstocking and maintained wages.

In his usual perceptive way, Campbell identified the essential talents of the cabinetmaker; he required

> a nice mechanic Genius, and a tolerable Degree of Strength, though not so much as the Carpenter; he must have a much lighter hand and a quicker Eye than the Joiner, as he is employed in Work much more minute and elegant.[71]

146

The cabinetmaker flourished in England in the eighteenth century and although five craftsmen were in London in 1696, none had an apprentice.[72] By the mid-eighteenth century numbers of cabinetmakers were established in the provinces. Thus in Warwickshire there were 11 masters with 19 apprentices (1751–79) and a single master in Coventry with one.[73] In 1767 there were 12 cabinetmakers listed in Birmingham, of whom 5 had apprentices.[74] In Wiltshire (1729–50) nine cabinetmakers indentured 18 apprentices, but of these, four men took 14 boys between them. James Begbie of Salisbury had the largest number bound in 1751, 1755, 1757 and 1759, while the Snow family at Salisbury and Henry Hill at Marlborough were also masters of three boys each.[75] At the same period, in both Sussex and Surrey fewer than ten boys were indentured to cabinetmaking.

The premiums paid to masters reflect the trade's prosperity and the high prices even some provincial furniture makers could command. The Wiltshire masters, who were chiefly in Salisbury, Devizes and Marlborough, frequently received a premium of £30, but the majority of sums were between £10 and £20; a similar pattern existed in Warwickshire with £20 or guineas the most commonly recorded premium.[76] The trade kept its status into the nineteenth century, and even when charity boys were apprentices they were from respectable families, frequently orphaned sons of fellow craftsmen. Thus, when James Morris Willcox of Warwick took apprentices in 1831 and 1832 one was the son of a local wheelwright and both were sponsored by borough charities.[77] Apart from local landowners, Willcox had patrons as far away as Manchester and Norfolk, giving his apprentices extensive experience; some of them reputedly built the elaborately carved summerhouse at Charlecote Park.[78]

The distinctions between the cabinetmaker and other interior designers were never clear, so that a man described when a master as a cabinetmaker, joiner or upholsterer might appear in a family's household accounts supplying other products or services. Upholsterers or upholders originally provided the fabric-covered parts of wooden furniture, but expanded to make bedding, curtains, draped toilet-tables, screens and wall hangings. They also furnished funerals, lining the church with black cloth, providing the mourners' gloves and hatbands as well as the horses' plumes. Eighteenth-century coffins were often cloth covered and studded, so that this too was their responsibility. Upholsterers provided and hung wallpaper when fabric was no longer fashionable and, from at least the mid-eighteenth century, were interior decorators advising clients on colour schemes rather than merely selling their craft skills.

Although they were established in London by the 1690s, single craftsmen worked in provincial cities (Bristol 1546–47 and Southampton 1660) at earlier periods, sometimes combining their skill with trunk making. In London in 1696 of the 11 upholders listed, the household of one man, John Bernard, may be typical; it comprised his wife, three daughters, two maids and one apprentice.[79] In the early eighteenth century the trade continued to be concentrated in London so that, of the eight Sussex boys bound to upholsterers, only two went to a Chichester master, John Short, while all the others went to London men; Surrey boys even more noticeably found apprenticeships in the City. Masters' premiums regularly reflected the exclusive nature of the trade; boys' parents were from professional and upper trade origins (gentleman, surgeon, clerk, stationer, haberdasher). Premiums were in the £10–£60 range, but with £30 and £40 most often recorded. The distinction between an upholsterer, who sold advice as well as goods, and the cabinetmaker, who made a product, can be seen when the same master indentured boys to both trades. Thus Gabriel Cruse of Devizes received only £10 when described as a cabinetmaker but £40 as an upholsterer in the 1750s.[80]

The social status of the upholsterer was markedly different from that of other craftsmen; in the accounts of Arbury Hall the upholsterer is called "Mr. Woodhouse", as was the architect, Mr. Couchman, while masons and other workers were referred to as "Prosser" or "John Alcott".[81] In the Duke of Chandos's household at Canons Park the upholsterer dined with senior members of the household staff, while the cabinetmaker ate with the servants.[82] There is evidence from family accounts that some very substantial landowners patronized small, local furniture makers in addition to the better-known London craftsmen. As well as buying furniture from London makers, the fourth Lord Leigh of Stoneleigh Abbey paid John York various sums (17 guineas, 15 guineas, £56 7s 6d) in the 1730s and 1740s for individual items of furniture.[83] York traded in Warwick as an upholder and in 1728 indentured his own son, James, for seven years with the help of a borough charity that paid the £5 premium.[84] In the 1740s Lord Leigh also paid £17 5s for furniture,[85] to Humphrey Hands, a joiner of Warwick, and master in 1729 and 1742 to two apprentices. He received 20 guineas and £12 as premiums;[86] his second apprentice, Thomas Biddle, was himself a master in 1765.[87] Even a century later upholsterers and cabinetmakers continued to overlap, and a firm such as Cookes of Warwick supplied furniture, made curtains and laid carpets for numerous substantial houses.

Like the leather industry, metal crafts had both local centres and men such as farriers and blacksmiths who were to be found everywhere. Although the terms "farrier" and "blacksmith" may appear synonymous, farriers specialized in shoeing and treating horses, while blacksmiths carried out general forged metal work as well as shoeing. Their social status was similar before about 1800, but the establishment of the London Veterinary College in 1791 began the farrier's upward move to become the veterinary surgeon of the nineteenth century. Their numbers, however, always differed, with the farrier a comparatively rare craftsman in contrast to the numerous blacksmiths. Their importance was great in a society where the horse was the only form of transport and source of power on the farm. The hypercritical Campbell noted the tasks of a farrier as making and fitting horseshoes, being "acquainted with all the Diseases incident to that useful Animal, and possessed of the Method of Cure", and having a "certain materia medica of his own adapted to the Constitution of his Patient" requiring "as much Judgment and Sagacity, though not quite so much learning" as the human surgeon.[88] Collyer was equally damning of the farrier as "generally very illiterate, and more rough and cruel in his operations than is necessary" but advised the farriery apprentice to "become thoroughly acquainted with the excellent works published"[89] during the years 1730–60, when in fact, a considerable number of instruction manuals for farriers appeared. Both farriers and blacksmiths had shops, but even in town centres they needed quite large premises for the forge and workrooms and Campbell suggested from £50 to £100 for setting up as a master.[90] In 1696 London had only three farriers listed among its inhabitants, none with an apprentice. At this period the farrier's status was fairly high so that, for example, in 1675 John Greswold, a gentleman, of Olton End, Solihull, was prepared to bind his son for seven years to a Walsall farrier, Thomas Morrisey, with a premium of £7.[91] That the premium for another midland boy, a yeoman's son, was only seven guineas by the mid-eighteenth century, may indicate the craft's reduced status.[92] By the early nineteenth century, their standing had so declined in civilian life that farriers' sons were bound to such humble trades as shoemaking and weaving; in the army, however, farriers continued to hold non-commissioned rank until modern times.

The distribution of farriers illustrates their comparative rarity in the community, so that in the first half of the eighteenth century only seven Surrey boys were apprenticed to the trade, while five boys in both Sussex and Wiltshire and four in Warwickshire were bound at the same period. Campbell had noted a premium of £5 or less in 1747,[93] but for the recorded apprenticeships in various counties sums were higher than this, for example £3–£10 in Wiltshire or two guineas to £10 in Warwickshire. The farriers' own prosperity can be judged from the trades to which their children were bound at the same period: to a mantua-maker with £9 13s 6d, a vintner (five guineas), a sailmaker (£20)[94] and, exceptionally, to a mercer in 1735 with £45.[95] To what extent farriers treated horses and other animals is difficult to assess, but among the Coventry farriers there were two who were also described as cow leeches, in 1790 and 1820, each of whom indentured his own son, and with an implication in their titles of more comprehensive animal treatment.[96] As late as 1850 William Micklewright and James Trickett were still in business as farriers in the city, where perhaps the old-style practitioner was preferred to the academically trained man.

In the early eighteenth century, the social status of the blacksmith, "one of those workmen whose assistance becomes necessary even in a rude state of society",[97] was among the upper ranks of skilled craftsmen. However, as the century progressed, while the blacksmith remained just as essential to society, his status within the community, reflected in both the premiums charged and the proportion of pauper to non-poor boys he apprenticed, seems to have deteriorated. The blacksmith's skills were as necessary to urban as to rural life, and this importance was emphasized in their very wide distribution throughout the whole country. The heavy physical work of the blacksmith's craft meant that the young, small or weak boy was of little use, and the majority of apprentices were 14 or more with a seven-year term predominant. The numbers of blacksmiths at all periods and in all areas indicate the importance of their services. The craft had seven men listed in London in 1696, typified by John Harris, whose household consisted of his wife, daughter, two "inmates" and his apprentice.[98] The social standing of blacksmiths can be judged by the same criteria that applied to other crafts, the size of premium, the social level of the parents putting sons to the trade and the numbers of pauper and charity children indentured. Blacksmiths' premiums, especially in the eighteenth century, had an enormously wide range, including the very high sum of £47 in 1720 to a Sussex master. Of this, £6 a year was for seven years' board and £5 "in money", paid by the boy's father, a Chichester carpenter.[99] The sum of £5 was most commonly recorded (28.2 per cent in Sussex, 25.7 per cent in Warwickshire, 24.8 per cent in Wiltshire and 32.8 per cent in Surrey) but £10 was paid quite often. Perhaps a typical example of an eighteenth-century blacksmith was Thomas Rose of Newbold Pacey (War.), apprenticed in 1763 to William Gilkes of Ashorne, a neighbouring village.[100] Rose was bound for seven years with a five-guinea premium. He settled in his home village as a blacksmith, married and had 11 children, the second of whom, James, he apprenticed to an unqualified young veterinary surgeon in Warwick about 1808. James Rose later took over the running of the Warwick practice when his master died, but even then his weekly wage was only 15s a week for four years and 17s for the next three years, in addition to his board and lodging. Later the family's status rose in the nineteenth century, with three qualified veterinary surgeons among them, one of whom was commissioned in the Fifth Lancers. It seems inevitable that blacksmiths suffered directly as a result of the rise of the veterinary profession for, as blacksmiths had always been secondary in status to farriers, the emergence of college-trained surgeons at the highest level of veterinary medicine proportionally diminished the status of the farriers and blacksmiths below them.

The majority of metal trades, however, were highly regionalized, their existence controlled by natural resources (fuel, minerals, water) as well as by economic development (communications, labour supply, markets). Many of these began as highly skilled, prosperous crafts, in individual workshops, but later became impoverished and overstocked as mass production developed. The gun trade, established in Birmingham in the 1690s when French imports were impossible, was always an urban, localized occupation, mechanized by the later nineteenth century. A city such as Salisbury, for example, had only two gunsmiths with apprentices (two each) in the first half of the eighteenth century, and in other English communities they were equally rare. Birmingham, however, had 97 masters with 124 apprentices at the same period.[101] There were also subsidiary branches of the gun trade in Staffordshire, mostly

gun-filers rather than smiths, who indentured pauper children to an impoverished part of the craft. With premiums chiefly in the £10–£20 range and
terms of seven years, it was a traditional trade that flourished particularly in
the eighteenth century, a period of almost constant warfare, and in Birmingham premiums noticeably increased after 1740, with masters there binding
several boys each. In the years 1710–60 at least 36 masters in Birmingham's
gun trade took apprentices, with Thomas Lane in the late 1750s indenturing
the largest number of boys (five in all). Lane's reputation in the trade was
such that with the apprentices indentured in 1753–8 the lowest premium he
accepted with one boy was ten guineas; with the other four boys, Lane was
paid £20 each. Perhaps an indication of rising premiums can be seen in the
four apprenticeships to Robert Willoughby during the years 1742–56. For the
first two of these, in 1742 and 1743, Willoughby was paid £10 with each
apprentice. A decade later, in 1753 and 1756, the premium had doubled to
£20.[102] Other masters, less famous than Thomas Lane, also charged higher
premiums as the middle of the century passed. Joseph Palmer received £10,
£15 and 15 guineas with his three apprentices in the years 1753 and 1755,
similar sums to those paid to William Richards at the same period when he
also indentured three boys, but Joshua Horton in the years 1751–7 regularly
received £20 and £21.[103] All these were masters on quite a large scale. However, comparison between masters in a smaller way of business, with only one
apprentice each, shows that rising premiums in the first half of the eighteenth
century were general. By the middle of the eighteenth century it could be
observed that

> the Trade of a Gun-Smith, in this fighting Age, is tolerably beneficial.
> The Trade is not much overstocked with Hands; and the Journeymen
> when employed earn Twelve or Fifteen Shillings a Week. A Boy may
> be bound at Fourteen, and requires no extraordinary strength or
> Education

although it had to be admitted that "It is a very ingenious Business, requires
Skill in the Tempering of Springs, a nice Hand at forming a Joint to make his
Work close, and a good Hand at the File to polish it handsomely" and there-
fore not a trade for a "dull, stupid boy".[104]

Other major metal trades were also based in the Midlands, so that nails,
chains and buckles were Black Country made, while watches were Coventry
and locks, toys, buttons and medals were Birmingham products, with needles
coming from the Worcestershire/Warwickshire border. All these industries
began as skilled crafts and were reduced to mass production, with children
and apprentices capable of doing the simple mechanized processes into which
manufacture became divided. As early as 1600 the nailing trade of Staffordshire was sinking to the status of sweated labour, with nailers petitioning the
justices to limit a master's apprentices (apart from his own children) to those

he lodged himself, which suggests an early dilution in traditional apprenticeship. By 1655 nailers were "enjoying nothing but misery and want".[105]

Nailing apprentices were generally younger than 14 when bound and premiums remained at £2 or below. The declining state of the Staffordshire trade in the eighteenth century may be seen in the premiums recorded for boys, pauper or not, who were indentured to nailers. From £6 3s in 1702 the premiums were reduced to £4 10s in 1719, £2 10s in 1733 and £1 in 1755–8. Whether nailing parishes sent children to masters within their own boundaries varied considerably, so that while Wednesbury put only a handful of its 240 children to the trade in the town in the years 1771–1809,[106] Old Swinford bound 323 of its 637 pauper children to nailing in the period 1670–1794 but kept 250 within the parish, sending the rest to 23 other communities.[107]

A contemporary Birmingham historian, William Hutton, had complacently observed that "Whatever the cut of the shoe it always demanded a fastening",[108] and bucklemaking was certainly to enjoy a boom period, of high premiums to masters, with few pauper and many prosperous apprentices indentured. However, buckles were replaced by buttons as a fashion accessory and the trade swiftly declined by the late eighteenth century. Until about 1770 Birmingham bucklemakers were able to attract premiums in a wide range from £2 to £21, but with £5 (28 per cent) and £10 (17 per cent) most often recorded. During this period there were 37 boys bound to 28 masters, so that although most men took only a single apprentice, there were five bucklemakers, such as Simeon Standley with four boys, who had apprentices training in their shop during a number of years. As the trade became less profitable the number of pauper entrants grew, bound until the age of 21 and often, as in the case of Richard Reeves's two apprentices aged 9 and 13, younger than normal.[109] Bucklemakers became more numerous in Birmingham in the 1740s and by 1767 there were 53 in the town,[110] of whom 23 have been identified as masters or apprentices. These men, however, illustrate the interchangeability of metal trades, for 14 of them practised a second craft (nine were also toymen, three buttonmakers, one a japanner and one an engraver). By 1770 their numbers had declined to 44 and by 1791 the situation was sufficiently serious for bucklemakers to petition the Prince of Wales to encourage the wearing of buckles, since more than 20,000 "in consequence of the prevalence of shoe strings and slippers were in great distress". A year later, in spite of royal support, a second petition had to be made, to the Duke and Duchess of York on this occasion, followed by an appeal to the king in 1800 to "crush the unmanly custom of wearing shoestrings".[111]

All these appeals had little effect on the trade's decline, and by 1803 the number of bucklemakers in Birmingham had fallen to 27. They were to be further considerably reduced by two external factors, the beginning of the Napoleonic Wars (for the French trade had previously been "all but unlimited") and by a military decision that buckles were dangerous to a soldier if they caught in his stirrups. Thus one of the great staple trades of Birmingham was dying out before the close of the eighteenth century, and by 1818 the town had only ten bucklemakers;[112] this number was halved by 1828.[113] Finally, in 1833, only two bucklemakers practised their trade in Birmingham, where in 1767 it had been possible to boast that "An infinite Variety are made both in White, Yellow, Bath Metal, Pinchback, and Soft White, also of Copper and Steel, and considering their Beauty and Elegance, the great Number of Hands, they go thro', etc. they are bought surprisingly Cheap, and this is the best Market for the Merchant."[114]

In contrast with Birmingham, the Staffordshire bucklemaking apprentices were almost entirely paupers, and of 29 Warwickshire children indentured there in the eighteenth century, 2 were charity boys, 6 were bound by their parents and 21 were poor. Their premiums reflect the impoverished Staffordshire trade, with three guineas the highest sum recorded and many children bound for the sake of their labour only. The large numbers of men in various branches of Staffordshire bucklemaking in the mid-eighteenth century (159 in Walsall, 25 in Wolverhampton, for example)[115] illustrate how overstocked and hence unprofitable the trade was.

Metal buttonmaking, however, was a branch of the toy trades, remained a Birmingham skill and was profitable into the mid-nineteenth century. Button manufacture rose from the decline of bucklemaking, with similar skills, labour force and raw materials required for the two products, each capable of being completely utilitarian or extremely fashionable according to cost. In 1767 there were 108 buttonmakers in Birmingham,[116] of whom only a minority indentured apprentices, although substantial child labour was implicit in buttonmaking. For example, none has been traced to John Taylor, reputedly with 500 workers in 1755. Although Lady Shelburne, a visitor to his factory in 1766 described the stamping process worked by women and children,[117] she did not indicate that they were apprentices. Premiums were extremely varied, up to £50, with £5 most commonly paid and only the master's status to explain sums such as the £30 that John Powell of Spiceal Street took with Thomas Owen in 1750.[118] It is possible to trace certain boys as they rose from apprentice to master; in 1729 and 1730 Joseph Hunt indentured two boys, John Gimblett with £2 and Edward Handson with £3, each for seven years.[119] By 1767 both boys were listed as masters, but there is also evidence that Hunt's third apprentice, John Chinn, a pauper, indentured in 1728, achieved master status by the 1750s, when he took two apprentices from his home parish.[120] By 1818 there were 78 buttonmakers in Birmingham,[121] and the number had scarcely changed a decade later,[122] for by the nineteenth century buttons had ousted buckles as one of Birmingham's chief products and buttonmaking remained a staple trade throughout the century.

Buttons, however, were only one of a range of decorative metal products in Birmingham, and many of the masters were also toymakers, engravers and medallists. Their apprentices, trained in these related skills, were flexible enough often to set up in a different trade from that specified in their indentures. The toy trade was named from one of its early staple products, the étui or metal case to hold small articles such as toothpicks or needles, earning Birmingham Burke's famous description as the "toyshop of Europe". Toys or trinkets included brooches, bracelets, watch chains, sword hilts, key-rings, purse-mounts and similar items made from steel; by 1767 there were 57 toymakers listed in the town.[123] These men included the small master (Samuel Bellamy with the single apprentice), the medium-sized enterprise of William Boden, with six apprentices, and the huge enterprise that Matthew Boulton had established at Soho.

In spite of assertions that industry expanded in Birmingham because of the lack of guild control over apprenticeship, the toy trades show all the traditional forms of apprenticeship, with the seven-year term and status-related premiums apparent. Most of the work was done in small family shops; many of these masters took several apprentices each, although most had only two. A trade with few paupers, its expansion in the 1750s was reflected in more apprenticeships and higher premiums, and in 1759 the town exported £500,000 worth of toys.[124] From a handful of boys early in the eighteenth century, by 1750–59 a total of 94 apprenticeships were recorded, although after 1770 numbers of entrants noticeably declined.

The overlapping of skills in the light metal trades was widely practised so that, for example, Edmund Birch, a toymaker, was also a steel-button and bucklemaker, Samuel Birch "slitteth and sells Iorn and rolled Steel", Thomas Clare was an engraver and die sinker, while John Moody was also a "Fillegree Worker".[125] This variety in their skills was reflected in the trades that boys, apprentices to toymen in 1767, later themselves practised as masters. George Dalloway had been bound to a brass founder, Thomas Hunt, during the years 1723–9, became a master by 1752, when he indentured, as a toyman, the young John Vashon for six years with a 100-guinea premium. Vashon was a master by 1767, but was then described as a bucklemaker. Obviously, such training gave apprentices basic skills that could be used in many branches of metal working. An apprentice taken by toymaker Thomas Lakin in 1750, William Parkes was a master by 1767, in Newhall Walk, but as a bucklemaker, not a toyman. Another master, John Lane, was both plater and toyman in 1751 when he apprenticed John Reynolds, who later himself set up as a master plater, a trade also followed by one of John Moody's boys. Further variety was provided by the apprenticeship of George Darby, bound to a toyman, Edward Riddell, in 1760, but by 1767 a planemaker in Swan Alley; by that of John Fox, apprenticed to a toymaker, Daniel Palmer, in 1741, but by 1767 a jeweller in Phillip Street, with three boys as his apprentices, and finally by that of Richard Parkes, bound to a watch-chain-maker, but a toyman himself in 1767. Several masters also seem to have taken in boys to these related trades; for example, in 1756 Benjamin Short was a master jeweller, with a £14 premium for the apprentice he indentured, and two years later, with a 12-guinea premium, was described as a toyman.

It is possible to gain an impression of the appearance of a toyman's apprentice if the boy for any reason absconded from the service of his master, who then advertised for his return in the local press. Such a runaway was James Glover, who was born at Eccleshall (Staffs.) and bound to Andrew Adams, a Digbeth toymaker. Glover was described as aged 19 and slender; he was well dressed with "blue grey breeches, blue harateen waistcoat, russett woollen and jersey coat all with metal buttons, a pair of black and white woollen jersey stockings, white wig and a middling good Hat crack'd at the corners". Another absconder was Thomas Hammond, bound in 1740 for seven years to Daniel Palmer, a toyman-jeweller, with a premium of £15. Palmer had in all three boys bound to him, for he subsequently indentured two boys after Hammond, in 1741 and 1742. Hammond was within four months of completing his term when he ran away, at the age of 20. Palmer described him as "strong set" with "thick legs and brown complexion". Hammond was tall – 5 feet 10 inches – and wore a "blue coat, with white metal buttons, a black waistcoat and brown hob wig".

An interesting example of the range of skills that a toyman's apprentice might have can be seen when John Moody advertised for the return of his runaway apprentice, James Knott, in 1750. The boy was 5 feet 7 inches tall, of "slenderish form" and appears to have taken two outfits of clothes with him, one of which he wore, comprising "a light grey coat, black shag waistcoat and breeches, a french grey coat, green frize waistcoat, scarlet breeches and Fustian breeches". He was described as "capable of working at Painting, Engraving and Plating of Spurs, and writes a very good Hand".[126] Another of Moody's apprentices, who did not run away and may also have had these abilities, was John Farmer, indentured during the period 1743–50 and later a master himself in 1753–4; however, by 1767 he was listed as a plater in *Sketchley's directory*, and must have had various skills to teach his apprentices. Although Matthew Boulton (1728–1809) was perhaps the most famous of Birmingham's manufacturers, information about his apprentices is erratically recorded. He had a known preference for "plain Country lads" as apprentices, but it has been said that he "set his face" against premium apprenticeship.[127] His father certainly indentured boys, including a relation, John Dyott, with £30 in 1751,[128] and Matthew Boulton claimed to have built and furnished a house for his apprentices.[129]

An example of the social standing of boys bound to toymen can be seen in the apprenticing of Sampson Lloyd to the toyman, John Green. Sampson Lloyd belonged to the wealthy and influential Quaker family, but obviously apprenticeship to the toy trade was not thought unsuitable.[130] One boy travelled from Shropshire to Birmingham and the trade also took in boys from Northfield (Worcs.) and Humber (Herefs.), as well as from Studley and Blackdown in Warwickshire. Premiums ranged up to 100 guineas, but £10,

£5 and £20 were most often recorded. However, a boy such as John Gimblett, with only a £2 premium when he was himself an apprentice button-maker, became a master toymaker and received sums of £20, £21, £30 and £35 with his apprentices in the 1750s.[131]

Another distinctively midland trade was japanning, begun in Pontypool (Mon.) and spreading to Staffordshire and Birmingham in the early eighteenth century. While japanning was carried out on tinplate in small, family shops, the resulting handmade goods were expensive. Once papier mâché was introduced as a heat-resistant material that could be lacquered, the whole process became cheap, mechanical and profitable. The Birmingham innovator of papier-mâché was John Baskerville, subsequently more famous for his printing ventures. He set up business at 22 Moor Street in 1740 and, five years later, made his home at Easy Hill, a fine house with eight acres of land beyond the edge of the town, where he "continued the business of a japanner for life".[132] He chiefly manufactured tea-tables, waiters (salvers) and trays[133] and described himself when apprenticing boys to the trade as "flower painter" as often as "japanner". From 1757 he was actively engaged in printing, but it is evident from the number of apprentices he indentured in the next decade that his japanning work continued to flourish, and in all Baskerville bound seven boys (the most of any japanner) during the years 1754-65.

The whole process was improved by a patented invention of Henry Clay, who has always been described as a pupil or apprentice of Baskerville. In fact he began his career bound to John Allport, a painter, with a £10 premium on 3 May 1753, indentured for six years,[134] the third of four apprentices. Perhaps Clay worked for Baskerville in the early 1760s, but by 1767 he was in partnership as a japanner with John Gibbons,[135] also described as a Baskerville employee. Clay made a fortune, with a London home and a workforce of 300. The cost of setting up as a master, in terms of space and labour, was considerable and premiums reflected the trade's prosperity and decline. Thus in the 1750s and 1760s Baskerville received a total of seven premiums of 10, 20 and 25 guineas, with one exception of only £5 5s in 1756. By the later eighteenth century the trade's recession was indicated by increasing numbers of poor boys indentured and lower premiums. For example, in 1763 John Willington was apprenticed to Samuel Troughton with a £40 premium; out of his time in 1770 he indentured a Warwick charity boy in 1792 with only £7,[136] a binding that would have been most unlikely in the trade's successful decades under Clay and Baskerville.

The other midland industry divided between Birmingham and Staffordshire was lockmaking, but it was particularly concentrated in Walsall, Willenhall and Wolverhampton. Locksmiths can be identified in Staffordshire in 1603 and 1660; with 84 hearths in Wolverhampton and 97 in Willenhall, it was one of the area's staple industries.[137] Although highly-skilled craftsmen such as John Wilkes and Thomas Blockley made expensive and beautiful products,[138] most lockmaking was coarse metal work, the masters able to attract only low premiums (below £3) and parish apprentices. Certainly highly skilled men could command more than this, so that Isaac Moore of Birmingham in 1750 received £20 with John Lovelock and nine years later Philip Chapman was paid twice this sum with a boy.[139]

It has been suggested that locksmiths' apprentices came mainly from their own families[140] and some evidence from indentures supports this. Locksmiths had few boys each, although rarely a master such as Abraham Whitwell of Willenhall would bind more; he had five boys in the years 1790–1819. However, certain large parishes, such as Tamworth and Coventry, were the source of pauper children sent to Staffordshire, of whom there is no evidence that they ever became masters themselves.[141] The working conditions of locksmiths' apprentices depicted by Disraeli and Dickens[142] never caused the general public unease of Kingsley's Tom in *The water-babies*, and by 1861 the number of apprentices in one area (Willenhall and Wednesfield) had reduced to 255 from 376 in 1851 and 613 a decade earlier, although St Monday continued to influence their lives. Locksmiths' apprentices were said to be generally young children,[143] but of 36 Warwickshire boys bound to Staffordshire masters in the mid-eighteenth century a quarter were aged 13 to 14 and none younger than 9.[144] By 1841 they were reported as coming chiefly from the Union workhouses of Willenhall and Wednesfield and the masters' cruel treatment in small shops was "unrestrained by public opinion [in] their methods of work and their treatment of the children".[145]

Although lockmaking was so distinctively a midland trade, locksmiths certainly worked and took apprentices in other areas, although usually only the single craftsman in a community, providing an essential service. How quickly a master might be established is illustrated by the career of Thomas Farre, a yeoman's son, bound to John Hedger, a Southampton locksmith, in 1630 for seven years. In 1639, two years out of his time, Farre himself took John Chidley, a Jersey cutler's son, as an apprentice.[146] Locksmiths are not always easy to identify in such records as poll or marriage tax returns, or even apprenticeship material, so that, for example, none is listed for London in 1696 or Wiltshire (1710–60), but are presumably among the many "smiths" recorded. By the early eighteenth century, however, London locksmiths were binding boys with £20 premiums and craftsmen were working in many provincial towns.

Watch- and clock-making showed similar patterns of development, with very few highly skilled men scattered thinly across pre-industrial England but a mass-production, concentrated industry in few areas by the early nineteenth century. Although the makers of watches and clocks might seem very similar, their distribution and numbers before the Industrial Revolution showed a clear distinction. Before the late eighteenth century clockmakers were more numerous than watchmakers, when public timepieces were usual (on church spires or market halls, for example) but individual watches were a rare luxury. Thus in Birmingham in 1767 there were only 4 watchmakers to 6 clockmakers,[147] or 24 clockmakers in Sussex compared with 8 watchmakers (1710–60).[148]

Only infrequently did villages support clockmakers' skills, but larger communities had several men who often travelled considerable distances to mend and adjust existing clocks, as well as making them in their own workshops.[149] Although by the early eighteenth century most provincial centres had clockmakers at work, numbers of apprentices went to London masters. The City had had craftsmen in the late seventeenth century, two in the ward of Farringdon Without, for example,[150] but none apparently with apprentices. However, by the early decades of the eighteenth century numbers of apprenticeships were recorded to City masters, including 24 Surrey boys and 3 from Sussex. At the same period provincial masters also indentured boys quite extensively; some, like William Monk of Berwick St John (Wilts.) took several apprentices; he bound at least four boys (1719–45) with £9 to £20 premiums.[151] Sussex particularly had a thriving clockmaking trade, with several masters in Lewes, Battle and Chichester and single craftsmen in eight other communities. Although the range of their premiums was wide (£1–£30 in Sussex, £1–£40 in Surrey, £9–£20 in Wiltshire, £2–£20 in Warwickshire) £10 and £20 were most often recorded, reflecting the status of the apprentices' parents, who included yeomen and large traders. The patriotic Campbell considered English workmanship very fine, although "but of modern Invention and of late improved . . . to the highest Perfection; we beat all Europe in Clocks and Watches of all sorts". He considered physical strength unnecessary, but a "smattering of Mechanics and Mathematics" was essential.[152]

While clockmaking remained an individual, quality and quite widespread craft, watchmaking changed entirely between the eighteenth and nineteenth centuries to a mass-produced, low-profit and overstocked trade, its skills diluted by massive numbers of apprentices into the deplored "Coventry system" of the early Victorian period. In the late seventeenth century the typical London watchmaker had a small household of a wife, children and an apprentice, but usually a maidservant or two.[153] By the early eighteenth century these London craftsmen, with a distinct proportion of foreign masters (names such as LeBlond, Brebent and Gautier) were able to attract premiums of up to 20 guineas from boys with distant homes in Cirencester or Northampton.[154] Sussex masters at the same period took even higher sums, from £8 to £30, as did men in Stratford-upon-Avon, Birmingham and Warwick. The watchmaker's prosperity until about 1760 contrasted sharply with his plight by the early nineteenth century, when cheap watches were produced in large numbers in centres such as Coventry.

Although there had been watchmakers in Coventry in the late seventeenth century, two firms were established there by 1750 and by 1781, when the city's apprenticeship registers began, there was a regular flow of boys to the trade. Campbell emphasized that the watchmaker usually did not himself personally make the watch, but "employs the different Tradesmen among whom the Art is divided, and puts the several Pieces of the Movement together, and adjusts and finishes it".[155] The craft had so expanded that, by 1817, it was possible to enumerate some 102 specialist branches of the trade when distressed Coventry watchmakers pleaded their case before a parliamentary committee.[156]

By 1815 William Field could observe that Coventry's "principal manufactures are ribbons, and watches . . . of the latter, a newly established trade, more, it is supposed are now made here than in the metropolis",[157] and in the next decade *Pigot's directory* claimed that in "the last thirty years the making of watches has brought great reputation to this city".[158] Numerically watchmaking employed a large proportion of highly skilled men. During the years 1781–1824, a total of 902 boys were indentured to watchmaking, in addition to 368 bound to other branches of the trade. These children were apprenticed to 105 masters in Coventry, either individuals, partnerships or firms. Ages were hardly ever specified, but the trade was traditional in the seven-year term for which boys were indentured; Campbell noted that a boy "may be bound about fourteen, or sooner if he is tolerably acute"[159] and four of the five witnesses in 1817 had themselves served a "regular" seven-year term. Premiums were recorded for none of the boys, but social origins were generally specified or implied.

There is considerable contemporary evidence to suggest that watchmakers were the skilled, respected craftsmen of the community, and their control of entry into the trade almost excluded the parish apprentice. It is noticeable in watchmaking how very few poor boys were indentured during the period 1781–1824. Only two paupers were bound to masters employing a single apprentice, one boy to a master in the next group (2 to 5 apprentices), six boys to men with 6 to 10 children, three paupers to masters in the next group (11 to 20 apprentices), only one to a master with between 21 and 30 boys and two to masters with over 30 apprentices. It is clear that the two largest firms (Bradshaw and Ryley, Vale and Howlett) employed no pauper male labour at all during this period.

Of the 1,266 apprentices to the various branches of watchmaking, a total of 162 boys (12.8 per cent) were indentured by the city's various charities, founded for this purpose by such philanthropists as Samuel Collins (established in 1717), Thomas Crow (1709), Thomas Jesson (1636), Joseph Symcox (1705) and Katharine Bailey (n.d.).[160] All the charity-sponsored boys were city children and a number were orphans. There were also 25 boys with widowed mothers in Coventry, 6 with mothers in the city who were not widows, and 3 boys whose mothers were named, but with no place of residence specified.

The social origins of watchmaking apprentices were, for such a numerically large group, relatively narrow, with no boys from the professional class (except one orphan). The boys' parents represented most of the city's occupations, with weavers' sons the largest group (28 per cent) followed by watchmakers' and leatherworkers' sons. The preponderance of weavers' sons clearly supports the view that watchmaking was considered a prosperous, expanding trade, with far better prospects of employment and wages than a weaver could expect for his son in his own occupation. Another group of boys, 22 in all, were the sons of deceased Coventrians, and a further 10 were orphans from beyond the city. It is noticeable that girls were excluded from watchmaking and an American visitor to Coventry in the mid-nineteenth century observed that, of the two thousand employed in the trade, less than a hundred were women or girls, in contrast to the ribbon industry.[161] The watchmakers' control of entry into their trade can be seen in the numbers of watchmakers' own sons bound to their fathers, for in addition to the 49 boys bound to watchmakers to whom they were not apparently related, there were a further 32 youths apprenticed to their own fathers, all smaller masters.

The two firms with the largest numbers of apprentices were Vale and Howlett, with 170 boys, and Bradshaw and Ryley with 79. Both firms were active in the 1780s, but whereas Vale's continued into the present century, Bradshaw's indentured no more children after 1815. In spite of the fact that watchmaking was a relatively modern craft in Coventry, watchmakers fairly quickly rose to importance and civic office within the community. By the mid-eighteenth century Samuel Vale had been four times mayor of the city; in 1743 he had been apprenticed for seven years to William Vale, a Coleshill clockmaker, and presumably a relative. His kinship to his master would account for the low premium of £3, in contrast to the 16½ guineas or £20 his fellow apprentices paid. By the early nineteenth century there were watchmakers in Coventry serving as constables, chamberlains, wardens and bailiffs. However, they were at their most successful later in the century, when large new building developments in Spon End and Chapel Fields were tangible evidence of the watchmakers' earnings and domestic comfort.

The watchmakers of Coventry suffered two periods of depression when their prosperity was seriously threatened. The first recession, in 1797, was as a result of government intervention, when Pitt imposed a tax on the wearing and use of watches and clocks, with 2s 6d levied on a silver or metal watch, 10s on a gold one and 5s on every clock.[162] Local opposition predictably was considerable, and the act was repealed a year later, but the years 1797–8 were marked by a noticeable fall in the numbers of boys indentured to watchmaking in the city, with a very considerable recovery by 1800. In 1798 the number of boys apprenticed to the craft fell to five, the smallest entry during the whole decade. Recovery was rapid, however, and by 1800 there were 30 boys apprenticed, the highest annual number then recorded. For the next two decades, watchmaking in Coventry prospered, and 1807 saw the largest number of boys bound to the craft (54) but by 1817 a serious situation had developed, according to contemporary opinion, entirely owing to the factory apprentice system, which produced more workmen than could be maintained in the trade, and also depreciated the value of labour, and in this year only 8 boys were apprenticed to watchmakers.

An indication of the watchmakers' own social values can be seen in their evidence to a parliamentary select committee, who were told that "the fraternity thought parish relief dishonourable, since the profession of a watch-maker had always been deemed that of a gentleman, and the higher order of Mechanics".[163] The fraternity were also unwilling to lose their votes for a year if poor relief were sought, for disenfranchisement was the penalty of receiving parish aid. The watchmaker's advantages over the weaver (greater skill pre-venting labour influx, fashions being less variable, wifely labour being unnec-essary) were emphasized in his superior living accommodation, but this superiority was achieved only after the trade had recovered from the 1817 recession. The decline of 1817 was attributed to various causes; the most important, in the petitioners' estimation, was the over-indenturing of appren-tices, with manufacturers offering bounties to induce boys to become appren-ticed.[164] It was claimed in 1817 that 12 watch manufacturers had between 150 and 160 boys indentured to them, with two firms having from 25 to 30 boys at one time. These assessments were, however, conservative, for 1810 saw almost the highest ever number of boys (52) beginning their apprentice-ships, completed by 1817, and at this date there were in all 230 boys serving their time to a total of 16 watchmakers or firms in the city. Thus, although in the period prior to the 1817 crisis a number of firms ceased to take in any boys at all (only two in 1811, three in 1813 and three more in 1816), the cumula-tive effect of the period before 1817 was already unavoidable. The reduction of apprentice entries prior to 1817 was echoed in the city's total watch pro-duction, which in 1817 fell to 14,000 watches in a year compared with 20,000 in previous, more prosperous times.[165]

There were in all five major witnesses who gave evidence on the state of Coventry's watch trade in 1817 to the parliamentary select committee; all were watchmakers who had worked at their trade in Coventry for consider-able periods. James Keene, with four boys indentured in the years 1807–15, had been in the trade since 1793; William Mayo, with three apprentices, had been born in Coventry and had worked as a watchmaker there since 1800, while Thomas Green had been engaged in the trade for nine or ten years. Of the final two witnesses, John Powell, a Coventry watchmaker since 1793, had recently moved to London to secure work, and Mark Noble Piercy had since 1787 been a manufacturer on his own account, but by 1817 described himself as "a workman". All five men were unanimous in stressing the declining state of the city's watch trade, and cited 1810–11 as the years when the decline began.

There was general agreement among the five Coventry witnesses about the cause of the distressed state of the watchmaking trade. Piercy recalled the ori-gins of watch factories in the city and the early beginnings of the "Coventry system of apprentices" that had been a failure in Birmingham when it began there about 1777, but that was successfully established in Coventry. He said there were 12 or 14 factories in the city, each with between 12 and 40 outdoor apprentices; he condemned the results of this system, because a "multitude of apprentices are brought into the trade, far beyond the probability of employment when they become journeymen, either in Coventry or elsewhere in the country". When apprentices finished their terms, their places were immediately filled by other boys as a source of cheap labour. A further cause of dissatisfaction in Coventry was the low standard to which boys were trained. James Keene, 24 years a watchmaker, expressed his disapproval of those manufacturers who were not "themselves brought up to the business" and employed ill-qualified men to teach their apprentices who, as a result, produced work of a low standard. Keene firmly stated that "the apprentice system, nothing else" was the cause of Coventry's distressed watch trade in 1817. He added that the low standard of work resulted from there being too many boys in one shop and the 102 separate branches that were taught, so that "a movement or spring maker is not able to work at any other branch of the business".

Of the five Coventry witnesses who gave evidence to the 1817 committee, four had themselves served apprenticeships within the city, of the traditional type rather than in a watch factory. Mayo, Green, Piercy and Powell had all been Coventry apprentices, and Mayo presented his own apprenticeship indenture to the committee to illustrate the method used in the city. Mayo said that he himself had one apprentice at that date and considered him "both for protection and teaching his art" exactly as his own son. He felt that indoor apprentices made the best workmen, with better moral characters, than those boys who lived at home with their parents and worked in the factories, for this latter group were under very little restraint, became corrupted and, when they had finished their day's work, thought they could do as they pleased. Two or three boys were as many as one master could properly instruct at the same time, and a change from outdoor to indoor apprenticeship would "restore the whole of the character of the Coventry watch trade". Another witness, Piercy, stressed that the factory system of "debauchery and depravity" was harmful, for where "large establishments of apprentices are kept, it may be truly denominated the asylum of vice and profligacy; for where youth are horded together in such large numbers, they contaminate the morals of each other, the master paying little or no regard to them".

The relationship between the workers' distress and the manufacturers' profits was mentioned by Thomas Green, who described how a master might have 30 boys apprenticed, each earning him from 18s to £1 4s a week, which enabled him to under-sell London and other manufacturers, for the boys were paid 4s 3d each a week as wages. The boys were harshly treated and their earnings were withheld when they were ill. At this period, the reputation of Coventry watches was generally poor, although Mayo emphasized that the city had good workmen, "fit to work at London or Liverpool", but that employers were prejudiced against taking on workmen trained in the city.[166] It has been claimed that watchmakers in Coventry formed a "working-class élite",[167] but their earnings, although higher than some other craftsmen's, were similar to the carpenter's or the mason's.[168] However, their steady employment, apart from the crises of 1797 and 1817, ensured an overall improvement in their living standards until, in a later prosperous period (1830–60) watchmakers were keeping their children at school until the age of 14.[169]

The craft of the watch-finisher was considered by the workmen themselves to be the most difficult branch of the trade, for he was responsible for putting the various parts of the watch together and setting it in motion.[170] Of the 1,266 boys apprenticed to the watch trade in Coventry in the period 1781–1824 only 25 were bound to finishers, but in 1817 all the witnesses spoke of general distress in the trade, regardless of the branch to which a boy was apprenticed.

After the harsh experiences of 1817, the watch trade in Coventry slowly recovered, so that by 1821 a watch was presented to Queen Caroline that had been made completely in the city by the firm of Mayo and Clark. It was described as a "favourable specimen of the perfection which the art of watch-making has attained in that city".[171] As well as illustrating the city's craftsmanship, such a gift was also an indication of the watchmakers' own radical views.

One response of Coventry watchmakers to the increased numbers of apprentices was by pamphlet protest; in 1817 an anonymous craftsman expressed to his "friends and Brother Artisans" his views on the "Evils . . . and Remedies" of half-pay apprenticeships. His sense of despairing resentment was similar to the feelings of other established, formerly honourable, craftsmen, such as the stockingers, whose whole livelihood and status were undermined by new work practices or machinery they could not control. The Coventry pamphleteer recalled how, seven or eight years ago, when parents

> put their children to the Watch Trade, they considered that by so doing they had given them the pledge of future comfort and respectability; but how miserably have they in this respect been disappointed, even in those who on the termination of their servitude have gained employ.[172]

Two years later one of Coventry's substantial watchmakers, John Powell, published a "Letter" to Edward Ellice MP, condemning at length but more dispassionately the evils of "large establishments" of apprentices, which produced "unfair competition, demoralisation of character, parish burthens, insufficient workmen, injured credit, and decay of trade".[173] The trade survived in the city throughout the nineteenth century in spite of all difficulties. Rotherhams still make specialist timepieces and industrial mechanisms.

Needlemaking has for so long been identified with Redditch (Worcs.) that its earlier origins in Long Crendon (Bucks.) and southwest Warwickshire are usually overlooked. Before 1700 needles were hand produced, often by European workmen, and served a variety of trades other than the domestic customer (sailmakers, bookbinders, leatherworkers, clothes trades). Production on the Worcestershire/Warwickshire border must have been in part due to the fast-flowing rivers of the area, the Avon and the Alne. A number of corn mills early in the eighteenth century were converted to needlemaking (Washford mill in 1730, for example) and as early as 1700 Studley was described as the "chief seat of the manufacture" of needles, with Birmingham a convenient source of wire as raw material. A number of charity children were bound to needlemaking, particularly girls, with £4 or £6 premiums, but parish officials with large numbers of paupers to bind also favoured needlemaking. Most of these children remained within their own parish or went to a neighbouring community, many indentured in small family groups. The needle trade had an exceptional number of apprenticeships in which children were paid, with 2s 6d or 3s increasing to 6s a week by the end of the term.[174]

As in many other industries at this period, for example, in cotton manufacture, there seem to have been close family relationships between the needle masters of the Alcester area so that Charles Rawlings of Alcester was the maternal uncle of Michael Morrall of Studley in 1820.[175] As with cotton masters, religion was a strong linking bond, for the majority of needlemakers were Roman Catholics (the Rawlings, Whissell, Hewitt, Alcock and Chatterley families) and the area had a strong recusant tradition. The adult careers of most parish apprentices have not been recorded, but of the 28 Alcester boys bound to needlemaking, at least two carried on their trade in the area into the mid-nineteenth century, for by 1850 one boy, Thomas Rimmer, apprenticed to George Pardoe of Alcester, was working in the town as a needle manufacturer in his own right, while another, William Boyce, apprenticed to James Whissell in 1808, was working at Sambourne in the same trade.[176]

Undoubtedly the highest-status metal craftsmen were those who worked in the most precious raw materials and used artistic skills to do so, the gold- and silver-smiths. One of the oldest London livery companies, the Goldsmiths held high civic office, endowed a wide variety of charities and, with high apprenticeship premiums and setting-up costs, remained "the most genteel of any in the Mechanic Way", consistently attracting boys from prosperous homes.[177] Goldsmiths traded chiefly in London, but many large provincial centres also had representative craftsmen, even though their work was assayed elsewhere (12 goldsmiths from Birmingham entered their marks at the London Assay office in 1773, for example).[178] In late-seventeenth-century London there were at least 38 goldsmiths listed, some of whom with apprentices were very substantial men indeed. Thus Sir John Johnson's one apprentice in 1693 was in a household consisting of Lady Johnson, three children, a journeyman, two lodgers, two servants and a coachman, while James Hallett, with two apprentices, had three servants and a footman.[179] A boy's progress to master is illustrated in the career of John Alcock from Southwark, bound in 1717 to Daniel Skinner, a City goldsmith, with £20. Out of his time by 1724 Alcock was himself a master nine years later to a Chichester boy, Thomas Peerman, with whom £42 was paid.[180] The dominance of the London trade was reflected in the proportion of provincial boys bound to City masters; thus all 22 Surrey boys (1711–31) and eight of the ten Sussex boys (1710–60) were sent to London goldsmiths. Exceptions were the handful of boys apprenticed to masters in Canterbury, Lewes, Salisbury and Devizes, for example. Goldsmiths' premiums were generally in the £20–£50 range suggested by Campbell,[181] with £20 most often recorded, but also included a minority that were considerably higher. For instance, three Surrey boys bound (1717–31) had premiums of £94, £120 and £200,[182] one Wiltshire master took £73 10s in 1759[183] and premiums for two Sussex gentlemen's sons were £100 each in the early eighteenth century.[184]

Although many goldsmiths were also silversmiths, there were other craftsmen who worked exclusively in silver, especially in London, where a distinct community of 25 silversmiths can be identified in the Gutter Lane area in 1698, of whom 12 had apprentices (three with two each).[185] Their status as lower than the goldsmith's is reflected in the few household servants, the scarcity of journeymen and more lodgers in divided dwellings. Although premiums were less than goldsmiths took, £10 was commonly recorded and some silversmiths were prosperous enough to afford higher sums than this to indenture their own sons. Thus a Chichester silversmith's son was apprenticed to a London apothecary in 1743 with £20,[186] while a Guildford craftsman bound his sons to a London merchant tailor with £45 and to a City draper with £50 in the early eighteenth century.[187] The relative scarcity of recorded apprenticeships to provincial silversmiths in the eighteenth century does not equate with the numbers of men practising the craft in the early nineteenth; for example, there were 26 silversmiths in Birmingham by 1828 but little evidence of their having been indentured.[188]

At the other end of the scale for apprentices in status, adult earning prospects and skills were children indentured to farm work. These apprentices formed a substantial minority of bindings in all counties, even those with large manufacturing enterprises, at all periods. Almost entirely pauper children, their overseers were prepared to pay small premiums to farmers in or beyond the parish as a considerable saving on the poor rate. The usual weekly maintenance for a poor child, either at home or fostered, was 1s 6d a week, plus clothes and shoes. Thus, as a poor child cost at least £3 18s a year to support, a single premium of even £5 plus clothes was an obvious economy. One of the abuses of industrial apprenticeship most often condemned was the indenturing of children aged 11 or younger far from home for terms of ten years or more. However, in agriculture such arrangements were common, for even a very young child on a farm could usefully be employed in such simple tasks as bean-setting, stone-picking or crow-scaring, requiring minimal supervision. The majority of agriculture apprentices, whether in an arable or pasture area, were these younger children. In 1735 one Yorkshire farmer noted in his diary that "James Lindley, aged 7 years, came to our house, as parish apprentice",[189] and such children appear in overseers' accounts from all English counties, especially those with few or distant industries. Thus remote Herefordshire parishes (Kingsland, Felton, Ocle Pychard and Aymestrey) bound all their apprentices to local farmers in the early nineteenth century.

In two equally rural areas of Suffolk a similar pattern can be seen, with 23 of the 46 children bound to farmers in the years 1770–83 but 90 out of 114 to agriculture by 1821–6 with changing labour demands on the land as well as increased pressure on the poor rate.[190] Even in a county as industrialized as Warwickshire, 594 children were apprenticed to farming (464 boys and 130 girls) during the later eighteenth and early nineteenth century, with at least 81 parishes participating. The pattern of apprenticeship was irregular, however, for certain large rural parishes (such as Wootton Wawen and Tanworth-in-Arden) indentured the majority of their children to ratepaying farmers, some of whom occasionally paid a £10 fine rather than accept an unsuitable pauper.[191] From the almost entirely industrialized town of Wednesbury there were only 13 apprentices to agriculture (5.4 per cent) in the period 1771–1809,[192] while only four of Old Swinford's 636 poor apprentices went to agriculture in the eighteenth century.[193]

Generally charity trustees did not bind their children to farming, preferring the traditional crafts of leather or building, so that one Derbyshire charity, with 258 children bound in the years 1685 to 1753, apprenticed none to agriculture.[194] Farming apprentices are also predictably missing from city apprenticeship records so that, although Portsmouth had 137 paupers to bind (1676–1776), they went chiefly to maritime occupations,[195] just as Coventry poor children entered textiles, rather than the surrounding countryside. Occasionally both boys and girls of non-poor parentage were bound to yeomen and husbandmen with various premiums, usually below £10. Thus, although Sussex apprentices generally went to crafts and trades both in the county and beyond, six (including two girls) were indentured to local yeomen and a further eight (three of whom were girls) to husbandmen, with appropriately lower premiums of £2 to £7. A similar pattern can be seen in Wiltshire, also a county of both agriculture and industry, with six apprentices (three girls) to yeomen and four (one girl) to husbandmen in the early eighteenth century. Although a few of the boys went to kinsmen, none of the girls did. They presumably worked in the dairy or buttery to learn the skills a future farmer's wife would need rather than in the fields or byres as a pauper apprentice.

In a quite separate category were those male apprentices indentured to yeomen with substantial premiums, equivalent to a saddler's or cabinet-maker's; for example, Richard Medhurst, bound in 1720 to Edward Turner of Hatfield (Herts.) had £20 as his premium[196] while John Monsley's premium for five years' apprenticeship to John Newcomb of Brinklow (War.) in 1752 was £50.[197] Such boys were presumably more like the modern farm pupil than apprentice, to be taught not labouring skills but management.

By the late nineteenth century there was considerable criticism of child labour on the farm, especially the discredited gang system. At an earlier period, however, farm apprentices may have been better off than children in industry, with less strict hours, some pleasant outdoor jobs and far more individual freedom. Even poverty was less acute in the country than the town, with opportunities for food- and fuel-gathering, legally or otherwise, to supplement the family income. Few factory apprentices could pick hedgerow crops on their way to work, or eat their dinner in the sunshine, or enjoy being with animals, and farm children worked only daylight hours, unlike most urban apprentices. At all periods the small farmer, as John Clare reminds us, worked his own family labour very hard[198] and clearly parish apprentices would be no better treated. However, once a child was out of his term, farm work was more regularly available than many other occupations for which only few adults were required, cotton spinning and watchmaking, for example. A farm worker or dairywoman could always find employment and may have given the pauper child better future prospects than many other apprenticeships did.

CHAPTER 8

The textile industries

The death of the factory girl

Who's stretch'd on that pallet
With lips ashy white,
And eyes that send forth
A wild, unearthly light?

It's the Child of the Factory
Destroy'd by its breath;
In it there's pollution,
In its precincts there's Death.

The Casement is open,
And on the chill blast,
That ill-omen'd sound
The Bell's heard at last.

She hears not its tones,
It tolls her death knell,
She hears holier strains
Than the Factory Bell.

CCRO, Miscellaneous cuttings (*c.*1830)

Of all the production industries that relied heavily on child labour, much of it apprenticed, textiles of every kind predominated. Although weavers worked in all counties at all periods, specific types of textile production were highly regionalized, depending initially on such factors as water-power, raw materials or a long-established craft skill, but by the early nineteenth century a supply of apprenticed labour was also critical. Weavers, however, were the first of such workers, irrespective of which fabric they produced. Most weavers worked at home, normally with family help, and their products ranged widely, from damask, lawn, orris, taffeta and quality broadcloth to fustian, ticking and provincial narrow goods. That the numbers of apprentices entering weaving depended on economic slump or boom can be seen, from an early date, where city records survive; for example, at Worcester the decade after 1610 was stable and prosperous, while in the 1620s and 1630s apprenticeships there declined as the weaving trade faltered.[1] Although weavers were always numerically a substantial group, their prosperity was by no means uniform, even in the decades before mechanization and fashion demands threatened their livelihood. Thus Worcester weavers in the sixteenth century left goods worth between £10 and £30 in their inventories, men with one or two looms each.[2] At the same period (1642) a south Warwickshire weaver, William Marshall of Butlers Marston, with books in his desk, had goods valued at £61 9s.[3] and an Essex weaver, Thomas Raynebeard, was worth only £22 14s 4d which included three old looms and "ymplements".[4] Early in the eighteenth century another country weaver could leave goods worth £60 13s 6d.[5] which, even in spite of contemporary inflation, was in sharp contrast to the numbers of weavers' children who were being indentured as pauper apprentices.

In the late seventeenth century, however, some weavers lived a modest but fairly comfortable existence; for example, in London, Daniel Gwilt had a wife, two children, maidservant and one apprentice comprising his household.[6] Of the six weavers at Melbourne in 1695 only one, John Parker, had an apprentice, who was presumably a relative.[7] At the same date in London the household of John Scarlett, a weaver in St Michael Bassishaw parish, consisted of his wife, three sons, two daughters, a bachelor, a maidservant and an apprentice.[8]

At the same period the established wool trade of the northwest counties (Cumberland and Westmorland) was preserving its apprenticeship premiums and the entry of boys from artisan homes. However, even in this traditional area premiums were fewer and of 97 stuffweavers' apprentices in Kendal (1709–36) premiums below £10 were paid for only 33 boys (34 per cent). The depressed status of weaving, including stuffweaving, is reflected in the high proportion of non-premium indentures, the largest group of apprentices among some 50 trades in the borough.[9] A similarly depressed state was recorded in another traditional cloth-weaving area, Somerset, in the same period.[10]

By the early eighteenth century there were two quite separate categories of weaver, the artisan receiving premiums of £5 or less and the clothier-weaver, to whom substantial sums were paid by parents such as yeomen. For example, of the 33 Surrey children indentured in the early eighteenth century only four were in this latter group, with premiums of £32, £40, £63 and £105 paid to London masters.[11] Even by the early eighteenth century in some areas weaving showed little of the pauperization it was to experience by 1800 so that, for example, of the parish apprentices bound by Old Swinford during this period only one per cent went to weavers.[12] By the late eighteenth century, however, the trade was overstocked, paid low wages and was reduced to taking increasing numbers of parish apprentices, with associated loss of status, especially in areas where more sophisticated textile work was introduced. Coventry was such a community of thriving medieval textile trades where, by the early nineteenth century, weavers were the poorest group in the city. In spite of their poverty, weaving apprentices were more than three-quarters of all the boys indentured; in 1790 of the city's 1,860 freemen, 64 per cent (1,200) were connected with the trade:[13]

Table 8.1 Weaving apprentices in Coventry, 1790–1889.[14]

	1790–1819							1860–89			
1790	121	1800	58	1810	56	1860	25	1870	2	1880	1
1791	144	1801	42	1811	83	1861	14	1871	6	1881	–
1792	89	1802	27	1812	51	1862	9	1872	7	1882	1
1793	102	1803	65	1813	45	1863	16	1873	3	1883	–
1794	49	1804	58	1814	94	1864	5	1874	2	1884	–
1795	40	1805	95	1815	113	1865	5	1875	2	1885	–
1796	60	1806	88	1816	100	1866	4	1876	2	1886	1
1797	58	1807	55	1817	44	1867	2	1877	2	1887	–
1798	52	1808	44	1818	64	1868	5	1878	1	1888	–
1799	39	1809	28	1819	90	1869	5	1879	1	1889	1

These figures were reflected in the numbers of weavers' apprentices in the surrounding north Warwickshire villages, where George Eliot sited Raveloe, the community to which Silas Marner came, one of those "pallid undersized men, who, by the side of the brawny country-folk, looked like the remnants of a disinherited race".[15] As the trade required only "moderate strength", apprentices to weaving could be younger than 14, but Campbell commented that such children were bound "more for the Advantage of the Master than any thing they can learn of the Trade in such Infant Years".[16]

Campbell suggested premiums of £3–£20,[17] but £5 was most often recorded. However, weavers' premiums seem to have varied very considerably, even when two children were indentured to a master at the same period, as in 1710 when William Simons of Kinwalsey (War.) bound firstly Elizabeth Mitchell, a Coventry butcher's daughter, with a £7 premium, but Thomas Jordan, son of a Coundon (War.) husbandman, with only £2;[18] presumably Simons's premiums depended on an apprentice's family circumstances. At the same period a weaver such as Nathan Lobb of Warwick varied his premiums according to the origins of the apprentice; in 1709 he took a fatherless boy from his own borough with whom only £1 was paid.[19] Seven years later, when the orphan's term had expired, he took a non-poor child, Isaac Lort from Tamworth, whose premium for the same term was £8.[20] After a further two years, in 1718, his third apprentice again came from Warwick, but he was, although a butcher's son, a pauper, and his premium was £2.[21] By the

1750s and 1760s some pauper and non-poor apprentices' premiums were paid in instalments, as happened when Francis Ralley of Bedworth was apprenticed to a local weaver, Anthony Drake, in 1718. His £3 10s premium was to be paid in four parts: 10s at the indenturing in September, £1 in three months, £1 in a year's time and the final payment of £1 in 1720, which at least ensured the overseers' contact with the master.[22] Another instalment premium was recorded for a Temple Balsall child, William Ebrall, who was bound in 1701 to a weaver in his own village. There was another Ebrall child also indentured by the overseers at the same period, so the family were presumably not prosperous.[23] However, for William Ebrall a premium of £13 was paid in four yearly instalments of £3 5s each, and he was one of the rare examples of a pauper's becoming a master, for by 1744 he was himself indenturing a poor boy from the village to serve until the age of 21, but with no premium recorded. Many of these weavers also had other occupations, sometimes related to textiles (such as a clothier or woolcomber), but also quite different, such as a gardener or butcher.

A new branch of the trade was developed with the establishment of engine-weaving in the mid-eighteenth century, reaching a peak in the 1790s, and increasingly apprenticing numbers of children to one master. Of 112 Coventry masters at this period only 35 had a single apprentice each, with 19 the most boys bound to one man. However, the declining prosperity of engine-weavers by the early 1800s was reflected in the numbers of pauper and charity children they bound. One of the largest masters, with 18 apprentices (1781–1816) was John Taunton. Until 1804 his apprentices' fathers were a brushmaker, two cordwainers, a schoolmaster, weaver and watchcase maker, apart from his own four sons. After this date he indentured two charity boys, three paupers, a sailor's and weaver's sons, clearly a group with less prosperous origins.[24] The reduced prosperity of weavers was particularly noticeable in contemporary law cases, since impoverished masters could no longer support their apprentices and often went bankrupt or absconded. The anonymous author of a contemporary pamphlet described how one "poor old weaver" who had several times been convicted of theft and had then actually left off his trade through weakness and old age had, when the child's premium was spent, thrown himself and the apprentice on the parish for relief.[25] Of the 73 cases involving apprentices brought to Coventry Quarter Sessions in the years 1757–63 and 1773–80 a dozen concerned weavers (as distinct from ribbon, silk or worsted weavers) and of these the master was poor, cruel or had absconded in eight instances and the apprentice had run away in four.[26] Although many of these traditional weavers must have turned their skills to newer products, such as figured ribbons, the decline in their wages, status and conditions was so serious that by the mid-nineteenth century the trade was subjected to various parliamentary enquiries, and in most deliberations over-indenturing of apprentices was blamed as a factor of decline.

Apprentices to cotton factories particularly became the concern of philanthropists and reformers. Certain characteristics of their apprenticeships, their
youthfulness, the distances they travelled to cotton factories, far from parents
and home, the low moral standard of factory life and the essentially dead-end
nature of their work, all attracted adverse comment. Their poor clothes or
food, living conditions or hours of work were less significant reasons for
reform in the contemporary mind, since many other apprentices were, as the
factory masters claimed, no better treated in these respects. The sending of
young children great distances from their homes was one of the abuses of
factory apprenticeship most strongly condemned by men such as Samuel
Romilly, who considered it an evil that had "grown of late years to a very
great magnitude".[27] Peel, on the other hand, asserted that the boys he indentured were potential pickpockets, and that "it was the happiest thing for them
to be removed from their former connexions". Another MP thought it "a
benefit" to take children away from their "miserable and deprived parents".[28]
While Peel's remarks may have been appropriate to the London children he
took, it seems unlikely that large numbers of juvenile pickpockets were bred
in the small, remote villages from which many of his apprentices came. Thus,
of the 230 Warwickshire children indentured to cotton enterprises 136 (59
per cent) remained within the county, but all except the Coventry boys travelled more than one parish away from their homes to factories in Warwick,
Tamworth and Fazeley. However, Warwickshire apprentices were also sent
further afield to Joseph Hulse at Amber Hill, to Bott, Birch and Company
at Nantwich, to John Bott at Tutbury, to Joseph Peel at Bury, to Thomas
Jewsbury and Joseph Wilkes at Measham, as well as to Benjamin Chambers at
Rolleston. Certain large parishes, such as Nuneaton and Stratford-upon-
Avon, were particularly involved in these arrangements as one solution to
their increased poor rates. A year of exceptional hardship, 1802, saw the
highest number of cotton apprenticeships, with 1800 and 1809 also significant.

Although factories were often far from children's homes, it is noticeable
that most masters indentured children in batches, presumably for more convenient travel and administration, but for the children this procedure had the
advantage of companionship among their own age group from their own
communities. It is also remarkable that, except Joseph Peel at Bury, all the
masters indentured two or more children from one family in a quarter of all
the cases recorded. Thus brothers and sisters travelled and worked together
and, especially if any of them were exceptionally young, must have helped
and protected each other to a considerable extent. It is also possible that a
weaker child was indentured along with a healthy sibling, as in the case of the
Buttlar family of Bedworth, whose four girls aged 10–14 were bound, with
their 8-year-old half-sister, Martha Warner, to Charles Harding of Tamworth
in 1809. Of these children, Comfort Buttlar was to die only three years later
at the age of 18.[29]

One group of young female apprentices were despatched from Warwickshire, not quite so far from their homes, in 1802, when John Bott of Tutbury indentured 15 girls from Coventry to work in his cotton-spinning enterprise. The Bott family already had interests in silk mills in the town, and in 1781 a water-powered cotton mill was built there when they entered the increasingly prosperous cotton sector. Doubt has been cast on whether they ever in fact spun cotton,[30] but their indenturing of 15 girl apprentices on 23 September 1802 specifies cotton-spinning as the children's intended task.[31] The indenture itself is unusual, since it is one composite document for all 15 girls, who were apprenticed by their overseers, for varying terms until they should all have reached the age of 21. At the time of signing the indenture, four girls were aged 10, four were 11, one was 12, three were 14 and three were 15. Two pairs of sisters were included in the group, and the indenture specified that the maximum hours of work were either to be 13 in every day or 11 in every night, Sundays excepted. John Bott agreed to provide "good and sufficient Meat Drink Apparel of all sorts Washing Lodging and all other Necessaries" for the children, who were to attend public worship on Sundays. In addition, as a further safeguard of the children's welfare, Bott agreed to produce the children to their parish officials each Wednesday after Christmas Day and to allow the children to be examined on another day in each year as to the treatment they received. Bott was entitled to discharge any child he found unsatisfactory, but had to provide at her dismissal clothing as good as the child had had at the time of signing the indenture; no premium was specified on the indenture.

Opportunities for industrial apprenticeships for poor children within Warwickshire were relatively few, for it was not an area with many large textile undertakings that required pauper labour. However, at Rock Mill, Emscote, halfway between Warwick and Leamington, there was a cotton-spinning factory that employed parish apprentices.[32] According to one local observer in 1815, some "50 hands" were employed there.[33] The owners of this firm were a family named Smart. Benjamin Smart senior (1733–1816) was a Quaker and a leading local personality in the late eighteenth and early nineteenth centuries.

Benjamin Smart senior had, from the 1770s, been a generous subscriber to Quaker funds and at his death the local press extolled this "exemplary and respectable inhabitant of this Borough".[34] His second son, Benjamin (1766–1839) was his partner in the Rock Mill enterprise, but apparently a less devout member of the Society of Friends, which he was forced to leave in 1794 when a paternity suit was brought against him. He was, however, reinstated in 1801, prior to his first marriage, but left the Society, apparently of his own accord, in January 1812.[35]

It has already been asserted that the close integration of families such as those of Wilkes and Arkwright, involved in the new manufacturing enterprises, owed much to the influence of non-conformity.[36] A similar situation occurred in Warwickshire when, in 1805, Benjamin Smart junior married as his first wife the middle-aged Quaker, Hannah Fowler of Tamworth, whose family owned Alder Mills in the town. It is interesting to speculate to what extent these two Quaker cotton manufacturers influenced each other in their use of child labour. However, surviving records show that Emscote Mill employed poor apprentices as early as 1797, while pauper girls from Warwickshire were not indentured at Tamworth until 1807.

It has long been thought that the Smarts' cotton enterprise began in 1792,[37] but there is now evidence that Benjamin Smart senior bought the mill and site from George Weale, a Warwick worthy, as early as 1772 for £200 and subsequently, in 1797, when Smart was 74 years old, leased it jointly to his sons, Benjamin junior and Thomas Clark Smart.[38] This later transaction mentions the mill as a dual-purpose venture for corn and cotton, very similar to Wilkes's early Measham enterprise when he used his Boulton and Watt engine for corn by night and cotton by day.[39] It is possible that the emphasis on 1792 as the year in which the Smart cotton enterprise began may be explained if this date is taken as the occasion when the Smarts rebuilt the old mill, for its present-day appearance, four storeys high, with a substantial brick-built house adjacent to it, confirms this later date (Fig. 8.1). In 1812, when the mill was to be sold or let, the property was described as comprising "Cotton-mill and Machinery upon the best Principles . . . modern Dwelling House . . . the Machinery is in good Repair, and the Buildings have mostly been erected

Figure 8.1 Emscote Mill, near Warwick, showing factory and house built by Benjamin Smart.

within a few years".[40] The 1797 lease described the "New Building or Warehouse . . . now occupied by . . . Benjamin Smart as a house for his apprentices", which is the first indication of apprentice children at Rock Mill, and five years earlier than other evidence.

The next suggestion of Smart's indenturing poor Warwickshire children as apprentices occurred in 1802, when there is also indication of how some, if not all, masters acquired parish labour for their mills. A minute in the Tysoe vestry book for 1802 reads

> 17 August. At a Vestry . . . this day at the church held Agreed that Charles Foster, that is at the Wid Claridges at the Upper Town should be put Apprenticed to Mr Smarts at Warwick in the Cotton Manufacterer If we can agree with him when he come upon Terms.[41]

Such an entry certainly implies that the cotton master would personally visit remote villages like Tysoe to recruit poor children as labour. However, young Charles Foster was not to become an apprentice at Emscote Mill, presumably because the Tysoe vestry members could not agree terms with Smart, for in October 1803, Foster was being boarded out with a parishioner at 2s a week, "the Parish to find him in all Manner of Wearing Apparel", and a year later (October 1804) he and his brother, Robert, were apprenticed to a shag weaver. In spite of the failure of Tysoe's negotiations with Benjamin Smart, the parish did not entirely lose touch with the cotton mill, for a decade later Sarah Caldicott of Upper Tysoe became an apprentice there.

There is conflicting evidence about the sending of Tysoe children to Benjamin Smart, for Joseph Ashby described how parish children were "taken into the families of the best-to-do ratepayers . . . [and] were maintained within some family circle",[42] while a later historian from the same family asserted that "Tysoe did not send its children in batches to the cotton mills or to any other industrial occupation".[43] However, in her biography of her father, Miss M. K. Ashby described how, in 1818, the overseers sent a "number of small Tysoe children in a wagon to a cotton factory at Guyscliffe, twenty miles away, to be apprenticed to the machines there, in a small building beside the picturesque Avon, the most romantic spot in Warwickshire".[44]

Examination of the vestry minutes and the overseers' accounts does not support either suggestion as correct in broad assumption or details. Tysoe actually sent one girl, Sarah Caldicott, to Emscote Mill in 1816 when she was aged 12. The decision was noted in the vestry minutes and her expenses recorded in the overseers' ledger. By 1817 Smart had ceased to indenture children (Sarah Caldicott was his last apprentice) and was already trying to dispose of his interest in the mill to concentrate his capital and energy into a new venture at Leamington Priors, the Marble Baths.

There is evidence that, like other factory masters of the Midlands,[45] Smart used the local press, as well as newspapers from further afield, to advertise for apprentices and for other employees such as joiners and millers. His notices appeared in at least four Midlands newspapers but not, apparently, in *Aris's Gazette*, perhaps because it was then publishing announcements of the "considerable Earnings" that boys and girls in the town could attain.[46] Each announcement brought a further supply of female apprentices to Emscote Mill. He always specified that his apprentices were to be healthy, active and aged 14. However, his enterprise remained a small one, with 40 to 50 apprentices there in 1804, but by 1807 their number was only "about 30", according to Smart's own estimate,[47] although in 1815 a local observer noted that there were some 50 hands employed at the mill.[48] Of these, 27 have been traced by name and for most of the girls a certain amount of additional information has survived.

During the years 1801–16 Benjamin Smart junior indentured poor children from 11 Warwickshire and at least 2 Oxfordshire parishes. In 1804 a widow's daughter from Tredington, Mary Phillips, was bound to Smart at the age of 17 for a term of four years. Her indenture did not record the payment of a premium, but the overseers of the poor's accounts for the parish indicate that 9s was spent on one occasion taking the girl to Warwick and a further sum of 18s 1½d for "taking Mary Phillips a second time to Warwick, [and] her mother" to the cotton mill. Her premium and incidental expenses came to a total of £6 9s 11d. During the year after Mary had been apprenticed, her mother received regular parish aid in the form of weekly cash payments of 2s, furniture repairs and coal during the winter. Widow Phillips died in April 1805,[49] having been ill for some months, so it may have been her mother's poor health that made the overseers send Mary Phillips to be a factory apprentice rather than have her remain as an orphan and a future liability on the parish.

A year later, in 1805, an orphan girl from Stratford-upon-Avon, Phoebe Lancaster, aged 14, was apprenticed for seven years by the parish officers, who paid a premium of £4 14s 6d with her. Two years later, in July 1807, three more girls, two of them sisters, aged 12 and 14, were also sent to Rock Mill as apprentices by the same parish.[50] On this occasion the overseers paid Smart a total of £15 as premiums for the girls at a period when Smart was advertising for "several active healthy girls as apprentices". A year before, in 1806, Smart was also advertising for apprentices but on this occasion his notice in the local press indicated that he required "BOYS and GIRLS, about 14 years of age",[51] the only time that he is known to have sought young male workers for the mill, and perhaps his terms, as Tysoe parish had found in 1802, were more favourable for the employment of girls than young boys. During 1808 Smart indentured two sisters from Southam, aged 13 and 16 and, three years later, another girl from the same village, also 16. The overseers' accounts for Southam are not extant for these years, and so the girls' premiums are not known, but Smart's concern for a girl's age was emphasized by endorsements on the indentures of the girls' baptismal dates, as for the Oxford apprentices.[52]

In 1812 the Stratford-upon-Avon overseers of the poor indentured to Smart (with a £5 premium) a girl from the parish, whose parents were described as "unknown", when she had reached the age of 16. Another Warwickshire parish to send an older apprentice to Smart's mill was Weston-under-Wetherley, whose overseers bound Sarah Moore aged 16 for five years in 1808. A further instance that has been traced of Smart's indenturing parish children occurred in 1810, when the overseers' accounts of Butlers Marston recorded their expenditure of £10 for "Sarah Nuet being Prentice" and 14s 6d for her "indenters". However, the premium of only £5 was entered in the apprenticeship register kept by the parish, with no apparent explanation for the discrepancy. Something is known of Sarah Newitt's origins, which were perhaps typical of other mill children's backgrounds. At the time of her apprenticeship, Sarah Newitt was 12 years old, the eldest daughter of Samuel and Elizabeth Newitt, who had been consistently aided by their home parish since 1800 with medical assistance, food, cash payments and house repairs.[53]

The final instance of a Warwickshire child's being bound as an apprentice to Emscote Mill was in March 1816, when 12-year-old Sarah Caldicott of Tysoe was indentured by the overseers. Sarah Caldicott was born in 1804, the eldest of the nine children of Mary and Samuel Caldicott, whose occupation was entered in the parish register as labourer. The eight other children were born at two-year intervals between 1807 and 1820. The parents' marriage in November 1803 was one of necessity, since the bride was already five months pregnant. During the years preceding Sarah's apprenticeship, her father regularly received 12s to 14s 6d a fortnight, with an extra 6d a week as round pay because he was "out of Employ".[54]

However, by the summer of 1815 Caldicott's weekly payment had been reduced to 2s, and in the autumn the overseers obtained a warrant for his arrest, while continuing to assist his wife and family. In March 1816, the overseers paid the parish constable 3s 6d for "taking Callicots Daugter away", presumably to Smart's mill, and in the same month the officials spent 6s for "Guarding Sam Callicott one night & 2 days" when he had tried to run away. He was finally taken to quarter sessions in March 1816, when the justices ordered that he be discharged,[55] and the local press reported his crime as that of "running away from his family".[56]

In addition to these known pauper children from Warwickshire parishes, there is evidence that Benjamin Smart junior sought labour further afield by advertising in at least one neighbouring newspaper, the *Oxford Journal*, three years after he had advertised similarly in the Warwick press. From a group of five letters written to one of the overseers of St Clement's parish, Oxford, in 1811–12 it is obvious that Smart already had established a connection with the parish, from whom he had indentured two poor girls, and was prepared to accept others.

Early in 1812 the *Oxford Journal* contained Smart's advertisement for "a few active healthy GIRLS, about 14 years of age, *not less than 4 feet 6 inches in height,* as APPRENTICES in the COTTON SPINNING BUSINESS. Two new dresses, and a premium of Five Pounds, with each, will be expected."[57] Smart's requirements were also specific in his letters – girls were to be active, healthy, of "a lively disposition", aged 14 or more and not less than 4 feet 6 inches tall. The elder Wallis sister was approved by Smart, who "felt no objection to her being bound immediately" after her arrival, when he had had opportunity to assess her suitability. He emphasized that he would only accept a girl "if upon seeing her I think she will answer my purpose", and was concerned to inform the parish officers that "if she returns" (as unsatisfactory) "I shall expect to be reimburs'd all the expenses incur'd on her account". Smart's uncertainty about accepting the 13-year-old Sarah Wallis in 1812 because "she is rather too young" was unhappily justified, for Sarah died at Emscote five years later aged 18.[58]

There is evidence that Warwick's minor industrial expansion did not last long or survive wartime needs very successfully.[59] After Smart had sold the mill for £5,000, having asked £12,000, a local landowner, who greatly disliked Smart, reported how he had gone to visit a "wretched pauper apprentice girl", formerly indentured to Smart, lodged in a cottage nearby with other apprentices "a sight of misery. How lucky that cotton business is over."[60] An unusual demonstration of public feeling against apprentices going to Smart occurred in June 1805 in Oxfordshire when he arranged to indenture six pauper girls from Witney. Three parishioners were brought before quarter sessions for their part, "with divers other evil disposed persons to the number of ten and more", in an unlawful and riotous assembly in the village at which they tried to prevent the overseers and constable from conveying the girls to Smart. Two of the parishioners, described as labourers, acted to "rescue" the children from the officials. The original plea of not guilty was changed to one of guilty before they were fined and discharged. In making their "very great riot, rout and tumult" they were said to be an "evil example" to others but certainly their unusual corporate action prevented the removal of village children to Emscote Mill.[61]

In addition to the Smart family's cotton enterprise there was also a Coventry cotton manufacturing company, Nickson and Browett, that took numbers of local children as apprentices. Calico weaving was introduced to Coventry in 1770,[62] but the earliest evidence of apprenticeship to the factory occurs in 1793, although the apprenticeship registers for the city began 12 years before that date. The partners in this enterprise were John Nickson and William Browett and their factory was situated on the east side of Hill Top, a narrow cobbled alleyway near the cathedral. The site of the factory can be clearly seen on Thomas Sharp's map of 1807, set among the ruins of the priory cells of Charterhouse.

The Coventry apprenticeship registers show that Nickson and Browett took in a total of 39 children, all boys, during the years 1793–1807. Between 1796 and 1801 William Browett apprenticed his sons, John, William and

Joseph, to the cotton-manufactory, as well as a relative, Joshua, from Northamptonshire, and there is evidence that his youngest son subsequently became the head of the firm in his father's place. In February 1812 William Browett died and his surviving partner, Nickson, "declined the trade";[63] the firm was continued for a short time on a limited scale by Browett's son, but it soon ceased trading.

Although many distinguished travellers, such as Maria Edgeworth, visited factories, their interest was more with the processes of manufacturing than the conditions of apprentices they saw. However, the inspectors who visited factories and reported to a parliamentary select committee in 1816 were particularly concerned with the working and living conditions of factory apprentices. The cotton mill at Emscote was one of those inspected by a local magistrate in May 1815; Theodore Price reported favourably in some respects on what he found there but finally he "inferred that cotton mills are all bad".

In spite of Price's impression that mill children "appeared as complete prisoners as they would be in gaol",[64] some undoubtedly tried to abscond. Only two young girls have been traced as runaways from Benjamin Smart's mill, one of whom twice tried to gain her freedom. In 1809 Sarah Cooke was sentenced at Warwick to 14 days in the House of Correction for running away from Rock Mill; three years later, in 1812, she was again caught running away and sentenced to one month's imprisonment and to be corrected as a further deterrent;[65] Rugby was her home to which she might have been returning.[66] Another girl, Diana Prestage, also ran away in May 1813, when her elder sister's term of apprenticeship ceased.[67]

If two girls were the only runaways from Emscote Mill out of a total work force of 30–50, this is a small proportion compared with the 15.2 per cent who absconded from Cuckney Mill during the same period,[68] although girls may have been less venturesome than boys, as Quarry Bank discovered. Smart's mill and Quarry Bank had much in common apart from preferring female apprentices; Greg required each girl to have a two-guinea premium as well as clothes (two shifts, two pairs of stockings, two frocks or bedgowns, two brats or aprons) and kept all apprentices a month on trial to "ascertain their probable healthiness".[69] Like Smart, the majority of his apprentices were local (from Staffordshire, Cheshire, Liverpool and Manchester) but Greg also had many children placed by their parents as paid workers.

Children apprenticed to worsted manufacture may have been fewer than those in cotton factories, or their records have survived less often. Stanley Chapman has described the intricate network of worsted pioneers in the Midlands among whom Sir Roger Newdigate of Arbury was unusual: the children at his Collycroft mill, managed by Henry Lane, have never been identified as apprentices. In the 1790s a French prisoner of war, le Quesne, drew a cross section through the mill, similar to that for Quarry Bank (c.1825). In his drawing 22 of the 50 figures are girls, wearing a blue uniform dress and frilled cap; at least 12 of the girls there can now be identified as Kenilworth apprentices, bound by their parish in 1792 and present when le Quesne made his sketches.[70]

Of the various branches of textiles, the production of silk was a very important industry in certain regions, providing apprenticeships for large numbers of children, especially females, but ranging from the great traders, often enormously wealthy, to the smallest artisans as masters. At the most prosperous end of the whole ribbon and silk industry were the manufacturer of ribbons and the silkman, who was the supplier of the essential raw material to the trade. Campbell, in 1747, noted that the silkman "buys raw Silk from the Importer, and sometimes imports it himself and sells it to the Manufacturer ... as a Ware-House-Keeper and Retailer, he requires no great Genius to acquire the Mistery of his Trade", but also described the "sums necessary to set up as Master" rather ominously as "unlimited", a rare term he used only for such occupations as insurer and money scrivener.

The apprentice to a silkman or ribbon manufacturer, however, contrasted in all respects with the child bound to a weaver in the two trades. The silkman's was "a very genteel and reputable trade", whose large capital requirements placed him in "the first rank of tradesmen". A gentleman's education, a "handsome fortune", polite behaviour, ability to write a "fair expeditious hand and be well versed in accounts" were essential qualities for the intending apprentice.[71] An entirely male occupation, with premiums in the £20–£45 range, family connections were significant in apprenticeship patterns. Substantial silkmen took quite large numbers of apprentices; in Coventry, Morris, Ratcliff and Smith had 18, Willerton and Theakstone had 13 and Thomas Cope had 12, many of them the industry's future leaders. The silk trade appealed to the professions and to wealthy tradesmen for their sons, but also to those men newly prosperous who wished their sons to enter an occupation more remote from personally selling or making a product. In spite of silk trade fluctuations, apprenticeships to manufacturers were surprisingly stable; silk and ribbon manufacturers very frequently formed partnerships of two or three men, not apparently related, presumably because of the high capital risks involved.[72] George Eliot, who lived among such ribbon masters in the 1830s and 1840s, noted their preference for their own social group in the Vincy family of "old manufacturers" who "could not any more than dukes be connected with none but equals, they were conscious of an inherent social superiority which was defined with great nicety in practice, though hardly expressible theoretically".[73]

The silk trade was established in Derbyshire, Cheshire, Staffordshire, London and Coventry and large numbers of apprentices were indentured by the early eighteenth century; contemporaries noted their extreme youth. Of the younger children, ten-year-olds were indentured particularly often, lacking strength, but deft-fingered, cheap and biddable, capable of repetitive work if supervised; William Hutton has left his own reminiscences of such an apprenticeship in Derby in the eighteenth century.[74] Most children, irrespective of age, were bound until the age of 21 with £2 or £3 premiums, and urban masters relied heavily on apprentices coming from surrounding country parishes or impoverished industrial communities with surplus children. As the silk trade was established well before ribbon-weaving, the abuses of traditional apprenticeship were less marked; most masters took only one or two apprentices each and resisted the half-pay system. Although one visitor in 1769 wrote disparagingly of Coventry's products as "ordinary sort of ribbands, chiefly black",[75] the silk trade there was an important thriving trade throughout most of the eighteenth century.

One Coventry silk-weaving family, the Gutteridges, spanned the various periods of prosperity and slump that affected the city from the 1780s to the mid-nineteenth century. The most articulate of them, Joseph Gutteridge, was the author of *Lights and shadows in the life of an artisan*, published in 1893. He had been born in Coventry in 1816; his father, Joseph, and his grandfather, William, were both silk-weavers. William Gutteridge took his first apprentice, a poor boy from Stoneleigh, in 1781, and another male pauper from Snitterfield in 1783, with whom he received an outfit of clothes and a five-guinea premium from the overseers.[76] By 1791 his second son, James, was old enough to be apprenticed, and a year later a Sutton Coldfield pauper, Thomas Taylor, joined the Gutteridge family. The eldest Gutteridge son, Thomas, had already been bound to a Coventry weaver, Joseph Coleman, in 1787 but the third, fourth and fifth sons, Joseph, William and John, served their apprenticeships with their father, and were bound in the years 1794, 1797 and 1801. For some unspecified reason, Thomas Taylor was assigned to another master, an engine-weaver, in 1798 when he had only one more year to serve, perhaps to make room for another Gutteridge son to join his father.

Joseph Gutteridge was born about 1780 and was, so his son declared, able to read and write well, as was the woman he married. Their eldest son, Joseph, was sent to a dame school at five and later to a local charity school; he practised reading by spelling out the names over shops as he walked to work. Joseph senior worked at Mrs Dresser's factory in St Agnes Lane, where young Joseph began his apprenticeship to his father in 1830. He did not serve his full term, for his father died before he could do so, but his observations on factory life were highly critical: he considered it "very demoralising to youths with any pretensions to refinement" and wished to avoid employment in a place where "moral depravity" resulted from the "indiscriminate association of adults and young people of both sexes but with little restraint in a tainted atmosphere".[77] However, Joseph Gutteridge and his family were not typical of most Coventry silk-weavers, for much general contemporary opinion described the work force as "heathenish", "disorderly" and "dissolute", while all observers noted that they were "wretchedly poor"[78] and even in the mid-eighteenth century Collyer had remarked that "the wages of Weavers in general are but poor".[79] All areas where silk was produced suffered from fashion changes and government import policies; flexibility was important for survival and the novelty of foreign goods was a constant challenge to English silk workers.

Fortunately for the silk trade, in the early nineteenth century fashion decreed ribbons with large purl (scalloped) edges, one of the weavers' more profitable products. Labour, however, was scarce, chiefly because adult males had enlisted. In response to the demand for purl-edged ribbons, large numbers of half-pay apprentices were engaged, girls from domestic service and men from agriculture. The whole silk trade was thus disastrously overstocked and the situation became acute when men were demobilized after 1815. The coming of steam power in the 1830s was a further blow to traditional apprenticeship. In Coventry the innovations of Thomas Stevens virtually rescued the industry; he had the foresight to develop mass-produced silk pictures, selling in a very wide price range, using new outlets, haberdashery shops. He secured government contract work as well as making individually commissioned quality silk goods; he had undeniable flair in publicizing his own products, travelling worldwide to trade fairs, where he wove commemorative silks, and establishing a London end to his business. He apprenticed several of his brothers to the trade in the later nineteenth century.

Although the Midlands ribbon trade was centred in Coventry, there were significant numbers of masters and apprentices in adjacent areas of the county and in these ribbon communities even greater distress was experienced than in the city itself. The trade's poverty was reflected in the virtually unchanged premiums across a century, for while £2 was an adequate sum in 1718 and modest by 1760, it was at pauper level by the 1820s. In a few instances, when a child was bound, the overseers agreed with the master the scale of wages the apprentice should be paid. In 1768, Jane Whadcock, a Fillongley widow's daughter, was indentured for seven years to William Page of Nuneaton, who was to give the child half-pay and "half candles" for the first five years and full pay (unspecified) for the last two years.[80] Twenty years later, in 1789, a similar arrangement was made by William Hurst when he indentured Ann Toon of Nuneaton for five years. For four years of her term she was to have half-pay and supply her own candles and in the final year she would receive journey wages.[81] These conditions were identical to those operating in Coventry 30 years later about which witnesses before the 1818 select committee complained so bitterly,[82] and seem to support the assertion to the Committee that the system began in the north. How a child fared at the end of the term generally cannot be assessed for lack of recorded evidence, but very rarely a master reported on how satisfactory his apprentice had been. Such a master was Robert Lester of Attleborough (War.) who took 13-year-old William Malabourn as an apprentice in 1789. After serving an eight-year term, Lester wrote to the boy's father: "Mr Marlobone I have freely gave your sun is time out & this is to sirtisfye any one that he is a good whorkman & a honest boy."[83]

In May 1818, the second parliamentary committee heard evidence about the distressed state of the town's ribbon-weavers from the rector of Bedworth, the Reverend Edward Finch. He reported that there was "plenty of work, but at very reduced prices . . . the price given to a worker for his labour is so small that a person cannot live upon his earnings". The parish made up the difference between wages and subsistence level. Edward Finch castigated the half-pay apprentice system as "one of the greatest evils of the ribbon trade".[84]

Not only the silk trade suffered from fashion changes, overstocking and poor apprentices, however, for in the late seventeenth and early eighteenth century handmade lace was an important English product, a rival to foreign imports, with substantial lacemen trading in London. Always a home industry, with female labour, the lace-maker of this period was able in some cases to attract quite good premiums from non-pauper girls. Thus in the first quarter of the eighteenth century apprenticeships were recorded to lace-makers such as Mary Leake of Salisbury, who took £10 in 1711,[85] Catherine Lane of Lambeth with the same sum in 1725,[86] or Mary Steele of Malmesbury, who received £8 in 1719.[87] Such premiums did not continue, however, as the trade became concentrated in the Bedfordshire, Buckinghamshire and Northamptonshire area, but with quality lace also made in Devon and Dorset. The trade experienced various slumps, but generally brought prosperity to the parishes where it was important, as Eden noted when commenting on the stable poor rates of these areas.[88] Although the Napoleonic Wars were a boom period, prices fell as fashions changed in the post-war years, especially as machine-made lace became available very cheaply. The 1843 Children's Employment Commission described the lace schools in these areas, but their pupils do not appear to have been apprentices. In an earlier period parish children had been bound to lace-makers, always young girls, usually until the age of 21 or marriage. Sometimes particularly troublesome paupers would be given a larger premium by a parish eager to be rid of them. Such a child was the illegitimate nine-year-old Alice Prickett, bound until the age of 25 in 1813 to a woman lace-maker in Bugbrooke with not only a seven-guinea premium but also clothes worth £1 8s 10d. As she came from a family prone to produce bastards to be supported by the parish, such an arrangement saved the poor rate for years to come.[89] Although the trade was overcrowded, often unhealthy and allegedly made girls incompetent housewives, it did provide the adult woman, even when married, with a source of domestic income. So acute was lace-makers' distress that newspapers appealed, even in non-lace areas, for ladies to buy the handmade product,[90] but its decline continued until the late nineteenth century.[91]

A closely related trade, framework knitting, extensively indentured apprentices from its earliest days; the proportion of apprentices to journeymen and the quota a master might take were constant topics of debate by the eighteenth century. As in watchmaking after 1800, many men saw overstocking with apprentices as the reason for all the trade's difficulties. Even when the trade was centred in London, individual stockingers in the provinces were working and taking apprentices. For example, at Kendal in the early eighteenth century, of the 17 stockingers' apprentices, premiums were paid for nine boys, from £2 to £10, but with £8 paid in four instances. Although four of these boys were orphans, their parents were not poor, and the fathers still alive were yeomen, a saddler, cordwainer and victualler.[92] Stockingers were never among the wealthiest citizens, however, so that in London in 1698 the household of Samuel Sheppard, who had one apprentice, consisted only of his sister and a male lodger, usually a sign of poor circumstances. However, two other city hosiers with apprentices at the same period each had a servant-maid in their households as well as wives, children and grandchildren.[93]

When the trade became concentrated in Nottinghamshire and Leicestershire in the 1730s, parish apprentices were seen as an immediate source of cheap labour, keeping production costs, especially journeymen's wages, low. However, young pauper apprentices produced inferior work that had to be sold cheaply, leaving fine work to London stockingers. The trade sought in 1745 to control apprenticeship entry and instruction, in the London style, with fines for non-compliance, but the numbers of paupers bound from many midland parishes in the later eighteenth century illustrate the weakness of these controls.[94] A few masters, on the Warwickshire/Leicestershire border near Hinckley, did not in fact indenture large numbers of apprentices, but of over 600 Warwickshire children who went to Leicestershire masters in the late eighteenth and early nineteenth century, the majority went to masters with several apprentices each. When contemporaries sought the reasons behind the trade's crisis of 1810 they found that "a vast increase had taken place in the numbers of apprentices taught by masters in more prosperous times, when hands were wanted to work the greatly enlarged body of machinery . . . at Hinckley two framework knitters had one hundred between them".[95] By 1812 two-thirds of the stockingers were said to be unapprenticed colts,[96] in addition to the large numbers of indentured children.

The qualities required by a stockinger were "some Ingenuity" and "some strengths",[97] but even as early as 1740 the phrase "poor as a stockinger" was heard.[98] By the later eighteenth century the most depressed industrial communities were a chief source of apprentices for stockingers, and their binding, at a peak in the middle years of the Napoleonic Wars, was reflected in the trade's distress of 1810, a prelude to the machine-breaking of 1811. Some contemporary observers, however, were aware that the "system of apprenticing children from the neighbouring parishes for the purpose of changing their settlement" was one of the principal causes of the stockingers' plight.[99] Although stockingers were known, with nailers, shoemakers and weavers, for their observance of St Monday, they themselves nostalgically recalled the prosperous years, when premiums up to £8 were recorded. However, when the bag-hosier, truck system and "cut-up" work all coincided with fashion preferences for plain not fancy products, the trade's response was the disastrous one of lowered premiums (two guineas) and more parish apprentices. Wages were further reduced by the entry of unapprenticed adult women, often the stockinger's own family, although very few girls could be indentured because the frame required physical strength. Stockingers were well represented among cruel masters, perhaps, however, because the trade was so numerous, and some overseers required a certificate of a master's character before their parish children were bound, as reassurance that the master was "of good fame and of sober life and conversation" or a "fit Person to take an apprentice".[100]

Perhaps of all categories of apprentices, those bound to textiles varied most, from the child indentured to the silkman or to the stockinger. For factory children, adult employment prospects were poor at the end of their terms; in domestic industries, although a former apprentice might rent a loom, weave for himself and even indenture his own apprentices, earnings were erratic and at certain periods below subsistence. Numerically large groups, both textile apprentices and their masters, figured disproportionately in legal proceedings, with masters who were cruel, bankrupt, runaways or even murderers, and apprentices who stole, absconded and were generally ill-behaved. As in other formerly honourable trades, textile apprentices, except those of the mercantile or management categories, suffered most acutely from trade variations and harsh masters, least able to protect themselves, except by absconding, and with little incentive of a prosperous future livelihood to make their apprenticeship more tolerable.

CHAPTER 9

Unsatisfactory apprentices

You shall do diligent and faithful Service to your Master for the Time
of your Apprenticeship, and deal truly in what you shall be trusted.
You shall often read over the Covenants of your Indenture, and see
and endeavour yourself to perform the same to the utmost of your
Power . . . You shall be of fair, gentle and lowly Speech and Behaviour
to all Men.

Instructions for the apprentices of the
London Company of Carpenters (*c.* 1750)

Since a child's apprenticeship to a master was a formal, legal arrangement,
requiring a written indenture, infringements of the agreement could exist on
both sides. Legal evidence suggests that the master rather than the apprentice
was usually at fault, and the apprentice was an unlikely plaintiff. Whereas the
master might ignore a single minor transgression, repeated misdemeanours
by the apprentice were punished. Apprentice behaviour was controlled by a
wide range of strictures, dictating conduct towards the master and his property and setting limits on personal conduct for the whole term. When apprentices embezzled a master's goods, passed on trade secrets, were disobedient or
transacted business without permission, they were breaking the essential conditions of the indenture. Equally, they might not leave a master without permission day or night, behave dishonestly towards the host family, gamble,
drink or attend theatres, nor might they enjoy sexual pleasures in or out of
matrimony. Thus even the prosperous apprentice could become a criminal
quite easily, even accidentally, and strict control of adolescent apprentices was
never achieved without difficulty.

It is understandable that Tudor and Stuart governments had a very strong
interest in encouraging and supporting the institution of apprenticeship
within the household, for it provided firm social control at local level over the
most potentially disruptive element in society: the young, unmarried males. It
is noticeable that certain complaints against apprentices by adults, often not
themselves masters, were common across a wide range of historical periods,

geographical areas, occupations and social classes. Collective rowdyism, modish dress, resistance to discipline and general impropriety were criticisms levelled against apprentices as often in the sixteenth as in the nineteenth century, particularly when they "intruded themselves" or behaved in other than a humble and deferential fashion. It is apparent that there were both written and traditional norms of behaviour within which apprentices were expected to confine themselves, except in times of permitted licence, such as Shrove Tuesday or May Day, when these strictures did not apply. It is equally clear that the term "apprentices" was widely applied by adults to adolescents in general in a pejorative sense in the way that "students" is used in the modern period.

From the early seventeenth century onwards there appeared in print, selling for about a shilling, a considerable number of manuals for the young male apprentice, giving him advice on his chosen occupation and how to conduct himself when he was indentured. The number of manuals published suggests that not every apprentice was observing the acknowledged rules and that they were defining in print a set of values and standards already under attack or no longer observed, but valued by traditionalists, or that they were for a social class new to apprenticeship. The advice manuals that began to appear in the early 1600s concentrated particularly on the child's dutiful relationship with the master and the host family. General domestic guidebooks also often included such advice, for example, William Vaughn's *The golden grove* in 1600, *A godly form of household government* by John Dod and Robert Cleaver in 1630 or Thomas Hilder's *Conjugal counsel* in 1653. Later manuals were particularly directed at the apprentice, such as Caleb Trenchfield's *A cap of gray hairs for a green head : or the father's counsel to his son, an apprentice in London* in 1671, Richard Burton's *The apprentice's companion* or William Mather's *The young man's companion*, both published in 1681. Sales of these works increased as apprentices became a larger proportion of the population (possibly as many as eleven thousand in London by the 1690s) and readership was wider as a result of greater literacy. More significantly, however, it is apparent that the advice manuals were intended for adolescents who were first-generation apprentices or who were entering an occupation and frequently a class very different from their parents' own. Undoubtedly the greater social mobility of the eighteenth century caused children to be apprenticed further from home and perhaps necessitated guidance for apprentices in new social situations, higher or lower than they had experienced, so that their manuals were similar to the handbooks of etiquette and polite behaviour that also began to appear at this period.

Authors such as Campbell and Collyer published manuals that set out, trade by trade, the educational and financial requirements a master would make to an intending apprentice. There were suggestions for the child's demeanour during the term, emphasizing the need for honesty, sobriety, sexual abstinence and, above all, diligent attention to the master's interests. Well-known novelists also produced advice manuals, which sold in surprising numbers; among Defoe's works in the genre were *The family instructor* (1715), *The great law of subordination consider'd* (1724) and *The complete English tradesman* (1738), self-explanatory titles that all gave advice on apprenticeship and its effective operation. Samuel Richardson, bound to a London printer, John Wilde, in 1706,[1] who "served a Diligent Seven Years . . . to a Master who grudged every Hour to me, that tended not to his profit", in 1733 published *The apprentice's vade mecum*. This work influenced the most successful of all the eighteenth-century advice manuals, *A present for an apprentice* in 1739, its subtitle an indication of its emphasis *(Or, a sure guide to gain both esteem and estate. With rules for his conduct to his master, and the world)*. The anonymous author was described as "late Lord Mayor of London" and the success of the work owed much to the writer as a role model and his personal rise in status in the legendary Dick Whittington manner. There were also a number of other anonymous publications throughout the eighteenth century, such as *The servant's calling: with some advice to the apprentice* (1725). This clearly distinguished between the two social categories of adolescents within the household and advised the apprentice against familiarity with young servants, whose company was tempting to the lonely youth in a strange community far from home, especially if they were in the same age group.

The significance of these and other advice manuals was reflected in contemporary literature and art; in Arthur Murphy's popular play, *The apprentice* (1756), one apprentice accuses another of reading "nothing but *The young man's pocket companion or The clerk's vade mecum*", while *A present for an apprentice* was highly praised in Fielding's *The champion* (1739–40). At the same period, in Hogarth's *Industry and idleness* (see Figs 9.1 and 9.2), while Frank Goodchild had his copy of *The prentice's guide* open before him, Tom Idle's lay mutilated on the workshop floor (see Figure 9.1) and Hogarth added two biblical quotations to emphasize the contrast (Proverbs 23, verse 21 and Proverbs 10, verse 4).

Even if apprentices did not commit actual crimes, their behaviour frequently displeased their masters and if they were sufficiently unruly they could, like young Joseph Clegg, be sent home to their parents. In 1730 James Clegg, a dissenting minister, had bound his son to a Manchester printer; after three years he received "afflicting tidings of the evil and unjust behaviour of Joseph to his master". It was the "worst report" he had ever had of any of his children, and hoped it was the only one. James Clegg visited the master and talked to his son "long" and "seriously", but the apprentice's behaviour did not improve and eighteen months later he was turned out for his "intemperance and injustice" towards his master. James Clegg felt the disgrace very keenly and a year later went to see the master again in an attempt to reinstate his son; the boy finally returned to Manchester.[2] Another cleric's sons, Thomas and John Josselin, proved equally unsatisfactory apprentices, returning home at intervals, changing masters and not completing their terms.[3]

Figure 9.1 "The fellow 'prentices at their looms", from Hogarth's *Industry and idleness.*

Although both Clegg and Josselin seem to have been loving fathers who took care in choosing masters for their sons, the details of the boys' behaviour is recorded in the fathers' diaries, both of which have a strong element of self-justification in the writing. It is possible that these boys lived severely disciplined lives in their fathers' parishes and, away from home, compensated by wild behaviour; they may even have been unruly adolescents at home whose fathers hoped apprenticeship would improve.

In spite of advice manuals and the force of the indenture, apprentices at different times broke all the conditions of apprenticeship, with violent behaviour that led to death, as well as offences against property and propriety. Their crimes against their master chiefly involved property, neglect of the master's interests and unsuitable personal behaviour. If only because of the obvious physical superiority an adult master enjoyed for most of the term, instances of apprentices committing the most serious crime, murder, were relatively rare. Not all such crimes were successfully accomplished, so that one goldsmith's apprentice who attempted to kill his master using "a short spere, the whiche he hid in the Kechyn . . . [that] served to open and to shete the wyndowys of the shoppe" was discovered; he asked to be assigned to another master but, understandably, none would have him. He was persuaded to forswear the craft and to leave London.[4]

Occasionally a murder attracted sufficient attention because of its unusual nature that it became a street ballad. In 1775, at the age of eight, the illegitimate Rebecca Downing, "of sensual Parents born", was indentured to a

Figure 9.2 "The industrious 'prentice a favourite, and entrusted by his master", from Hogarth's *Industry and idleness*.

70-year-old farmer, Richard Jarvis of East Portlemouth (Devon). Her work was picking stones and weeds from the fields and tending cattle. At her trial, when she was 15, she was described as insolent and sullen, a girl who frequently needed chastising. She was found guilty of poisoning her master with arsenic, which she added to his breakfast potion of parched wheat prepared as coffee. Jarvis's granddaughter was suspicious and said that, when he became ill, she tried to force Rebecca to drink a cup of the same liquid, but that the apprentice spat it out. "The girl confessed her guilt to the physician, and assigned a desire of being free from servitude as the motive." In gaol she was found to know nothing of Christianity and had "never been told anything about having a soul". After being sentenced, she was "drawn on a sledge to the place of execution attended by an amazing concourse of people, where, after being strangled, her body was burnt to ashes". Separate reports of the occasion describe Rebecca as "more stupified than grieved by her situation" and as "insensible to every kind of admonition". Her execution in July 1782 was exceptionally severe, presumably because the crime was premeditated and might have proved an encouragement to other pauper apprentices who were wretchedly treated. Although ballads were frequently produced about such sensational events (Tom Idle's execution was thus described), Rebecca Downing's story also had a woodcut illustration of her death at the stake at the top of the printed broadsheet.[5]

Although deliberate crimes of this kind were rare, unpremeditated physical attacks by apprentices, driven beyond endurance by their masters, occurred more often. In spite of physical disadvantage, even the younger apprentice might be goaded to attack his master if he were treated with unwarrantable severity; girls when apprentices hardly ever seem to have turned to physical violence. Francis Place described how his father had been apprenticed to a baker, a "sad brute"; one day, when cutting up wood for the oven, the master threw his bread-weights at the apprentices, who picked them up and dropped them down a well nearby. "Doubly enraged at this, the master took up a billet of wood and threw it at them." The wood, striking Place's father, hurt him and "on the impulse of the moment [he] swung the hatchet he had in his hand at his master and cut him across the buttocks. He fled immediately and came on foot to London."[6] When his master hit him with a gun-barrel, another apprentice responded by throwing a basin of dirty water at him before absconding.[7] A more unusual crime for an apprentice to commit was arson, but one young London apprentice attempted to set fire to his master's house by putting a red-hot poker in his bed; the boy had tried to do so on three previous occasions and failed.[8] Although murder by an apprentice remained a rare crime, other stories of violence and revenge against masters were not uncommon experiences in the eighteenth century from the evidence of court proceedings and newspaper reports in all parts of England.

Crimes against a master's property were far more often committed and could also carry the death penalty. One female apprentice who died in 1735 for theft was Mary Wootton, aged nine; 14 months earlier she had been indentured to the wife of John Easton in London. She stole 27 guineas from her mistress by breaking open a chest of drawers; she ran away but was soon captured at Rag Fair and sentenced to death.[9] Apprentices who stole from their masters, of course, broke the law as well as the terms of the indenture, so that absconding was often the only course open, usually followed by an irregular or even criminal existence. Thus, joining a fairground trader, Cheap John, was the fate of one Shrewsbury draper's apprentice who got into bad company, and then robbed his master to "keep up his unlawful wants". This young runaway had been "very respectably brought up . . . an excellent scholar, and in every way a genteel young fellow". Another youth, who had stolen a customer's £20, intended for paying an account to his master, a cabinetmaker, absconded, and then took to begging and had "often been in quod [prison] and could make plenty of tin; when one dodge failed he tried another".[10] Since an apprentice with only part of the term complete could not legally work in the trade for another master it is not surprising that crime provided an inevitable livelihood.

By far the largest number and greatest variety of complaints about apprentices concerned infringements of the indenture conditions restricting the adolescent's personal behaviour. Apart from the indenture, some guilds had sought to control their apprentices locally with additional strictures from the Middle Ages onwards. In London apprentices were not allowed to attend tennis courts, bowling alleys, dances, cock-fights or brothels, while the

Merchant Adventurers of Newcastle upon Tyne prohibited "daunce dice mum . . . or any musick".[11] There were also numerous regulations about an apprentice's personal appearance and dress and the frequency with which such rules were made or reiterated in all the major ancient trading centres (Bristol, Coventry, Lincoln, London, Newcastle upon Tyne, Norwich and York) suggests that apprentices regularly flouted existing rules and that their behaviour caused new ones to be devised.

Although adolescents were allowed in many ways to work, behave and dress as adults, apprentices were precluded from enjoying many pleasures available to their contemporaries and elders; such restrictions seem to have been both resented and avoided when possible. The first of these limitations was placed on apprentices' entering a tavern, inn or alehouse, although children were used to drinking alcohol, if only small beer, from an early age. In the mid-eighteenth century a Coventry magistrate sought to stop apprentices from drinking by rewarding informants,[12] which cannot have been easy in a community with 126 taverns.[13] Although apprentices were normally used to fetch and carry alcohol for their masters, so that in many workshops they were "turned into pot-boys",[14] both Campbell and Collyer emphasized the importance of sobriety to the apprentice, although this must have often been difficult for the adolescent in view of the availability of alcohol in most occupations and its role in ceremonial occasions.

In one important aspect of behaviour, their sexuality, the indenture specifically limited what apprentices might or might not do; they might not commit fornication or contract matrimony. For this reason too the apprentices were not allowed to "haunt" taverns, because of the unsuitable acquaintances they would make there. Restricting the adolescent male's opportunities for female company was not as difficult as it now might seem. Living-in apprentices were constantly under the eye of the master, his wife or the journeymen; servants also in the larger household were regular observers of assignations. Apprentices received little or no money wages and their hours of work were very long, even in the professions and prosperous trades; both factors made it difficult for apprentices to seek company. Lack of domestic privacy in the host household further reduced the apprentice's opportunities for courtship. All these conditions help to explain why a substantial number of male apprentices eventually married their masters' daughters or other female relations.

When apprentices did fornicate, they were usually caught when a bastard child was sworn to them before the local magistrates. In 1633 Richard Harrison, an apprentice to Richard Parr of Alvechurch (Worcs.) was accused of fathering her child by Jane Parr, presumably related to the master if not his daughter,[15] while at Solihull (War.) in the same decade a servant girl, Elizabeth Bull, brought a paternity suit against her master's apprentice, Edward Watton.[16] Masters recognized the temptation that young, living-in maids might prove to their apprentices; some, like William Lucas's Quaker master, sought to avoid this difficulty by providing the apprentices with their own servant, who was "selected for her absence of all charms on account of the young men; and never did anyone see such a rapid succession of swearing, gin-drinking, thieving, canting, ugly old women as we had".[17]

A master's supervision of his apprentice's morals varied very considerably from the laxity experienced by Francis Place to the strictness of a Quaker master endured by William Lucas and if only work supervision were exercised by the master, as Place claimed in London by the later eighteenth century, the old values of apprenticeship had clearly disintegrated. At the same period in the provinces, however, in even a fairly modest trade, watchmaking, the master still enforced the traditional terms of the indenture, not permitting the apprentice to be absent without permission and treating the boy as his own son. In London there is evidence that male apprentices frequented brothels, undeterred by the warnings of George Barnwell; for example, in 1764 the master of a brothel near Temple Bar was arrested and a number of clients, including many apprentices, were taken up.[18] In the same year a woman was committed to Clerkenwell bridewell for keeping a bawdyhouse in Charterhouse Lane and encouraging young apprentices; many aged less than 16 were found in her house.[19]

Clearly the problem of adolescent sexuality was a considerable one, exacerbated by such social and economic factors as late marriages and the uncertainty of life expectancy. Since puberty was reached at about sixteen years and marriage was delayed for male apprentices until the age of 21 or even 24 when they had finished their term, it is not surprising that both organized and amateur prostitution flourished.[20] Defoe complained that the increase of bachelorhood by the early eighteenth century, with deferred marriage even among the poorer classes, led directly to a rise in prostitution,[21] and it has been estimated that there were some twenty to thirty thousand bachelor apprentices in London by the eighteenth century.[22] Brothels for them were sufficiently a part of the city scene to be illustrated in a contemporary sketch[23] and their association with the occupants to cause one newspaper to comment that, as a holiday approached, "the Alewives of Islington, Kentish Town, and several other adjacent Villages, are in great expectation of a considerable Trade from the Citizens, as Harlots are from their Apprentices".[24] Not only in London, however, was prostitution a threat to the young apprentice: in 1756 a Coventry magistrate condemned the 14- and 15-year-olds who had been taken into the fields by a "dirty, disordered strumpet", adding that on Sundays this was a common practice; he was particularly incensed that apprentices were thus kept away from divine service.[25] Association with a prostitute was one of the steps Hogarth illustrated in Tom Idle's path to the gallows.

The reasons for apprentices increasingly breaking the rule of their indenture forbidding fornication from the late seventeenth century onwards seem to be threefold. First, there was a natural and widespread reaction against the Puritan restrictions of the 1650s; secondly, apprentices must have felt that they should be able to participate in the greater sexual permissiveness of the eighteenth century; thirdly, the growth of money wages and living out for some apprentices made control over their sexual behaviour almost impossible. The severity of a guild punishment for a sexual lapse indicates how seriously this clause in the indenture was regarded; thus, when one London apprentice, John Rolls, was found in bed with his master's maidservant, Margaret Byllington, both naked, in an "unthrifty" (wanton) manner, the Goldsmiths' Company had him stripped and beaten by two members of the craft, particularly because, since the event the apprentice had been boasting "often and openly" and providing an "yll ensample to other young men apprentices of the same craft".[26]

Although apprentices were to avoid fornication, they were denied the pleasures of lawful marriage according to the terms of the indenture and from the Tudor period onwards authority had been concerned at the increase of poverty attributable to "over-hasty marriages and over-soon setting-up of households by the youth".[27] Although female apprentices might have their indentures cancelled if they married before the term was complete, male apprentices were dismissed and were no longer allowed to work at their craft if they married while still bound. If for no other reason, marriage for a living-in apprentice was impossible because of accommodation problems and, in the period before money wages were paid, the young couple would have no income on which to subsist. Collyer, among many eighteenth-century commentators, advised all male apprentices against an unsuitable match. He warned that the "strongest temptation" they would meet was that which "arises from women" and that they should "despise the allurements of [their] master's female servants", for many men were ruined by marrying a maidservant, socially inferior to the apprentice and unfitted to be the wife of the craftsman or tradesman he would become.[28]

Not all apprentices were circumspect, however, and improvident marriages were made, although more difficult after Lord Hardwicke's Marriage Act of 1753, and the literate, thoughtful men, who subsequently wrote reminiscences of apprenticeship, particularly resented this restriction. Three such authors married while still apprenticed, all to women equally poor. James Dawson Burn, apprenticed to a hatter, earning 10s a week,[29] and Joseph Gutteridge, bound to the silk trade, both married in the early nineteenth century; however, if married apprentices were symbolic of the decline of provincial apprenticeship traditions, in London the changes were earlier, for Francis Place had married, aged only 19 in 1791, an impoverished 17-year-old.[30] Gutteridge was clearly aware that he was breaking a clause in his indenture, "exceeding the bounds of legality in thus contemplating matrimony . . . [he] yet considered [himself] morally entitled to choose and to follow the course which appeared most certain to lead to happiness".[31] None of these three men would have agreed with Defoe that "a married apprentice will make a repenting tradesman".[32]

Since the apprentice was to live at close quarters with the host family for between 7 and 14 years, the personal relationship with them was obviously important and the indenture specified that "in all Things as a faithful Apprentice he shall behave himself towards his said Master and all his during the said term". The pauper child was to "demean himself" towards the master and his family "honestly, orderly, and obediently". Therefore, when one London apprentice attacked his mistress, the Goldsmiths' Company punishment was that he should be beaten by his master until he bled and then, kneeling, should ask for forgiveness.[33] In practice, the apprentice was obliged to follow not only the master's orders but also those of his womenfolk, sons and older apprentices, a common complaint and cause of resentment among apprentices, especially the rule of the master's wife in trade matters. Collyer advised the apprentice to strive for domestic harmony, for it was "base and disengenuous" to "carry tales out of the family" or to entertain his friends at the expense of the reputation of his master and mistress.[34] Such an apprentice as John Coggs, with his stories of domestic strife, could have caused considerable embarrassment to his master if he had told them to his friends rather than written them in code in his commonplace book.[35] In order to prevent family friction, Collyer considered, the apprentice should not interfere in domestic concerns, not "tattle" or repeat servants' gossip, nor carry tales between his master and mistress. Most writers emphasized that the child's life could be greatly affected by the master's wife, if only on the level of domestic comfort and diet. If she ruled her husband the apprentice might then be "obliged to spend some years in running of her errands, and doing the drudgery of the house" instead of receiving his craft training.[36] This was exactly the situation young George Herbert experienced in Banbury, even having to tend a baby, until his father protested to the master that George's time was to be spent in learning shoemaking rather than in domestic tasks.[37]

In addition to forbidding the alehouse and sexual activity, the indenture also proscribed other forms of amusement for apprentices. They were not allowed to "play at Cards, Dice, Tables or any other unlawful Games", nor might they attend the playhouse. Hogarth chose gambling as the first of Tom Idle's crimes in his progress to Tyburn in 1747, playing at hustle-cap with three pickpockets during divine service, using a level tombstone as a table. The poor young craft apprentices had small means with which to gamble, but if dishonest, they could use the master's cash, goods or credit as a stake. In Leeds ten men were fined £2 each for allowing "apprentices and servants" to play at skittles on their premises,[38] while the Coventry apprentices' gambling was condemned by the magistrate, John Hewitt, along with their other unacceptable behaviour.[39] Forbidden taverns and female company, the prosperous apprentice might indulge in various forms of gambling, and John Coggs noted in his commonplace book, in code, spending the cash his mother and indulgent aunt had given him on games of cards until late at night.[40] Collyer advised his readership to avoid any form of gambling, especially for money,

196

along with singing, "hops" and the company of women.[41] One country lady, well aware of the dangers her godson might face in city life, in 1743 wrote to warn him of the "Temptations and Snares". Having advised observance of the sabbath and loyalty to his master, she added

> One thing I must give you a particular Caution of the loose Women that walk the Street on purpose to entice and pick up Men and lead them into evil, shun them as you would the Plague and be sure never to hear what they would say to you, for they are like the Devil going about seeking whom they may devour. To prevent falling into their hands you must not drink to disorder your selfe for then you may be their prey for a Drunken Man is fitt for any thing and many times commits such things when he is drunk that he repents of all his Life, and never capable of atoning for his fault.[42]

Although not forbidden by the conditions of their indentures, it was the apprentices' capacity for collective rowdyism that most frequently offended adults and it was this aspect of their corporate behaviour that roused fear and indignation among respectable citizens as apprentices became more numerous and public disorder apparently more widespread. Their numbers made them particularly active in London and they often acted against a quite specific social group, as on Evil May Day 1517, when they had rioted in Southwark against the excessive influence of foreign traders.[43] By 1592 the Privy Council was obliged to pass an act to ensure that apprentices were kept indoors by their masters on Midsummer night, but also closing their meeting places, such as playhouses.[44] In the seventeenth century London apprentices began to gather together for political and religious reasons, usually to the displeasure of adults. To justify their activities, the anonymous author of *The honour of London apprentices* (1647) stressed the important role apprentices had played in famous historic events, such as the Crusades, Edward III's French wars, in Spain with the Black Prince and, finally, how they had decided the outcome of the Wars of the Roses. The pamphlet was obviously intended to strengthen a feeling of fraternity among apprentices, who had "a kind of supernatural sympathy, a general union, which knits their hearts in a bond of fraternal affection".[45] Shortly after its publication apprentices actually interrupted parliament and purged it of the leaders of the pro-army faction. They had already engaged in distinctly political activities and in 1642 had petitioned the government for peace because they foresaw "the face of our own ruin, in our masters' present condition . . . the violation of our religion by papists and sectaries, the breach of our own laws, the invasion of the subjects' liberties, the general decay of trade". They insisted they had behaved in an orderly manner, although claims were made that they had carried weapons, for "though a multitude, we humbly conceive ourselves no tumults".[46]

In the late seventeenth century a satirist noted apprentices, "brave intent" of taking up a political role instead of their traditional adolescent sports, seeking to "advise the King and Parliament".[47] They were particularly active during the Exclusion Crisis of 1679, when some three hundred Whig apprentices in London formed themselves into an association to draw up a petition which, they claimed, had 30,000 signatures.[48] Activities such as these indicate how politicized the London apprentices had become by the end of the century, capable of considerable organization. At the same period they also held religious meetings, arranging their own services and assemblies.[49] Although there is some evidence that similar activities took place in the provinces,[50] the London apprentices' numbers were their strength, while politics may have been more actively discussed in the City than in the provinces, far from power and government.

With religion as an excuse the London apprentices continued to play a part in eighteenth-century popular disturbances, including the Gordon Riots of 1780, when 70 houses and four gaols were burned in London on a wave of anti-Catholic feeling. Of the 450 arrested and the 160 persons tried for their part in the riots, 36 were identified as journeymen and apprentices, collectively described by Walpole as "apprentices, convicts and all kinds of desperadoes",[51] a typical contemporary attitude to apprentices and the bad company they kept. In contrast, the rowdyism of provincial apprentices and their companions, although condemned by the local magistrates when youths "lurked" in the streets and robbed gardens of produce, was of a distinctly non-political kind. Many contemporary newspaper reports noted the presence of youths at occasions of public disorder (elections, food riots, trade disputes or hangings) and usually referred to them collectively as apprentices.

Apart from institutionalized, group violence, male apprentices assaulted each other fairly often, and their apprentice status was always cited in reports of these incidents, usually accurately. When two shoemaker's apprentices quarrelled, one stabbed the other "in the belly with a knife", while at a Birmingham umbrella factory a 17-year-old apprentice, described as "pert", as a result of a squabble with "two young men in his master's workshop, challenged them both to a trial of strength in the fashionable art of pugilism, and, in a desperate royal, had tipped them a black eye apiece à-la-Mendoza".[52]

The conditions of the indenture which bound the apprentice to serve the master faithfully, keep his secrets, obey his lawful commands and be honest with the master's possessions were important clauses for cancelling an agreement if an apprentice proved genuinely unsatisfactory or if the master, for any reason, wished to be rid of the child. Neglecting work and disobedience were the two most often cited reasons for dismissing an apprentice if the master went to law and the formal wording of the indenture was wide enough to cover almost any misdemeanour the apprentice might commit at work or leisure.

All writers of advice manuals, conforming to contemporary deference, considered that not only was obedience essential for an apprentice but that the master must be obeyed "chearfully and willingly, without Hesitation, Murmuring or Reluctance".[53] Typical of masters who complained was one man who said his apprentice was "idle, loose and disorderly",[54] another whose boy had committed "divers misdemeanours against him ... partly by running away ... repeatedly and behaving himself dishonestly, disorderly and disobediently",[55] while a third asserted that though his female apprentice "hath been several times for her such Misdemeanour committed to and punished in Bridewell ... [she] remains incorrigeable".[56] It was possible for a master to complain that, for an unspecified reason, his apprentice was "totally unfit and incapable of learning or ever exercising his said Trade"[57] (that of a silkweaver), while mental or physical disabilities (such as blindness) could also be cited as reasons for cancelling an indenture.

All apprentices brought to court for disobedience seem to have been guilty of repeated offences and, in such cases, the justices invariably cancelled an indenture, since a persistently disobedient apprentice was a constant source of disruption in the master's business and was demonstrably not behaving according to the letter or the spirit of the indenture. A month's hard labour in the local house of correction was a common sentence for neglectful work, absence at night or disobedience; discharge of the apprentice and loss of the premium was the punishment for repeating such behaviour.

The refractory apprentice was, according to Defoe, a greater problem as premiums grew larger in the eighteenth century, for apprentices felt "they did not give such sums of money to be confin'd like prisoners, or to be used like footboys",[58] while a master tartly observed that "now we get a hundred pound, or two or three hundred apiece with them, they are too high for reproof or correction".[59] Undoubtedly an increase in the numbers of gentlemen's sons entering trade as the seventeenth century progressed made apprentices more difficult to control. One contemporary pamphleteer was convinced that large premiums and several wealthy apprentices indentured together in the same household made for unruly behaviour, because

> apprentices must live high, and wear finer clothes than formerly they did; wait on their masters abroad and do none of the servile work, that formerly they used to do, which kept them humble. And if they were now obliged to do the same, it would keep them from growing so proud and scornful as they are, or taking the liberty they now do, of taunting at their superiors, quarrelling with their services, usage, and diet, and going from them when fit to do service.[60]

Much advice in handbooks was meant for the new provincial apprentices, adolescents like the three Isham brothers from Northamptonshire, bound to London mercers, or the stepbrothers of Sir George Sondes, indentured to merchants in the late seventeenth century.[61] These first-generation apprentices were literate but unused to city manners or life in homes other than their own and neighbouring country houses, perhaps particularly susceptible to the pleasures and dangers of London. The sons of minor gentry had presumably no personal experience of apprenticeship, although boys from legal or medical families might seek advice from their own fathers who had been apprenticed. However, difficult apprentices existed even in the godly household, for one of William Lucas's fellow apprentices to a Quaker master spent Sundays "in a way he would give no account of, and he treated [the master] with the utmost contempt . . . call him names, swear at him and abuse him in the most outrageous manner".[62] An apprentice such as John Coggs typified boys from prosperous families bound with large premiums to substantial London masters, not badly behaved enough to be dismissed, but sorely trying the master's patience by gambling, staying out late with rowdy friends, spending too much time at a rival firm and quarrelling with his master and mistress on several occasions.[63]

One of the conditions of the indenture stated that the apprentice should not be absent from the master's service day or night unlawfully, but this restriction on personal freedom was frequently ignored, especially by the more prosperous adolescent. *The apprentice's vade mecum* emphasized that

> keeping late Hours, and sometimes tarrying out whole Nights, which is in itself one of the most unwarrantable Things, (and still more pernicious in its Effects), that can possibly be committed by a young Man, is wholly inexcusable; and yet it is the natural and almost unavoidable Consequence of the haunting of Taverns and Playhouses.[64]

In the nineteenth century an apprenticeship could still be cancelled for such behaviour, as William Lucas's fellow apprentice discovered when his master observed him "with some low companions sallying out of a low court in Drury Lane",[65] exactly the kind of activity that brought parental disapproval on the young William Hickey in the 1760s.[66] One of Defoe's model apprentices described part of a master's duty as keeping a boy from doing what he should not do, "playing in the fields, or streets, or church yard, all sermon time". The apprentice's opportunities for absenting himself were few and were usually observed by someone in the household. One master's wife noticed their youngest apprentice was

> keeping bad hours . . . It is certain he has a haunt somewhere in the town, that he steals out in the morning before day, and comes softly in again as if he were a thief; and every evening, as duly as it comes, he is abroad, nobody knows where . . . it is a great pity the boy should be ruined, he was a pretty sober lad when he came thither.[67]

Even the rebellious John Coggs secured his master's permission to go and visit his aunt and the distinction between an apprentice and other adolescents in this respect was clearly and widely understood; thus when one of Pepys's household was chastised for visiting her mother, she retorted that she was not "an apprentice girl, to ask leave every time she goes abroad".[68] A century later in London the situation in the lower trades had apparently changed so greatly that Francis Place could describe the leisure hours he and his fellow apprentices enjoyed that contravened all the conditions of the indenture, with masters powerless or unwilling to intervene.

Even if temporary absence might be overlooked by a master, absconding was a very serious offence and masters were prepared to offer rewards for the return of runaways. Absconders were generally the older apprentices, better able to support themselves, predominantly male and from the manual trades rather than from the prosperous occupations. Details of many runaways have survived in settlement examinations, for a number of these apprentices ultimately needed parish aid. Usually the examinations simply state that the pauper served a number of years with a particular master before absconding, but occasionally more information was given. For example, in 1817, when seeking relief, Philip Burbidge described how he had been apprenticed when "young" to Robert Harris of Gotherington (Glos.) for seven years, and "being at that time very wild, he frequently ran away from his master's service, but always returned, and his master received him", but finally let him go, presumably glad to be rid of a troublesome adolescent.[69]

In the eighteenth century, a period of almost continuous warfare for England, it was easy for a runaway to remain uncaught by enlisting, and even some non-poor boys did so,[70] responding to the call of Captain Plume and his fellow recruiting officers. Thus William Bowles, indentured to a prosperous silversmith for seven years in 1801, "enlisted for a soldier" after only four years and ten months, while William Job, bound to his own father, a cordwainer, joined the marines with two years of his seven-year term left to serve.[71] Not all masters were prepared to let absconders go unpunished, as quarter sessions cases record. In 1678 a tanner's apprentice from Ashby-de-la-Zouch (Leics.) was confined to the house of correction for not completing his term[72] while another boy was secured in the dungeon "for neglect of service" in the hope that "it may reform his conduct on his return".[73] When a master sought to cancel an indenture because of "ill behaviour" and his own "want of employment" it is doubtful which was the true motive for going to law.[74] For repeatedly unacceptable behaviour the magistrate cancelled the indenture, allowing the master to retain the premium.[75]

The really unmanageable apprentice might also find himself consigned to the armed forces as a punishment. In 1779, John Clerk, "ag'd ab^t 12 & 4 feet 1 inch in heighth" appeared at Warwickshire Quarter Sessions for running away several times from his master, embezzling his property and being a "vagrant idle & disorderly person". The justices sentenced him to three months hard labour unless he would join the navy, and the Secretary of the Marine Society was to be asked to approve his entry.[76] Some apprentices ran away from their masters and later returned voluntarily; John Lilburne's apprentice, William Kiffin, heard a sermon preached on the fifth Commandment while playing truant and returned full of remorse.[77] Other apprentices ran away not because they "had any complaints to make against their employer; they had left him . . . because they wanted to see their mothers"[78] and simple homesickness must have been an important emotion for some younger apprentices.

If premeditated, the decision to leave a master was a serious one, and a seventeenth-century dyer's apprentice sought an astrologer's guidance on the subject. At the age of 21, having been a soldier, he wished to know "whither it is best to stay wth my Master all my Tyme out or noe & whither it will bee for my good?" His doubts may have related to his own health, for in casting his horoscope William Lilly noted that this brown-haired young man, with a scarred face, "plumpe and fatt", but of straight stature, was "subject to the stone, gravell in the kidneys etc".[79] Taking such advice was, however, exceptional; many apprentices absconded on the spur of the moment, especially if a quarrel with the master or excessive physical punishment had occurred, but a number of adolescents, like William Hutton, carefully planned their escape, preparing food and clothes for the journey. The number of newspaper advertisements that referred to apprentices absconding with spare clothes suggests some premeditation in their flight.

It is noticeable that runaways were chiefly from manual rather than from the more prosperous occupations, first, because those apprenticed with substantial premiums were supposed to be treated as part of their master's family. Secondly, wealthy parents were more likely to protest at undue harshness to their children and the apprentice was motivated to complete the term and reap the rewards of a profitable adult livelihood. Even with a premium of £250 and in a Christian household, Lucas wrote home of his poor food, long hours, uncomfortable quarters and teasing,[80] but the promise of a secure future career for such apprentices made them endure their misery. In good families too supervision was stricter and absconding more difficult. These factors did not operate in the poorer trades; parish or charity children's parents were unlikely to protest on their behalf, even if they knew of harsh treatment, for communication with their families was difficult for such children. Blatant cruelty, visible to a craftsman's neighbours, however, could occasionally make intervention possible, as in the case of little William Taylor in Spitalfields (Ch. 10). In addition, there was small prospect of a prosperous future as an incentive, so that absconding must have seemed preferable to remaining with an intolerably hard master. From the evidence of local newspapers and quarter sessions records, it is apparent that absconding increased in the years of warfare, and in one midland county, Warwickshire, a peak was reached in 1810–11:[81]

Table 9.1 Runaway apprentices in Warwickshire, 1806–12.

Year	Number of apprentices absconding
1806	11
1807	23
1808	39
1809	56
1810	86
1811	83
1812	77

It is apparent that, by this period, masters were making far less effort to recover their missing apprentices by advertising for them in the local press. However, a master's complaint that an apprentice was a persistent runaway usually secured a discharge and masters seem more anxious to have older apprentices, in the last year or two of the term, returned to them because such apprentices were, at this stage, useful and even profitable workers, apprised of the master's trade skills or secrets. According to the anonymous author of *Low life*, most London apprentices chose to abscond between the hours of 1am or 2am on Sunday mornings, "packing up their cloathes that they may make off by the help of the trap-door at the top of the house, while all the family are fast asleep". Undoubtedly harsh treatment of the more independent or truculent apprentice caused absconding and in two typical contemporary accounts of men describing their running away from their masters, cruelty was the reason given. In 1741, at the age of 17, William Hutton ran away from his uncle, a Nottingham stockinger, who was his second master, for Hutton had already served one term between the ages of 7 and 14 in a Derby silk mill. He was starved by his uncle, denied warm clothing in the winter and underpaid; he had endured his aunt's spite for some years before planning to abscond. Hutton described how he took with him a loaf of bread, his Bible, some clothes, his best wig and hat, as well as 2s, and set out for Birmingham, 50 miles away, in constant fear of recapture.[82]

Another runaway, with a good premium of £50, was Christopher Wright, apprenticed to a Staffordshire clockmaker and gunsmith in the early nineteenth century. His master unwisely gave the young apprentice a "valuable fowling piece" to clean and, when he spoiled it in the process, his master

> took hold of the gun with a countenance distorted with rage [and] shouted, "I'll try the temperature of this gun on your skull and see which is the harder". He then dealt me a blow with the barrel which indeed proved the thickness of my skull, for it was saved by Providence from damage.

The master, Richard Baker, had always thought "nothing of cuffing [him] about the head and ears if he thought [the apprentice] slow in mastering a new process which needed careful application", but in his memoirs Wright expressed his remorse at absconding, for

> had my master been of a more kindly disposition I would certainly have returned, as nothing can extenuate the crime (without great provocation) of running away from an apprenticeship, such recklessness branding the party in after life as a vagabond and wastrel.[83]

Although such memoirs tend to be self-justificatory, there is no indication in Wright's attitude that the traditional values of apprenticeship had deteriorated. The punishment for absconding was a month in prison and by 1766 the crime was so commonplace that an act was passed to add the length of time the apprentice was missing on to the end of the term.[84]

Although most runaway apprentices were male, girls did abscond, some repeatedly, and press advertisements for their return give interesting descriptions of the runaways. In 1800, for example, a Chilvers Coton (War.) ribbon-weaver, George Cooper, sought the return of his apprentice, Sarah Sergeant, who had absconded "without any cause or provocation". She was described as "about 17 years of age, of a Fair Complexion, has light hair, is of a middle Stature, and had with her two Gowns, one of them Printed, and rather of a light Colour".[85]

Such girls, however, were a minority both in advertisements and in court proceedings; of the runaways at Coventry Quarter Sessions (1757–80) only 2 were girls, while 11 were boys, but one of these girls, Mary Hunt, indentured to a ribbon-weaver, ran away several times.[86] When runaway girls were parish apprentices their absconding sometimes caused their village overseers to investigate, as, for example, in 1813, when the overseers of Astley (War.) spent 7s travelling to Hinckley (Leics.) about "Joseph Tompson's girl running away from her master Edward Woodcock".[87] A number of female runaways turned to crime or prostitution after absconding, since respectable employment or continued apprenticeship was impossible without a sponsor or reference. Such a career was that of Sarah Millege, a prisoner in Salisbury gaol in 1786. In her examination she said she believed she was aged 21 and had been born in Stapleton (Som.); she was "brot up in the poor house there – was apprenticed to her aunt, Susannah Smith of Kingswood. Run away, after servg. three years". She then supported herself by "carrying Meat and Garden stuff in Bristol Market", living in a room she rented from a shoemaker. She left Bristol for Bath, where she joined up with two minor criminals. When arrested, she had fifteen and a half guineas as well as 5s in her pocket, with silver shoe buckles, new clothes and new cloth in her bundle, all stolen.[88] It is noticeable in such cases that criminals of all kinds, from Tyburn to the small local court, referred to their broken apprenticeships as a step of some importance and, whether true or not, cited apprenticeship as an acknowl-edged symbol of good character and former respectability.[89]

The frequency with which apprentices ran away may be judged from the popularity of societies to reclaim them, as in Nottinghamshire,[90] and from the numerous advertisements in newspapers all over England, sometimes with an illustration, a woodcut of a running man, to attract the reader's eye (Appen-dix 3). The notices state the apprentice's trade, appearance (often unflatter-ing), any distinctive features or deformities and age, followed by the master's offer of a reward and a warning not to aid or harbour the runaway. A typical advertisement in 1760 was for the return of John Binns:

> Run away (late in the custody of John Eccles). On Monday, the 14th of July, 1760, about 11 o'clock in the forenoon, John Binns, of Norland, 24 years of age, about 5ft 5in. Had on a dirty drab coat, a dark coloured waistcoat, an old hat, uncocked, stitched round the edges with white thread, blackish lank hair and a long visage. Who-ever will give information of him so that he may be retaken . . . shall receive half-a-guinea reward.[91]

During the term of the apprenticeship it was obviously essential that the master could trust the apprentice with money, goods and reputation. The stupid apprentice could be deceived by a dishonest customer as, for example, a "sharper" who cheated one apprentice in the master's absence out of silver spurs and a pair of boots,[92] while the more prosperous apprentice had greater opportunities for theft.[93] Both Campbell and Collyer stressed the importance of the apprentice's keeping careful, accurate accounts, and John Coggs's com-monplace book shows how he struggled with percentages, foreign currency and discounts.[94] Clearly the more an apprentice was trusted the greater the opportunity to be dishonest. Some thefts were on a grand scale and one youth in a large shop in London's Cheapside, "of serious abstinent character", was found to have made £1,000 by stealing out of the till and by overcharging customers for six years; he invested his gains in the funds.[95]

Small-scale cheating of customers and petty larceny were fairly common crimes by apprentices against their masters, as was the theft of craft imple-ments when absconding. One Oxfordshire tailor's apprentice stole his mas-ter's goose (a special tailor's iron)[96] and a barber-surgeon's absconding apprentice took with him a number of surgical implements when he ran away to sea.[97] Such thefts may have been to enable the apprentice to work, to sell for food or even to inconvenience the master. Although in many trades per-quisites were permitted to journeymen (the tailor's cabbage, the shipwright's chips or the weaver's thrums), these benefits seem never to have been for apprentices.[98] Apart from legal deterrents, there were also the fines and physical punishments the guilds themselves imposed for theft, ranging from a few pence to a public whipping. Thus the Armourers' Company, urging their members not to go to law, themselves punished an apprentice, Peter Morris; he had initially stolen 6d from his mistress's purse and then persuaded a 14-year-old maidservant to "take a knife and pick her Mistress' Chest of 12d and give it to him" as well as stealing a penny or two for him each time she bought meat. The maidservant denied the charges, but the Armourers decided the apprentice should be whipped; he then confessed, kneeling, to ask forgiveness of his master.[99]

The criminality of apprentices was such that, in certain gaols, exclusive accommodation was provided for them, as at Birmingham and Coventry.[100] The Merchant Adventurers of Newcastle upon Tyne set up their own gaol, supervised by a specially appointed official, to which wayward apprentices could be sent. While in prison the apprentice was to be "relevyed at the charge of his master or mistress, in some stricte manner, having regard to the preservation of his or their healthes". The prison official was to "see them saifflie kept accordinglie; not sufferinge them to plaie anie ghames whatsoever, or to have the companies of anie other person or persons, or to have conference with anie at all", except with the consent of the governor of the company and of the apprentice's master. One apprentice, Allen Gilpin, who was accused of using foul language to a woman, and not apparently showing remorse, was put in the gaol on a daily diet of two-penny worth of bread and a quarter of small beer.[101]

By the early nineteenth century the problem of the absconding apprentice's turning to crime still caused concern to the authorities and in a classification of "juvenile delinquents" in London in 1822 the seventh and worst category was made up of boys who "live with prostitutes, and subsist by house-breaking etc". These were found to be "mostly parish apprentices" with some "respectably connected and refractory apprentices" among them,[102] a situation deplored by Dickens in the next decade.

The apprenticeship indenture did not specify how apprentices were to dress, but their appearance must have caused their masters some annoyance at different periods to judge from the numbers of guild regulations that were passed to control apprentices' clothes and hair. To be "apparaylden as a prentice" was acknowledged from the medieval period onwards as a form of social control, of status definition and of peer recognition, similar to any uniformed group, and the Bridewell apprentices, for example, could be easily distinguished in popular disturbances by their distinctive blue liveries.[103] The importance of identifying the apprentice when outside the master's house or shop may be seen by the use of apprentice badges by some guilds; that of the London Tin-Plate Workers had the apprentice's name and date of indenture on one side and the company emblem on the other (see Fig. 9.3).[104] The Vintners' apprentices wore a distinctive cap badge for the same purpose.[105] That such strictures were resented and ignored can be seen by the numbers of apprentices punished by their guilds for flouting these regulations. In the late sixteenth century apprentices were to wear blue gowns in winter, or blue

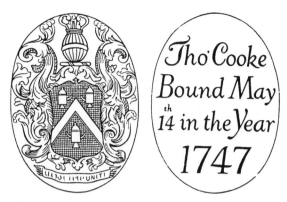

Figure 9.3 An apprentice badge from the Tin Plate
Workers' Company, 1747.

calf-length coats in summer, with flat cloth caps, shining shoes and plain
stockings. No silk was to be worn and the only weapon permitted was a
pocket-knife; how little notice was taken of these restrictions may be judged
from a mayoral statute of 1582 forbidding the wearing of colourful clothes.[106]
The master himself, according to the indenture, was responsible for clothing
the apprentice at all levels of prosperity or poverty and it was possible for a
master to be fined for dressing an apprentice improperly.[107] Presumably the
master's choice was of clothes suitable for work, hard-wearing, economical,
unfashionable and even overlarge to last longer, while the adolescent would
have preferred more stylish garments. The London Curriers forbade their
apprentices to wear hats "or anything but a woolen cap", silk ruffles or any
cloth enriched with gold, silver or silk. They were not allowed embroidered
pumps and slippers, jewellery or a sword, dagger or anything but a knife.[108]
The Grocers' Company, in about 1611, specified in even greater detail how
apprentices might dress; the doublet collar was to have neither "poynt, well
[whale] bone, or plaits", but to be made, as were the breeches, only of "cloth,
kersey, fustian, sackcloth, canvasse, English leather or English stuffe", costing
not more than 2s 6d a yard. Apprentices' stockings were to be of woollen,
yarn or kersey, and they were not to wear "Spanish shoes with Polonia
heels".[109] In 1608 any apprentice unsuitably dressed for his position, "rather
beseeming some courtier", wearing gold or silver buttons, lace or jewels, was
to lose his finery at the first offence and be punished for the second.[110]

That such excesses were not practised only in London may be seen in the
passing of "an acte for the apparrell of apryntyces" empowering the mayor,
alderman and sheriffs of Newcastle upon Tyne to make severe regulations to
control apprentices' dress. Masters were to be fined if their apprentices'
appearance did not conform and the apprentices were to forfeit the years
of their term they had already served. The Newcastle Adventurers were
particularly active against apprentices' finery and set limits in the late seven-

teenth century on what their clothing should cost. It was to be "plain and of cloth under x^s the yarde, or of fustian of or under iij^s the yeard, nor to wear any velvate or lace . . . neither any silke garters".[111] Such strictures and the measures to enforce them indicate a very fashionable group of young men far from London.

A problem for any apprentice who acquired additional clothes was where to store them in the essentially unprivate accommodation in the master's house and in order to make it more difficult for adolescents to gather a wardrobe together, the keeping of trunks and chests without permission was specifically forbidden by a number of guilds. Thus the Curriers' apprentices were not allowed to keep clothes anywhere except the master's house, whose connivance meant a fine of 6s 8d to the poor of his parish.[112] Although Richardson caricatured the apprentice who aped the man of fashion, a contemporary also hoped that some

> good Law were thought of, to restrain the far more destructive Practices of our modern Apprentices, viz. those of Whore and Horse-keeping, frequenting Taverns Clubs and Playhouses, and their great Excesses in Cloathes, Linen, Perriwigs, Gold and Silver Watches, &c.[113]

The wearing of clothes inappropriate to the apprentice's status was always seen as an attempt to be mistaken for someone of higher rank, even as insubordination, so that "attorney's clerks and city apprentices dress like cornets of dragoons".[114] However, regulations to control the personal style of apprentices' dress were intended for the more prosperous rather than the poorer adolescent, lacking a parent's money to spend. Even poor youths, however, had personal preferences in dress and Place noted the drab and unattractive clothes thought suitable for apprentice boys, with "no taste no attention to their convenience . . . the ugly dress of an ill-dressed man was common to them".[115] It is not surprising that, in the 1790s, apprentices hired finery to wear on Saturday nights[116] or that factory children at Measham spent some of their earnings on "trifling Articles of Dress; somewhat superior to the usual apparel worn".[117]

With little money to spend, poorer apprentices could still indulge in hairstyles that were individual, and "weare their haire long [and] locks at their eares like ruffians". During the Commonwealth, long hair was particularly attacked as signifying disorderliness and guild regulations were made that every apprentice "shall cutt his haire from the crowne of the heade, keepe the foreheade bare, his lockes (if any) shall not reache belowe the lapp of his eare, and the same length to be observed behynd". After two months nine boys in Newcastle had still not complied, so their heads were shaved and they were imprisoned.[118] In London too apprentice grocers' hair was to be worn without any "tufte or lock, but cut short in decent comely manner"[119] while a pewterer's apprentice had his unseemly hair summarily cut off. The City Ironmongers refused his freedom to any apprentice in 1638 if he had not "orderly cutt and barbed his hayre", since boys had recently worn their hair "overlong, more like to ruffians than citizens apprentices".[120] As soon as false hair became fashionable in the late seventeenth century apprentices were forbidden to wear long or short wigs that cost more that 15s.[121] Beards were also not allowed to older apprentices in some crafts; the barber-surgeons, for example, permitted an apprentice no more than 15 days' growth of beard, or his master would be fined half a mark. The cutting of overlong hair was a hated punishment used to humiliate the unmanageable apprentice; such a boy, in 1647, after "evill and stubborne behaviour" and frequent absences, was brought before the barber-surgeons' court. There he behaved

> rudely and most irreverently . . . towards his said M^r and the whole Court in sawcy Language and behaviour using severall oathes protesting he [would] not serve his M^r whatever [should] come of it. The Court did therefore cause the Haire of the said apprentice, being indecently long, to be cut shorter.[122]

These severe restrictions on apprentices' fashionable inclinations must be seen in contemporary terms, when dress was a visual form of status, rather than in modern terms as a form of self-expression. At a period when people of all ages were judged by their appearance, to dress above one's station was to confuse accepted social norms and to trick one's acquaintances. Many commentators inveighed against fashionable extravagances and contemporary drama was full of deceivers and their dupes as characters. Richardson was at pains to point out to the young apprentice the evils of "pride and affectation" in dress as

> one of the epidemick Evils of the present Age, immers'd, from the Highest to the Lowest, in Luxury and Sensuality. It is an Evil with terrible Consequences and lifts up the young Man's mind far above his Condition as an Apprentice. This Vice has inverted all Order and destroy'd all Distinction; and you shall now hardly step into any Shop, but you shall see a starch'd powder'd Youth, that, but for his Station behind the Counter, your Fathers would have address'd to rather as the Son of a Man of Condition, than Servant put to learn a Trade for his future Subsistence . . . nothing can be more incongruous to his Situation and Circumstances of Life, as an Apprentice, or shew a more light and frothy Mind, and greater Depravity of Manners, than this Apish Affectation and Vanity of Dress, which must make him despis'd by the sober Part of Mankind, and valued by no one living but himself.[123]

Apart from unsuitable or criminal behaviour, it was also possible for an apprentice to be discharged for being in some way disabled, unfit to learn a trade skill. The London craft companies were particularly aware of this problem and some, for example, the Carpenters and Clothworkers, specified that their court was to see a potential apprentice "be not lame croked ne deformed".[124] Some children were obviously unsuitable for any kind of apprenticeship, which did not prevent their parish officials seeking to arrange one and so remove a long-term burden from the ratepayers. One such child was Edward Coles, bound to George Geydon of Northampton for seven years with a £5 premium and £1 in addition for clothes, which Geydon claimed he had spent in six months. Geydon produced witnesses to swear that the apprentice was

> subject to this infirmity that he can neither lie dry in his bed nor keep himself cleanly in his apparel but doth void his excrements in both, whereby he becomes troublesome and loathsome to the whole family where he lieth.

Geydon insisted that the "infirmity was altogether concealed from him" when he indentured the boy, who was duly returned to his home parish; the master repaid £3 6s 8d to the apprentice.[125] Another apprentice was, when blind, consigned to the workhouse by his master, who sought to cancel the indenture.[126] Special provisions for one apprentice were made by Stratford-upon-Avon overseers who, binding a partially sighted boy in 1786 to a local woolcomber, endorsed the indenture to allow for the eventuality of his becoming totally blind.[127] Placing a blind child with a master was obviously a considerable problem, and some were re-apprenticed; thus John Ensor, a "poor blind child", had been bound by Bedworth overseers to a ribbon-weaver in an adjacent parish in 1788 but after two years was re-indentured to a Coventry weaver, with whom he apparently remained.[128] Some apprentices were impossible to bind, so that John Bowlt, a shipwright's apprentice, had had two masters, but another man would not take him "because of disease".[129]

Some children could be apprenticed by offering an additional premium to an intending master[130] but such arrangements could bring their own problems. One Nottingham alderman had taken an interest in "a very symple boye, littell better than a naturall foole" and had him bound to a local tailor, from whom the boy then stole. The alderman was obliged to intercede for the apprentice, so that he was not punished because of diminished responsibility.[131]

In assessing the level of unsatisfactory or actual criminal apprentices it is impossible to determine what proportion of the whole they formed. Two aspects of the problem remain. First, that their numbers varied very greatly depending on the overall economic and even political situation in England

and also in their own localities, so that harvest failure, war, production levels of particular goods and population growth or decline made more or fewer apprentices rebellious or obedient, tractable or criminal. Secondly, they seem to have engendered public comment in most decades, generally in an unfavourable way, for their personal behaviour, even if this did not become criminal, when they broke the norms expected of their recognized status in society, and they were subjected to additional strictures from their own guilds, who sought conformity and a respect for established standards. Apprentices were clearly a recognizable social group by at least the Tudor period, with distinct crimes of which they were regularly accused, particularly theft, dishonesty and absconding. Although the terms of the indenture were quite specific about what apprentices might and might not do, it also contained such wide generalizations about their personal behaviour that almost any of their activities could be interpreted as an infringement of the indenture by a master who wished to be free of his apprentice. It seems inevitable that the majority of misdemeanours by apprentices were punished by their masters in the traditional ways of corporal punishment or deprivation of privileges, with recourse to the law or to the craft guild only when such measures failed and allowances could not be made for behaviour as adolescent high spirits.

CHAPTER 10

Harsh and criminal masters

A few days since the Murder of an Apprentice Girl to a Nailer at Oldbury, was, by Suspicion, discover'd at the Time of her Funeral; when upon opening her Coffin, many wounds were found in her given with Rod Iron when red-hot, since which the Coroner's Inquest have sat on the Body, and brought in their Verdict Wilful Murder; upon which her Master was committed to Shrewsbury Gaol.

Aris's Birmingham Gazette (21 December 1747)

The complex relationship between master and apprentice, defined both in law and customary practice, required each participant to contribute skills and receive either service or instruction in exchange. The master was obliged by the indenture to provide for the apprentice "proper" meat, drink, clothes, lodging, washing and "all other things fit", which might include medical attention. The pauper's master at the end of the term was to provide "double apparel", two complete outfits for the apprentice, for work and holiday wear; he was in addition to ensure that the child did not become a charge on the parish. The master of a non-poor apprentice contracted to teach the child a specified trade. A minority of indentures allowed the master to administer due physical correction, but it was an infrequent clause and presumably inserted only for the potentially troublesome child. Thus a master might break any of these undertakings and become a criminal, deliberately or accidentally. No indenture specified how apprentices should be treated, and the master, *in loco parentis*, might punish a child saving only life and limb. Only when masters exceeded these limits and treated apprentices with extreme cruelty or caused their death was an indenture cancelled and the masters punished, but such cases are extremely rare in court proceedings.

The popular concept of a master's duty was a biblical one, that, as Abraham, he would "command his children and his household",[1] an aspect of paternal control that was stressed by pamphleteers and dramatists in many different decades as a vital aspect of apprenticeship. The criteria for an ideal master were set out in the eighteenth century by most writers on the subject. All agreed with Defoe's fictional master that he was

> a parent to the boy tho not a father, and that the duty of taking care of him, both soul and body, was mine . . . 'tis but murdering youth, and robbing their fathers, to take young men and keep them under no government.

His wife insisted that apprentices, "by their indentures, are entirely subjected to their master's government".[2] A change in this relationship was noted and deplored by Defoe as early as 1727, when he suggested that in recent years apprentices had become unruly, "more like gentlemen than servants", and he blamed high premiums for this. His remedy was that apprenticeship ought

> in justice to be a school to [the apprentice], where he ought to learn everything that should qualify him for his business, at least everything his master can teach him; and if he finds his master backward or unwilling to teach him, he should complain in time to his own friends that they may supply . . . the defect.[3]

The master's duties, however, involved not only teaching craft skills but also a moral responsibility for the apprentice's formal religious training, including preparation for Anglican confirmation.[4] In all apprenticeships, in any economic situation, the calibre of the master was vital; his qualities and attitudes determined the success of the technical training, the moral standards inculcated and the daily treatment the child received. Collyer considered that "the grossest errors [were] frequently committed" in the choice of a suitable master and that "for want of sufficient care in this particular, the unhappy youth is inevitably ruined"; he added that the boy's happiness chiefly depended upon the master. The ideal master should be a man of "perfect integrity, humanity, and piety", for a dishonest master would teach a boy to be a knave, while a reprobate would sow the seeds of "vice and profaneness". The master's skills were vital, for a poor craftsman-teacher produced an apprentice who was a bungler all his life. Collyer recognized a master could be at fault by withholding his trade secrets and using his apprentices as "slaves", contravening both the spirit and the letter of the indenture.[5]

When the specific conditions of the indenture were not fulfilled, the aggrieved party could complain to quarter sessions and request the arrangement be cancelled. An interesting collection of complaints and infringements has survived in the quarter sessions for Coventry, where apprenticeship was traditionally valued, for the years 1757–63 and 1773–80 (13 years in all),[6] when there were 74 cases involving apprentices and masters in breach of their indentures. There were 12 categories into which these cases fell, but the majority of misdemeanours (68.9 per cent) were the fault of the master rather than the apprentice:

Table 10.1 Apprenticeship cases at Coventry Quarter Sessions, 1757–63 and 1773–80.

Reason for cancellation	Number of cases	% of total
Master ran away	22	29.7
Master poor	12	16.2
Master cruel	10	13.5
Apprentice ran away	7	9.4
Apprentice misbehaved	7	9.4
Mutually agreed	6	8.1
Master neglected apprentice	3	4.1
Master immoral to apprentice	2	2.7
Apprentice ill	2	2.7
Apprentice unfit to teach	1	1.3
Master bankrupt	1	1.3
Master imprisoned for debt	1	1.3

The commonest complaint, that of a master's absconding, was most frequently recorded during the years 1775–9, when 15 of the cases occurred. These men were from various trades, not all impoverished (a baker, weaver, breeches-maker, barber, capper, tailor, shagweaver and engine-weaver), as well as silk- and ribbon-weavers. Such cases often came to court at the instigation of local overseers of the poor, obliged to provide for destitute apprentices abandoned in the master's parish or returned to their home area. In some cases the absconding master's family went with him, but in others his wife and family were deserted along with the apprentices of the runaway Coventry masters; two were said to be hiding in London. A master's poverty and inability to maintain the apprentice was also a common reason for cancelling an indenture and the Coventry tradesmen in this category included a flax-dresser, weaver, ribbon-weavers (five) and silk-weavers (two), all of whom could no longer afford to keep their apprentices in the necessities of food and clothes specified in the indenture. In one case both the master, a ribbon-weaver, and apprentice had become inmates of the workhouse. Another master, a silk dyer, had been imprisoned for debt, while a printer left Coventry to become "a strolling player about the country";[7] in both cases their apprentices became chargeable to the parish.

After a master's absconding and poverty, in the third category of cases, the master's cruelty to his apprentice, there was deliberate harshness rather than misfortune or accident. Such men were accused of beating, immoderately correcting, abusing or "greatly misbehaving" towards the child, rather than of failing to provide adequate food or clothes. One Coventry master, a brass founder, threatened to "be the death" of his apprentice,[8] while in another case the child gave "full Proof of the Truth of . . . having been cruelly beaten and abused" to the court.[9] Two Coventry chimney-sweep's apprentices were discharged in 1774 because he had greatly misused and ill-treated them by beating.[10] The petitioners on behalf of the two climbing-boys were their mothers, a widow and a porter's wife, both from Birmingham, with whom the children must have retained some kind of contact. The sweep, Thomas Morgan, pleaded guilty, but he had indentured two young Warwick boys a decade earlier, one a pauper,[11] and there was no suggestion that they were ill-treated. Fines for masters in such circumstances were usually low; 6s 9d in 1774, for example.[12]

Apprentices might also seek to be discharged because they had been sexually abused by their masters, and two of the Coventry cases were in this category. The infrequency of such cases may mean that masters did not, as they were *in loco parentis*, break the incest barriers, or that cases were not brought to court because so notoriously difficult to prove. In 1760 Elizabeth Payne, apprenticed to Edward Warren of Coventry, a silk-weaver, complained of the "Misbehaviour of her said Master towards her by frequently attempting to seduce her Chastity and by having ben guilty of great indecencies towards her". The girl gave "full Proof of the Truth of the said Complaint" and was freed from her apprenticeship. In the following year a substantial Coventry ribbon merchant, William Burgess, was accused by his apprentice, George Farmer, of "misusing and evil intreating the said Apprentice by Sodomitical practices towards him and against his Consent"; the master could not disprove the accusation and the indenture was cancelled.[13]

Although Coventry had a substantial apprentice population, and therefore such cases were perhaps more frequent, other areas of England show a similar variety of neglectful or cruel masters in their quarter sessions and assizes, contemporary newspapers, pamphlets and broadsheets. Teaching his occupational skills was a master's duty to the prosperous or charity child, but not an undertaking to a pauper. Contravention of this particular clause was greatly resented, especially when the apprentice was made to do domestic or menial tasks unconnected with the specified occupation. Such infringements occurred in even the wealthy trades; an apothecary's apprentice objected to being an errand boy and having to put up and take down the shop shutters[14] while a goldsmith's apprentice protested when "wholly employed in drawing potts of drink and carrying the same out to his customers".[15] Even a pump-maker's apprentice, one of Campbell's humbler trades, complained to the justices when he was "almost constantly employed in drawing of beer, both Sundays and working days".[16] Minding the master's children was equally resented, especially by male apprentices, one of whom described how his time was spent in "making [the] fires and doing other household work and also looking after [the] young child of about some eight months old". When he told his father that he was spending his apprenticeship taking the master's baby for walks, the situation was quickly rectified, without recourse to the law, when his father complained directly to the shoemaker.[17] Not all complaints were treated seriously, however, so that when one weaver's apprentice alleged he was taught only simple, unskilled work, the case was dismissed as "vain and frivolous and grounded upon the humour of the apprentice's mother".[18]

Apart from providing instruction, the master was obliged to feed, clothe and lodge an apprentice and, if trade fell off, economies could easily be made on the child's maintenance. The parish premium clearly encouraged a poor master to indenture a child, whom he could not afford to keep once the money was spent and for whom he had insufficient work; such masters could either go on parish relief or abscond, but in either case the apprentice suffered greatly. A pitiable example of a master in these circumstances was recorded in the case of a Warwick charity boy, William Taylor, a labourer's son, bound to a Spitalfields master in the 1830s. In January 1837 the boy's father received a letter from London:

> No 13 Norton Folgate
> Corner White Lion Sr
> Shoreditch
>
> Jany 17 1837

Mr Taylor

Sir

I am sorry to be compelled to act the part of a Mediator with you for your poor Lad who lives with Mr Moon Tailors Shop in York Street Spitalfields. He has [declared] to me that he is half starved never having more than two indifferent meals a day & frequently not any & as to his Clothes he is like a Beggar having nothing but Rags and wearing no Shirt. Now I cannot think that a Parent can Patiently bear this – for his distressful condition is enough to move the heart of the most indifferent – besides being occasionally beat & illtreated by both Mr & Mrs Moon. I do hope you will not mention my name when you send for him (though I would not advise you to send the Money to Mr Moon to have him conveyed home, for I think he would not part with him for a mere message) as I am related to Mr Moon & it would make great unpleasantness – you have only to confront your Son in the presence of Mr & Mrs Moon & I doubt not you will be satisfied at least if he relates the same deplorable history that he gave me.

I am Sir
Yours Respec^y

N. Norton[19]

Not providing adequate clothing was a common complaint against poor masters, typified by a Shoreditch baker who

> had not allowed [his apprentice] sufficient clothing, and being bare-foot, gave him sixpence to buy a pair of shoes. Not being able to buy a pair for sixpence he durst not go home for fear of his master's furious passion till about eight o'clock of the night, when the master refused to admit him in and the next day caused him to be sent to the House of Correction where he has remained ever since at hard labour.

Another child described how she was given only one stuff gown and a baize petticoat during her five-year term. Lack of an adequate diet was, however, a more serious and constant cause of apprentices' complaints, and one girl was so ill-fed that she had to beg bread from her master's neighbours. In this case her accommodation was also unsatisfactory, for she slept on "a very small flock bed and six of them lays therein, some at the foot and some at the head". Her master, a hair-twister, was actually serving a six-month sentence in Newgate at the time, leaving the child destitute.[20] Even a more prosperous master might keep a child "barfoote and bare-legged in the Winter, and fasting", as a Nottingham butcher's apprentice claimed when seeking the restitution of his premium (£5 and two loads of coals).[21] If a master were at fault and an indenture cancelled, returning the apprentice's clothes was usual; at Hertfordshire Quarter Sessions in 1772 a grocer-tallow chandler, guilty of ill-treating his apprentice, handed back all the boy's clothing, a coat, three waistcoats, breeches, aprons and stockings.[22]

An apprentice's treatment was clearly related to the master's prosperity and in lower crafts and trades harshness might be expected. However, there was little a master gained by so cruelly punishing or ill-treating an apprentice that the child became incapable of work. Undoubtedly the abuse that reached the courts and press was of a very serious nature indeed. A master such as John Crofts, with his wife, committed a terrible catalogue of cruelties against their female apprentice, including some form of sexual abuse:

> *imprimis*, the sayd John Crofts . . . is not to make nor medle with her, upon anye Condition.
> *Item*, since hee hath beaten her in her heade most greeveiously sundrie tymes.
> *Item*, moreover, hee hath beaten her upon the face, which were most greivous, that she had almost lost one of her eyes.
> *Item*, since that tyme, hee hath beaten her and punched her with his fiste upon her syde, that she was scarse able to take her winde.
> *Item*, that by him and by her, she was so beaten and pinched upon her armes divers tymes, that they were so black, it would pittie any Christian to behold.

Item, he hath beaten her upon the face, that he hath made her byte her lipps with her owne teeth

In such serious cases direct protests to the master were of little avail, for he had already sworn that she would have even worse treatment because she had complained publicly.[23]

The apprenticeship indenture defined the physical punishment a master might administer as "due" or "moderate" so that when a Wiltshire man whipped his nine-year-old apprentice with 60 stripes at a time, the indenture was cancelled. Death at a master's hands remained a rare category of murder, however, and in the same county, of nearly 3,000 coroner's bills for the mid-eighteenth century, only nine were of deceased apprentices. Of these, one committed suicide, a climbing-boy suffocated and two died from natural causes. However, three of the nine were murdered by their masters and two died of ill-treatment, but not "wilful intent to destroy".[24] The majority of masters accused of murdering their apprentices were acquitted or only lost the premium, while a minority were hanged, in contrast to other murderers in Georgian England. Thus one Nottinghamshire master and his wife were only bound over for beating and abusing their apprentice "inasmuch as he dyed upon itt within halfe a yere after as is affirmed by ye childs mother in Court".[25] Sometimes it was possible to protect a child from repeated violence at a master's hands but continue the apprenticeship and in Norwich, when a man had unreasonably corrected his apprentice, he entered into a bond not to do so again.[26]

Physical violence to apprentices was common in a majority of trades for spoiled work, disobedience or unruly behaviour and to many inarticulate men physical correction was the only punishment they knew how to give, in spite of William Hutton's comment that "when correction is often made it steels the breast of the inflictor"[27] and apprentices had few privileges or wages to be reduced as an alternative to corporal punishment. Undoubtedly many men were unfit to be masters as, for example, the gunmaker who nearly killed his apprentice for spoiling a valuable fowling-piece as he cleaned it (Ch. 9). This apprentice later absconded.[28] Even older apprentices near the end of the term could be beaten by their master, as Henry Cary's swain was for quitting his work when Sally went by, "My master comes like any Turk/ And bangs me most severely."[29] However, only repeated, persistent cases of cruelty were likely to go to court and as an apprentice's parents, relatives or friends usually made the complaint, contact with the family was essential. Illiterate, poor parents were unlikely to protest about any kind of master.

Overseers of the poor only rarely took cruel masters to court, for the parish would have been unwilling to take children back if the indentures were cancelled, while only exceptional overseers enquired about a master's character and standing before their apprentices were bound. Some abuses were exposed through the intervention of a cruel master's neighbours. Thus when a

Hackney tambour-worker named Jouveaux treated his 17 parish apprentices cruelly and five died "in a decline" he was found guilty of

> assaulting and very cruelly beating Susannah Archer, a child of fifteen years of age, his apprentice; of employing her to work in his business . . . beyond her strength, at unseasonable hours and times; of neglecting to provide for her proper clothing and necesaries, whereby she was stated to be emaciated and her health impaired.[30]

These girls embroidered on muslin from 4am or 5am until 11pm or midnight, sometimes till 2am or 3am in the morning. Their food was bread, water and rice; they ate while sitting at their embroidery frames and they slept in a garret on three beds. The neighbours' concern was aroused when they heard the girls shrieking and saw them hunting for food in the pig trough. The force of public opinion made Jouveaux move his workshop to Stepney Green at 4am because his neighbours cried "Shame!" at him.[31] In such cases, it is impossible to assess personal spite as a factor, but there were often numbers of witnesses to tell the same story.

There are striking differences in the punishments for masters found guilty of murdering their apprentices; "wilful" cruelty ending in the child's death might result in a capital sentence or manslaughter verdict. By the later eighteenth century new legislation enabled members of the public to act when they suspected a master of intolerable cruelty towards apprentices, particularly the parish children most at risk. An interesting case of this kind was that of Elizabeth Robbins, so harshly treated that she died, but her sufferings were noted by her master's neighbours and the assize judge made the trial an occasion for pronouncing on the duties of those who indentured parish apprentices.

Elizabeth Bott Robbins, baptised at Kenilworth on 22 May 1793,[32] was apprenticed by her home parish on 23 November 1803[33] with a premium of £3 to Thomas Swift of Coventry, a ribbon-weaver, who had had a male apprentice seven years earlier. Elizabeth's father, Richard, was serving in the Foot Guards in London when she was indentured, although she may, from the evidence of her middle name, have been a stepchild or illegitimate. In 1810, when she was 16, an inquest was held in Coventry and, after 12 hours' investigation, a verdict of "wilful Murder by starving" was pronounced against Thomas Swift and Ursula, his wife.[34] The Swifts were acquitted of murder, but later tried for a misdemeanour, assaulting and ill-treating Elizabeth. During the trial three other young girls, also Swift's apprentices, and three neighbours gave evidence about the "several instances of harsh and severe treatment" the children received. The adult witnesses all observed that the apprentices seemed "to want the necessary quantity of food". The matron of Coventry workhouse, Mrs Sturley, referred to the "Distressed situation in which the children were when they were taken away from the [Swifts] and placed in her care". Three medical practitioners were unanimous about

Elizabeth's condition. Bradford Wilmer, an eminent Coventry surgeon with Poor Law experience, said that "the quantity of food which the deceased was allowed, as described by the other apprentices, was not sufficient to support the health and strength of a girl of her age, who worked as she did". Joseph Collins, another surgeon, agreed, while the third medical witness, Dr Terry, testified that "the small quantity of food which the deceased received, with the work she performed, would have produced much debility and impaired her constitution".

In his summing up to the jury, the judge emphasized the value of the medical evidence, which he thought "the most important part of the case". He remarked that "young persons [might] carry a case far beyond its fair hearing", but added that it was "remarkable" the Swifts did not produce as witnesses for their defence any local tradesmen, butchers or bakers, from whom they had bought the apprentices' food, and so prove the quantity purchased. He then advised the jury that if the unanimous medical evidence had satisfied them "the weak state of this child was brought on by want of proper and necessary food", then they must find Swift guilty, but of manslaughter, not murder. The case provides good firsthand evidence of the ribbon-weaving apprentice's hours and general living conditions in a poor family. Swift's female apprentices worked a 15-hour day in winter, longer in summer; their diet was inadequate and monotonous, greatly deficient in protein and vitamins for adolescents. Deliberate cruelty was described by two apprentices; Swift beat Elizabeth Robbins on several occasions, threatened to kill her, pulled her ears until she bled, forced a candle into her mouth and tried to induce another apprentice to beat her. Further harshness was inflicted by isolating the girl from social contacts, complaining when she visited a neighbour and watching her wherever she went, even to the privy. She seems to have been particularly victimized by her master and two witnesses commented that she was "not so well used as the other apprentices". In his summing up the judge insisted the case had wide implications and the local press commented that "his observations claim our attention". His Lordship said that apprentices in general were involved in this case, for

> it is the duty of masters, and it should be distinctly known so, that the health of their apprentices should not be impaired either by excess of labour or for want of wholesome and proper nourishment . . . it is to the master that the apprentices ought to look for support. By taking apprentices he takes upon himself to support them, and if he cannot support them in a manner they should be supported, he ought to give them up . . . it ought to be publicly made known, that masters, who take apprentices, are bound to supply them with what is necessary to their health and comfort, and if they do not, the law will punish, and punish severely, all those who are guilty of such cruelty and inhumanity.

Swift was sentenced to two years' imprisonment and hard labour in the House of Correction, while his wife was acquitted as a result of the judge's advice to the jury that it was Swift, as the master, who was responsible for the apprentices' welfare.

Popular opinion was some form of protection to apprentices if it were suspected that the master had blatantly violated the norms of the relationship. When a Nuneaton master took three of his apprentices before the magistrates for "their disobedience of his orders in not appearing at his door on the Sunday preparatory to going to church" the boys were sent to Bridewell and whipped. A local diarist noted "people generally . . . very indignant at the severety of Mr Stowe"; in the following year the townspeople threatened to donkey him for employing blackleg labour during a strike.[35]

Community protest when apprentices were ill-treated is occasionally recorded; in 1812 Martha Cave was convicted of cruelty to her parish apprentice, the court pronounced against her "barbarity" and, in the pillory, she was "much pelted with mud and filth by the populace".[36] Cruelty to an apprentice could be so extreme that it became the topic of a contemporary pamphlet; such was the case of Ann Hands, who died in March 1783 as a result of her ill-usage. Apprenticed as a 14-year-old orphan by Birmingham workhouse, sent to a Chilvers Coton ribbon-weaver, John Clay, "upon likes" (on trial), she endured a year of beatings, injuries and starvation. Her condition was reported by a local curate to the magistrate, Sir Roger Newdigate, who quickly removed her from Clay's house and lodged her, with medical care, for a month. Ann's health recovered, but the brutal treatment began again when she returned to Clay and she died. At the trial nine witnesses described her time as an apprentice; Clay's defence was that he beat her because she did not work hard enough. The post-mortem examination revealed that she died from lack of food. The local press added a rare editorial comment to the report of the trial:

> The conduct of the prisoner towards the deceased was so compleatly cruel as scarcely to be equalled by any former instance of barbarity, and such that could only be exercised by a person possessed of a heart steeled against every feeling of humanity.

After his execution at Warwick, Clay's body was carried on a cart through Coventry and then gibbeted at Tuttle Hill, near Nuneaton, a rare event watched by more than 4,000 people.[37] A local diarist noted the murder and the fact that Clay was "hung in Cheans".[38] The evidence against Clay was so damning that the jury took only ten minutes to reach a verdict.[39] An enhanced punishment for a master who murdered his apprentice could be, as at Worcester in 1760, for his body to be anatomized after the execution.

The varieties of cruelty a master might inflict on apprentices were very great, sometimes resulting in permanent physical damage, as experienced by one shoemaker's apprentice whose master beat his head and body with a great leathern strap and afterwards with a broomstick so that he has been disabled in his left hand ever since. His master tied him to a bedpost, so that he was in danger of losing his left eye.[40]

The only punishment for such a man was usually the loss of the apprentice's service and frequently having to return all or part of the premium. The child, however, might be permanently harmed by the experience. Thus Rebecca Giles, a pauper of St Giles, Cripplegate, was discharged from her indenture after having been "beat and abused by her master that her right arm was so much bruised that [she] might have lost the use of it but for [the Lord Mayor's] clemency in getting her into S. Bartholomew's Hospital". As in many cases, physical violence was only part of general ill-treatment, for this girl's master had

kept her so low in clothes and other necessaries that in the hard winter . . . she was obliged to wear shoes without soles, and for want of necessary apparel (her clothing being in a tattered condition) was almost perished with cold.[41]

Occasionally a master neglected his apprentice because he was himself in difficulties; thus when a dissenting tailor was jailed, his apprentice asked local magistrates to cancel the indenture.[42] A master might also be a common felon, and this too was a valid reason for discharging an apprentice to seek another master.[43]

As well as physical cruelty, some apprentices clearly suffered sexual abuse from masters. In Elizabeth Robbins's case the judge was particularly concerned to discover if her master had ever gone to her chamber at any time, and undoubtedly apprentices were potentially at risk when living in their master's house, away from friends and relations. Such serious complaints are recorded in Coventry in the late eighteenth century by both boys and girls,[44] while four charity children were returned to the London Foundling Hospital because "debauched" by their master in the 1770s.[45] Apart from the difficulty of proving such cases, their infrequency may indicate that sexual abuse of the apprentice was acknowledged as a violation of the paternal role and so tantamount to incest.

Various cases of sadistic behaviour, however, were recorded; one female apprentice was hanged, naked, by her thumbs and lashed 21 times, while on a different occasion she had seven-pound weights locked round her waist.[46] In the same court another apprentice reported having been beaten, salted and held naked next to a fire.[47] One of the more bizarre incidents involving the sexual abuse of apprentices occurred in 1764 at Malmesbury (Wilts.), where a farmer was accused of maiming and castrating his two apprentices, aged 8 and 16. The master, Henry Timbrell,

[had] assumed divers characters to support a life of indolence and laziness: sometimes he was a Methodist Preacher or an Anabaptist Teacher, but of late he made a practice of breeding up bastard children for a stipulated sum. Two of the boys he tried to dispose of by throwing them in the way of the smallpox. Failing at that, he decided to castrate them in the hope of selling them as singers to the Opera. One night, when they were in bed, he proceeded to wicker them, after the manner in which poor rams are castrated.

Timbrell was indicted for "maiming" Tommy Hay, "an infant, about eight years, by depriving him of both of his testicles" and for the same crime against Robert Brown, aged 16, his other apprentice, "by depriving him of one of his testicles". For each of the offences Timbrell was fined 13s 4d and sentenced to two years' imprisonment. In addition, on his release, he had to give £50 as security for his good behaviour for life and also two sureties of £25 before he was let out of prison.[48] Timbrell seems unaware that by this decade, eighteenth-century musical taste appreciated castrati far less. The eighteenth-century regional press invariably reported such cases in great detail. Thus, when an Oldbury nailer's apprentice was murdered in 1747, the red-hot rod marks on her body were noted. The master, with a show of indifference, then madness, was executed at Shrewsbury gaol four months later.[49]

In spite of the harshness many apprentices experienced, it seems unlikely that most masters intended to kill them, but to cause suffering as a form of discipline which, *in loco parentis*, they were permitted. There were, however, some masters and mistresses who actually meant their apprentices to die, for example, Henry Oughton, a husbandman, who took Anne Ragg for 11 years with a £7 premium. Quarter sessions heard how he treated her for five years with "undue and inordinate correction" before trying to poison her. She did not die and was released from her master, who was ordered to repay £4 of her premium to her parents.[50] In 1783 a farmer's wife was accused of murdering Mary Allen, a parish apprentice, by beating and starvation. Although the woman was found not guilty of murder, the burial register carried a most unusual annotation by the incumbent:

11 September : Mary Allen, 10 Years of Age; murdered by her Mistress, Ann Pratt, a farmer's Wife of Leather-Iron in this Parish, where she lived in the Capacity of a Parish Apprentice. This, however, was the Verdict of the Jurors; N. B. But at the Assizes the Verdict was Manslaughter.[51]

Since the relationship between master and apprentice was a familial one, the possibility of violence was always present. The physical closeness in which life was endured could easily lead to hostility, intolerance and open violence, with the apprentice an easy victim, especially if young or small. For the inarticulate master a blow was the easiest form of correcting poor work, lateness or other misdemeanours. There was enormous popular interest when apprentices were murdered by their masters, illustrated in ballads and broadsheets. Thus *The cryes of the dead* told of a recent murder in Southwark by Richard Price, a weaver, who "most inhumanly tormented to death a boy of thirteene yeares old, with two others before, which he brought to untimely ends":

> Many poore Prentisses to himself did he bind,
> Sweet gentle children all of a most willing mind:
> Serving him carefully in this his weaving art
> Whome he requited still with a most cruel heart.[52]

By the late eighteenth century, with an increase in street literature and newspapers, as well as greater literacy, the death of apprentices at their masters' hands became a topic of considerable publicity, and detailed reports were frequently printed immediately after the trial, as with John Clay. In two notorious cases the apprentices' deaths were caused by their mistresses and were thus even more sensational, especially as both women came from a prosperous level of London trades. In the late eighteenth century Mrs Sarah Meteyard and her daughter kept a haberdashery in fashionable Bruton Street, where parish apprentices made nets and mittens. The workroom for four girls was "a little slip about two yards wide at one end and comes off like a pennyworth of cheese", according to one witness. One of the girls, aged 13, had died from starvation and beatings; Sarah Meteyard and her daughter were executed.[53] In the same decade the case of Mrs Brownrigg was particularly notorious; she was a successful midwife, married to a painter and plasterer, with a house in Fetter Lane where they "lived in credit". She had two female apprentices as domestic servants; the first girl, Mary Jones, had been indentured by the Foundling Hospital, to which she returned by escaping from the Brownriggs on Sunday morning as they slept. One of her eyes was so badly injured it was feared she might lose her sight; the hospital governors secured her discharge from the Brownriggs. Two years later Mrs Brownrigg killed an 11-year-old parish apprentice after torture and ill-treatment had reduced her to "all one wound from her head to her toes", according to the surgeon who examined her. A third apprentice was discharged and Mrs Brownrigg was executed at Tyburn on 14 September 1767.[54] Her cruelty gained her a place in popular mythology, for in 1829, when Esther Hilman, a tambour-worker, was also executed for starving and beating a ten-year-old pauper apprentice to death, Francis Place recorded a contemporary ballad about the case, linking it to the Brownriggs. It was subsequently proved that Esther Hilman had had three apprentices die while in her charge:

> Since Mother Brownrigg's ancient doom,
> Now sixty years and more,
> Such treatment to poor infants
> Was never heard before.[55]

In spite of such incidents, apprentices' lives were not normally at risk from their masters, who wished to benefit from their labour. A child's safeguard was the interest of family and friends, really only possible if the child were not too far from home. Neighbours would occasionally report a master's behaviour, but motives of personal spite cannot be ignored in such cases. Legal protection for apprentices, especially for parish children, greatly increased in the nineteenth century, but in contemporary literature the unhappy apprentice and the brutal master were a popular, stereotyped theme (*Peter Grimes, Oliver Twist, The water-babies*). It is important to judge masters by the standards of their own times, since men who themselves worked 14 hours a day for six days a week saw nothing wrong in thus preparing children for doing so in an adult worker's life. Even in the prosperous occupations and professions the master's personal comfort had always to be set aside in favour of a customer, client or patient, for whom competition was keen. Collyer particularly emphasized this aspect of apprentice duties, stressing that they, like the master, must be prepared to leave a meal willingly to attend to a customer. All occupations accepted the necessity of extended hours when an emergency occurred or large orders were possible, for extra work meant greater profit and in such circumstances exploiting apprentices was customary.

It is clear from a variety of sources that a pauper apprentice's life was at greater risk from a harsh master than a more prosperous child's. As early as 1738 it was possible for a reformer to comment that

> a master may be a tiger in cruelty, he may beat, abuse, strip naked, starve or do what he will to the poor innocent lad, few people will take much notice, and the [parish] officers who put him out least of anybody.[56]

That not all overseers of the poor were uncaring of their apprentices may be seen from the occasional notes in their account books when they recorded visiting or enquiring about a pauper child about whom concern had been expressed: "18 May 1784 Mr Snow and my journey and expence going to Warwick on compleant of Dame Woodfield that her son who is bound prentice to Thos Dale by this p'ish was ill used 5s 0d".[57] Predictably the worst-treated parish child was likely to be the orphan, bastard and stepchild, or even one from a very large poor family, unwilling to have an apprentice returned home because of the cost of maintenance. Perhaps, as Adam Smith commented, these parish children were the worst, most intractable apprentices, "usually bound for more than the usual number of years, and they generally turn out very idle and worthless".[58] Compulsory allocation of apprentices must have encouraged harsh treatment and made masters resent apprentices they had not freely chosen. The willingness of prosperous parishioners to pay fines rather than take pauper apprentices indicates how unacceptable and unwanted such children were, welcome only to be exploited.

There were no particular trades or crafts whose masters were, from the evidence of court proceedings, particularly cruel, although the overstocked sweated occupations were most often recorded as ill-treating apprentices. Such trades were more numerous, increasingly unprofitable and with uneducated masters who were themselves desperately poor, treating apprentices as they themselves had been used. Both boys and girls appear to have suffered incredible cruelty from a minority of sadistic masters, but boys were always more able and inclined to abscond in such circumstances, especially if they could enlist. The pauper's premium must often have been a temptation to the poor artisan, enabling him to buy tools, stock or materials, pay debts and gain a small capital sum. However, such a master's resources might not have been adequate to support the extra member of the household for years or even to find work for the apprentice. Cruelty was clearly status-related. In prosperous occupations there were powerful incentives to treat the apprentice well; an educated master had received a substantial premium and children could communicate with parents. Complaints at this level involved inadequate comfort or inept instruction, not physical cruelty. As there were so many potentially unfavourable factors in the relationship of the apprentice and master it is not surprising that such arrangements turned out ill; it is perhaps amazing that they were ever successful.

CHAPTER 11

Apprentices at the end of the term

I think I am entitled to credit for one act of wise determination, and that was in serving my apprenticeship to a trade. I look upon this as the grand turning point in my existence; to me it was the half-way house between the desert of my youth, and the sunny lands of my manhood. I have reason to reflect with pleasure upon my conduct as a journeyman; I entirely escaped the leading vice of the profession at the time, which was intemperance.

J. D. Burn, *The autobiography of a beggar boy* (1882)

One of the most powerful, traditional and appealing aspects of apprenticeship was as the road to fame and wealth for a child of humble origins symbolized by Dick Whittington. In spite of the fairy-tale nature of his story, he typified the worthy apprentice's success; he held high office, married his master's daughter, endowed charities and died worth over £7,000. Three centuries later Hogarth was to repeat the essential elements of his story in the *Industry and idleness* series of engravings, contrasting the virtuous Frank Goodchild with the unworthy Tom Idle. Achieving a master's status was important in any occupation for the apprentice who wished to progress beyond a journeyman's wage and profit from the labour of others. There were four ways in which a male apprentice might become established as a master: by marriage, inheritance, purchase or setting up. Of these, the first two usually cost the young man nothing, but partnership or purchase of an existing business or setting up cost varying sums of money.

The advantages for an apprentice of marrying his master's daughter were obvious; he had a ready-made livelihood, no setting-up expenses, needed no assistance from his parents, acquired an existing clientele and good prospects of ultimately taking over the whole business. In addition, he would have known his future wife for a long time, unlike some arranged marriages where the participants were almost strangers. For the master too such a marriage could be advantageous. He gained a young partner, trained in his ways, who would keep the enterprise profitable when his own earning power began to fail, who would protect trade secrets and would not, when out of his time, become a rival's journeyman or set up for himself, taking valued customers with him. A smaller dowry for his daughter was a further benefit, but the arrangement was unlikely to bring the master any payment for goodwill, which was a welcome injection of capital for the smaller tradesman.

Attaining a master's status by marriage was generally publicly approved, mentioned, for example, in obituary notices. When Nathaniel Thomas, a native of Leeds, died in 1781, the local press described how he became a wealthy London alderman from a humble shop-boy; "his behaviour there soon gained him both the respect of his Master, and the affections of his Master's daughter, whom in a few years he married, was taken into partnership by his late father-in-law".[1]

An apprentice whom he knew was undoubtedly a suitable son-in-law to many masters, a popular theme in drama, and sometimes the relationship was recorded in a man's will. Thus one wealthy wool merchant, John Mitchell, left each of his daughters £800, urging Hannah to marry his former apprentice, which she did,[2] and it has been estimated that in the early seventeenth century some 8 per cent of London aldermen had been apprentices who had married their masters' daughters.[3] In the artistic occupations an apprentice seems often to have become his master's son-in-law; Hogarth married Sir James Thornhill's daughter and Philip Reinagle was father-in-law to his former apprentice, Henry Howard. Not only in the most prosperous occupations were such marriages arranged, however, for two of Thomas Tompion's apprentices married their master's nieces[4] while a tailor's apprentice in Myddle (Salop) married his master's sister.[5] Not every apprentice who wished to marry his master's daughter gained parental support; James Clegg strongly opposed his son's marriage to the daughter of Mr Parks, who also "sufficiently expressed his aversion to the match". Although Clegg had "serious discourse" with his son to "diswade him from marrying" his efforts were unsuccessful and John finally married without his father's consent.[6]

An apprentice newly out of his time might also marry his master's widow and take over running the firm or shop, although a degree of public disapproval can be discerned towards marriages where there was a great age difference.[7] Even into the nineteenth century, however, such marriages were quite common, and in a large range of occupations wives helped in simple, repetitive processes, served in the shop and often ran a business in the master's absence or illness. Marriage with a former apprentice enabled the business to continue trading and gave the widow a more secure future than if she had simply sold up. In dangerous but quite prosperous trades, such as plumbing or farriery, women were often widowed young, and continued to manage the firm with the help of journeymen and apprentices; marriage was an obvious and practical solution.

It was also possible for an apprentice to become a master by inheriting his master's business; a very early bequest of this kind was that made by Richard le Barber, the first master of the Barber-Surgeons' Company, who in 1310 left his apprentice his shop in London's Bread Street.[8] Equipment and tools were valuable in helping an apprentice set up and occasionally these too were bequeathed. In 1512 Richard Barton of Bedford left his apprentice, Thomas Comendale, his best doublet and hose, two shirts, his best shoes, shop gear belonging to the craft and 6s 8d, a sum he also left to his other apprentice.[9] A century later a country blacksmith, John Trickett, left "my prentis John Cattels two hammers and three payres of tongs belonging to the shop" out of his total estate worth £17.[10]

Joining or succeeding his father in a craft or business was an important way of apprentices becoming masters. Family links were particularly striking in certain occupations, especially those at the top (the professions, manufacturers, wholesalers) and bottom (weavers and hatters). Retail trades (grocer and butcher) and traditional crafts (blacksmith, wheelwright) were also often in the same family, with apprenticeships regularly recorded, for decades. An inherited business was clearly an excellent opportunity for an apprentice. If he were entering any of the high-risk capital occupations, such as manufacturing, with large sums of money tied up in plant, machinery, stock and wages, the costs of setting up could be enormous and beyond any young man's resources unaided. Trading ventures, involving the purchase and holding of large stocks, extended credit, the cost of premises and the risks to capital, were equally impossible for a former apprentice without family support. Putting up his plate in the professions was the cheapest way of establishing a medical or legal practice, but produced only a modest living for some years, with bad debts and patients or clients who were incurable or difficult. If a newly qualified man could join his father in a practice he immediately acquired goodwill, premises and equipment, as well as his father's clientele, reputation and experience; a surprising number of modern medical, legal and veterinary practices have this strong family element. It was also quite common for a boy apprenticed to an uncle who was childless to inherit the firm or business. Thus William Stout of Lancaster bequeathed an ironmonger's shop to his nephew[11] and William Lloyd was left a house, shop and land in Shrewsbury by his "uncle Jewkes" to whom he had been apprenticed.[12]

Sometimes masters took apprentices into partnership without money changing hands. A man who had a particularly talented pupil was presumably glad to do so and prevent the young journeyman from setting up against him and taking his clients; for this reason Thomas Tompion made his former apprentice, Stephen Horseman, a partner.[13] The exceptionally talented apprentice could always develop his own enterprise so that, for example, Henry Clay, indentured in 1753, improved on his master's method of making papier mâché, patented his new ideas and set up a London outlet for his goods, becoming a very wealthy man in the process. In trades where large capital was required and apprentices from modest origins could never hope to become masters, there was the possibility of rising within the firm. A number of Matthew Boulton's department heads at Soho had once been his apprentices, "young plain Country Lads", whom he trained, but who were gifted designers and craftsmen.[14] It was also possible for an apprentice out of his time to be given a branch of the main enterprise to run; so William Cookworthy, apprenticed in 1719 in London to the Quaker apothecary, Silvanus Bevan, was put to manage a wholesale branch his master had set up at Plymouth.[15]

The importance of his master's training and repute to the newly established craftsman may be judged from the numerous examples of men who advertised the name of their former master as an indication of their skills. Such advertisements were common throughout the eighteenth and nineteenth centuries, even for well-known craftsmen who had worked in a district for some years, and Thomas Waller, a printer, who had been "an Apprentice and Journeyman with G. Wright of Leeds upwards of 20 Years", thought it necessary to remind readers of the fact.[16] Sometimes such advertisements were in response to a new rival in the area and certainly outlining a career, including apprenticeship, was usual, especially in the medical and related occupations:

> Horse Farrier. James Cook (late apprentice to James Cheatham, a very eminent Farrier at Preston) is come to settle in Leeds and may be found at the House of the late Doctor Nash, in Vicar-Lane, where he intends carrying on the Farrying Business in all its Branches, such as Docking, Nicking, Cropping, Firing, Gelding, etc. as well as the Physical Part of both Horse and Cow.[17]

When a master died apprentices sought to retain the old customers and work in hand; so George Graham advised readers he was

> Nephew of the late Mr Thomas Tompion, who lived with him upwards of seventeen years, and managed his trade for several years past, whose name was joined with Mr T.'s for some time before his death, and to whom he left all his stock and work, finished and unfinished, continues to carry on the said trade at the late Dwelling House of the said Mr T. at the sign of the Dial and Three Crowns at the corner of Water Lane in Fleet Street, London, where all persons will be accommodated as formerly.[18]

Masters who, like William Stout, helped their apprentices to set up, putting business their way and lending them money, appear to have been exceptional. In providing for his nephew to begin trading as an ironmonger Stout gave him £32 to buy goods in Sheffield, the shop equipment (weights, scales, boxes and utensils worth £20) as well as the use of premises. The cost of stocking a retail shop could be substantial; Stout's other nephew, John, had £300 to spend in London for his proposed draper's shop in about 1740.[19] At the same period Campbell published a list of the costs of setting up in over 300 trades in

Table 11.1 Costs of setting up as a master in London, in 1747.

£	Trade
0–5	Watch-chain maker
0–10	Bugle maker, seal engraver
0–20	Saddle riveter, thongmaker
0–50	Silver/gold buttonmaker, watch-spring maker
5–10	Button-ring maker, coach-bucklemaker, bucklemaker, spangle-maker
10–20	Glass-frame maker, shoe-buckle maker, vellum maker, watch-movement maker
10–50	Bodicemaker, button-mould maker, mop-maker
10–100	Bellows maker
10–200	Barber
10–500	Broom maker, cart wheeler
15–20	Waterman
15–200	Shagreen case-maker
20–50	Flax dresser, girth weaver, hour-glass maker, locksmith, pipemaker, screw maker, stirrup-maker, saddle-tree maker, watch-case-cap maker
20–100	Boxmaker, butcher, chaser, fan maker, fish-hook maker, hoop-petticoat maker, mantua-maker, snuffbox maker, wool-card maker
20–200	Poulterer
40–200	Fuller
50+	Armourer
50–100	Bookbinder, calendar-frame carver, coach carver, cap maker, carpet maker, cork cutter, cook, enameller, copper-plate engraver, edge-tool maker, farrier, fisherman, frame-maker, glass grinder, gilder, gold finder, holster-case maker, hot presser, iron cooper, last-maker, needlemaker, parchment maker, plane-maker, robe maker, smith, snuff shopkeeper, tweezer maker, watchmaker, watch finisher, whip maker, woolcomber, woodcutter
50–200	Apothecary, basket maker, bit maker, bridle cutter, brush maker, breeches-maker, buckram stiffener, bone lace-maker, chair carver, ship carver, chocolate maker, clogmaker, coach carver, collar maker, cutler, embroiderer, wood gilder, gold beater, loom maker, millwright, floor cloth painter, plasterer, piece broker, pin maker, pump maker, spinner, jacksmith, staymaker, surgical-instrument maker, wax figure maker
50–300	Back maker, birdcage maker, plaster-figure maker
50–500	Anvil smith, house carpenter, carpet weaver, grate founder, fruiterer, glover, lapidary, music-shopkeeper, saddler, screen maker, stucco maker, turner (ivory and silver), undertaker
50–1,000	Mohair-buttonmaker, print seller
50–5,000	Maltster
to 100	Child's-coatmaker, house painter, pattern drawer, quilter
100–200	Clay-figure maker, coach-harness maker, diamond cutter, paper printer, pattern maker, perfumer, saw maker, smith, tallow chandler, wire drawer, worsted man

£	Trade
100–300	Boat builder, comb maker, confectioner, earthenware shopkeeper, miller
100–500	Baker, blue maker, brickmaker, card maker, cheesemonger, sword cutler, drysalter, dyer, gardener, glass seller, glazier, horner, joiner, mason, musical-instrument maker, net maker, pamphlet seller, pastry cook, printer of stuffs, plumber, scale maker, seed-shop keeper, shoemaker, stocking weaver, tin man, vintner, wax chandler, weaver, whalebone man, wine cooper
100–1,000	Attorney, brazier, bricklayer, coppersmith, fishmonger, gunsmith, hatter, mathematical-instrument maker, milliner, orrice weaver, salesman, tanner, upholder
100–2,000	Haberdasher, hair merchant, rag man, sailcloth-maker, stationer, statuary, skinner, tapestry weaver
100–5,000	Jeweller, tobacconist
200–500	Block maker, cooper, trunk maker
200–1,000	Coach-leather currier, colour shop keeper, lighter builder, rope maker
200–2,000	Calico printer, cabinetmaker
300–500	Leather cutter, packer
300–1,000	Pewterer, tea-shopkeeper
300–2,000	Leatherseller
400–3,000	Silk throwster
to 500	House carver, tailor
500–1,000	Chemist, nurseryman, optical-instrument maker, oil shopkeeper, printer, sailmaker, starch maker, thread man
500–2,000	Anchor smith, pawnbroker, cloth worker, druggist, engine maker, fellmonger, grocer, ironmonger, leather dresser, letter founder, refiner, shipbuilder
500–3,000	Coachmaker, goldsmith
500–5,000	Bookseller, distiller, hosier
1000–5,000	Linen draper, timber merchant, sugar baker, woollen draper
1000–10,000	Coal factor, laceman, mercer, wool stapler
2000–5,000	Soap boiler
2000–10,000	Brewer
20,000+	Banker, insurer, merchant, money scrivener, notary, silk man, vinegar maker
Not stated	Architect, arrowmaker, bowyer, broker, burnisher, bell hanger, caul maker, chandler, chimney-sweep, counsellor at law, coffee man, conveyancer, diviner, doctor of civil law, fan painter, fine drawer, founder, fringe maker, girdler, glass blower, knife grinder, hatband maker, china shop keeper, innholder, land surveyor, musician, paper maker, parish clerk, paviour, physician, potter, proctor, sailor, sawyer, scrivener, scourer, sergeant at law, ship's carpenter, silk spinster, slop shopkeeper, chancery solicitor, spectacle maker, surgeon, tassel maker, tyre woman, wood monger

London as part of his advice manual to the parents and guardians of intending apprentices (see Table 11.1).[20]

It is apparent that for all but the humblest occupations some degree of family help was important to a young man setting up, and sometimes bequests of money were made for this purpose. Ralph Josselin spent £50 to set up his son, Thomas, in Essex as a haberdasher after his London apprenticeship ended in 1667[21] and in Myddle (Salop) Richard Gough described how his neighbours' sons were aided by their fathers. Perhaps Gough commented on them only because they were remarkably unsuccessful. One boy, bound to a London leatherseller, subsequently failed in business, as did another indentured to a Bristol merchant, but who was later enabled by his mother to set up in Wolverhampton, where he "grew mellancolly and dyed". A Shrewsbury grocer's apprentice from Myddle set up by his father also failed, as did a hatter's apprentice, "such an insatiable drunkard, that although hee is a good workman, and was sett uppe severall times by his father, yet hee still spent all, and sold his tooles, and hardly [kept] cloathes on his back". In all Gough mentioned 16 apprenticeships of village boys, as well as of pauper children: of these several were not completed because the boys died (including his own son who caught smallpox at Shrewsbury), gave unsatisfactory service to a master, or because of intemperance. The other boys finished their terms and became craftsmen in the village or further afield.[22]

There were, however, exceptional apprentices who, without family backing, once out of their time, invented a product or process that was completely new, appealed to customers and sold well immediately. Such men as Robert Ransome, apprenticed to an ironmonger, with his patent cast-iron plough shares,[23] John Baskerville with his type-founts, or Thomas Stevens with his woven silk pictures, all provided a novel product which was so successful that capital was not a problem. The commonest way for most apprentices to become a master was to set up in business for themselves, and from high-capital to poor craft occupations, expect a low income while becoming established. In some trades a set of tools was the only requirement, as some activities were performed entirely on site, with little workshop preparation beforehand. For other trades a workshop or yard was essential, so that whereas a plasterer or bricklayer could arrive at work with no materials needed beforehand, a craftsman such as a carpenter or joiner would often have to make preparations before he reached the site, and a carver or mason did the greater part of the work in his workshop or yard.

For the smaller man, establishing himself as a master required at least some credit and a degree of self-confidence, especially in view of the high rate of bankruptcies recorded in the eighteenth-century press. Place recognized that if he "continued to work as a journeyman and depended on the savings [he] might make . . . [he] never should have the means of becoming a master, and should therefore remain a journeyman as long as [he] lived". He was sure he would have a large family, for whom only wretchedness waited unless he could "get into business". Place related in detail how he arranged for short credit with three mercers and two drapers, paid punctually and in four years was creditworthy in the wholesalers' eyes; he had expected that it would take six years to achieve this.[24] George Herbert also had short credit for three months with London suppliers for his "uncommon" leathers, until a local incumbent loaned him £20 to go to Paris and arrange to import his own.[25] A few indentures specified that the master would provide the new young journeyman with stock or tools to help set him up; one Norwich cooper agreed to provide his apprentice at the end of seven years with 150 hoops, of three different kinds, to start him in the trade, but such arrangements seem to have ceased once premiums became standardized.[26] For the less prosperous but not pauper apprentice various charities existed to help a young person set up at the end of the term, usually with interest-free loans, although such charities were far fewer than those to indenture the child originally. Successful merchants were usually the founders, who presumably understood the difficulties faced by a journeyman without prosperous parents. The charity founder generally specified the area from which an applicant should come and those assisted formed only a very small proportion of journeymen each year. A number of these charities are still functioning according to the founders' wishes.[27]

Responsibility for setting up an apprentice was clearly his father's, as Mandeville reminded his readers, so that matching a premium with ultimate setting-up costs was essential. Mandeville particularly deplored the ambitious parent who managed to find the premium, although beyond his means, for

> a Man that gives Three or Four Hundred Pounds with his Son to a great Merchant, and has not Two or Three Thousand Pounds to spare against he is out of his Time to begin the World with is much to blame not to have brought his child up to something that might be follow'd with less Money.[28]

Campbell seemed critical of all parental choice and Collyer was equally opposed to parents who, "from vanity or inconsideration", judged a trade by the largest premium they could afford.[29]

Apart from the occupational advantages, in some communities apprenticeship brought franchise rights, access to specific charities and local privileges (such as grazing in the common fields) and so admission to freedom status was an important step for the former apprentice. Freedom was also attained by purchase or patrimony, but by apprenticeship was a means of advancement for boys of modest families, new to a trade or city. Franchise rights were highly valued by freemen, lost if poor relief were claimed, and in Coventry in 1790, for example, men returned from London to the city to vote.[30]

Just as poor apprentices were unlike others in important conditions of their indenture, at the end of their term provisions for beginning their adult work differed. The pauper's master agreed to ensure that the apprentice would not be a charge on the parish and provide "double apparel" for the boy or girl at the end of the term. In certain cases the apprentice was also given the basic trade tools. The provision of double apparel, one outfit for work and one for holy days, given at the end of the term, was intended to replace the two outfits with which the poor apprentice arrived as a child, enabling the adult to be decently clad when beginning work. Although the term "double apparel" was widely used and understood, some indentures itemized the actual clothes the master was to provide and in 1689 Ann Castleman was to leave her apprenticeship with "two new gowns, two new petticoats, one paire of boddyes, two paire of stockings, one pair of shoes, two new shifts, two new Aprons, one straw Hatt, two suites of head Clothes and two handkerchiefs",[31] which was considerably more generous than the basic outfits provided for most apprentices coming out of their time.

By the eighteenth century such clothing provisions were common for poor children but in an earlier period a master's responsibility for clothes at the end of the term was also negotiated for more prosperous apprentices. At Southampton (1609–1740) both groups of apprentices had clothes provided, less often for girls than boys, however. Although normally the garments were not listed, those provided by a clothier for his apprentice in 1673 were itemized; he was to have two "sufficient" suits of "woollen apparell", with four shirts, four bands and four handkerchiefs. For a third of the apprentices a cloak was an addition to the two outfits. In a handful of cases when the master had not provided clothes during the term he did not do so at its conclusion; very exceptionally the apprentice was provided with only a single item, such as a pair of shoes, or with money in lieu of clothes.[32]

By the end of the eighteenth century only the poor child was regularly given clothes at the end of the term; sometimes the indenture would be endorsed to reduce the apparel to one suit of clothes[33] or to make exceptionally generous provision for the apprentice, for example, six shifts and 10s for one poor girl.[34] Other indentures specified the master should give the apprentice two suits "as good as he received". By the late eighteenth century endorsements about clothes at the end of the term were particularly common for factory apprentices, but even these conditions varied, so that the indenture might specify one or two suits of clothes or even none, as Harding of Tamworth negotiated.[35]

As well as clothes at the end of the term the apprentice might also receive tools or, very rarely, money from a former master; these extra conditions were written into the indenture or added as an endorsement. Some charity apprentices were entitled to sums of money from the trustees so that, for example, Webb's charity of Warwick provided the substantial sum of £5 for each apprentice at the end of his time if the master certified the boy had been satisfactory.[36] Helping an apprentice to begin a working life by providing tools or implements applied only in certain craft occupations; thus a nailer's apprentice in 1733 was provided by his West Bromwich master with a "hammer, bore, bicker Anard & cloves and 1 bundle of Iron".[37] Other craftsmen who provided tools were the bricklayer, carpenter (broad-axe, handsaw, chisel and mallet), clothworker (shears), cooper (adze, axe, heading knife), shoemaker, tailor (pressing iron and shears), silk-weaver, woolcomber (pair of combs) and barber (razor, knife, shaving cloths). The shipwright's tools were particularly numerous, comprising an axe, adze, augur, mallet, claw-hammer, handsaw, chisel, maul and caulking iron.[38]

Thus in theory and usually in practice at the end of seven years the apprentice was trained in occupational skills that would provide a livelihood for a man and his family for 30 years or more and for a woman until marriage or in widowhood. Apprenticeship attracted both criticism and praise for its essential characteristics, its detractors and supporters often selecting the same facet for comment. It guaranteed entry to various crafts, protecting the practitioner from overstocking, low wages, unqualified competitors and poor workmanship. It provided legal rights, membership of a distinctive social group, with its own privileges, that would help members and their families who fell on hard times. Ideally apprenticeship made possible the transmission of craft skills along with the master's own moral standards and way of living which the apprentice would expect to attain in due time. It relied on the apprentice's accepting the principle of deferred gratification in adolescence to secure a future and parental willingness to pay the premium and lose wage-earning capacity for a number of years. The essential benefits of apprenticeship were as valid in 1800 as in 1600, but its critics resented the privileges of craft membership and objected to the restrictions faced by the unapprenticed in finding work. Some who had themselves been apprentices condemned its rigidity, for in times of economic boom or crisis work might be available for many more workers, but extra hands could not be produced quickly under the strictures of apprenticeship. One of the assets of seniority in a craft, exceeding the quota of apprentices, also caused resentment among humbler masters denied this privilege.

However, when times were desperate in many trades, large numbers of apprentices were illegally bound, swelling the workforce, increasing output, even if with poor quality products, and causing adult journeymen to be laid off. Although the population increases of the later eighteenth century meant that there were many more parish children to be bound, the problem of over-apprenticing had existed in certain poor trades, nail-making, hosiery and weaving, a century before. Thus apprenticeship came to be regarded as both the cure for and the cause of a trade's poverty and it is noticeable that those prosperous craftsmen who never over-apprenticed children, such as the saddler or the cabinetmaker, retained their status and consistently supported apprenticeship. When apprenticeship came to be abused on a large scale by indenturing children in factories, using the traditional formula, with premium and term, but without the essential features of living in a master's family and receiving personal instruction for an adult livelihood, its survival was threatened. The factory child and the climbing-boy were symbols of this abuse and through public concern at their working conditions apprenticeship as a whole came under attack and by 1814 was no longer legally enforceable to practise a craft. When the letter but not the spirit of apprenticeship was used to exploit adolescents the institution itself could not survive. In spite of abuses, apprenticeship remained for many the path to a secure future and social advancement, of however modest a kind. Apprenticeship has retained a high place in the esteem of many and continued to thrive into the present century, for in the ancient trading cities its influence has always been considerable. Even today former apprentices declare at which particular engineering works they served their time, with a sense of pride and belonging that their eighteenth-century equivalents would have recognized and found entirely appropriate.

CHAPTER 12

The decline of apprenticeship

[Apprenticeship] should be discontinued as a worn-out vestige of the past, and instead a system of pupilage should be instituted compatible with freedom of action, the intelligence of the present age, and the progressive state of modern institutions.

Transactions of the National Association for the Promotion of Social Sciences (1863)

Of all the *rites de passage* a child could come to experience, puberty, marriage, parenthood and death, apprenticeship was less a matter of personal choice or natural forces than of parental influence and youthful duty. In theory it was available to both boys and girls, poor or affluent, educated or illiterate, but in practice recruitment was affected by such powerful forces as parental status, prospering occupations, consumer demand and population numbers. However, apprenticeship surprisingly retained its standing for some three centuries in spite of such vicissitudes and was really rejected as a training method only under the modern external pressures of universal education and a raised standard of living.

The crucial importance of a good master, competent to teach and, *in loco parentis*, to behave in a kindly manner to the apprentice, was widely acknowledged. The best master would provide more than basic care as, for example, when the eminent Dr Robert Barry was summoned to treat Farington's apprentice in 1798[1] or when Bewick paid two medical bills for Robert Johnson in 1792–3.[2] The famous master was always in demand and there was a generally accepted acknowledgement that such a man would produce distinguished pupils, as in the case of Scheemaker's teaching the sculptor's art to Nollekens or James Thornhill indentured to Thomas Highmore. Sometimes, however, arrangements could turn sour, and one of Lawrence's apprentices left because he claimed he was not being properly taught by the famous portraitist.[3] The publicity value of a well-reputed master, even though known only in his local community, was considerable and many craftsmen considered it worthwhile to advertise the name of the master with whom they had served their term. Inheriting a master's clientele at his death was widely recognized and John Wright of Worcester, a talented plasterworker, wrote to Lord Archer in 1736 on the death of his master, Joshua Needham, to secure a commission for himself: "I Live at Worcester and as my Mr Needham is Dead and your Bed Room at the end of your Great Parlour is not finish'd I shall be Glad of the Honr of being imployd by your Woorship."[4] Such a man would have learned his master's values, skills and methods as a youth, sharing all aspects of the business and, as Defoe had advised, been taught how to judge and buy raw materials, to keep accounts and to become acquainted with the clients, customers and suppliers.

The everyday practices in an apprenticeship are very difficult to uncover, but Nicholas Blundell of Little Crosby frequently noted the tasks Lancashire apprentices performed, for example, collecting cash ("I payed Richard Hetons Prentice all I ought his Master"), delivering goods ("Samuel Rigby sent his Prentice hither with a Pair of Glass Scaunces") and completing tasks ("Gill the Painter sent his Prentice to paint the Sashes with Whit in the Parlor").[5] Thomas Bewick, indentured in 1767 to Ralph Beilby, a general engraver at Newcastle, learned the simple and complex branches of the trade, working for a great diversity of customers. Unfortunately, his own apprenticeship experiences were not repeated in Bewick's relationship with Robert Johnson, his ablest apprentice, on whose tuition he bestowed "unceasing pains":

> I . . . behaved to him uniformly with the kindness of a Father or a Brother & have watched with every pains in my power to instruct him – been liberal to him in pecuniary matters – employed the best physician to attend him when he was unwell – let him want for nothing – paid him his wages besides, whether at work or not . . . used every endeavour in our power to advance him in the world, & when all this was done, he shewed not a particle of gratitude, but observed that any "cartman would take care of his Horse".[6]

As early as 1726 Defoe was bewailing the insubordination of apprentices, "more like gentlemen than tradesmen; more like companions to their masters, than like servants",[7] and many masters must have feared that an able former apprentice, newly a journeyman, would set up in the locality as a rival, perhaps with lower charges, even more obliging, with less work in hand but the same skills, and so undermine the older man's livelihood. Bewick was careful not to do so, but moved to London rather than compete with Beilby.

Superficial conceptions and impressions of male apprentices changed little over several centuries. They were always seen as potentially unruly, even politically threatening, and as abused cheap labour by detractors, but as the skilled, respectable craftsmen of the future by supporters of apprenticeship. Perhaps the answer lies in numbers, so that an elite, upwardly mobile youth, proceeding to freeman status in an occupation that could not suffer from overstocking, part of a respected social group, was the ideal Frank Goodchild figure that made apprenticeship a traditional goal for a fortunate minority. However, when England's population swelled, as infant mortality declined, and as sweated occupations grew to meet consumer demands, children were indentured and called apprentices although virtually all the established criteria were distorted.

In the early modern period an industry could see its strength and influence in the numbers of apprentices bound, as in the Worcester cloth trades,[8] and in the legal proceedings skilled men undertook to stop the unapprenticed from working as rivals. The majority of such apprentices were adequately fed, clothed, lodged and taught, with a degree of guild and community supervision. It is not surprising, therefore, especially after the Civil War, that a gentleman such as Sir William Dugdale would arrange an apprenticeship to a London surgeon for his son.[9] The influence and visible wealth of the great provincial trading companies was a further incentive in such choices; the Sheffield Cutlers' accounts illustrate how they controlled new admissions, the term served and numbers of apprentices each man might take. However, their new purpose-built hall of 1728 and their expenditure of £100 in 1746 to "raise men & armes to oppose ye Rebells" indicate functions beyond simply controlling the craft.[10] Guild mutualism remained a powerful force well beyond its medieval origins. Clearly, traditional apprenticeship was exclusive and reinforced its elitism by ceremonies of private initiation and public display, including distinctive dress. The youth's desire to belong to a particular group must account for accepting the distressing rituals of being admitted. Most initiations required physical endurance, even courage, and all were intended to humiliate the newcomer, who would eventually inflict the experience on other novices. Such ceremonies surprisingly survived into the present century, almost unaltered in some trades, widely regarded as a bonding factor, the death of a 17-year-old youth in Lancashire in 1989 from such a ceremony a tragic recent example.[11] Public displays of membership also existed to remind society at large that the group existed, such as patron saints' parades or the Cutlers' celebrations on Oak Apple Day.[12]

However, just as the successful apprentice was almost a stereotyped figure, the failed, the runaway or the criminal was equally well publicized, if only as a warning to others. Clearly, the most striking failures of all were apprentices who died on the scaffold, where claims to have been apprenticed seem unequalled as a mark of former respectability. In London particularly, by 1700 concern was felt at their sheer numbers and the potential link between crime and ill-controlled apprentices. Men as notorious as Jack Sheppard, Jonathan Wild and Dick Turpin were all formerly apprentices; some blamed their masters' laxity for their downfall and it has been shown that two-fifths of those hanged at Tyburn in the eighteenth century had served an apprenticeship. London, of course, differed in scale from provincial cities, but similar claims to former respectable apprentice status could be heard in the English counties from those on the scaffold. Thus "Thomas Summers, who was executed at Coventry on Wednesday April the 28th, 1784, persuant to his sentance for Beastiality with a Cow . . . was apprenticed to his Father, by Trade a Taylor" while in the same city Josiah Neale Dayus, executed for housebreaking two years later, had

> industrious parents, who gave him as good an education as their circumstances would allow, after which he was bound apprentice to his father, by trade a butcher. During his servitude, he discovered a natural propensity to vice and immorality.[13]

Peter Linebaugh has shown that butchers' apprentices were prominent among the London hanged (10 per cent) and that of the 1,242 men and women hanged there in half a century (1700–50), 40 per cent (498) had been apprenticed to a trade.[14] The *Newgate calendar* noted 12 of the 42 case studies as former apprentices, including those bound to an apothecary, a cabinetmaker and a maltster,[15] none an impoverished occupation and, with a large middle-class readership, criminal biographies were best-sellers in Georgian England, a literary equivalent to Hogarth's engravings.

Although the word "apprentice" has slowly slid down the social scale, well into the eighteenth century it was possible for a youth like John Howard, later the prison reformer, to have a separate apartment, with his own servant and two horses, when he was indentured to a wholesale grocer, even though such young men were always a privileged minority. Not all arrangements, even at the highest level, however, were successful, for Timothy Goodwin, second son in a Warwickshire gentry family, was apprenticed to a London brewer and seems to have spent a life in the capital entirely devoted to amusements. At 18, he had left his respectable lodgings for Peel's coffee-house and lived "a useless existence" there. His widowed mother was most anxious about his future. He later went bankrupt but, at his elder brother's death in 1766, inherited the Arlescote estate.[16] His portrait by Allan Ramsay, to whom he was related, shows a confident, well-dressed apprentice (Fig. 12.1), exactly the youthful, uncontrollable stereotype of whom Defoe complained. Loyalty was so crucial a part of the master–apprentice relationship that, when apprentices committed the greatest crime, murdering a master, it was considered as "petty treason", only slightly less than treachery to the monarch. To emphasize the heinous nature of the crime, the guilty apprentice was drawn on a sledge, not a cart, to the gallows. Such cases were always given wide publicity, as with Rebecca Downing in 1782 or James Hall, who had killed his master in 1741 (Fig. 12.2).

Perhaps the most striking quality about apprenticeship was its conservatism and certainly apprentices were supporters of the traditional; thus they attacked shops as far apart as Bristol, Bury St Edmunds, Norwich and York in

Figure 12.1 Timothy Goodwin, a brewer's apprentice, by Allan Ramsay (*c.* 1740). By permission of Warwickshire Museum.

the years after the Civil War when parliament wished to keep premises open on Christmas Day.[17] Apprenticeship was valued for its traditional standards, to judge from the numbers of bequests made to enable orphaned children to be bound. Perhaps there were no other obvious alternatives that were perceived as securing a young person's future and John Hanbury, a Worcester gentleman, left £20 each to his two nephews in 1644 for this purpose.[18] Certainly, an apprenticeship should have provided complete welfare for a child, including spiritual guidance, and philanthropists such as Thomas Coram saw apprenticeship as a means to an end for foundlings, "the only gateway" for an independent future. On a more modest scale, the many provincial apprenticing charities had similar aims, although in 1815 there were said to be only 15 of the 38 English counties with charities exclusively dedicated to apprenticing poor children. This, however, is an underestimate, for Coventry's are omitted and many others may also have been excluded.

Apprenticeship would have changed little, nevertheless, in status and popular esteem, but for the devaluation that was caused by the vast numbers of

245

Figure 12.2   James Hall murdering his master, Mr Penny of Clement's Inn, from *The Tyburn Chronicle* (1768).

children, often very young, sent to work in factories and domestic sweated trades and all called apprentices. Clearly the basic details of the indenture, term, tuition, premium, were common to prosperous and pauper alike, but the abuses of the out-apprentice, of paying apprentices, with no personal master–child relationship and with no skilled adult livelihood ahead, all meant that traditional apprenticeship was no longer well regarded by ambitious, even respectable parents. Overstocking existed by the later seventeenth century in a minority of desperately impoverished trades, but was not common across a wide range of occupations until a hundred years later, bringing apprenticeship itself into disrepute. Strikingly, however, apprenticeship for the very best careers, especially the professions, remained effective and even expanded into the early twentieth century. By the later nineteenth century, however, social changes meant that many originally apprenticed occupations henceforward preferred theoretical and formal education, in college and university, and after the repeal of the Statute of Artificers in 1814 practising a skill though unapprenticed was no longer illegal.

For the many new occupations of the nineteenth century apprenticeship was inappropriate, in retail and clerical work, for example, as well as in the wide range of "blue-collar" jobs that emerged. The conflict with mass-produced goods, especially clothes and food, meant that many labour-intensive crafts survived only in the luxury, handmade sector for a minority of traditional, wealthy customers. Thus the nature of work and the pace of work changed as customers' tastes widened and in a modern consumer-based economy apprenticeship seemed inflexible to adults and unacceptably strict to young people. The advantages of apprenticeship in controlling the quality of work, in preventing unfair competition and in fixing rates, all came to be disregarded in an atmosphere of *laissez-faire*. The one-to-one relationship between master and apprentice could go wrong, children's contact with their families was weakened and, as educational expectations were raised for all, apprenticeship must have seemed increasingly archaic in nineteenth-century England, a relic of the past to match maypole festivities. Even achieving freeman status and the right to vote lost its power. The accusations against apprentices and apprenticeship centred on the poorest categories and the most exploited workers, especially the factory children, but in all areas of England the Poor Law Commissioners described excessive harshness and abuses, so that apprenticeship declined because perceptions of childhood changed. The present-day "Modern Apprenticeships", introduced by the government in 1993, while offering technical skills incomprehensible to their predecessors, nevertheless include aims that the eighteenth century would both have acknowledged and valued, "competence to do the job . . . customised training . . . motivated young people . . . signing a pledge".[19]

The main clauses in apprenticeship indentures

A pauper apprenticeship indenture (eighteenth century)

This indenture made the . . . day of . . . in the . . . year of the Reign of Our Sovereign Lord . . . by the Grace of God of Great Britain, France and Ireland, King, Defender of the Faith etc; and in the Year of our Lord . . . Witnesseth that . . . Churchwardens of the Parish of . . . and . . . Overseers of the Poor of the said Parish, by and with the Consent of His Majesty's Justices of the Peace of the said . . . whose Names are hereunto subscribed, have put and placed, and by these Presents do put and place . . . a poor Child of the said Parish Apprentice to . . . of . . . with h . . . to dwell and serve from the Day and Date of these Presents, until the said Apprentice shall accomplish h . . . full Age of . . . according to the Statute in that Case made and provided; During all which Term the said Apprentice h . . . said Master faithfully shall serve, in all lawful Business according to h . . . Power, Wit and Ability; and honestly, orderly, and obediently in all Things demean and behave h . . . self towards h . . . said Master and all his during the said Term. And the said Master doth Covenant and Grant for himself, his Executors and Administrators, to and with the said Churchwardens and Overseers, and every of them, their and every of their Executors & Administrators, and their and every of their Successors for the time being, by these Presents, that he the said Master the said Apprentice, . . . And shall and will during the Term aforesaid find, provide and allow unto the said Apprentice meet, competent and sufficient Meat, Drink, Apparel, Lodging, Washing, and all other things, necessary and fit for an Apprentice. And also shall and will so provide for the said Apprentice that h . . . be not any way a charge to the said Parish, or to the said Parishioners of the same; but of and from all charge shall and will save the said Parish and Parishioners harmless and indemnified, during the said Term. And at the end of the said Term shall and will make, provide, allow and deliver unto the said Apprentice double Apparel of all sorts, good and new, that is to say a good new Suit for the holy Days, and another for the Working days. In Witness whereof the Parties abovesaid to these present Indentures interchangeable have put their Hands and Seals, the Day and Year above-written.

A charity apprenticeship indenture (1732)

This Indenture Witnesseth that William Adams Son of Richard Adams of Kenelworth in the County of Warwick Labourer doth put himself Apprentice unto John Axson of Kenelworth in the said County of Warwick, Blacksmith to learn his Art and with him after the manner of an Apprentice to serve from the 26th Day of December Anno Domini 1732 unto the full end and term of Eight years from thence next ensuing and fully to be compleat and ended: during which Term the said Apprentice his said Master faithfully shall and will serve his Secrets keep his lawful Commandments every where gladly do he shall do no damage to his said Master nor see to be done of others; but to his Power shall lett or forthwith give Notice to his said Master of the Same: The Goods of his said Master he shall not waste nor lend them unlawfully to any Hurt to his said Master he shall not do cause or procure to be done he shall neither sell nor buy without his Masters leave. Taverns Inns or Alehouses he shall not haunt At Cards Dice Tables or any other unlawful Game he shall not play. Matrimony he shall not contract nor from the Service of his said Master Day nor Night shall absent himself but in all Things as an honest and faithful Apprentice shall and will demean and behave himself towards his said Master & all his during all the said Term. And the said John Axson for and in Consideration of the Summ of Five Pounds of lawful Money of Great Britain to him in hand well and truly paid by Wm Best Richd Betty & John Heath the Minister and Churchwardens out of Mr. Waits Charity (the Receipt whereof is hereby acknowledged) the said Apprentice in the Art and Skill of a Blacksmith which he now useth shall teach and instruct or cause to be taught and instructed the best way and manner that he can finding and allowing unto the said Apprentice sufficient Meat Drink & all Apparrel Washing Lodging and all other Necessaries during the said Term. (WCRO, DR 296/71)

A "normal" apprenticeship indenture (1701)

This Indenture witnesseth that John Greswold son of Henry Greswold of Solehull in the County of Warwick decd doth put himself Apprentice to Henry Lyell Citizen and Tallow Chandler of London to learn his Art and with him (after the manner of an Apprentice) to serve from the day of the date hereof unto ye full end and term of Seven years, from thence next following to be fully complete and ended During which term the said Apprentice his said Master faithfully shall serve, his Secrets keep his lawful Commandments everywhere gladly do, He shall do no damage to his said Master nor see to be don of others, but he to his power shall let or forthwith give warning to his said Master of the same. He shall not wast the goods of his said Master nor lend them unlawfully to any. He shall not commit Fornication nor contract Matrimony within the said term. He shall not play at Cards, Dice, Tables or any other unlawful Games, whereby his said Master may have any loss with his own goods or others during the said term without licence of his said Master he shall neither buy nor sell. He shall not haunt Taverns or Playhouses, nor absent himself from his said Masters service day nor night unlawfully. But in all things as a faithful Apprentice he shall behave himself towards his said Master and all his during the said term: And the said Master his said Apprentice in the same Art which he useth, by the best means that he can shall teach and instruct or cause to be taught and instructed, finding unto the said Apprentice meate, drink apparel, lodging and all other necessaries, according to the Custom of the City of London, during the said term. And for the true performance of all and every the said Covenants and Agreements, either of the said parties bind themselves unto the other by these presents. In witness whereof the parties above named to these Indentures interchangeably have out their Hands and Seals the Eighteenth day of December in the Thirteenth Year of the Reign of our Sovereign Lord William the Third King over England 1701. (WCRO, CR 1291/489 p. 97)

Trade initiation ceremonies for apprentices

(These examples of twentieth-century initiations have been collected by Mr Brian Clifford; he kindly made them available to me in 1978.)

Date	Age*	Boy/ girl	Occupation	County	Initiations reported
1912	12	boy	heavy engineering	n.s.**	oiling of genital area; sent for left-handed spanners; dipped in fire-buckets; Epsom salts in tea
1913	14	boy	engineering works clerk	Sussex	wore three-cornered hat made of newspaper
1915	16	boy	steel works	Essex	debagged by women; greasy cotton waste applied to genital area; smacked
1917	16	boy	film laboratory	London	genital area dyed
1919	12	boy	cotton mill	Lancs.	new boys and girls had genitalia greased
1920	13	boy	coal mining	"North"	coal dust on genital area
c.1912	n.s.	boy	printing	"Country"	sprayed with water from banging wet type together; sent for striped ink; debagged and genital area painted with ink
1924	14	boy	pattern maker	"North"	bought beer all round; had to clean tools; not spoken to for a week; painted with mixture of sawdust and paraffin
1925	14	boy	furniture factory	London	held headfirst in lavatory
1930s	n.s.	boy	car factory	Staffs.	genital area greased; sent for glass hammer, etc.; had to give message to "deaf" man; girls' "bloomers" filled with horsehair
1932	n.s.	girl	cotton-mill errand girl	Lancs.	sent for a "long stand"
1938	n.s.	boy	silversmith's errand boy	Yorks.	women debagged boys, painted them with "green rouge" and feathers; made them kneel and "bow to Allah"

Date	Age*	Boy/ girl	Occupation	County	Initiations reported
1939	n.s.	girl	cotton mill	Lancs.	lunch-box chained down; sent for smallest/largest tools; fancy dress for some workers
c.1943	n.s.	boy	engineering firm	Lancs.	Shrove Tuesday: boys' jackets nailed to floor and pockets filled with iron filings
n.d.†	n.s.	boy	engineering workshop	n.s.	put headfirst in water tank; rolled in barrel; genital area painted

* Most mentioned that the initiations happened on their first jobs after leaving school, therefore aged about 14.
** n.s.: not stated
† n.d.: no date

Advertisements for the return of runaways

Aris's Gazette, 30 April 1744

Francis Cook, Apprentice to Francis Stringer of the Parish of Neen Savage, Salop, Taylor, did on 1st Inst absent himself from his said Master and took several Things with him in a felonious Manner. The said Francis Cook is about 18 years . . . 5 feet 7 inches . . . a pale Complexion, strait brown Hair . . . wearing a White Rug Coat, Waistcoat and Breeches when he went off.

Coventry Mercury, 21 November 1757

Run away from Michael Elliot, Silk-weaver, in the Parish of Foleshill . . . on the 24th of October last, Joseph Cox and John Mills, his Apprentices – Joseph Cox is about 13 Years old, has a fresh Complexion, wears a Woollen Cap, light colour'd Waistcoat, and Leather Breeches. – John Mills is about 13 Years old, has Pock Holes in his Face, had on a brown Linen Frock, blue Waistcoat, and Leather Breeches.

Leeds Intelligencer, 23 October 1770

Run Away from his Master at Swillington Wind-Mill, on Sunday last, Henry Harvey, an Apprentice, about 13 years of age, had on when he went off, a blue coat, green Waistcoat, Leather Breeches, and black Stockings, is of a brown Complexion, with dark full Eyes . . . if he will return to his Master's service again, he will be kindly received.

Leeds Mercury, 20 July 1779

Run Away, on Sunday the 27th of June last, Joshua Dawson, Apprentice to Thomas Kemp, Painter of Leeds. He is 17 years of Age, of fair Complexion, low made, a good deal in-kneed, wears his Hair tied, of light Colour; had on a light Drab Coat, brown Waistcoat, and new Leather Breeches.

Indenturing a pauper child, 1679

	£	s	d
Itt. Charges at the binding Jo. Glover Apprentice sevall neighbours being with us		1	00
Itt. paid Phillip Coe for John Glover 33 ld. by the weeke 2 weekes	1	13	00
Itt. paid for cloth to make Jo. Glover Apparrell		11	09
Itt. paid for John Glover's Indentures & a bond for the performance(?) of Covenants		2	00
Itt. paid for 4 ells of cloth to make John Glovers shirts		4	06
Itt. paid for a hat for him		1	06
Itt. paid for a paire of shooes for Jo. Glover		2	08
Itt. charges when John Glover was bound and for trimming for John Glover's clothes		2	00
Itt. paid to Sam Yeates with Jo. Glover	2	00	00
Itt. paid for 2 paire of stockens for John Glover		2	02
Itt. paid to Sam Yeates the remaining _____? of his money with John Glover	2	00	00
Itt. paid Sam Yeates for makeing John Glovers Apparrell		5	06
Itt. paid for 4 bonds for John Glover		1	04

(WCRO, DR 296)

Notes

Place of publication is London unless otherwise stated.

Introduction

1. 5 Eliz. I c. 4.
2. *House of Commons journals*, XXVIII (1814), p. 564.
3. M. W. Flinn, *British population growth, 1750–1850* (1970), pp. 12–13.
4. T. E. Tomlins, *The law dictionary* (1835).
5. F. R. Batt, *The law of master and servant* (1967), pp. 603–5.
6. *Ibid.*, pp. 607–9.
7. 39 Eliz. I c. 3.
8. 43 Eliz. I c. 2.
9. 13 and 14 Car. II c. 12.
10. 8 & 9 Wm III c. 30.
11. 8 Anne c. 9.
12. 20 Geo. III c. 19.
13. 4 & 5 Wm & Mary c. 23.
14. 30 Geo. II c. 24.
15. 6 Geo. III c. 25.
16. 8 Geo. III c. 28.
17. 20 Geo. III c. 36.
18. 28 Geo. III c. 48.
19. 32 Geo. III c. 47.
20. 33 Geo. III c. 55.
21. 42 Geo. III c. 73.
22. 42 Geo. III c. 46.
23. PP, III (1816), pp. 122, 124.
24. 56 Geo. III c. 139.
25. *Aris's Gazette*, 6 May 1816.
26. *Warwick Advertiser*, 25 May 1816.
27. Somerset Record Office (SRO), DD/SF, Box 55, 1102; I am grateful to Dr Robin Clifton for this reference.
28. C. R. Dobson, *Masters and journeymen* (1980), p. 56.
29. *Ibid.*, pp. 154–70.
30. O. J. Dunlop & R. D. Denman, *English apprenticeship and child labour* (1912), p. 45.

Chapter 1

1. P. Morgan, *Warwickshire apprentices in the Stationers' Company of London, 1563–1700* (Dugdale Society, 1978).
2. M. M. Medlicott (ed.), *No hero, I confess* (1969), pp. 11, 17.
3. W. Lucas, *A Quaker journal*, I (1934), p. 19.
4. F. G. Stokes (ed.), *The Blecheley diary of the Rev. William Cole, 1765–7* (1931), p. 76.
5. A. Macfarlane (ed.), *The diary of Ralph Josselin, 1616–1683* (1976), p. 453.
6. E. Hughes, *North country life in the eighteenth century* (1965), pp. 88–9.
7. *Aris's Gazette*, 7 May 1744.
8. *Coventry Mercury*, 7 December 1807.
9. J. D. Burn, *The autobiography of a beggar boy* (1978 reprint), p. 59.
10. T. Cooper, *The life of Thomas Cooper, written by himself* (1872), pp. 9–10.
11. F. M. Eden, *The state of the poor*, 1928 edn (1797), pp. 248–58, 311–15.
12. *Aris's Gazette*, 22 December 1783.
13. V. S. Doe (ed.), *The diary of James Clegg of Chapel-en-le-Frith, 1708–55* (Derbyshire Record Society, 1978–9).
14. A. Raistrick, *Quakers in science and industry* (Newton Abbot, 1950), p. 203.
15. Shakespeare Birthplace Trust Records Office (SBTRO), BRT 8/199.
16. F. G. Emmison (ed.), *Some Bedfordshire diaries*, 40 (Bedfordshire Historical Record Society, 1960), p. 107.
17. Hughes, *North country life*, p. 89.
18. W. Hutton, *Life of William Hutton, stationer, of Birmingham* (1816), p. 8.
19. G. Herbert, *Shoemaker's window* (1971 edn), p. 7.
20. M. Thale (ed.), *The autobiography of Francis Place* (1971), p. 71.
21. J. Burnett (ed.), *Useful toil* (1974), p. 307.
22. *Ibid.*, p. 331.
23. J. Collyer, *The parent's and guardian's directory* (Cambridge, 1761), p. 16.
24. *Warwick Advertiser*, 14 March 1818.
25. 2 & 3 Anne c. 6.
26. J. Lane, *Apprenticeship in Warwickshire, 1700–1834* (PhD thesis, University of Birmingham, 1977), p. 325.
27. W. Felkin, *A history of machine-wrought hosiery and lace manufacture* (1867).
28. R. Campbell, *The London tradesman* (1747), p. 219.
29. *Ibid.*, pp. 218–19.
30. Lane, *Apprenticeship in Warwickshire*, p. 358.
31. *Ibid.*, p. 484.
32. *Ibid.*, p. 264.
33. PP, III (1816), pp. 123–4.
34. Manchester City Library (MCL), C5/5/1–225; C5/5/2/1–98; C5/3/1–125; C5/8/22.
35. Campbell, *The London tradesman*, p. 328.
36. Collyer, *The parent's and guardian's directory*, p. 101.
37. Warwickshire County Record Office (WCRO), DR 52/5; SBTRO, BRT 8/199.
38. WCRO, DR 280/83.
39. Coventry City Record Office (CCRO), Apprentice Registers I, II.
40. PP, III (1816), p. 18.
41. Campbell, *The London tradesman*, p. 260.
42. Dunlop & Denman, *English apprenticeship*, p. 32.
43. *Ibid.*, p. 47.
44. CCRO, A 99, fol. 17.
45. Morgan, *Warwickshire apprentices*, p. 6.
46. A. C. Merson (ed.), *A calendar of Southampton apprenticeship registers, 1609–1740*, XII (Southampton Records Series, 1968), p. xix.

47. Cumbria Record Office (CRO), WSMB/K.
48. Public Record Office (PRO), I. R.1. The registers are arranged on a regional basis and five counties' entries have been extracted and published by local record societies. They are: *Bedfordshire apprentices*, IX (Bedfordshire Historical Record Society, 1925), pp. 147–76, by Mrs H. Jenkinson; *Surrey apprenticeships, 1711–31*, X (Surrey Record Society, 1929) by H. Jenkinson; *Sussex apprentices and their masters, 1710–52*, XXVIII (Sussex Record Society, 1929) by R. G. Rice; *Warwickshire apprentices and their masters, 1710–60*, XXIX (Dugdale Society, 1975) by K. J. Smith; *Wiltshire apprentices and their masters, 1710–60*, XVII (Wiltshire Archaeological and Natural History Society, 1961) by C. Dale. Future references to these titles are under the editors' names.
49. H. Jenkinson, p. x.
50. Rice.
51. D. Guthrie, *A history of medicine* (1945), pp. 215–65.
52. Anon., *Book of trades* (1818), p. 3.
53. W. E. Tate, *The parish chest* (Cambridge, 1960), p. 225.
54. S. D. Chapman, *The early factory masters* (Newton Abbot, 1967), pp. 230–40.
55. WCRO, DR 225/340–41.
56. Hereford and Worcester Record Office (HWRO), F 71/77.
57. MCL, C5/5/1–225; C5/5/2/1–98; C5/5/3/1–125.
58. D. Defoe, *The complete English tradesman* (1738), p. 147.
59. D. Defoe, *The great law of subordination consider'd* (1724), pp. 10–11.
60. Dunlop & Denman, *English apprenticeship*, p. 200.
61. A. Plummer, *The London Weavers' Company, 1600–1970* (1972), p. 75.
62. Dunlop & Denman, *English apprenticeship*, p. 204.
63. *Ibid.*, p. 200.
64. Merson, *A calendar of Southampton apprenticeship registers*, pp. xvii–xviii.
65. R. E. Leader, *Sheffield cutlers*, I (1906), p. 45.
66. Dunlop & Denman, *English apprenticeship*, p. 202.
67. D. Defoe, *The trade of England reviv'd* (1681), p. 30.
68. J. Aikin, *A description of the country from thirty to forty miles round Manchester* (1795), p. 182.
69. Cited in Dunlop & Denman, *English apprenticeship*, p. 202.
70. D. Defoe, *The family instructor*, II (1715), p. 261.
71. *House of Commons journals*, XIX (21 January 1718/19) p. 78.
72. K. J. Smith, nos. 1261, 2236, 1182.
73. H. Jenkinson, nos. 69, 132, 592, 703, 760, 1077, 1499, 1500, 1854, 2091, 2205, 2261, 2262, 2631, 2642.
74. HWRO, 008.7.
75. A. F. Cirket (ed.), *English wills, 1498–1526*, XXVII (Bedfordshire Historical Record Society, 1957), p. 37.
76. CCRO, Accn. 76/18.
77. R. Parker, *The common stream* (1975), p. 165.
78. J. G. L. Burnby, *Apprenticeship records*, I(4) (British Society for the History of Pharmacy, 1977), p. 159.
79. Hughes, *North country life*, pp. 93–5.
80. D. F. McKenzie (ed.), *Stationers' Company apprentices, 1701–1800*, NS XIX (Oxford Bibliographical Society, 1978), pp. 222, 174.
81. Dale, nos. 2129, 1219.
82. Campbell, *The London tradesman*, pp. 331–40.
83. Anon., *Book of trades*, pp. 3, 231.
84. R. J. Blackham, *London's livery companies* (n.d.), p. 263.
85. H. Nockolds, *The coachmakers* (1977), pp. 48–9.
86. Plummer, *The London Weavers' Company*, p. 76.

87. Burnby, *Apprenticeship records*, p. 151.
88. H. Jenkinson, no. 1595.
89. *Ibid.*, no. 1108.
90. Rice.
91. Dale, no. 2337.
92. *Ibid.*, nos. 1802, 2195.
93. Dunlop & Denman, *English apprenticeship*, p. 204.
94. Lane, *Apprenticeship in Warwickshire*, p. 157.
95. Plummer, *The London Weavers' Company*, p. 76.
96. Rice.
97. K. J. Smith, nos. 675, 2343.
98. Lane, *Apprenticeship in Warwickshire*, p. 158.
99. Burnby, *Apprenticeship records*, p. 145.
100. WCRO, DR 126, Box 19.
101. W. T. Baker (ed.), *Records of the borough of Nottingham*, V (1900), p. 407.
102. E. Pursehouse, "Waveney Valley studies", *East Anglian Magazine*, 1963, p. 207.
103. WCRO, DR 296/45.
104. S. C. Ratcliff & H. C. Johnson (eds), *Warwick county records*, VII (Warwick, 1946), pp. 41, 89.
105. Pursehouse, "Waveney valley studies", p. 207.
106. J. D. Peden, "The apprentices of Pitminster", *Studies in Somerset History* (Department of Extra-mural Studies, University of Bristol, 1971), p. 4.
107. Dunlop & Denman, *English apprenticeship*, p. 203.
108. Merson, *A calendar of Southampton apprenticeship registers*, pp. ix–lxxvi.
109. N. R. Perry (ed.), *The Poor Law settlement documents of the church of St. Mary, Old Swinford, 1651–1794* (Birmingham & Midland Society for Genealogy and Heraldry, 1977), pp. 63–105.
110. WCRO, DR 79, DR 318, CR 369/57.
111. Lane, *Apprenticeship in Warwickshire*, p. 154.
112. *Ibid.*, p. 155.
113. WCRO, DR 198/119.
114. HWRO, G 73/2.
115. D. Marshall, *The English poor in the eighteenth century* (1926), p. 198.
116. Macfarlane, *The diary of Ralph Josselin*, pp. 545–6.
117. S. Richardson, *The apprentice's vade mecum* (1734), p. 35.
118. Collyer, *The parent's and guardian's directory*, p. 9.
119. British Library (BL), MS Eng. misc., f.78.
120. Thale, *The autobiography of Francis Place*, p. 446.
121. Macfarlane, *The diary of Ralph Josselin*, p. 446.
122. Hutton, *Life of William Hutton*, p. 9.
123. W. Blake, *Songs of innocence* (1789).
124. *Charity Commissioners' Report* (1837), p. 160.
125. WCRO, WA 6/270, WA 6/272, WA 6/267, WA 17/129–30, WA 16/10–11, WA 6/256–7.
126. *Ibid.*, DR 225/340.
127. C. W. Cunnington & P. Cunnington, *Handbook of English costume in the eighteenth century* (1972), p. 342.
128. WCRO, DR 296/45.
129. SBTRO, BRT 8/199.
130. Leeds City Libraries, Archives Department, DB/196/1.
131. WCRO, 250/50.
132. *Ibid.*, WA 6/257/Box 70.
133. *Ibid.*, DR 432/29.
134. *Ibid.*, DR 296/25.

135. *Ibid.*
136. SBTRO, BRT 8/99.
137. PP, III (1816), p. 215.
138. Bodleian Library Oxford (BLO), MS DD. Par. Oxf. St. Clements, b.24.
139. *Worcester Journal*, 25 September 1806.
140. *Oxford Journal*, 23 January 1812.
141. J. Brown (ed.), *A memoir of Robert Blincoe* (Manchester, 1832), p. 19.
142. Chapman, *The early factory masters*, p. 172.
143. WCRO, CR 136/V65.
144. Ratcliff & Johnson, *Warwick county records*, V, p. 205.
145. Plummer, *The London Weavers' Company*, p. 95.
146. Dunlop & Denman, *English apprenticeship*, p. 195.
147. Macfarlane, *The diary of Ralph Josselin*, pp. 447, 546.
148. WCRO, CR 1908/211.

Chapter 2

1. Herbert, *Shoemaker's window*, p. 7.
2. Campbell, *The London tradesman*, pp. 331–40.
3. Collyer, *The parent's and guardian's directory*, p. 26.
4. Campbell, *The London tradesman*, p. 219.
5. Felkin, *A history of machine-wrought hosiery*, p. 118.
6. S. Timmins (ed.), *Industrial history of Birmingham and the midland hardware district* (1866), p. 183.
7. PP, VI (1817), p. 43.
8. I. & P. Opie (eds), *The Oxford nursery rhyme book* (1960), pp. 95, 81.
9. J. Vanbrugh, *The provok'd wife* (1697), Act VI, sc. i; Anon., Broadside printed by Ford of Chesterfield.
10. Thale, *The autobiography of Francis Place*, p. 216.
11. For example, A. L. Lloyd, *The singing Englishman* (1944), pp. 52–4; J. Reeves, *The idiom of the people* (1958), p. 156; Opie, *The Oxford nursery rhyme book*, p. 195; BL, Add. MS 27825.
12. J. Hewitt, *A journal of the proceedings of J. Hewitt*, III (Coventry, 1779), pp. 1–4.
13. Anon., "A chapter of cheats", in *A touch on the times*, R. Palmer (ed.) (1974), p. 179.
14. *Ibid.*
15. R. Porter (ed.), *Patients and practitioners* (Cambridge, 1985).
16. Campbell, *The London tradesman*, p. 205.
17. *Ibid.*, p. 237.
18. 8 & 9 Wm III c. 30.
19. PP, XXVIII (1834), pp. 432–5.
20. PP, XXIV (1840), p. 78.
21. B. Mandeville, *The fable of the bees*, I (1714), pp. 74–5.
22. Cited in D. Marshall, *The English domestic servant in history* (Historical Association pamphlet 13, 1968), p. 9.
23. Campbell, *The London tradesman*, pp. 227–8.
24. Collyer, *The parent's and guardian's directory*, pp. 195–6.
25. W. Bailey, *A treatise on the better employment and more comfortable support of the poor in workhouses* (1758), p. 5.
26. J. Fielding, *An account of the origin and effects of a police* (1758), p. 50.
27. E. E. Butcher (ed.), *The Bristol corporation of the poor, 1696–1834*, III (Bristol Record Society, 1931), p. 85.

28. PP, IX (1818), pp. 14, 24.
29. PP, XIV (1843), pp. f.172–3.
30. *Ibid.*, p. f.58.
31. 42 Geo. III c. 73.
32. PP, XIX (1834), D1, pp. 168–9.
33. R. Pearsall, *The worm in the bud* (1971), p. 259.
34. CCRO, A 133, p. 128.
35. E. Mayer, *The curriers of the City of London* (1968), pp. 28–9.
36. Burn, *The autobiography of a beggar boy*, p. 120; eighteenth-century novels, *Tom Jones* and *Joseph Andrews*, for example, seem preoccupied with the risk of older women to the young, attractive man.
37. Campbell, *The London tradesman*, pp. 21–2.
38. Cited in S. & B. Webb, *English poor law history: part I* (1963), p. 204.
39. PP, VI (1817), pp. 75–89.
40. PP, XXVIII (1834), Appendix A, p. 7a.
41. Anon. *Book of trades*, pp. 43, 203, 308, 387.
42. A. Meiklejohn, "John Darwall, MD (1796–1833) and Diseases of artisans", *British Journal of Industrial Medicine* 13, 1956, pp. 142–51.
43. B. Ramazzini, *A treatise on the diseases of tradesmen* (1705), p. 142.
44. *The universal British directory*, II (1791), p. 208.
45. Meiklejohn, "John Darwall, MD", pp. 142–51; I am grateful to Professor J. M. Harrington for drawing my attention to this reference.
46. WCRO, DR 447/1, CR 1618, WA 6/43/7.
47. *The Gentleman's Magazine*, LII (1782), p. 526.
48. F. A. Wenderborn, *A view of England towards the close of the eighteenth century* (1791), I, p. 246.
49. Campbell, *The London tradesman*, p. 164.
50. C. T. Thackrah, *The effects of arts, trades and professions on health and longevity* (1832), pp. 102–3.
51. Corporation of London Records Office (CLRO), Complaint Book of the Chamberlain's Office, 1787.
52. Anon., *Medical tracts, 1765–85* (1818), pp. 124–5.
53. R. Southey, *Letters from England*, I (1808), p. 192.
54. Ramazzini, *A treatise on the diseases of tradesmen*, p. 40.
55. W. Richardson, *Chemical principles of the metallic arts* (1790), pp. 193–5.
56. Campbell, *The London tradesman*, p. 221.
57. *Monthly Magazine* (1800), p. 340.
58. Anon., *Book of trades*, p. 198.
59. Thackrah, *The effects of arts, trades and professions*, p. 122.
60. *Ibid.*, p. 155.
61. Ramazzini, *A treatise on the diseases of tradesmen*, pp. 83–4.
62. *Ibid.*, pp. 175–6.
63. Thackrah, *The effects of arts, trades and professions*, p. 71.
64. Meiklejohn, "John Darwall, MD", pp. 146–8.
65. PP, III (1816), pp. 4–26.
66. Meiklejohn, "John Darwall, MD", pp. 142–51.
67. Ramazzini, *A treatise on the diseases of tradesmen*, pp. 145–6.
68. L. P. Pugh, *From farriery to veterinary medicine* (Cambridge, 1962), p. 76.
69. Ramazzini, *A treatise on the diseases of tradesmen*, p. 28.
70. *Ibid.*, p. 54.
71. *Aris's Gazette*, 9 September 1745, 12 May 1746.
72. Ramazzini, *A treatise on the diseases of tradesmen*, p. 194.
73. Thackrah, *The effects of arts, trades and professions*, p. 30.

74. C. W. & P. Cunnington, *Handbook of English costume in the seventeenth century* (1972), p. 412.
75. *The Gentleman's Magazine*, LV (1785), pp. 938–9.
76. Ramazzini, *A treatise on the diseases of tradesmen*, p. 195.
77. BL, Add. MS 34, 245B., ff.3–16.
78. PP, IX (1818), p. 7.
79. PP, XXI (1833), B.1, p. 1.
80. PP, VI (1817), p. 74.
81. Thackrah, *The effects of arts, trades and professions*, p. 200.
82. *Ibid.*, p. 199.
83. Ramazzini, *A treatise on the diseases of tradesmen*, p. 189.
84. *Report of the National Truss Society* (1842).
85. Cited in D. M. George, *London life in the eighteenth century* (1925), p. 203.
86. *Monthly Magazine* (1797), p. 202.
87. Cited in George, *London life in the eighteenth century*, p. 203.
88. G. Sturt, *The wheelwright's shop* (1963), pp. 84, 109.
89. Thackrah, *The effects of arts, trades and professions*, pp. 198–9.
90. Ramazzini, *A treatise on the diseases of tradesmen*, p. 144.
91. *Ibid.*, p. 219.
92. Campbell, *The London tradesman*, p. 252.
93. PP, VI (1817), pp. 74, 78.
94. PP, XIV (1843), p. 225.
95. *Ibid.*, p. f.55.
96. Eden, *The state of the poor*, II, p. 549.
97. PP, XIV (1843), p. f.7.
98. Thackrah, *The effects of arts, trades and professions*, p. 198.
99. Ramazzini, *A treatise on the diseases of tradesmen*, p. 157.
100. Thackrah, *The effects of arts, trades and professions*, p. 41.
101. Review of C. T. Thackrah's, *The effects of arts*, in *Edinburgh Medical and Surgical Journal* (1831).
102. *Warwick Advertiser*, 24 December 1819.
103. *Ibid.*, 3 August 1818.
104. WCRO, MI 261/2.
105. MCL, C/5/8/27.
106. *Warwick Advertiser*, 10 February 1816.
107. *Ibid.*, 18 December 1819.
108. Sturt, *The wheelwright's shop*, p. 210.
109. Ramazzini, *A treatise on the diseases of tradesmen*, preface.
110. MCL, C5/5/1, C5/5/2, C5/5/3, C5/5/4.
111. Chapman, *The early factory masters*, p. 169.
112. CCRO, Apprenticeship Register I.
113. W. M. Rising & P. Millican (eds), *An index of indentures of Norwich apprentices enrolled with the Norwich assembly, 1500–1752* (Norfolk Record Society, 1959).
114. E. J. Buckatzch, "The place of origin of immigrants into Sheffield, 1624–1799", *Economic History Review*, second series, II, 1950, p. 145.
115. Dale.
116. K. J. Smith, no. 168.
117. *Ibid.*, no. 856.
118. Rice.
119. Mrs H. Jenkinson.
120. G. D. Ramsay, "The recruitment and fortunes of some London freemen in the mid sixteenth century", *Economic History Review*, second series, XXXI(4), 1978, pp. 527–36.
121. Morgan, *Warwickshire apprentices*, p. 17.

122. S. L. Thrupp, *The merchant class of medieval London* (Chicago, 1948), p. 211.
123. B. W. E. Alford & T. C. Barker, *The history of the Carpenters' Company* (1968), pp. 73, 116.
124. M. Graham (ed.), *Oxford city apprentices, 1697–1800* XXI (Oxford Historical Society, 1987), p. xix.
125. D. J. Rowe (ed.), *Records of the Company of Shipwrights of Newcastle-upon-Tyne*, II (Surtees Society, 1971), pp. 237–83.
126. A. D. Dyer, *The city of Worcester in the sixteenth century* (Leicester, 1973), pp. 182–3; D. Hollis (ed.), *Calendar of the Bristol apprentice book, 1532–65*, part I (Bristol Record Society, 1949), pp. 15, 197.
127. Buckatzch, "The place of origin of immigrants", p. 305.
128. Bristol City Record Office (BCRO), Apprentice Rolls, 1711–24, f.74.
129. CCRO, Apprenticeship Register I.
130. Burnby, *Apprenticeship records*, p. 153.
131. E. M. Hampson, *The treatment of poverty in Cambridgeshire, 1597–1834* (Cambridge, 1934), p. 153.
132. S. A. Cutlack, *The Gnosall records, 1679–1837* (Staffordshire Record Society Collections, 1936), p. 53.
133. Cited in Tate, *The parish chest*, p. 221.
134. H. Fearn, "The apprenticing of pauper children in the Incorporated Hundreds of Suffolk", *Proceedings of the Suffolk Institute of Archaeology*, XXVI (1955), pp. 96–7.
135. Lane, *Apprenticeship in Warwickshire*.
136. Merson, *A calendar of Southampton apprenticeship registers*, p. xxxiii.
137. L. Stone, *The family, sex and marriage in England, 1500–1800* (1977), p. 58.
138. Plummer, *The London Weavers' Company*, p. 87.
139. Rowe, *Records of the Company of Shipwrights*.
140. K. J. Smith; Dale.
141. L. Stone, "Social mobility in England, 1500–1700", *Past and Present* 33, 1965, p. 53.
142. E. Ralph & N. M. Hardwick (eds), *Calendar of the Bristol apprentice book, 1532–65*, part II (Bristol Record Society, 1980).
143. Merson, *A calendar of Southampton apprenticeship registers*, p. xxxi.
144. Stone, "Social mobility in England, 1500–1700", p. 53.
145. Morgan, *Warwickshire apprentices*, p. 18.
146. H. Jenkinson.
147. Rice.
148. K. J. Smith.

Chapter 3

1. Stone, *The family*, p. 149.
2. Morgan, *Warwickshire apprentices*, p. 2.
3. Cited in J. Brewer, *Party ideology and popular politics at the accession of George III* (Cambridge, 1976), p. 159.
4. Collyer, *The parent's and guardian's directory*, p. 1.
5. *Aris's Gazette*, 11 June and 17 September 1750.
6. *Leeds Mercury*, 12 October 1779.
7. Campbell, *The London tradesman*, pp. 239, 178, 171, 158, 160, 167, 114, 234, 244.
8. *Ibid.*, pp. 142, 189, 194–5, 249, 65.
9. Campbell, *The London tradesman*, p. 51; Collyer, *The parent's and guardian's directory*, p. 269.

10. S. Young, *Annals of the barber-surgeons* (1890), pp. 354, 312.
11. Campbell, *The London tradesman*, p. 123.
12. *Ibid.*, p. 293.
13. Cited in J. Lawson & H. Silver, *A social history of education in England* (1977), p. 181.
14. *Leeds Mercury*, 6 April 1773.
15. Merson, *A calendar of Southampton apprenticeship registers*, p. xxii.
16. Rising and Millican, *An index of indentures*, p. 3.
17. Merson, *A calendar of Southampton apprenticeship registers*, p. xxii.
18. S. Harmer, *Vox populi* (1642).
19. Mandeville, *The fable of the bees*, p. 288.
20. J. & M. Tonkin, *The book of Hereford* (1975), p. 115.
21. F. White, *Directory of Warwickshire* (Sheffield, 1850), p. 15.
22. D. Wardle, "Education in Nottingham in the age of apprenticeship, 1500–1800", *Transactions of the Thoroton Society*, 1967, p. 47.
23. Aikin, *A description of the country*, p. 394.
24. C. Gill & A. Briggs, *A history of Birmingham*, I (Oxford, 1952), p. 82.
25. Wardle, "Education in Nottingham", pp. 49–50.
26. H. C. Barnard, *A short history of English education* (1947), p. 7.
27. W. Cobbett, *Cottage economy* (1979 edn), pp. 6–7.
28. *Charity Commissioners' report* (1837), pp. 241, 160.
29. WCRO, DR 318/7, N2/358, DR 126.
30. W. G. Briggs, "Records of an apprenticeship charity, 1685–1753", *Derbyshire Archaeological and Natural History Society Journal* LXIII, 1953, p. 48.
31. Merson, *A calendar of Southampton apprenticeship registers*, pp. xxii and lii.
32. C. Jackson & S. Margerison (eds), *Yorkshire diaries and autobiographies in the seventeenth and eighteenth centuries*, LXXVII (Surtees Society, 1883), p. 16.
33. Rising & Millican, *An index of indentures*, p. 3.
34. Wardle, "Education in Nottingham", p. 34.
35. Stokes, *The Blecheley diary*, p. 59.
36. J. Powell, *A parson and his flock, 1690–1740* (Warwick, 1981), p. 10.
37. Collyer, *The parent's and guardian's directory*, pp. 75, 92.
38. Sturt, *The wheelwright's shop*, p. 207.
39. Burnett, *Useful toil*, pp. 304–5.
40. V. E. Chancellor (ed.), *Master and artisan in Victorian England* (1969), p. 89.
41. Burnett, *Useful toil*, pp. 304–5.
42. SBTRO, PR117; CCRO, Accn. 201.
43. S. D. Chapman, *William Felkin* (MA thesis, University of Nottingham, 1960), p. 24.
44. T. Secker, *Works*, III (1792), p. 153.
45. Stone, *The family*, p. 309.
46. *Charity Commissioners' report* (1837), pp. 1–3.
47. WCRO, W 16/11.
48. I. Gray (ed.), *Cheltenham settlement examinations, 1815–26* (Bristol and Gloucestershire Archaeological Society, 1969).
49. R. S. Schofield, "Dimensions of illiteracy, 1750–1850", *Explorations in Economic History*, 2nd series, 10(4), 1973, pp. 437–54.
50. Burn, *The autobiography of a beggar boy*, p. 132.
51. Eden, *The state of the poor*, pp. 139, 263, 331.
52. W. Field, *The town and castle of Warwick* (Warwick, 1815), p. 92.
53. Aikin, *A description of the country*, p. 221.
54. PP, XXI (1833), B.1, pp. 1–2.
55. Chancellor, *Master and artisan*, p. 89.
56. PP, XII (1820), p. 360.
57. PP, XXI (1833), B.1, pp. 1–2.

58. *Ibid.*, p. 4.
59. MCL, C5/8/9/4.
60. C. Colvin (ed.), *Maria Edgeworth: letters from England, 1813–44* (1971), p. 31.
61. Brown, *A memoir of Robert Blincoe*, p. 37.
62. Secker, *Works*, III, p. 153.
63. Burn, *The autobiography of a beggar boy*, p. 94.
64. *Book of Common Prayer*, Order of Service for Candidates for Confirmation.
65. C. Hill, *Society and Puritanism in pre-revolutionary England* (1964), pp. 446, 471.
66. 34 & 35 Hen. VIII c. 1.
67. 35 Eliz. I c. 1.
68. Hill, *Society and Puritanism*, pp. 451, 455.
69. *Circular letter of the SPCK to its clergy correspondents* (1714).
70. WCRO, W 16/11.
71. W. Chamberlaine, *Tyrocinium medicum: or, a dissertation on the duties of a youth apprenticed to the medical profession*, 2nd edn (1819), p. 156.
72. Lucas, *A Quaker journal*, I, p. 44.
73. CCRO, Accn. 139, 142.
74. Burnett, *Useful toil*, pp. 341, 331.
75. Brown, *A memoir of Robert Blincoe*, pp. 28–9.
76. Burnett, *Useful toil*, p. 313.
77. *Ibid.*, p. 349.
78. CCRO, Accn. 139, 142.
79. Burnett, *Useful toil*, p. 348.
80. *Aris's Gazette*, 25 December 1780.
81. Medlicott, *No hero*, p. 22.
82. Herbert, *Shoemaker's window*, p. 8.
83. V. M. Crosse, *A surgeon in the early nineteenth century, the life and times of John Crosse Green* (1968), pp. 14–15.
84. Chancellor, *Master and artisan*, pp. 97–8.
85. C. Shaw, *When I was a child* (1903), p. 16.
86. Medlicott, *No hero*, p. 22.
87. Sturt, *The wheelwright's shop*, p. 19.
88. Burnett, *Useful toil*, p. 314.
89. Herbert, *Shoemaker's window*, p. 11.
90. Defoe, *The complete English tradesman*, pp. 6–16.
91. BL, MS Eng. misc., f.78.
92. R. L. Brett, *Barclay Fox's journal* (1979), p. 94.
93. Henry Jephson, letter: in private hands.
94. Aikin, *A description of the country*, p. 139.
95. Raistrick, *Quakers in science*, p. 279.

Chapter 4

1. SBTRO, BRT 8/199.
2. HWRO, G 45/52.
3. SBTRO, BRT 8/199.
4. HWRO, G 73/2.
5. Eden, *The state of the poor*, p. 315.
6. CCRO, Apprenticeship Register I.
7. PP, XXVIII (1834), Appendix A, part I, p. 8a.
8. *Ibid.*, p. 7a.

9. Campbell, *The London tradesman*, pp. 21–3.
10. Secker, *Works*, pp. 21–3.
11. WCRO, DR 250/50.
12. PP, XVIII (1834), Appendix 1, p. 779.
13. Tysoe vestry minutes, 19 October 1810; in private hands.
14. PP, XVIII (1834), Appendix 1, p. 432.
15. *Ibid.*, p. 789.
16. *Ibid.*, p. 783.
17. J. Farrar, *The autobiography of Joseph Farrar, JP* (Bradford, 1889), p. 52.
18. WCRO, DR 75/4–5.
19. N. Mitchelson, *The Old Poor Law in East Yorkshire* (1953), p. 10.
20. J. C. Atkinson (ed.), *Quarter sessions records*, VII (North Riding Society, 1889), pp. 176, 186.
21. N. Bacon, *Annals of Ipswich* (1884), pp. 306, 398.
22. *Warwick Advertiser*, 31 January 1818.
23. *Leeds Mercury*, 3 December 1782.
24. T. Gisborne, *An enquiry into the duties of men* (1794), p. 292.
25. Middlesex Quarter Sessions, Minutes, 29 May 1800.
26. Butcher, *The Bristol corporation*, p. 60.
27. WCRO, DR 198/119.
28. A. Young, *Annals of agriculture*, XXVII (1796), p. 334.
29. Fearn, "The apprenticing of pauper children", p. 96.
30. Stokes, *The Blecheley diary*, p. 56.
31. G. Crabbe, "Peter Grimes", letter XXII in *The borough* (1810).
32. *The charities in the county of Warwick* (1839).
33. R. Newton, *Eighteenth century Exeter* (Exeter, 1984), p. 28.
34. *The charities in the county of Warwick*, p. 516.
35. *Ibid.*, p. 61.
36. E. Hobhouse (ed.), *The diary of a West Country physician, 1684–1726* (1934), p. 106.
37. Cited in B. Rodgers, *The cloak of charity* (1949), p. 12.

Chapter 5

1. Cited in Dunlop & Denman, *English apprenticeship*, p. 56.
2. *Ibid.*, p. 99.
3. Campbell, *The London tradesman*, pp. 331–40.
4. J. D. Chambers, *Nottinghamshire in the eighteenth century* (1966), p. 295.
5. Herbert, *Shoemaker's window*, pp. 11–12.
6. Chancellor, *Master and artisan*, p. 99.
7. *Warwick Advertiser*, 7 April 1810.
8. PP, XIV (1843), pp. 204–5, 235.
9. Lucas, *A Quaker journal*, p. 45.
10. Chamberlaine, *Tyrocinium medicum*, p. 156.
11. Chapman, *The early factory masters*, pp. 199–209.
12. PP, III (1816), pp. 131–2.
13. Brown, *A memoir of Robert Blincoe*, pp. 30–31, 63.
14. CCRO, Poor Law correspondence, unnumbered.
15. PP, III (1816), p. 121.
16. Burnett, *Useful toil*, p. 307.
17. PP, XII (1843), p. 109.

18. Lucas, *A Quaker journal*, p. 44.
19. Jackson & Margerison, *Yorkshire diaries*, p. 11.
20. Aikin, *A description of the country*, p. 183.
21. Blackham, *London's livery companies*, p. 104; *Hereford Times*, 18 February 1955.
22. BLO, Eng. MS misc., f.78.
23. Hutton, *Life of William Hutton*, p. 8.
24. *Warwick Advertiser*, 7 April 1810.
25. Cf. a contemporary song by John Freeth of Birmingham:
    Six days out of seven poor nailing boys get
    Little else at their meals but potatoes to eat;
    For bread hard they labour, good things never carve,
    And swore 'twere as well to be hanged as to starve.
    R. Palmer (ed.), *A touch on the times* (1974), p. 274.
26. Burnby, *Apprenticeship records*, p. 155.
27. Rice, p. 66.
28. Chapman, *The early factory masters*, Chapter 10.
29. Aikin, *A description of the country*, p. 183.
30. Lucas, *A Quaker journal*, p. 46.
31. J. D. Marshall (ed.), *Autobiography of William Stout of Lancaster, 1665–1752* (1967), p. 67.
32. Thale, *The autobiography of Francis Place*, p. 79.
33. Lucas, *A Quaker journal*, p. 44.
34. Plummer, *The London Weavers' Company*, p. 95.
35. Stone, *The family*, pp. 254–5.
36. Macfarlane, *The diary of Ralph Josselin*, p. 205.
37. J. D. Marshall, *Autobiography of William Stout*, p. 66.
38. J. Brasbridge, *The fruits of experience* (1824), p. 26.
39. F. Collier, *Workers' family economy in the cotton industry* (1964), p. 45.
40. PP, III (1816), pp. 125–6.
41. E. P. Thompson & E. Yeo, *The unknown Mayhew* (1971), pp. 438–9.
42. Plummer, *The London Weavers' Company*, p. 90.
43. Mayer, *The curriers*, p. 118.
44. M. James, *Social problems and policy during the Puritan revolution, 1640–1660* (1930), p. 179.
45. *Victoria County History, War.*, II, p. 180.
46. Rising & Millican, *An index of indentures*, p. 179.
47. Hutton, *Life of William Hutton*, p. 9.
48. Merson, *A calendar of Southampton apprenticeship registers*, nos. 164, 167, 8.
49. *Ibid.*, no. 386.
50. Cited in E. Lipson, *History of the woollen and worsted industries* (1921), p. 27.
51. WCRO, DRB 56/Box 11.
52. Thale, *The autobiography of Francis Place*, p. 74.
53. SBTRO, BRT 8/199.
54. *Ibid.*
55. Chancellor, *Master and artisan*, p. 97.
56. Burn, *The autobiography of a beggar boy*, p. 124.
57. Burnby, *Apprenticeship records*, p. 156.
58. Merson, *A calendar of Southampton apprenticeship registers*, nos. 408, 371.
59. MCL, C5/8/9/4.
60. Burnett, *Useful toil*, p. 306.
61. WCRO, DR 126/692.
62. Thale, *The autobiography of Francis Place*, p. 74.
63. BLO, Eng. MS misc., f.78.

64. For a discussion of leisure, see R. W. Malcolmson, *Popular recreations in English society, 1700–1850* (Cambridge, 1973).
65. For a survey of St Monday, see D. A. Reid, "The decline of Saint Monday, 1766–1876", *Past and Present* 71, 1976, pp. 76–101.
66. Staffordshire Record Office, quarter sessions rolls, Epiphany, 1636, no. 19.
67. S. Rudder, *A new history of Gloucestershire* (1779), p. 619.
68. J. Brand, *Observations on popular antiquities*, I (1870), p. 88.
69. *Ibid.*, p. 91.
70. C. Hole, *A dictionary of British folk customs* (1978), p. 231.
71. C. Wharton, "Warwickshire calendar customs", *Warwickshire History* I(5), 1971, p. 3.
72. Brand, *Observations on popular antiquities*, p. 77.
73. Malcolmson, *Popular recreations*, pp. 48–9.
74. Collyer, *The parent's and guardian's directory*, p. 5.
75. *Northampton Mercury*, 2 February 1788.
76. *Leeds Intelligencer*, 27 February 1770.
77. SBTRO, PR 117.
78. F. Burbidge, *Old Coventry and Lady Godiva* (1952), p. 73.
79. *Warwick Advertiser*, 19 February 1814, 6 March 1824.
80. *London Daily Advertiser*, 7 March 1759.
81. Malcolmson, *Popular recreations*, p. 29.
82. Hewitt, *A journal of the proceedings of J. Hewitt*, I, p. 41.
83. Dunlop & Denman, *English apprenticeship*, p. 190.
84. *Ibid.*, p. 189.
85. W. Hutton, *History of Derby* (1791), p. 218.
86. Brand, *Observations on popular antiquities* (1870), p. 90. In 1614 Sir Thomas Overbury observed of one of his *Characters*, Macquerela, "in plaine English, a bawde", that nothing daunted her as much as "the approach of Shrove Tuesday", while another, a "Roaring Boy", was "a supervisor of brothels, and in them is a more unlawful reformer of vice than prentises on Shrove Tuesday". In Nabbe's comedy, *Tottenham Court* (1638), a character says he has "less mercy than Prentices at Shrovetide".
87. R. Latham & W. Matthews (eds), *The diary of Samuel Pepys*, IX (1995), pp. 130–32.
88. "Poor Robin" (1707):
    February welcome, tho' cold and bitter:
    Thou bringest Valentine, Pan-cake and Fritter;
    But formerly most dreadful were the knocks
    Of Prentices 'gainst whore-houses and cocks.
89. E. M. Thompson, *The Chamberlain letters* (1966), pp. 139–40.
90. Hole, *A dictionary of British folk customs*, pp. 191–206.
91. For example: P. Stubbes, *The anatomie of abuses* (1583) and T. Hall, *Funebriae florae* (1661).
92. Cited in C. Phythian-Adams, *Local history and folklore* (1975), p. 10.
93. Ratcliff & Johnson, *Warwick county records*, III, pp. 271–2.
94. Bedfordshire Record Office, HSA 1672, 550 (24 July 1672).
95. N. F. Hulbert, "A survey of Somerset fairs", *Somerset Archaeological and Natural History Society Proceedings*, LXXXII (1936), pp. 86 ff.
96. *Pigot's commercial directory* (1828), pp. 761–842.
97. G. A. Cooke, *A topographical and statistical description of the county of Hereford* (1830), pp. 23–4.
98. Essex Record Office, Q/SBb 225/16.
99. Herbert, *Shoemaker's window*, pp. 11–12.
100. Brown, *A memoir of Robert Blincoe*, p. 41.
101. Thale, *The autobiography of Francis Place*, p. 72.
102. *Ibid.*, p. 64.

103. *Ibid.*, pp. 65–6.
104. B. Jonson, G. Chapman, J. Marston, *Eastward ho!* (1605) Act 1, sc. i.
105. Defoe, *The family instructor*, p. 230.
106. Cited in L. de Mause (ed.), *The history of childhood* (New York, 1976), p. 319.
107. F. W. Dendy (ed.), *The records of the merchant adventurers of Newcastle-upon-Tyne*, XCIII (Surtees Society, 1895), p. 25.
108. Richardson, *Chemical principles*, p. 13.
109. PRO, H. O.43/26; letters from Robert Spillman, 25–6 August 1793.
110. N. Z. Davis, "The reasons of misrule: youth groups and charivaris in sixteenth century France", *Past and Present* 50, 1971, pp. 41–75.
111. J. O. Halliwell (ed.), *The autobiography and personal diary of Dr Simon Forman, the celebrated astrologer, from AD 1552 to AD 1602* (1849), p. 9.
112. C. Cibber, *An apology for the life of Mr Colley Cibber*, V (1740), p. 340. That apprentices were familiar with plays is illustrated in Quicksilver's ability in *Eastward ho!* to quote from *Tamburlaine* and *The Spanish tragedy*, while A. Murphy's apprentice refers to the attractions of the London "Spouting Club", which was a "meeting of prentices and clerks, and giddy young men, intoxicated with plays".
113. *Aris's Gazette*, 1 March 1755, 2 August 1752.
114. PP, XIV, 1843, p. 173; White, *Directory of Warwickshire*, p. 55.
115. Thale, *The autobiography of Francis Place*, pp. 78–82.
116. *London Chronicle*, 18 February 1764.
117. BLO, MS. Eng. misc., f.78.
118. Macfarlane, *The diary of Ralph Josselin*, p. 525.
119. Leader, *Sheffield cutlers*, p. 112.
120. Rising & Millican, *An index of indentures*, p. 76.
121. MCL, C5/2/5, /28.
122. Chancellor, *Master and artisan*, pp. 23, 21.
123. *Ibid.*, p. 98.
124. PP, XXIV (1840), p. 696.
125. J. D. Burn, *A glimpse at the social conditions of the working classes of the United Kingdom, during the early part of the present century* (c. 1868), p. 39.
126. J. Hunter (ed.), *The life of Mr Thomas Gent, Printer of York, written by himself* (1832), p. 16.
127. See Appendix 2.
128. Burnett, *Useful toil*, pp. 349–50.
129. Lucas, *A Quaker journal*, p. 44.
130. *Worcester Journal*, 7 February 1751.
131. *The Philanthropist*, 1 September 1836.
132. J. Rule, *The experience of labour in eighteenth century industry* (1981), pp. 198–9.
133. Burnett, *Useful toil*, pp. 308–9.
134. BCL, nos. 394954, 662306.
135. T. Evans, *Fifty years recollections of an old bookseller* (1837), p. 47.
136. A. D. McKillop, "Samuel Richardson's advice to an apprentice", *Journal of English and German Philology* XLII, 1943, pp. 40–54.
137. Lucas, *A Quaker journal*, p. 45.
138. Chancellor, *Master and artisan*, p. 85.
139. *Leeds Mercury*, 6 August 1774.
140. *Ibid.*, 15 August 1769.
141. Letters of Henry Jephson, MD, in private ownership.
142. Chancellor, *Master and artisan*, pp. 141–51.

Chapter 6

1. Campbell, *The London tradesman*, p. 276.
2. Thale, *The autobiography of Francis Place*, p. 20.
3. Campbell, *The London tradesman*, p. 331.
4. Lane, *Apprenticeship in Warwickshire*, pp. 366–7.
5. *Sketchley's Birmingham, Wolverhampton & Walsall directory* (Birmingham, 1767), p. 4; Lane, *Apprenticeship in Warwickshire*, pp. 367–8.
6. *Pigot's commercial directory* (1828), p. 818; Lane, *Apprenticeship in Warwickshire*, p. 368.
7. Lane, *Apprenticeship in Warwickshire*, p. 368.
8. R. E. Chester Waters, "A statutory list of the inhabitants of Melbourne, Derbyshire in 1695", *Journal of the Derbyshire Archaeological and Natural History Society* VII, 1885, p. 17.
9. Corporation of London Records Office (CLRO), marriage tax assessment, 69.3.
10. Campbell, *The London tradesman*, p. 276.
11. *Ibid.*, p. 281.
12. Collyer, *The parent's and guardian's directory*, p. 83.
13. Campbell, *The London tradesman*, p. 188.
14. CRO, WSMB/K.
15. *Ibid.*
16. K. J. Smith, no. 2012.
17. H. Jenkinson.
18. Macfarlane, *The diary of Ralph Josselin*, p. 546.
19. Dale.
20. CRO, WSMB/K.
21. Rice.
22. Campbell, *The London tradesman*, p. 189.
23. For example: L. G. Mitchell (ed.), *The Purefoy letters, 1735–53* (1973) and W. Thackeray, *Vanity fair* (1847–8).
24. Campbell, *The London tradesman*, p. 339.
25. CRO, WSMB/K.
26. Waters, "A statutory list", pp. 11, 15, 18, 20, 21.
27. CLRO, marriage tax assessment, 69.3.
28. Waters, "A statutory list", p. 11.
29. CRO, WSMB/K.
30. CLRO, marriage tax assessment, 73.16.
31. H. Jenkinson; Rice; Dale.
32. Lane, *Apprenticeship in Warwickshire*, pp. 388–9.
33. Campbell, *The London tradesman*, p. 227.
34. Dale.
35. H. Jenkinson.
36. Dale, nos. 787, 2014, 2068.
37. K. J. Smith. nos. 768, 1068, 1155; PRO, I. R.1, 54/104.
38. H. Jenkinson, nos. 403, 841.
39. D. V. Glass (ed.), *London inhabitants within the walls, 1695*, 2 (London Record Society, 1966), p. 192.
40. CLRO, poll tax assessment, 69.3.
41. Dale, nos. 2427, 896.
42. *Sketchley's directory*, pp. 44–5.
43. Lane, *Apprenticeship in Warwickshire*, pp. 397–400.
44. Campbell, *The London tradesman*, p. 336.
45. *Ibid.*, p. 224.

46. Collyer, *The parent's and guardian's directory*, p. 263.
47. Campbell, *The London tradesman*, p. 225.
48. I. Pinchbeck, *Women workers and the Industrial Revolution, 1750–1850* (1969), p. 290.
49. *Sketchley's directory*, pp. 50–51.
50. *Pigot's commercial directory*, pp. 804–5.
51. Campbell, *The London tradesman*, p. 197.
52. *Ibid.*, p. 340.
53. Collyer, *The parent's and guardian's directory*, p. 301.
54. Glass, *London inhabitants*.
55. CLRO, poll tax assessment, 69.3.
56. Merson, *A calendar of Southampton apprenticeship registers*, nos. 93, 157, 178, 258, 308.
57. Rice, p. 11.
58. Campbell, *The London tradesman*, pp. 196–7.
59. *Ibid.*, p. 197.
60. *Ibid.*, p. 336.
61. Ralph & Hardwick, *Calendar of the Bristol apprentice book*.
62. Merson, *A calendar of Southampton apprenticeship registers*.
63. CRO, WSMB/K.
64. *Ibid.*
65. Glass, *London inhabitants*.
66. Rice.
67. Compassionate Conformist, *England's vanity, or the voice of God against the monstrous sin of pride in dress and apparrell* (1693), p. 107.
68. P. Kalm, *Account of his visit to England in 1748* (1892), p. 94.
69. R. S. Fitton & A. P. Wadsworth (eds), *The Strutts and the Arkwrights* (1958), p. 62.
70. Campbell, *The London tradesman*, p. 331.
71. CRO, WSMB/K.
72. Dale.
73. *Sketchley's directory*, pp. 45–7.
74. CRO, WSMB/K.
75. R. Palmer, "Joseph Hill, his book: the diary of a Stratford-upon-Avon wigmaker", *Warwickshire History* IV(6), 1980–81, pp. 192–202; SBTRO, PR 117.
76. WCRO, DR 126; Boddington later moved to Birmingham and was a master there in 1818 to a Kenilworth charity boy with whom he took a £5 premium (WCRO, DR 296/73).
77. Marshall, *The English domestic servant*, p. 195.
78. Lane, *Apprenticeship in Warwickshire*, p. 492.
79. Ralph & Hardwick, *Calendar of the Bristol apprentice book*.
80. Macfarlane, *The diary of Ralph Josselin*, p. 543.
81. WCRO, DR B 19/82–88; DRB 68; DRB 19/55.
82. HWRO, G.61/1; G.45/52; G.54/29; A.9/26 I.
83. West Devon Record Office, 731/279–833.
84. Campbell, *The London tradesman*, p. 328.
85. 28 Geo. III c. 48.
86. Lane, *Apprenticeship in Warwickshire*, p. 503.
87. WCRO, DR 126.
88. CCRO, A 134, pp. 66–7.
89. *Ibid.*, Apprenticeship Register I.
90. For example, WCRO, DR 28/83.
91. PP, III (1816), p. 4.
92. Anon., *Report of the society for superceding the necessity of climbing-boys* (1829), p. 15.
93. CCRO, Apprenticeship Register II; White, *Directory of Warwickshire*, p. 553.
94. C. Kingsley, *The water babies* (1863), p. 8.
95. Ralph & Hardwick, *Calendar of the Bristol apprentice book*.

96. Glass, *London inhabitants*.
97. CLRO, marriage tax assessment, 62.10.
98. *Ibid.*, 72.20.
99. CRO, WSMB/K.
100. H. Jenkinson.
101. Dale, nos. 1802, 2195.
102. S. Foart Simmons, *The medical register for the year 1783* (1783), p. 16.
103. K. J. Smith, nos. 815, 1484.
104. Campbell, *The London tradesman*, p. 339.
105. Collyer, *The parent's and guardian's directory*, p. 270.
106. Rice.
107. WCRO, CR 1279/16.
108. "Couching" was a surgical procedure for cataract.
109. B. Wilmer, *Cases and remarks in surgery* (1779).
110. N. Penlington, "Sir Theodosius Boughton and laurel water", *Warwickshire History* IV(4) 1979–80, pp. 145–53.
111. J. Lane, "Eighteenth century medical practice: a case study of Bradford Wilmer, surgeon of Coventry, 1737–1813", *Society for the Social History of Medicine Bulletin* III(3), 1990, pp. 369–86.
112. PRO, I. R.1/58, 66, 67; CCRO, Apprenticeship Register I. I am grateful to Dr J. Burnby for the London references.
113. Merson, *A calendar of Southampton apprenticeship registers*.
114. Glass, *London inhabitants*.
115. CLRO, marriage tax assessment, 62.15.
116. Burnby, *Apprenticeship records*, p. 158.
117. Rice.
118. H. Jenkinson, no. 1302.
119. Campbell, *The London tradesman*, p. 331.
120. *Ibid.*, p. 71.
121. Dale.
122. K. J. Smith.
123. Rice, p. 168.
124. Campbell, *The London tradesman*, p. 331.
125. Rice.
126. J. Boswell, *Life of Samuel Johnson* (1831), I, p. 385.

Chapter 7

1. Waters, "A statutory list" p. 18.
2. Rice.
3. Dale.
4. K. J. Smith.
5. Campbell, *The London tradesman*, p. 338.
6. Dale.
7. K. J. Smith.
8. Campbell, *The London tradesman*, p. 338.
9. K. J. Smith, nos. 234, 1901, 2004.
10. Campbell, *The London tradesman*, pp. 234–5.
11. Collyer, *The parent's and guardian's directory*, p. 119.
12. *Ibid.*, p. 119.
13. *Ibid.*

14. H. Jenkinson, no. 191.
15. Dale, no. 958.
16. K. J. Smith, nos. 1165, 257, 1173.
17. *Sketchley's directory*, p. 21.
18. *The universal British directory*, II, p. 234.
19. J. H. Clapham, *Economic history of modern Britain*, I (Cambridge, 1930), p. 169.
20. CLRO, marriage tax assessment, 62.5.
21. Waters, "A statutory list", p. 20.
22. Merson, *A calendar of Southampton apprenticeship registers*.
23. Lane, *Apprenticeship in Warwickshire*, pp. 413–22.
24. Campbell, *The London tradesman*, p. 219.
25. Anon., *Low life* (1764), frontispiece.
26. Anon., *Book of trades*, p. 349.
27. George, *London life in the eighteenth century*, p. 201.
28. T. B. Dudley, *A complete history of Royal Leamington Spa* (1896), pp. 53–6, 84, 110.
29. WCRO, WA 6/267.
30. *Warwick Advertiser*, 21 June, 21 July 1806.
31. Campbell, *The London tradesman*, p. 158.
32. Collyer, *The parent's and guardian's directory*, p. 75.
33. CLRO, marriage tax assessment, 73.114.
34. Campbell, *The London tradesman*, p. 159.
35. *Ibid.*, p. 160; Collyer, *The parent's and guardian's directory*, p. 173.
36. CLRO, marriage tax assessment, 62.3.
37. Waters, "A statutory list" p. 22.
38. CLRO, marriage tax assessment, 73.12.
39. H. Jenkinson, no. 592.
40. Lane, *Apprenticeship in Warwickshire*, pp. 437–43.
41. Campbell, *The London tradesman*, p. 160.
42. Collyer, *The parent's and guardian's directory*, p. 92.
43. G. Tyack, *Warwickshire country houses* (Chichester, 1994), p. 68.
44. K. J. Smith, no. 1393.
45. PRO, I. R. 1. 55/38.
46. Dale, nos. 2632, 2705.
47. Merson, *A calendar of Southampton apprenticeship registers*.
48. Rice.
49. CLRO, marriage tax assessment, 62.13.
50. Waters, "A statutory list", pp. 16, 15.
51. Campbell, *The London tradesman*, p. 159.
52. *Ibid.*, pp. 158–9; Collyer, *The parent's and guardian's directory*, p. 188.
53. K. J. Smith, no. 288.
54. WCRO, DR 126.
55. *VCH War.*, VIII, pp. 474, 508, 531, 451.
56. WCRO, DR 126.
57. *Ibid.*, WA 6/122.
58. *Ibid.*, CR 136/A582–637.
59. CCRO, Apprenticeship Registers I and II.
60. White, *Directory of Warwickshire*, p. 559.
61. Campbell, *The London tradesman*, p. 164.
62. H. Jenkinson.
63. Dale.
64. Rice.
65. CCRO, Apprenticeship Registers I and II.
66. Rice, p. 67.

67. J. Lane, "Robert Moore of Warwick 1711–83", *Country Life*, 28 June 1984.
68. Campbell, *The London tradesman*, p. 163.
69. Glass, *London inhabitants*.
70. H. Jenkinson.
71. Campbell, *The London tradesman*, p. 171.
72. Glass, *London inhabitants*.
73. K. J. Smith; Lane, *Apprenticeship in Warwickshire*.
74. *Sketchley's directory*, p. 17.
75. Dale, nos. 378, 70, 1351, 8, 1378, 1250, 1298, 1434, 1695, 2245.
76. Dale; K. J. Smith.
77. WCRO, WA 6/256/Box 70.
78. A. Stevens, *The woodcarvers of Warwick* (1980), pp. 13–16.
79. CLRO, marriage tax assessment, 62.13.
80. Dale, nos. 2317, 2354, 1392, 2353.
81. WCRO, CR 136/A582–637.
82. C. H. Baker & M. I. Collins, *The life and circumstances of James Brydges, first Duke of Chandos* (1949), p. 196.
83. SBTRO, DR 18/17/3.
84. WCRO, CR 1240/2.
85. SBTRO, DR 18/17/3.
86. K. J. Smith, nos. 1792, 213.
87. PRO, I. R.1, 50/154.
88. Campbell, *The London tradesman*, p. 237.
89. Collyer, *The parent's and guardian's directory*, p. 136.
90. Campbell, *The London tradesman*, p. 334.
91. WCRO, CR 299/604.
92. SBTRO, BRT 8/199.
93. Campbell, *The London tradesman*, p. 334.
94. H. Jenkinson, nos. 1611, 2499, 2034.
95. Rice, p. 166.
96. CCRO, Apprenticeship Registers I and II.
97. Anon., *Book of trades*, p. 350.
98. CLRO, marriage tax assessment, 62.1.
99. Rice, p. 41.
100. PRO, I. R.1, 55/38.
101. Lane, *Apprenticeship in Warwickshire*, p. 238.
102. K. J. Smith, nos. 324, 475, 1922, 2155, 2380.
103. *Ibid.*, nos. 18, 1011, 1518, 1761, 1822.
104. Campbell, *The London tradesman*, p. 242; Collyer, *The parent's and guardian's directory*, p. 157.
105. J. F. Ede, *History of Wednesbury* (1964), pp. 134–7.
106. Lane, *Apprenticeship in Warwickshire*, p. 227.
107. Ede, *History of Wednesbury*, p. 134.
108. Perry, *The Poor Law settlement documents*, pp. 64–105.
109. Lane, *Apprenticeship in Warwickshire*, pp. 218–20.
110. *Sketchley's directory*, pp. 10–11.
111. *Wrightson's new triennial directory of Birmingham* (Birmingham, 1818), p. 153.
112. *Pigot's commercial directory*, p. 786.
113. *Sketchley's directory*, p. 10.
114. *Ibid.*, pp. 88–90, 81–2.
115. *Ibid.*, pp. 13–17.
116. *VCH War.*, VII, p. 95.
117. K. J. Smith, no. 1593; *Sketchley's directory*, p. 16.

118. K. J. Smith, nos. 865, 962.
119. WCRO, DR 856/Box 11.
120. *Wrightson's directory*, pp. 153–4.
121. *Pigot's commercial directory*, p. 787.
122. *Sketchley's directory*, pp. 13–16.
123. *House of Commons journals*, XXVIII (1759), pp. 492–7.
124. *Sketchley's directory*, pp. 13, 57.
125. *Aris's Gazette*, 11 June 1750, 19 January 1757, 17 September 1750.
126. BCL, Boulton & Watt letter book, 1768–73, 1 October 1770.
127. H. W. Dickinson, *Matthew Boulton* (1936), p. 62.
128. K. J. Smith, no. 675.
129. BCL, Boulton & Watt letter book, 1768–73, 1 October 1770.
130. K. J. Smith, no. 1330.
131. *Ibid.*, nos. 865, 2416, 2384, 1268, 1376.
132. Hutton, *Life of William Hutton*, pp. 122–3.
133. *Sketchley's directory*, p. 37.
134. *VCH War.*, VII, p. 95; Timmins, *Industrial history of Birmingham*, p. 567.
135. K. J. Smith, no. 461.
136. Lane, *Apprenticeship in Warwickshire*, p. 241.
137. *VCH Staffs.*, II, p. 251.
138. G. B. Hughes, "Handsome locks for English doors", *Country Life*, 1 August 1963.
139. K. J. Smith, nos. 1346, 2006.
140. N. W. Tildesley, *A history of Willenhall* (1951), p. 140.
141. WCRO, CR 369/57.
142. *Sybil* was published in 1845; *Barnaby Rudge* (1841) showed Simon Tappertit as apprentice to Gabriel Vardon, a locksmith.
143. Timmins, *Industrial history of Birmingham*, p. 91.
144. Lane, *Apprenticeship in Warwickshire*.
145. PP, XIII (1843), p. 307.
146. Merson, *A calendar of Southampton apprenticeship registers*, nos. 301, 313.
147. *Sketchley's directory*, pp. 20, 59.
148. Rice.
149. The Paris family of Warwick were clockmakers, blacksmiths and gunmakers of note by the early eighteenth century, responsible for church clocks as far afield as Somerset and Oxford.
150. CLRO, marriage tax assessment, 69.3.
151. Dale, nos. 959, 217, 1638, 1988.
152. Campbell, *The London tradesman*, pp. 250, 252.
153. CLRO, marriage tax assessment, 62.14, 62.25.
154. H. Jenkinson, nos. 2863, 622.
155. Campbell, *The London tradesman*, pp. 250–51.
156. PP, VI (1827), p. 77.
157. Field, *The town and castle of Warwick*, p. 437.
158. *Pigot's commercial directory*, p. 817.
159. Campbell, *The London tradesman*, p. 252.
160. *VCH War.*, VIII, pp. 399–407.
161. E. Burritt, *Walks in the Black Country and its green borderland* (1868), p. 391.
162. 37 Geo. III, *c.* 108.
163. PP, VI (1817), p. 43.
164. J. Prest, *The Industrial Revolution in Coventry* (1960), pp. 28, 82–7.
165. *Ibid.*, p. 204.
166. PP, VI (1817), pp. 73–87.
167. *VCH War.*, VIII, p. 227.

168. Prest, *The Industrial Revolution in Coventry*, p. 72.
169. C. Bray, *The industrial employment of women* (1857), pp. 8–10.
170. PP, VI (1817), p. 77.
171. *Warwick Advertiser*, 9 June 1821.
172. Anon., *An address to the public shewing the evils and pointing out the remedies of the present injurious system of apprenticeing boys to the watch trade* (Coventry, 1817), p. 6.
173. J. Powell, *A letter to Edward Ellice, Esq.* MP (1819).
174. CLRO, marriage tax assessment, 69.3, 84.
175. WCRO, DR 360/79/4.
176. White, *Directory of Warwickshire*, p. 749.
177. Campbell, *The London tradesman*, p. 142.
178. Timmins, *Industrial history of Birmingham*, p. 502.
179. CLRO, marriage tax assessment, 69.3, 4.
180. H. Jenkinson, no. 21; Rice, p. 147.
181. Campbell, *The London tradesman*, p. 335.
182. Jenkinson, nos. 1660, 1614, 72.
183. Dale, no. 2734.
184. Rice, p. 202.
185. CLRO, marriage tax assessment, 69.3, 10–13, 18, 26–8, 44, 61, 76, 78, 91.
186. Rice, p. 202.
187. H. Jenkinson, nos. 1775–6.
188. *Pigot's commercial directory*, pp. 803–4.
189. Jackson & Margerison, *Yorkshire diaries*, p. 329.
190. Fearn, "The apprenticing of pauper children", pp. 85–97.
191. Lane, *Apprenticeship in Warwickshire*, pp. 358–64.
192. Ede, *History of Wednesbury* p. 134.
193. Perry, *The Poor Law settlement documents*, pp. 64–105.
194. Briggs, "Records of an apprenticeship charity", pp. 50–52.
195. E. G. Thomas, "The apprenticeships and settlement papers of the parish of St Thomas, Portsmouth: pauper apprenticeship", *Portsmouth Archives Review* IV, 1979–80, pp. 12–24.
196. Rice, p. 124.
197. K. J. Smith, no. 1474.
198. John Clare tells how he spent the winter, "the season of . . . imprisonment in the dusty barn", while in spring and summer he tended animals, scared birds and weeded corn. E. Blunden (ed.), *Sketches in the life of John Clare by himself* (1931), p. 48.

Chapter 8

1. Dyer, *The city of Worcester*, p. 110.
2. *Ibid.*, p. 98.
3. HWRO, 008.7.
4. F. W. Steer, *Farm and cottage inventories of mid-Essex, 1635–1749* (1969), p. 81.
5. WCRO, CR 112/Ba 65.
6. CLRO, poll tax assessment, 69.3, 32.
7. Waters, "A statutory list", p. 21.
8. CLRO, marriage tax assessment, 73.11.
9. CRO, WSMB/K/no. 5.
10. SRO, DD/SF, box 55, 1102.
11. H. Jenkinson, nos. 2877, 52, 2719, 382.
12. Perry, *The Poor Law settlement documents*, pp. 64–105.
13. Lane, *Apprenticeship in Warwickshire*, pp. 339–46.

14. CCRO, Apprenticeship Registers I and II.
15. G. Eliot, *Silas Marner* (1861), p. 4.
16. Campbell, *The London tradesman*, p. 260.
17. *Ibid.*, p. 340.
18. K. J. Smith, no. 1468.
19. WCRO, DR 126.
20. K. J. Smith, no. 1343.
21. WCRO, DR 126.
22. *Ibid.*, DR 225/340.
23. *Ibid.*, CR 112/Ba 115.
24. Lane, *Apprenticeship in Warwickshire*, p. 352.
25. Cited in A. Briggs (ed.), *How they lived, 1700–1815* (1969), pp. 221–2.
26. CCRO, A133–135.
27. S. Romilly, *Memoirs* (1840), II, p. 378.
28. *Ibid.*, p. 399.
29. WCRO, MI 261/2.
30. Chapman, *The early factory masters*, p. 90.
31. CCRO, Poor Law correspondence, unnumbered.
32. It is not mentioned in Chapman, *Early factory masters*, p. 240.
33. Field, *The town and castle of Warwick*, p. 78.
34. *Warwick Advertiser*, 30 November 1816.
35. Bull Street, Birmingham, Friends' Meeting House records, items 128, 237.
36. Chapman, *Early factory masters*, p. 104.
37. *VCH War.*, VIII, p. 508; Field, *The town and castle of Warwick*, p. 78.
38. WCRO, CR 770/Box 23.
39. Chapman, *Early factory masters*, p. 86.
40. *Warwick Advertiser*, 13 June 1812.
41. Tysoe vestry minutes, in private hands.
42. *Warwick Advertiser*, 11 February 1911.
43. A. W. Ashby, "A hundred years of Poor Law administration in a Warwickshire village", in *Oxford studies in social and legal history*, P. Vinogradoff (ed.), III (1912), p. 137.
44. M. K. Ashby, *Joseph Ashby of Tysoe* (1974), p. 283.
45. Chapman, *Early factory masters*, p. 157.
46. *Aris's Gazette*, 19 November 1804.
47. *Coventry Mercury*, 14 September 1802, 9 June 1804.
48. Field, *The town and castle of Warwick*, p. 78.
49. WCRO, DR 79/153, 154; DR 79/3.
50. SBTRO, BRT 8/203, /204.
51. *Warwick Advertiser*, 19 April 1806; *Worcester Journal*, 25 September 1806.
52. WCRO, DR 584/64/23, /25, /32.
53. *Ibid.*, DR 458/52; DR 96/8.
54. *Ibid.*, DR 288/3, /8, /17.
55. *Ibid.*, QS 39/12, f.158.
56. *Warwick Advertiser*, 23 April 1816.
57. *Oxford Journal*, 23 January 1812.
58. BLO, MS DD. Par. Oxf. St Clements, b.24; WCRO, DR 524/5.
59. *VCH War.*, VIII, p. 508; *Warwick Advertiser*, 21 March 1819.
60. WCRO, CR 1707.
61. Oxfordshire Archives, quarter sessions records, unnumbered bundle, Trinity 1805.
62. B. Poole, *Coventry: its history and antiquities* (1870), p. 359.
63. *Ibid.*, pp. 359–60.
64. PP, III (1816), p. 125.
65. *Warwick Advertiser*, 21 March 1812.

66. WCRO, DR 230/59.
67. *Warwick Advertiser*, 8 May 1813.
68. Chapman, *Early factory masters*, p. 170.
69. MCL, C5/8/22, C5/8/9/2.
70. WCRO, QS 73/1; DR 296/61; CR 136/V65.
71. Campbell, *The London tradesman*, pp. 77, 338, 302.
72. CCRO, Apprenticeship Registers I and II.
73. G. Eliot, *Middlemarch* (1871), p. 245.
74. Hutton, *History of Derby*, p. 191.
75. Anon., *England displayed* (1769), II, p. 13.
76. WCRO, DR 139/8.
77. Chancellor, *Master and artisan*, chaps 1–3.
78. CCRO, accn. 201.
79. Collyer, *The parent's and guardian's directory*, p. 251.
80. WCRO, DR 484/94/2.
81. *Ibid.*, DR 280/68.
82. PP, IX (1818), pp. 16–17.
83. WCRO, DR 280/68.
84. PP, IX (1818), pp. 185–6.
85. Dale, no. 1041.
86. H. Jenkinson, no. 1160.
87. Dale, no. 1339.
88. Eden, *The state of the poor*, pp. 140–43, 262–6.
89. WCRO, DR 458/52.
90. For example: *Warwick Advertiser*, 22 January 1820.
91. F. Thompson, *Lark Rise to Candleford* (1939), p. 79, described the few old village women still able to make pillow-lace on the Oxfordshire/Northamptonshire border in the 1880s.
92. CRO, WSMB/K.
93. CLRO, poll tax assessment, 69.3, 31, 85.
94. G. Henson, *The . . . history of the framework-knitters* (Nottingham, 1831), pp. 168, 178.
95. Felkin, *A history of machine-wrought hosiery*, p. 435.
96. PP, II (1812), p. 235.
97. Campbell, *The London tradesman*, p. 215.
98. Henson, *The . . . history of the framework-knitters*, p. 101.
99. *Hansard* (1815), pp. 533–4.
100. WCRO, DR 148/119; DRB 46/84.

Chapter 9

1. McKenzie, *Stationers' Company apprentices*, p. 377.
2. Doe, *The diary of James Clegg*, I, pp. 132–3, 171, 201, 204, 206–7.
3. Macfarlane, *The diary of Ralph Josselin*, pp. 446–558.
4. W. Herbert, *The history of the twelve great livery companies of London* (1837), II, pp. 168–9.
5. Devon Record Office, 9972/E37; *Exeter Flying Post*, 2 August 1782; PRO, Misc. Rolls of the Exchequer LTR (E70/42, f.23).
6. Thale, *The autobiography of Francis Place*, p. 19.
7. Medlicott, *No hero*, p. 23.
8. *London Chronicle*, 17 December 1764.
9. Cited in George, *London life in the eighteenth century*, p. 232.
10. Burn, *The autobiography of a beggar boy*, pp. 99, 119.

11. I. Pinchbeck & M. Hewitt, *Children in English society* (1969), I, p. 223.
12. Hewitt, *A journal of the proceedings of J. Hewitt*, I, pp. 41–2.
13. *VCH War.*, VIII, p. 225.
14. *Birmingham Journal*, 26 September 1855.
15. Stone, *The family*, p. 254.
16. Ratcliff & Johnson, *Warwick county records*, I, p. 179; VI, p. 55.
17. Lucas, *A Quaker journal*, p. 44.
18. *London Chronicle*, 1 August 1764.
19. *Ibid.*, 3 February 1764.
20. P. Laslett, *The world we have lost* (1965), pp. 103–5; J. R. Gillis, *Youth and history* (New York, 1974), p. 7. In the late seventeenth century expectation of life for most of the population was 32 years and even for the aristocracy it was only 34.7 for men and 33.7 for women. By the early eighteenth century these figures had improved, for the prosperous sector of society, to 45.8 for males and 48.2 for females.
21. D. Defoe, *Some considerations upon streetwalkers* (n.d.), pp. 6–7.
22. Stone, *The family*, p. 616.
23. *Ibid.*, plate 41.
24. *Weekly Journal*, 4 June 1720.
25. Hewitt, *A journal of the proceedings of J. Hewitt*, I, p. 60.
26. W. Herbert, *The history of the twelve great livery companies*, I, pp. 423–4.
27. Stone, *The family*, p. 50.
28. Collyer, *The parent's and guardian's directory*, pp. 309–11. As Gillray illustrated in his *Plaisirs de mariage* the consequences of an imprudent marriage could be
    A smoky house, a failing trade,
    Six squalling brats and a scolding jade. (BL, Catalogue of Political and Personal Satires, V, no. 5938).
29. Burn, *The autobiography of a beggar boy*, p. 129.
30. Thale, *The autobiography of Francis Place*, p. 104.
31. Chancellor, *Master and artisan*, p. 113.
32. Defoe, *The complete English tradesman*, I, p. 155.
33. Herbert, *The history of the twelve great livery companies*, II, pp. 169–70.
34. Collyer, *The parent's and guardian's directory*, pp. 303–16.
35. BLO, MS Eng. misc., f.78.
36. Collyer, *The parent's and guardian's directory*, p. 31.
37. Herbert, *Shoemaker's window*, p. 138. It was also possible for the male apprentice to behave too familiarly towards his master's wife, a common enough situation to become a popular rhyme:
    My master he did cudgel me
    For kissing of my dame.
38. *Leeds Intelligencer*, 16 July 1771.
39. Hewitt, *A journal of the proceedings of J. Hewitt*, I, pp. 41–2.
40. BLO, MS Eng. misc., f.78.
41. Collyer, *The parent's and guardian's directory*, pp. 303–16.
42. S. Markham, *John Loveday of Caversham, 1711–89* (Wilton, 1984), p. 348.
43. J. J. Scarisbrick, *Henry VIII* (1968), pp. 98–9.
44. *Acts of the Privy Council*, XXII, p. 549.
45. Anon., *The honour of London apprentices exemplified in a brief historical narrative* (1647).
46 Anon., *An humble declaration of the apprentices and other young men of the city of London* (1642), reprinted in *Harleian miscellany*, VIII (1811), pp. 593–7.
47. Anon., *A satyre against separatists* (1675). In 1660, in Tatham's play, *The Rump*, apprentices were depicted as a riotous mob who claimed considerable rights in government. They threatened revenge on a one-eyed shoemaker, who had risen in rank under Cromwell, and demanded a free parliament, later burning rumps of mutton in public, shouting "Roast the

Rump!" (Act IV, scene i and Act V, scene i).

48. J. Dunton, *The life and errors of John Dunton* (1705), p. 50.

49. S. R. Smith, "The London apprentices as seventeenth-century adolescents", *Past and Present* 61, 1973, pp. 149–61.

50. B. Capp, "English youth groups and *The pinder of Wakefield*", *Past and Present* 76, 1977, pp. 127–9.

51. P. Cunningham (ed.), *The letters of Horace Walpole, Earl of Orford* (1891), VII, p. 391.

52. *Warwick Advertiser*, 30 June 1819.

53. Richardson, *The apprentice's vade mecum*, p. 3.

54. CCRO, A 134, p. 136.

55. WCRO, DRB 19/86.

56. CCRO, A 135, p. 166.

57. *Ibid.*, p. 26.

58. Defoe, *The great law of subordination consider'd*, p. 13.

59. Defoe, *The family instructor*, pp. 260–61.

60. Anon., *The grand concern of England explained* (1673); reprinted in *Harleian miscellany*, VIII (1811), p. 576.

61. J. Thirsk, "Younger sons in the seventeenth century", *History* 54(182),1962, pp. 358–77.

62. Lucas, *A Quaker journal*, p. 15.

63. BLO, MS Eng. misc., f.78.

64. Richardson, *The apprentice's vade mecum*, p. 19.

65. Lucas, *A Quaker journal*, p. 15.

66. P. Quennell (ed.), *Memoirs of William Hickey* (1975), p. 39.

67. Defoe, *The family instructor*, p. 173.

68. Latham & Matthews, *The diary of Samuel Pepys*, VII, p. 273.

69. Gray, *Cheltenham settlement examinations*, p. 15.

70. For example, in the opening scene of George Farquhar's *The recruiting officer* (1706), set in provincial Lichfield, Sergeant Kite invites "as many apprentices as have cruel masters" to enlist.

71. Gray, *Cheltenham settlement examinations*, pp. 20, 12.

72. Ratcliff & Johnson, *Warwick county records*, VII, p. 104.

73. BCL, MS 218/1.

74. Atkinson, *Quarter Session records*, p. 234.

75. Ratcliff & Johnson, *Warwick county records*, VII, p. 35.

76. WCRO, QS 39/8.

77. Hill, *Society and Puritanism*, p. 451.

78. Collyer, *The parent's and guardian's directory*, p. 44.

79. BLO, MS Ashm. 178, f.8 R, MS Ashm. 385, p. 128.

80. Lucas, *A Quaker journal*, p. 43.

81. *Warwick Advertiser*, 1806–12; I am grateful to Professor R. E. McGowen for this analysis.

82. Hutton, *Life of William Hutton*, p. 11.

83. Medlicott, *No hero*, pp. 23–5.

84. 6 Geo. III c. 25.

85. *Coventry Mercury*, 13 January 1800.

86. CCRO, A 135.

87. WCRO, DR 373/32.

88. BCRO, quarter sessions bundle, 1786.

89. P. Linebaugh, *Tyburn, a study of crime and the labouring poor in London during the first half of the eighteenth century* (PhD thesis, University of Warwick, 1975).

90. Chambers, *Nottinghamshire in the eighteenth century*, p. 231.

91. H. Wright, "Sowerby parish apprentices", *Transactions of the Halifax Antiquarian Society*, 1934, p. 63.

92. *Oxford Journal*, 10 July 1765.

93. For example, in Massinger's *The city madam* (1659) ways of short-measuring fabric are given.

94. BLO, MS Eng. misc., f.78.

95. *London Chronicle*, 16 July 1764.

96. *Oxford Journal*, 17 August 1765.

97. Young, *Annals of the barber-surgeons* (1890), p. 262.

98. Rule, *The experience of labour*, pp. 126–7.

99. Blackham, *London's livery companies*, p. 193.

100. BCL, MS 218/1; VCH *War.*, VIII, p. 276.

101. Dendy, *The records of the Merchant Adventurers*, pp. 23, 169, 154.

102. BL, Add. MSS 27826, f.201; letter from Henry Wilson to Robert Peel.

103. *Weekly Journal*, 2 June 1716.

104. Illustrated in O. Warner, *A history of the tin-plate workers* (1964), p. 24.

105. Blackham, *London's livery companies*, p.147.

106. C. W. Camp, *The artizan in Elizabethan literature* (New York, 1923), pp. 5–6.

107. *Ibid.*, p. 3.

108. Mayer, *The curriers*, p. 82.

109. Herbert, *The history of the twelve great livery companies*, I, pp. 166–7.

110. BL, Add. MSS, 18,913.

111. Dendy, *The records of the Merchant Adventurers*, pp. 20, 22.

112. Mayer, *The curriers*, p. 82.

113. W. Maitland, *History of London* (1739), p. 160.

114. *The World* (1755).

115. Thale, *The autobiography of Francis Place*, p. 63.

116. J. H. Plumb, "The new world of children in eighteenth century England", *Past and Present* 67, 1975, p. 91.

117. Anon., *Printed accounts of the borough of Stratford-upon-Avon, 1794–5* (1796), p. 20.

118. Dendy, *The records of the Merchant Adventurers*, pp. 22–3.

119. W. Herbert, I, p. 167.

120. Cited in Dunlop & Denman, *English apprenticeship*, p. 192.

121. Dendy, *The records of the merchant adventurers*, p. 25.

122. Young, *Annals of the barber-surgeons*, pp. 261, 269.

123. Richardson, *The apprentice's vade mecum*, pp. 33–5.

124. Alford & Barker, *The history of the Carpenters' Company*, p. 30; Blackham, *London's livery companies*, p. 101.

125. Ratcliff & Johnson, *Warwick county records*, I, pp. 257–8.

126. CCRO, A 125, p. 255.

127. SBTRO, BRT 8/199.

128. WCRO, DR 225/340; CCRO, Apprenticeship Register I.

129. Rowe, *Records of the Company of Shipwrights*, p. 74.

130. HWRO, G 73/2.

131. Baker, *Records of the borough of Nottingham*, pp. 193–4.

Chapter 10

1. Defoe, *The family instructor*, p. 238.

2. *Ibid.*, pp. 258–61.

3. Defoe, *The complete English tradesman*, I, p. 15.

4. *Book of Common Prayer*: Order of Service for Candidates for Confirmation.

5. Collyer, *The parent's and guardian's directory*, p. 31.

6. CCRO, A 133, A 134, A 135.

7. *Ibid.*, A 135, p. 236.

8. *Ibid.*, A 133, p. 215.

9. *Ibid.*, A 133, p. 110.

10. *Ibid.*, A 134, pp. 66–8.

11. WCRO, DR 126.

12. CCRO, A 133, p. 103.

13. *Ibid.*, A 133, p. 128.

14. Lucas, *A Quaker journal*, p. 44.

15. Middlesex Sessions, Calendar, April 1722.

16. *Ibid.*, April 1755.

17. Herbert, *The history of the twelve great livery companies*, p. 8.

18. Plummer, *The London Weavers' Company*, p. 71.

19. WCRO, WA 6/257, Box 70.

20. Middlesex Sessions, Calendar, April 1711.

21. *Ibid.*, February 1729/30.

22. Baker, *Records of the borough of Nottingham*, pp. 156–7.

23. *Ibid.*, pp. 109–10.

24. *Historical MSS committee report on MSS in various collections (Wilts.)*, I (1901), p. 117; R. F. Hunnisett (ed.), *Wiltshire coroners' bills, 1752–96*, XXXVI (Wiltshire Record Society, 1981), nos. 174, 569, 1324, 1433, 1619, 1820, 1861, 1892.

25. H. H. Copnall (ed.), *Nottinghamshire records* (1915), p. 128.

26. W. Hudson & J. C. Tingey (eds), *Records of the city of Norwich*, II (1910), p. 176.

27. Hutton, *History of Derby*, p. 209.

28. Medlicott, *No hero*, pp. 23–25.

29. A. Quiller-Couch (ed.), *The Oxford book of English verse* (1949), p. 522.

30. *Lancaster Gazetteer*, 4 July 1801.

31. *The Times*, 23 May 1801.

32. WCRO, DR 101/5.

33. *Ibid.*, DR 296/60.

34. *Warwick Advertiser*, 7, 21 April 1810.

35. Nuneaton Public Library, Anon., *Memorandum book of occurrences at Nuneaton*, I, 1818–19.

36. *Warwick Advertiser*, 18 January, 1 February 1812.

37. *Coventry Mercury*, 10 March, 7, 14 April 1783.

38. CCRO, A 128/17.

39. Anon., *Proceedings at large on the trial of John Clay for the wilful murder . . . of Ann Hands, his apprentice* (Coventry, 1783).

40. Middlesex Sessions, Calendar, October 1728.

41. CLRO, Guildhall Sessions papers, 1742.

42. Ratcliff & Johnson, *Warwick county records*, V, p. 15.

43. *Ibid.*, p. 127.

44. CCRO, A 133, pp. 103, 128.

45. R. K. McClure, *Coram's children: the London Foundling Hospital in the eighteenth century* (1981), p. 134.

46. Middlesex Sessions of the Peace, Sessions Book, 70/19, 32.

47. *Ibid.*, 148/41.

48. *London Chronicle*, 25 February 1764; *Salisbury Journal*, 19 March 1764.

49. Ratcliff & Johnson, *Warwick county records*, I, p. 212.

50. *Coventry Mercury*, 29 September 1783.

51. WCRO, DR 536/2.

52. H. E. Rollins (ed.), *A Pepysian garland* (1922), p. 223.

53. J. Villette, *The annals of Newgate*, IV (1776), p. 167.

54. *The Gentleman's Magazine* (1767), pp. 433 ff.

55. BL, Add. MSS, 27828, f.113.
56. Anon., *An enquiry into the causes of the increase and misery of the poor of England* (1738), p. 43.
57. WCRO, N4.
58. Cited in George, *London life in the eighteenth century*, p. 230.

Chapter 11

1. *Leeds Intelligencer*, 21 February 1781.
2. Jackson & Margerison, *Yorkshire diaries*, p. 19.
3. R. D. Lang, *The greater merchants of London in the early seventeenth century* (DPhil thesis, University of Oxford, 1963).
4. Raistrick, *Quakers in science*, pp. 228–9.
5. R. Gough, *The history of Myddle* (1981), p. 228.
6. Doe, *The diary of James Clegg*, I, pp. 222–3.
7. E. P. Thompson, "'Rough music': le charivari anglais", *Annales* 2, March–April 1972, p. 295.
8. Young, *Annals of the barber-surgeons*, p. 25.
9. Cirket, *English wills*, p. 62.
10. N. W. Alcock, *Stoneleigh villagers, 1597–1650* (University of Warwick, 1975), p. 41.
11. Marshall, *Autobiography of William Stout*, p. 72.
12. Gough, *The history of Myddle*, p. 210.
13. Raistrick, *Quakers in science*, p. 230.
14. Dickinson, *Matthew Boulton*, p. 60.
15. Raistrick, *Quakers in science*, p. 203.
16. *Leeds Intelligencer*, 5 December 1775.
17. *Leeds Mercury*, 21 December 1779.
18. *London Gazette*, 28 November 1713.
19. Marshall, *Autobiography of Wiliam Stout*, pp. 71–2.
20. Campbell, *The London tradesman*, pp. 331–40.
21. Macfarlane, *The diary of Ralph Josselin*, p. 353.
22. Gough, *The history of Myddle*, pp. 97, 113, 228, 216, 101, 196, 206.
23. *Norwich Mercury*, 23 April 1785.
24. Thale, *The autobiography of Francis Place*, pp. 137–8.
25. Herbert, *Shoemaker's window*, p. 21.
26. Rising & Millican, *An index of indentures*, p. 18.
27. For example, Sir Thomas White in 1542 left land producing £70 a year and £1,400 in money to provide for apprentices from Coventry, Northampton, Leicester, Nottingham and Warwick; loans were to be repaid after nine years. In 1990 the charity distributed £654,539.
28. Mandeville, *The fable of the bees*, pp. 58–9.
29. Collyer, *The parent's and guardian's directory*, pp. 27.
30. Prest, *The Industrial Revolution in Coventry*, p. 28.
31. Bedfordshire Record Office, P 64/14.
32. Merson, *A calendar of Southampton apprenticeship registers*.
33. For example, WCRO, DR 225/340.
34. *Ibid.*, DR 156/21.
35. *Ibid.*, DR 225/41.
36. *Ibid.*, WA 6/256, Box 70.
37. *Ibid.*, DR 123/10.
38. Merson, *A calendar of Southampton apprenticeship registers*, nos. 164, 343.

Chapter 12

1. K. Garlick & A. Macintyre (eds), *The diary of Joseph Farington*, III (1798), p. 983.
2. I. Bain, *The watercolours and drawings of Thomas Bewick and his workshop apprentices* (1981) I, p. 66.
3. K. Garlick & A.Macintyre (eds), *The diary of Joseph Farington*, p. 2027
4. SBTRO, DR 37/Box 181; I am grateful to Miss Mairi Macdonald for this reference.
5. J. J. Bagley (ed.), *The great diurnall of Nicholas Blundell*, II; III (London and Cheshire Record Society, 1968–72), p. 110; p. 80.
6. Bain, *The watercolours*, p. 66.
7. Defoe, *The complete English tradesman*, p. 16.
8. Dyer, *The city of Worcester*, p. 109.
9. W. Hamper, (ed.), *The life, diary and correspondence of Sir William Dugdale* (1827), pp. 100–101.
10. Cutlers' Hall, Sheffield, account books (1625–1790).
11. *Daily Mail*, 19 December 1989.
12. Markham, *John Loveday of Caversham*, p. 196.
13. Coventry Local Studies Library, unnumbered.
14. P. Linebaugh, *The London hanged* (1991), pp. 62, 105, 102.
15. G. T. Wilkinson, *The Newgate calendar* (1991 edn).
16. Markham, *John Loveday of Caversham*, pp. 331, 418, 424.
17. R. Hutton, *The rise and fall of merry England* (1994), pp. 244, 210–11.
18. HWRO, 1644/58.
19. *The Times*, 1 December 1993: "Prospects: work-based training: modern apprenticeships" (Coventry and Warwickshire Training and Enterprise Council brochure, n.d.).

Bibliography

Apprenticeship material abounds in English record offices, whether as single items or in collections; the quantity is as daunting as its often uncatalogued state. Apprenticeship registers and indentures have primarily been scanned by genealogists for the names they contain. Few registers or collections can be considered complete, either because single items have been lost or because certain categories of apprentices (paupers or girls, for example) were deliberately excluded; under-registration must always be suspected. Newspapers for all areas contain miscellaneous apprenticeship references, as do records of quarter sessions, assize courts and official publications in general. Published secondary sources on apprenticeship are few since Dunlop & Denman's work of 1912, but Dorothy George, the Webbs and Dorothy Marshall among older writers give the institution careful attention, while modern historians, especially John Rule and C. R. Dobson, emphasize its importance in labour history generally.

I. Primary sources

a. Official publications

Abstract of returns on the maintenance of the poor in England, 1818.
Charity Commissioners' reports.
Historical MSS committee report on MSS in various collections (Wilts.), I (1901).
House of Commons journals.
Report of the committee on several petitions relating to the apprentice laws, PP, IV (1812–13).
Report . . . on parish apprentices, PP, V (1814–15).
Report . . . on the state of children in manufactories, PP, III (1816).
Report . . . on the employment of boys in sweeping chimneys, PP, VI (1817).
Report . . . on the poor laws, PP, IV (1817).
Report . . . on the petitions of the watchmakers of coventry, PP, VI (1817).

Report . . . on the laws relating to watchmakers, PP, IX (1818).

Reports . . . on the silk ribbon weavers' petitions, PP, IX (1818).

Report . . . on the silk trade, PP, XIX (1831–2).

Report . . . on the labour of children in mills and factories, PP, XV (1831–2).

Report . . . on the employment of children in factories, PP, XXI (1833).

Report . . . on the administration and practical operation of the poor laws, PP, XXVIII (1834).

Report . . . on the state of the hand-loom weavers, PP, XXIV (1840).

Report . . . on the employment of children in trades and manufactures, PP, XIV (1843).

b. Newspapers and periodicals

Aris's Gazette
Birmingham Journal
Coventry Mercury
Daily Mail
Exeter Flying Post
Hereford Times
Lancaster Gazetteer
Leeds Intelligencer
Leeds Mercury
London Chronicle
London Daily Advertiser
London Gazette
Monthly Magazine
Northampton Mercury
Norwich Mercury
Oxford Journal
Salisbury Journal
The Gentleman's Magazine
The Lady's Magazine
The Philanthropist
The Times
The World
Warwick Advertiser
Weekly Journal
Worcester Journal

c. Printed sources

Place of publication is London unless otherwise stated.

Aikin, J. *A description of the country from thirty to forty miles round Manchester* (1795).

Anon. *A satyre against separatists* (1675).

Anon. *An address to the public shewing the evils and pointing out the remedies of the present injurious system of apprenticeing boys to the watch trade* (Coventry, 1817).

Anon. *An ease for overseers of the poor* (1601).

Anon. *An enquiry into the causes of the increase and misery of the poor of England* (1738).

Anon. *An humble declaration of the apprentices and other young men of the city of London* (1642).

Anon. *Book of trades* (1818).

Anon. *England displayed* (1769).

Anon. *Low life* (1764).

Anon. *Medical tracts, 1765–85* (1818).

Anon. *Memorandum book of occurrences at Nuneaton*, I, (1818–19).

Anon. *Printed accounts of the borough of Stratford-upon-Avon, 1794–5* (1796).

Anon. *Proceedings at large on the trial of John Clay for the wilful murder . . . of Ann Hands, his apprentice* (Coventry, 1783).

Anon. *Reflections on the relative situations of master and servant* (1800).

Anon. *Report of the Society for superceding the necessity of climbing boys* (1829).

Anon. *The honour of London apprentices exemplified in a brief historical narrative* (1647).

Anon. *The servant's calling, with some advice to the apprentice* (1725).

Atkinson, J. C. (ed.). *Quarter sessions records*, VII (North Riding Society, 1889).

Bailey, W. *A treatise on the better employment and more comfortable support of the poor in workhouses* (1758).

Baker, W. T. (ed.). *Records of the borough of Nottingham* (1900).

Brand, J. *Observations on popular antiquities* (1870).

Bray, C. *The industrial employment of women* (1857).

Brett, R. L. *Barclay Fox's journal* (1979).

Brown, J. (ed.). *A memoir of Robert Blincoe* (Manchester, 1832).

Burn, J. D. *The autobiography of a beggar boy* (1978 reprint).

Burn, J. D. *A glimpse at the social conditions of the working classes of the United Kingdom, during the early part of the present century* (c. 1868).

Burnby, J. G. L. *Apprenticeship records* (British Society for the History of Pharmacy, 1977).

Burnett, J. (ed.). *Useful toil* (1974).

Burritt, E. *Walks in the Black Country and its green borderland* (1868).

Butcher, E. E. (ed.). *The Bristol corporation of the poor, 1696–1834* (Bristol Record Society, 1931).

Campbell, R. *The London tradesman* (1747).

Chamberlaine, W. *Tyrocinium medicum: or, a dissertation on the duties of a youth apprenticed to the medical profession* (2nd edn, 1819).

Chancellor, V. E. (ed.). *Master and artisan in Victorian England* (1969).

Chitty, J. *A practical treatise on the law relative to apprentices and journeymen and to exercising trades* (1812).

Cirket, A. F. (ed.). *English wills, 1498–1526*, XXVII (Bedfordshire Historical Record Society, 1957).

Cobbett, W. *Cottage economy* (1979 reprint).

Collyer, J. *The parent's and guardian's directory* (1761).

Colvin, C. (ed.). *Maria Edgeworth: letters from England, 1813–44* (1971).

Compassionate Conformist, *England's vanity, or the voice of God against the monstrous son of pride in dress and apparrell* (1693).

Cooper, T. *The life of Thomas Cooper, written by himself* (1872).

Copnall, H. H. (ed.). *Nottinghamshire records* (1915).

Crosse, V. M. *A surgeon in the early nineteenth century, the life and times of John Crosse Green* (1968).

Cunningham. P. (ed.). *The letters of Horace Walpole, Earl of Orford*, VII (1891).

Cutlack, S. A. *The Gnosall records, 1679–1837* (Staffordshire Record Society Collections 1936).

Dale, C. (ed.). *Wiltshire apprentices and their masters, 1710–60*, XVII, (Wiltshire Archaeological and Natural History Society, 1961).

Defoe, D. *Some considerations upon streetwalkers* (n.d.).

Defoe, D. *The complete English tradesman* (1738).

Defoe, D. *The great law of subordination consider'd* (1724).

Defoe, D. *The trade of England reviv'd* (1681).

Defoe, D. *The family instructor* (1715).

Dellow, E. (ed.). *Svedenstierna's tour of Great Britain, 1802–3* (1973).

Dendy, F. W. (ed.). *The records of the Merchant Adventurers of Newcastle-upon-Tyne* XCIII (Surtees Society, 1895).

Doe, V. S. (ed.). *The diary of James Clegg of Chapel-en-le-Frith, 1708–55*, (Derbyshire Record Society, 1978–9).

Dunton, J. *The life and errors of John Dunton* (1705).

Eden, F. M. *The state of the poor* [3 vols] (1797).

Emmison, F. G. (ed.). *Some Bedfordshire diaries* (Bedfordshire Historical Record Society, 1960).

Evans, T. *Fifty years recollections of an old bookseller* (1837).

Farrar, J. *The autobiography of Joseph Farrar, JP* (Bradford, 1889).

Fearn, H. "The apprenticing of pauper children in the Incorporated Hundreds of Suffolk", XXVI *Proceedings of the Suffolk Institute of Archaeology* (1955).

Felkin, W. *A history of machine-wrought hosiery and lace manufacture* (1867).

Field, W. *The town and castle of Warwick* (Warwick, 1815).

Fielding, J. *An account of the origin and effects of a police* (1758).

Freshfield, E. (ed.). *The vestry minutes of S. Christopher le Stocks* (1886).

Garlick, K. & A. Macintyre (eds). *The diary of Joseph Farington*, III (1798).

Gisborne, T. *An enquiry into the duties of men* (1794).

Glass, D. V. (ed.). *London inhabitants within the walls, 1695* (London Record Society, 1966).

Gough, R. *The history of Myddle* (1981 reprint).

Graham, M. (ed.). *Oxford city apprentices, 1697–1800*, XXI (Oxford Historical Society, 1987).

Gray, I. (ed.). *Cheltenham settlement examinations, 1815–26* (Bristol and Gloucestershire Archaeological Society, 1969).

Hamper, W. (ed.). *The life, diary and correspondence of Sir William Dugdale* (1827).

Hanway, J. *A sentimental history of chimney sweepers* (1785).

Henson, G. *The . . . history of the framework-knitters* (Nottingham, 1831).

Herbert, G. *Shoemaker's window* (1971 reprint).

Herbert, W. *The history of the twelve great livery companies of London* (1837).

Hobhouse, E. (ed.). *The diary of a West Country physician, 1684–1726* (1934).

Hollis, D. (ed.). *Calendar of the Bristol apprentice book, 1532–65*, part I (Bristol Record Society 1949).

Hudson, W. & J. C. Tingey (eds). *Records of the city of Norwich* (1910).

Hunnisett, R. F. (ed.) *Wiltshire coroner's bills, 1752–96*, XXXVI (Wiltshire Record Society, 1981).

Hunter, J. (ed.) *The life of Mr Thomas Gent, Printer of York, written by himself* (1832).

Hutton, W. *History of Derby* (1791).

Hutton, W. *Life of William Hutton, stationer of Birmingham* (1816).

Jackson, C. (ed.). *Yorkshire diaries and autobiographies in the seventeenth and eighteenth centuries*, LXV (Surtees Society, 1865).

Jackson, C. & S. Margerison (eds). *Yorkshire diaries and autobiographies in the seventeenth and eighteenth centuries*, LXXVII (Surtees Society, 1883).

Jenkinson, Mrs H. (ed.). *Bedfordshire apprentices*, IX (Bedfordshire Historical Record Society, 1925).

Jenkinson, Sir H. (ed.). *Surrey apprenticeships, 1711–31*, X (Surrey Record Society, 1929).

Johnson, H. C. & J. H. Hodson (eds). *Warwick County Records*, VIII (Warwick, 1953).

Johnson, H. C. & N. J. Williams (eds). *Warwick County Records*, IX (Warwick, 1964).

Kalm, P. *Account of his visit to England in 1748* (1892).

Lane, J. (ed.). *Coventry apprentices and their masters, 1781–1806*, XXXII (Dugdale Society, 1982.

Latham, R. & W. Matthews (eds). *The diary of Samuel Pepys*, [9 vols] (1995).

Lucas, W. *A Quaker journal* (1934).

Macfarlane, A. (ed.). *The diary of Ralph Josselin, 1616–1683* (1976).

McKenzie, D. F. (ed.) *Stationers' Company apprentices, 1701–1800*, N. S. XIX (Oxford Bibligraphic Society, 1978).

Maitland, W. *History of London* (1739).

Mandeville, B. *The fable of the bees* (1714).

Marshall, J. D. (ed.). *Autobiography of William Stout of Lancaster, 1665–1752* (1967).

Medlicott, M. M. (ed.). *No hero, I confess* (1969).

Meiklejohn, A. (trans.). "John Darwall, MD (1796–1833) and diseases of artisans", *British Journal of Industrial Medicine* 13 (1956).

Merson, A. C. (ed.). *A calendar of Southampton apprenticeship registers, 1609–1740*, XII (Southampton Record Series, 1968).

Missoni, H. *Memoirs and observations in his travels over England* (1719).

Morgan, P. *Warwickshire apprentices in the Stationers' Company of London, 1563–1700* (Dugdale Society, 1978).

Palmer, R. (ed.). *A touch on the times* (1974).

Perry, N. R. (ed.). *The Poor Law settlement documents of the church of St Mary, Old Swinford, 1651–1794* (Birmingham & Midland Society for Genealogy and Heraldry, 1977).

Playfair, W. *A letter to the Rt Honourable and Honourable the Lords and Commons of Great Britain on the advantages of apprenticeships* (1814).

Powell, J. *A letter to Edward Ellice, Esq. MP* (1819).

Quennell, P. (ed.). *Memoirs of William Hickey* (1975).

Ralph, E. & N. M. Hardwick (eds). *Calendar of the Bristol apprentice book, 1532–65*, part II (Bristol Record Society, 1980).

Ramazzini, B. *A treatise on the diseases of tradesmen* (1705).

Ratcliff, S. C. & H. C. Johnson (eds). *Warwick county records*, I–VII (Warwick, 1935–46).

Rice, R. G. (ed.). *Sussex apprentices and their masters, 1710–52*, XXVIII (Sussex Record Society, 1929).

Richardson, S. *The apprentice's vade mecum* (1733).

Richardson, W. *Chemical principles of the metallic arts* (1790).

Rising, W. M. & P. Millican (eds). *An index of indentures of Norwich apprentices enrolled with the Norwich Assembly, 1500–1752* (Norfolk Record Society, 1959).

Romilly, Sir S. *Memoirs* (1840).

Rowe, D. J. (ed.). *Records of the Company of Shipwrights of Newcastle-upon-Tyne*, II (Surtees Society, 1971).

Rudder, S. *A new history of Gloucestershire* (1779).

Secker, T. *Works* (1792).

Shaw, C. *When I was a child* (1903).

Smith, A. *The wealth of nations* (1976 edn).

Smith, K. J. (ed.). *Warwickshire apprentices and their masters, 1710–60*, XXIX (Dugdale Society 1975).

Southey, R. *Letters from England* (1808).

SPCK. *An account of the charity schools in Great Britain and Ireland* (1711).

Steer, F. W. *Farm and cottage inventories of mid-Essex, 1635–1749* (1969).

Stokes, F. G. (ed.). *The Blecheley diary of the Rev. William Cole, 1765–7* (1931).

Sturt, G. *The wheelwright's shop* (1963).

Thackrah, C. T. *The effects of arts, trades and professions on health and longevity* (1832).

Thale, M. (ed.). *The autobiography of Francis Place* (Cambridge, 1971).

Thomas, A. H. *Calendar of pleas and memoranda rolls . . . at the Guildhall* (1929).

Thompson, E. M. *The Chamberlain letters* (1966).

Timmins, S. (ed.). *Industrial history of Birmingham and the midland hardware district* (1866).

Tomlins, T. E. *The law dictionary* (1835).

Townsend, J. *A dissertation on the poor laws* (1786).

Ure, A. *The philosophy of manufactures* (1835).

Villette, J. *The annals of Newgate*, IV (1776).

Wenderborn, F. A. *A view of England towards the close of the eighteenth century* (1791).

Young, A. *Annals of agriculture*, XXVII (1796).

II. Secondary sources

Alcock, N. W. *Stoneleigh villagers, 1597–1650* (University of Warwick, 1975).

Alford, B. W. E. & T. C. Barker. *The history of the Carpenters' Company* (1968).

Ariès, P. *Centuries of childhood* (1962).

Ashby, A. W. A hundred years of Poor Law administration in a Warwickshire village. In *Oxford studies in social and legal history*, P. Vinogradoff (ed.) (1912).

Ashby, M. K. *Joseph Ashby of Tysoe* (1974).

Bacon, N. *Annals of Ipswich* (1884).

Bagley, J. J. (ed.). *The great diurnall of Nicholas Blundell* [3 vols] (Lancashire and Cheshire Record Society, 1968–72).

Bain, I. *The watercolours and drawings of Thomas Bewick and his workshop apprentices*, [2 vols] (1981).

Baker, C. H. & M. I. Collins, *The life and circumstances of James Brydges, first Duke of Chandos* (1949).

Barnard, H. C. *A short history of English education* (1947).

Batt, F. R. *The law of master and servant* (1967).

Blackham, R. J. *London's livery companies* (n.d.).

Brasbridge, J. *The fruits of experience* (1824).

Brewer, J. *Party ideology and popular politics at the accession of George III* (Cambridge, 1976).

Burbidge, F. *Old Coventry and Lady Godiva* (1952).

Burke, P. *Popular culture in early modern Europe* (1978).

Camp, C. W. *The artizan in Elizabethan literature* (New York, 1923).

Chambers, J. D. *Nottinghamshire in the eighteenth century* (1966).

Chapman, S. D. *The early factory masters* (Newton Abbot, 1967).

Clapham, J. H. *Economic history of modern Britain* (Cambridge, 1930).

Collier, F. *Workers' family economy in the cotton industry* (1964).

Colvin, H. M. *A biographical dictionary of British architects, 1660–1840* (New Haven, 1995).

Cunnington, C. W. & P. Cunnington. *Handbook of English costume in the eighteenth century* (1972).

Cunnington, P. & C. Lucas. *Occupational costume in England* (1967).

Dickinson, H. W. *Matthew Boulton* (Cambridge, 1936).

Dobson, C. R. *Masters and journeymen* (1980).

Dudley, T. B. *A complete history of Royal Leamington Spa* (1896).

Dunlop, O. J. & R. D. Denman, *English apprenticeship and child labour* (1912).

Dyer, A. D. *The city of Worcester in the sixteenth century* (Leicester, 1973).

Ede, J. F. *History of Wednesbury* (1964).

Fitton, R. S. & A. P. Wadsworth (eds). *The Strutts and the Arkwrights* (1958).

Flinn, M. W. *British population growth, 1750–1850* (1970).

George, D. M. *London life in the eighteenth century* (1925).

Gill, C. & A. Briggs, *A history of Birmingham*, [2 vols] (Oxford, 1952).

Gillis, J. R. *Youth and history* (New York, 1974).

Glass, D. V. (ed.). *London inhabitants within the walls, 1695* (London Record Society, 1966).

Guthrie, D. *A history of medicine* (1945).

Hampson, E. M. *The treatment of poverty in Cambridgeshire, 1597–1834* (Cambridge, 1934).

Herbert, W. *The history of the twelve great livery companies of London* (1887).

Hewitt, J. *A journal of the proceedings of J. Hewitt . . . of the city of Coventry* (Coventry, 1779).

Hill, C. *Society and Puritanism in pre-revolutionary England* (1964).

Hole, C. *A dictionary of British folk customs* (1978).

Hughes, E. *North country life in the eighteenth century* (1965).

Hutton, R. *The rise and fall of merry England* (1994).

James, M. *Social problems and policy during the Puritan revolution, 1640–1660* (1930).

Jones, M. G. *The charity school movement* (1938).

Laslett, P. *The world we have lost* (1965).

Lawson, J. & H. Silver. *A social history of education in England* (1977).

Leader, R. E. *Sheffield cutlers* (1906).

Leonard, E. M. *The early history of English poor relief* (1965 reprint).

Linebaugh, P. *The London hanged* (1991).

McClure, R. K. *Coram's children: the London Foundling Hospital in the eighteenth century*, 1981.

Malcolmson, R. W. *Popular recreations in English society, 1700–1850* (Cambridge, 1973).

Markham, S. *John Loveday of Caversham, 1711–89* (Wilton, 1984).

Marshall, D. *The English domestic servant in history* (Historical Association pamphlet 13, 1968).

Marshall, D. *The English poor in the eighteenth century* (1926).

Mause, L. de (ed.). *The history of childhood* (New York, 1976).

Mayer, E. *The curriers of the City of London* (1968).

Mitchelson, N. *The Old Poor Law in East Yorkshire* (1953).

Musgrove, F. *Youth and the social order* (1964).

Newton, R. *Eighteenth century Exeter* (Exeter, 1984).

Nockolds, H. *The coachmakers* (1977).

Parker, R. *The common stream* (1975).

Pearsall, R. *The worm in the bud* (1971).

Phythian-Adams, C. *Local history and folklore* (1975).

Pinchbeck, I. *Women workers and the Industrial Revolution, 1750–1850* (1969).

Pinchbeck, I. & M. Hewitt. *Children in English society* [2 vols] (1969, 1973).

Plummer, A. *The London Weavers' Company, 1600–1970* (1972).

Poole, B. *Coventry : its history and antiquities* (1870).

Porter, R. (ed.). *Patients and practitioners* (Cambridge, 1985).

Powell, J. *A parson and his flock, 1690–1740* (Warwick, 1981).

Prest, J. *The Industrial Revolution in Coventry* (1960).

Pugh, L. P. *From farriery to veterinary medicine* (Cambridge, 1962).

Raistrick, A. *Quakers in science and industry* (Newton Abbot, 1950).

Rodgers, B. *The cloak of charity* (1949).

Rudé, G. *The crowd in history* (New York, 1964).

Rule, J. *The experience of labour in eighteenth century industry* (1981).

Scarisbrick, J. J. *Henry VIII* (1968).

Schofield, R. S. "Dimension of illiteracy 1750–1850", *Explorations in Economic History*, 2nd series, 10(4), 1973.

Stone, L. *The family, sex and marriage in England, 1500–1800* (1977).

Tate, W. E. *The parish chest* (Cambridge, 1960).

Thompson, E. P. & E. Yeo. *The unknown Mayhew* (1971).

Thrupp, S. L. *The merchant class of medieval London* (Chicago, 1948).

Tildesley, N. W. *A history of Willenhall* (1951).

Tyack, G. *Warwickshire country houses* (Chichester, 1994).

Unwin, G. *The guilds and companies of London* (1963 reprint).

Warner, O. *A history of the tin-plate workers* (1964).

Webb, S. O. & B. *English poor law history: parts 1 and 2* (1963 reprint).
Wilkinson, G. T. *The Newgate calendar* (1991 edn).
Wilmer, B. *Cases and remarks in surgery* (1779).
Young, S. *Annals of the barber-surgeons* (1890).

a. Articles

Abrams, P. Rites de Passage: the conflict of generations in industrial society. *Journal of Contemporary History* 5(1), 1970, pp. 175–90.

Beattie, J. M. The pattern of crime in England, 1660–1800. *Past and Present* 62, 1974.

Briggs, W. G. Records of an apprenticeship charity, 1685–1753. *Derbyshire Archaeological and Natural History Society Journal* LXIII, 1953, pp. 43–61.

Buckatzch, E. J. The place of origin of immigrants into Sheffield, 1624–1799. *Economic History Review*, second series, II, 1950.

Capp, B. English youth groups and *The pinder of Wakefield*. *Past and Present* 76, 1977.

Davis, N. Z. The reasons of misrule: youth groups and charivaris in sixteenth century France. *Past and Present* 50, 1971.

Derry, T. K. The repeal of the apprenticeship clauses in the Statute of Apprentices. *Economic History Review* III, 1931–2.

Fox, L. The Coventry guilds and trading companies. *Birmingham Archaeological Society Transactions* 78, 1962.

Lane, J. Eighteenth century medical practice: a case study of Bradford Wilmer, surgeon of Coventry, 1737–1813. *Social History of Medicine* III(3), 1990, pp. 370–86.

McKillop, A. D. Samuel Richardson's advice to an apprentice. *Journal of English and German Philology* XLII, 1943, pp. 40–54.

Plumb, J. H. The new world of children in eighteenth century England. *Past and Present* 67, 1975.

Pursehouse, E. Waveney Valley Studies, *East Anglian Magazine*, 1963, pp. 206–10.

Ramsay, G. D. The recruitment and fortunes of some London freemen in the mid sixteenth century. *Economic History Review*, second series, XXXI, 1978.

Reid, D. A. The decline of Saint Monday, 1766-1876. *Past and Present* 71, 1979, pp. 76–101.

Smith, A. The folklore of industry. *Local Historian*, May, 1974.

Smith, S. R. The London apprentices as seventeenth century adolescents. *Past and Present* 61, 1973, pp. 149–61.

Stone, L. Social mobility in England, 1500–1700. *Past and Present* 33, 1965, pp. 16–55.

Thirsk, J. Younger sons in the seventeenth century. *History*, 54(182), 1962, pp. 358–77.

Thomas, E. G. The apprenticeships and settlement papers of the parish of St Thomas, Portsmouth: pauper apprenticeship. *Portsmouth Archives Review* IV, 1979–80, pp. 12–24.

Thompson, E. P. Rough music: le charivari anglais, *Annales* 2(March–April), 1972.

Thompson, E. P. Time, work discipline and industrial capitalism. *Past and Present* 38, 1967.

Wardle, D., Education in Nottingham in the age of apprenticeship, 1500–1800. *Transactions of the Thoroton Society*, 1967, pp. 285–312.

Waters, R. E. Chester. A statutory list of the inhabitants of Melbourne, Derbyshire in 1695, *Journal of the Derbyshire Archeological and Natural History Society* VII, 1885.

Wharton, C. Warwickshire calendar customs. *Warwickshire History*, I(5), 1971, pp. 2–11.

Wright, H. Sowerby parish apprentices. *Transactions of the Halifax Antiquarian Society*, 1934, pp. 57–73.

b. Directories

Foart Simmons, S. *The medical register for the year 1783* (1783).

Pigot's commercial directory (1828).

Sketchley's Birmingham, Wolverhampton & Walsall directory (Birmingham, 1767).

The universal British directory [5 vols] (1791–8).

White, F. *Directory of Warwickshire* (Sheffield, 1850).

Wrightson's new triennial directory of Birmingham (Birmingham, 1818).

c. Theses

Chapman, S. D. *William Felkin* (MA thesis, University of Nottingham, 1960).

Lane, J. *Apprenticeship in Warwickshire, 1700–1834* (PhD thesis, University of Birmingham, 1977).

Lang, R. D. *The greater merchants of London in the early seventeenth century* (DPhil thesis, University of Oxford, 1963).

Linebaugh, P. *Tyburn, a study of crime and the labouring poor in London during the first half of the eighteenth century* (PhD thesis, University of Warwick, 1975).

Index of names and places

Index of subjects